Transactions of the Royal Historical Society

SIXTH SERIES

IV

LONDON 1994

British Library Cataloguing in Publication Data

Transactions of the Royal Historical Society.
 —6th Series, vol. IV (1994)
 1. History—Periodicals
 I. Royal Historical Society
 905 DI
ISBN 0-86193-139-4

Made and printed in Great Britain by Butler & Tanner Ltd, Frome and London

CONTENTS

POLITICAL IDEOLOGIES IN TWENTIETH CENTURY BRITAIN

TRANSACTIONS OF THE

ROYAL HISTORICAL SOCIETY

PRESIDENTIAL ADDRESS

By R. R. Davies

THE PEOPLES OF BRITAIN
AND IRELAND 1100–1400
1. IDENTITIES

READ 19 NOVEMBER 1993

PEOPLES are back on the historian's agenda. Their return to the historical limelight, or at least out of the historical shadows, is doubtless in part a response to the growing awareness of the power of ethnicity in our own contemporary world. So it is with changes of historical fashion at all times. But it also no doubt arises in part from the growing recognition that the centrality that academic historians have so long given to the unitary nation state as the natural, inevitable and indeed desirable unit of human power and political organisation is itself a reflection of the intellectual climate in which modern academic historiography was forged in the nineteenth century. The linear development of the nation state is no longer of necessity the overarching theme and organising principle in the study of the past that it once was. Once our historical gaze could be shifted from the state and its institutions and from the seductive appeal of its prolific archives, other solidarities and collectivities could come more clearly into historical focus. Some of them seemed to have as great, if not occasionally greater, depth and historical resilience than did the nation state. At the very least they deserve to be studied alongside it. Not least in prominence among such collectivities are the peoples of Europe.

Nowhere arguably are these issues of more historical and contemporary significance than in the British Isles. Nowhere in medieval Europe was the potential of a nation state realised at an earlier date than in England, where the *gens Anglorum* and *regnum Anglie* came early to be regarded as co-terminous; nowhere were the institutions of an

I

effective state power developed so precociously. 'The nature and origins of the English state, the mysteries of its long continuity and power', as James Campbell has observed, 'are truly interesting (questions)'.[1] And from at least Bishop Stubbs's day those questions have prompted one of the most intellectually satisfying and comprehensive of academic historical constructs, that of continuous English, especially English constitutional, history. That this construct has appeared to be increasingly inadequate of late is due not only to its apparent teleological certainties but also to the fact that it was triumphantly and exclusively English. It marginalised the histories of the rest of the British Isles and Ireland, at worst by ignoring them, at best by converting them into subsidiary appendages to its own central theme. Paradoxically the historians of Ireland, Scotland and Wales returned the compliment by composing their histories likewise in largely self-contained units; but they returned the compliment even more directly, indeed derivatively so, by adopting the assumptions and even the chronology of English political history as the framework of their own national histories. Perceived in this light, the history of the British Isles is no more than the sum of the histories of its component countries, nations or whatever we care to term them. That may well be how it was, and should be. But now that the academic establishment is in apparently full retreat from the concept of continuous English history, now that courses on English history are being repackaged apologetically, if not always substantively, as British history courses, and now that a search for a British dimension is in vogue in the study of almost all centuries of the past from the medieval period to our own day, it may be opportune to ask what constitutes the identities of the different parts of the British Isles. Several answers readily suggest themselves. One, I beg to submit, is the identities of its different peoples.

To say as much is to invite, and probably deserve, instant criticism. Few concepts are so nebulous, slippery and insubstantial as that of 'a people'; it is at best a will o' the wisp, at worst a delusion. It lacks the hard institutional substance and ample archival sediment which would qualify it for serious historical study. 'National consciousness', so we have been authoritatively told, 'required embodiment in working institutions in order to acquire enduring reality'.[2] The concept of a people is a carefully-cultivated myth which conceals the brutal realities of the struggle for political power. Furthermore, it is a myth which has been essentially – and certainly until the age of democracy and universal education – the preserve of cerebral intellectuals and power-seeking and self-serving élites: it bears little relation to the aspirations and

---

[1] James Campbell, *Stubbs and the English State* (The Stenton Lecture 1987, Reading), 9.
[2] G. R. Elton in *Nationalismus in Vorindustrieller Zeit*, ed. Otto Dann (Munich, 1986), 77.

thought-worlds of the ordinary people of the pre-industrial age. Indeed the notion of a people is not only utterly elusive and fatally wishy-washy, it is also infected with the biological and racial descent-myths so widely propagated in the nineteenth century but so rightly castigated today as pernicious nonsense. Even if, contentiously, we dress up the word 'people' in the more respectable word 'nation', we will be told 'in its modern and basically political sense the concept of nation is historically very young', barely older than perhaps the early nineteenth century.[3] Some of the crucial features of modern nationhood—a powerful state bureaucracy, the extensive use of the printed word and mass propaganda, and capitalist and industrial economic formations—are patently lacking from the medieval world; its bonding agents were familial, hierarchical and dynastic, while the existence of supra-national organisations (notably the church) on the one hand and the essential localism of rural society on the other inhibited the development of what might be truly called national consciousness.

It is best to test such a critique against the evidence itself and that as far as the medieval British Isles is concerned is the aim of these addresses; but it might not be amiss, before engaging with some of that evidence, to venture some prefatory observations. Peoples may not be an 'enduring reality', whatever that is; but perceptions, myths and sentiments should surely be legitimate items for the historian's agenda if we mean to try to reconstitute the experience of the past in the round and on its own terms. Illusions, if such they be—and our own included—are likewise an essential item on that agenda. The gap between the Great Tradition, cultivated by and accessible to the articulate few and prominent in the historical evidence, and the Little Tradition of the unrecorded majority is, of course, a real problem; but might it not be a form of patronising condescension to assume that it could rarely be bridged? When we hear of Welsh peasants in Elizabeth's day congregating in mountain-top assemblies to intone their genealogies and to hear their bards recount ancient victories over the Saxons, or when we note the way that 'the freeholders and whole community of the realm' of Scotland were associated, in propaganda and in life, with the struggle for independence, we may at least be tempted to wonder whether the sense of being a people is merely the illusion of intellectuals and the propaganda of politicians.[4] As to the myths of biological descent they may well have acquired particular connotations and spurious scientific validation in the nineteenth century: but they were also of

[3] E. J. Hobsbawm, *Nations and Nationalism since 1780* (Cambridge, 1990), 18.
[4] *A Catalogue of Manuscripts relating to Wales in the British Museum*, ed. E. Owen (Cymmrodorion Record Series, 1900–22), I, 72; A. A. M. Duncan, *The Nation of Scots and the Declaration of Arbroath (1320)* (Historical Association, 1970), 21, 31, 34.

course the veriest commonplaces of the historical mythology of the medieval world. Modern historians are indeed entitled to claim that the nations and nationalism they describe are historically recent phenomena: what even the most unassertive historian of the medieval period is bound to retort is that medieval peoples themselves seem frequently to have believed that they belonged to nations (*naciones*) and peoples (*gentes*).[5] That modern historians and medieval peoples were not talking about the same phenomenon may, possibly if very arguably, be conceded; that we should try to discover what medieval men and women meant by coralling themselves verbally into collectivities which they called 'peoples', rather than judging whether they were such by our own *a priori* and time-bound criteria, is surely proper.

That, of course, still begs the question of what is, or rather was, a people. The definition is, not unexpectedly, as elusive as the concept itself. We might well appropriate for our purposes Benedict Anderson's famous definition of a nation as 'an imagined community', imagined by itself and/or by others and accepted as such, so long as we recall that a people was, and is, only one of several such imagined communities.[6] A people co-exists, and is often in direct competition, with these other imagined communities. Its claim on the affections and loyalties of those who could be conceived, or claim, to be among its members range from the minimal, or less, to the total. It is frequently being reshaped, redefined and renamed. It is alternatively a prominent and a strangely evanescent concept; as one distinguished sociologist has put it, referring to ethnic communities, they are characterised by a 'curiously simultaneous solidity and insubstantiality'.[7] Such, despairingly, are the communities which I would wish to explore with you in these addresses.

The medieval world was undoubtedly a world of peoples, *gentes*. It could hardly be otherwise. The books of the Old Testament recounted the story of a chosen people and its covenant with God. Rulers had ringing in their ears the words of Jeremiah: 'Behold I have set you over

[5] S. Reynolds, 'Medieval *Origines Gentium* and the Community of the Realm', *History* LXVIII (1983), 375–90 (an article to which I am deeply indebted); also *idem*, *Kingdoms and Communities in Western Europe 900–1300* (Oxford, 1984), esp. chap. 8. For the early medieval period: P. Amory, 'The meaning and purpose of ethnic terminology in the Burgundian laws', *Early Medieval Europe* II (1993), 1–28.

[6] Benedict Anderson, *Imagined Communities. Reflections on the Origins and Spread of Nationalism* (1983). Cf. the comment of J. M. Wallace-Hadrill in *EHR* LXXIX (1964), 137–9: 'But when is a people a people? The answer seems to be "when it has *Zusammengehörigkeisgefuhl*". That is what it comes to.'

[7] Anthony D. Smith, *The Ethnic Origins of Nations* (1986), 2. Cf., for the early middle ages, the comments of Edward James in *EHR* CVI (1991), 941.

the peoples (*gentes*) and the kingdoms (*regna*)'.[8] If God had chosen to organise human society into such groupings, who were they to demur? The words for these groupings—nation (*nacio*) and people (*gens*, occasionally *populus*)—were appropriately slippery ones.[9] In some contexts it is clear that a nation could contain several peoples. One of King Edgar's law codes, for example, speaks of 'all the nation, whether Englishmen, Danes or Britons'.[10] Indeed the word 'people' might be used in almost a pejorative sense in comparison with the superior collectivity of the 'nation': thus one of the English chancery memoranda produced during the 1330s seems rather deliberately and pointedly to have drawn a distinction between England as a nation and the Scots as merely a people (*gens*) inhabiting a land.[11] But in spite of such examples and in spite of the distinction which might have been drawn between the two words in the Roman world, medieval practice used the words 'people' and 'nation' in their Latin forms interchangeably and haphazardly.[12] Indeed both words had a huge gamut of meanings in contemporary sources: *natio*, for example, was often used in the same text, especially in Ireland, both for nation in the modern sense and for lineages and affinities.[13]

Terms might be loose and interchangeable; but there could be no doubting that for medieval authors the world was, and had always been, a world of peoples. That was the opinion and, more important, the assumption of encyclopaedists and chroniclers alike. Such was the assumption also in the farthest corners of the European world: an old Irish scholarly poem, for example, contains a list of the nations of the earth not dissimilar to the very early so-called 'Frankish Table of Peoples'.[14] From Isidore of Seville in the early seventh century to Bartholomew Anglicus in the thirteenth, and doubtless beyond, learned commentators and systematisers displayed remarkable ingenuity in

[8] Jeremiah I, 10.

[9] There is an excellent discussion of the terminology in G. A. Loud, 'The Gens Normannorum—Myth or Reality?', *Proceedings of the Battle Conference*, IV (1981), 104–17.

[10] IV Edgar 2.2 in *English Historical Documents c.500–1042*, ed. D. Whitelock (second edition, 1979), 435.

[11] Michael Prestwich, 'England and Scotland during the Wars of Independence', *England and Her Neighbours 1066–1453, Essays in Honour of Pierre Chaplais*, ed. Michael Jones and Malcolm Vale (1989), 187.

[12] As in the dedicatory preface of Gerald of Wales's *Descriptio Kambriae*: 'Kambriae nostrae descriptionem, *gentis*que naturam, aliis alienam *nationibus* et valde diversam' (*Opera*, ed. J. S. Brewer et al (Rolls Series. 1861–91), VI, 155). For Gerald's views on ethnicity: Robert Bartlett, *Gerald of Wales 1146–1223* (Oxford, 1982), 187–94.

[13] James Lydon, 'The middle nation', *The English in Medieval Ireland*, ed. James Lydon (Dublin, 1984), 3–4; J. B. Smith, *The Sense of History in Medieval Wales* (Aberystwyth, 1991), 11.

[14] D. Ó. Corráin, 'Nationality and kingship in pre-Norman Ireland', *Historical Studies* XI (1978), 5; S. Reynolds, in *History* LXVIII (1983), 375.

organising and classifying the peoples of the known world. Certain features of their taxonomic exercises are readily apparent. Peoples to them were communities of common descent; the elementary etymology of the words *natio* and *gens*, derived as they were from the Latin terms for birth and begetting, confirmed that undoubted fact immediately. Isidore expressed it with his usual crispness: 'a *gens* is a multitude sprung from one principle; ... a *gens* is named from *generatio*'.[15] All that remained to be done was to work out the descent of each people from its founding patriarch, with the Bible and classical legends providing a convenient, and often combined, pantheon of candidates. Since a people was formed by descent, blood was the vehicle for its consolidation and expansion from one generation to the next. This was no matter of rarefied intellectual theory; it was the yardstick by which a person's legal status might be defined. Welsh law-texts, for example, proclaimed that an individual born to Welsh parents on both sides (*Cymro vamtad*) was by definition a gentleman (*bonheddig cynhwynol*); the distinction between such a noble-born Welshman and a foreigner was a basic principle of Welsh jurisprudence.[16] Nor of course was the definition of membership of a people by purity of blood-descent a Welsh peculiarity. The Welsh indeed could find themselves at the receiving end of such a definition: an Englishman might receive a privilege exempting him from being convicted in Wales other than by fellow Englishmen 'by birth and by blood', and Welshmen often found their social advancement blocked by the taint of Welsh blood in their veins.[17]

Membership of a people, however, was not merely a matter of blood and descent; it was also regularly and externally revealed in what can only be called national character. We, of course, fight shy of such simplistic labels; medieval men had no such inhibitions. They regularly compiled lists, ranging from the descriptive to the scurrilous, of the characteristics of each people—in temperament, character, habits, lifestyle and so forth.[18] These were innate differences genetically, as we would say, transmitted; but they were also very substantially shaped by

---

[15] *Isidori Hispalensis Episcopi. Etymologiarum sive originum librum XX*, ed. W. M. Lindsay (2 vols., Oxford, 1911), IX, ii, 1.

[16] *Cyfreithiau Hywel Dda yn ôl Llyfr Blegywryd*, ed. S. J. Williams and J. E. Powell (Cardiff, 1942), 58; *Llyfr Du or Weun. Facsimile of the Chirk Codex of the Welsh Laws*, ed. J. Gwenogvryn Evans (Llanbedrog, 1909), 62, ll. 22–3.

[17] For examples and discussion: R. R. Davies, *Lordship and Society in the March of Wales 1282–1400* (Oxford, 1978), 306–7. Contemporaries often spoke of nation, blood, language (and other common characteristics), together, e.g. 'Quidam eorum nacionis sue et sanguinis et lingue partem tenentes', *The Annals of Ireland by Friar John Clyn and Thady Dowling*, ed. R. Butler (Dublin, 1849), *s.a.* 1325.

[18] Accessible and popular examples may be found in *On the Properties of Things, John Trevisa's translation of Bartholomew Anglicus De Proprietatibus Rerum. A Critical Text* (3 vols., Oxford, 1975–88), 760–1, 769, 812 etc.

external factors, as classical scholarship had indeed recognised—not least by climate, physical surroundings, and astrological conditions.[19] Such characteristics distinguished one people from another: as Gerald of Wales put it when he came to describe the Welsh, their nature as a people (*gens*) made them stand out, and be truly different, from other peoples (*nationes*).[20] Given that a people was identifiable by origin, blood, descent and character—in other words that it was an objective and 'enduring reality'—any fudging of the boundaries between peoples should, at least theoretically, be construed as literally unnatural. Of course in practice peoples mingled, intermarried, evolved, changed their identities and borrowed each other's customs; but in particular between peoples who were in an unequal relationship, especially in numbers and power, such easy-going intermingling was regarded as reprehensible and pernicious. It eroded and undermined the identity of a people. Fourteenth-century English government officials, especially in their comments on and policy towards Ireland, had a revealing label for it. It was degeneracy, literally defecting from and compromising one's own identity as a people or *gens*.[21]

The medieval construction of the world, therefore, was one which defined it as a collection of peoples; whatever modern historians care to believe, contemporaries were not in doubt about the reality and solidity of such communities. Nor was this merely a matter of intellectual constructs so beloved of scholars in all ages. Chroniclers and historians, whom we in this Society like to think are both more hard-headed and sure-footed than most of their fellow intellectuals, likewise saw the world, and specifically Britain, in such terms. For Bede there were three peoples and languages in Britain before the coming of the Anglo-Saxons—British, Picts and Irish (*Scotti*); and since he regarded, and indeed may in some senses be said to have invented, the English as a single people, that made a total of four.[22] 'Nennius' concurred, even if he used the word Saxons (*Saxones*) rather than English (*Angli*).[23] It was a view of the ethnic composition of Britain which many of their successors echoed. Thus when the author of the *Regularis Concordia* heaped praise on King Edgar he saluted him as 'king of the English

[19] For comments on medieval views of the impact of external factors on national character: Paul Meyvaert, ' "Rainaldus est malus scriptor Francigenus". Voicing National Antipathy in the Middle Ages', *Speculum* LXVI (1991), 743–63; Robert Bartlett, *Gerald of Wales*, 179–80, 201–10; Alexander Murray, *Reason and Society in the Middle Ages* (Oxford, 1978), 251–7.

[20] Giraldus Cambrensis, *Opera*. VI, 155; cf. V, 59 (*Topographia Hibernica* I, xxvi).

[21] J. A. Watt in *A New History of Ireland. II Medieval Ireland 1169–1534*, ed. A. Cosgrove (Oxford, 1987), 310–12, 384–90. The earliest legislation against degeneracy was in 1297.

[22] *Bede's Ecclesiastical History of the English People*, ed. B. Colgrave and R. A. B. Mynors (Oxford, 1969), i, 1 (pp. 16–19), iii, 6 (pp.230–1), v, 23 (pp.560–1).

[23] 'Nennius', *British History and the Welsh Annals*, ed. J. Morris (1980), c.7.

and of the other peoples (*gentes*) within the ambit of the Brittanic Isles', while the Anglo-Saxon chronicle's obit on Edward the Confessor noted how he had 'governed the Welshmen, ... ruled Britons and Scots, Angles and Saxons, his eager soldiers'.[24] If we cross the dividing line of the Norman conquest, it might be objected that Geoffrey of Monmouth is not perhaps the most reliable of sources for the present, let alone the past. But he was, of course, an influential author, and he opens his *History* with a snapshot of the island of Britain now 'inhabited by five peoples (*populi*): Normans, Britons, Saxons, Picts and Scots'.[25] There is much that is derivative and repetitive in such phrases; but it is the fact that they are so commonplace which makes them noteworthy. The idea that the island of Britain was occupied in the present as in the past by distinct peoples remained a commonplace throughout our period. When Ranulf Higden came to compile his immensely popular *Polychronicon* in the fourteenth century he divided Britain into its component parts and rehearsed the origin-legends and characteristics of each of its peoples.[26] Higden's near contemporary, John of Fordun, was much more of a pioneer; he single-handedly created a history of the Scottish people—for such it is even if it lacks the title *eo nomine*—which became the authorised version of their past for generations to come. His was the story of how the single Scottish people had been shaped over time, both in the distant past as the Greeks and the Egyptians, their aboriginal forebears, were united, and more recently as the peoples (*gentes*) of Northumbria and Cumbria and Scots and Danes 'were now long since faithfully assimilated as if a single people' (*gens*): and a people which was, of course, quite distinct from the English.[27]

If we press the question as to what such men and medieval men of affairs in general—as opposed to encyclopaedists and theoreticians—meant by the word people, we can perhaps arrange our answer under two broad headings. First, a people might be characterised negatively as a community which was, and believed itself to be, and was seen as, different from other peoples. Ethnic identity is relational; it is otherness

---

[24] 'Gloriosus ... Eadgar ... Anglorum ceterarumque gentium intra ambitum Britannicae insulae degentium rex egregius', *Regularis Concordia*, ed. T. Symons (1953), 1. *Anglo-Saxon Chronicle s.a.* 1065, ed. D. Whitelock (1961), 139.

[25] *Historia Regum Brittannie of Geoffrey of Monmouth. I Bern Burgerbibliothek*, Ms.568, ed. N. Wright (Cambridge, 1985), c.5.

[26] Ranulph Higden, *Polychronicon*, ed. C. Babington and J. R. Lumby (9 vols., Rolls Series, 1865–86), I, 328–431; II, 2–174.

[27] Johannis de Fordun, *Chronica Scotorum*, ed. W. F. Skene (2 vols., Edinburgh, 1871–2), II, 1–30; 1156 (I, 164, 'Northumbriae ... gentes et Cumbriae, Scotis et Danis jam diu fideliter tanquam una gens conglutinatae'. For comment on Fordun: Marjorie Dexeer, 'Fluid Prejudice. Scottish Origin Myths in the later Middle Ages', *People, Politics and Community*, ed. J. Rosenthal and C. Richmond (Gloucester, 1987), 60–76.

which often best serves to confirm and underline identities for both parties. 'The Welsh', said one rather resigned and world-weary English official in a famous comment in 1296, 'are Welsh'.[28] What more need be said, he clearly implied: the simple word 'Welsh' conjured a whole host of sentiments and characteristics, most of them doubtless unflattering, about this distinctive people. Isidore was at hand to provide his own pithy definition: 'a people (*gens*) is a multitude ... distinct from another people (*natio*) in terms of its own aggregation (*collectionem*)'.[29]

This fault-line of being distinguished from other peoples was one of the commonest identifiers of a people throughout the British Isles. No country could be more fragmented politically and so obviously lack any regnal solidarity other than a temporary overkingship than medieval Ireland. Yet the country, and especially its professional learned classes, were deeply imbued with a sense that the Irish, in spite of all their divisions, were a single people. The basic distinction in chronicle and historical mythology alike was that between the Goídil (*Gaedhil*), the native Gaelic Irish, and the Gaill, a blanket term for all foreigners, even often those who had long since been resident in Ireland.[30] Later, it is true, a distinction might be drawn between the 'English by birth' (Saxain) and what we might call the Anglo-Irish (Gaill); but the latter, it should be noted, still remained 'foreigners'.[31] Much the same distinction was made in Wales between native and true-born Welshmen and foreigners, and in Gaelic Scotland between Scots (mac Gaoidhil) and strangers (mac allmharagh).[32] These were the theoretical distinctions of self-absorbed and intensely conservative societies, and especially of their professional bardic, legal and clerical élites. Things were different in the much more open and mobile society of the kingdom of England. There, it is not so much in terms of blood and mythology that a people was defined, as by land of birth and regnal affiliation. No one should be disparaged by being married 'to men who are not of the nation of the kingdom of England', said the Petition of the Barons in 1258.[33] The terms of reference may be different, but the end result

---

[28] The letter is printed in J. G. Edwards, 'Edward I's Castle-Building in Wales', *Proceedings of the British Academy*, XXXIII (1950), 80–81 and in translation in *The History of the King's Works*, ed. H. M. Colvin, I (1963), 398–9.

[29] Isidore, *Etymologies* (as in n.15 above). IX. ii, 1.

[30] *A New History of Ireland. II, 1169–1534*, li. For the possible etymology of the word: F. J. Byrne, *Irish Kings and High Kings* (1973), 8.

[31] A. Cosgrove, *Late Medieval Ireland, 1370–1541* (Dublin, 1981), 74.

[32] D. Jenkins, *Cyfraith Hywel* (Llandysul. 1970), 16, 20; J. Bannerman, 'The King's Poet and the Inauguration of Alexander III', *Scottish Historical Review*, LXVIII (1989), 144.

[33] *Documents of the Baronial Movement of Reform and Rebellion 1258–1267*, ed. R. F. Treharne and I. J. Sanders (Oxford, 1973), 80. In 1295 Edward I decreed that Helié Daubeney should be deemed to be a 'pure Englishman'; *Rolls of Parliament* I, 135.

is much the same: a people is defined in part by reference to who they are not and who are not of them. Being English, the barons of 1258 might have said, is not being foreign. *Plus ça change*...

There was, unfortunately, rather more to this awareness of being different from other peoples than the observation of distinctions. From that fairly neutral position it was all too easy to move into attitudes of suspicion, thence to contempt and so to hatred. The identities of peoples in the medieval as in the modern period were all too often affirmed and strengthened on that basis. It was, of course, war and conflict which were the great generators of hatred and so the confirmers *par excellence* of a people's self-identity. It was no accident that it was out of the wars against the Welsh and the Scots (and the French) that some of the most strident, abusive and self-congratulatory English political poems of the period emerge. 'The English,' remarks one of them, 'like angels are always conquerors ... As though a swine should resist the valour of the lion, the filthy Scots attack England.'[34] Demonising the enemy works wonders for people's self-identity. 'The two nations', commented Archbishop FitzRalph of Armagh, 'are always opposed to one another from traditional hatred, the Irish and Scots being always enemies of the English.'[35]

Yet peoples are not defined simply by antipathy to each other. There were recognised distinguishing features which also served to identify one people from another, both to themselves and especially to others. Two quotations from either end of the period I have chosen to discuss may indicate what contemporaries considered to be among these distinguishing features. The first comes from a letter which Bernard, the first Norman bishop of St David's, wrote to the Pope around 1140. 'The people' of Wales, he commented, differed by implication from those of England, 'entirely as a nation (*natione*), in language, laws, habits, modes of judgement and customs.'[36] Bernard, of course, had an axe to grind; he wanted to highlight the individuality of the Welsh in order to justify the case for them to have an archbishopric of their own, for which Bernard was the self-evident candidate. But there is no need to dismiss his statement for this reason; it contained a list of the attributes of a people which was utterly unexceptional in the middle ages. Just over two centuries

---

[34] *The Political Songs of England from the Reign of John to that of Edward III*, ed. T. Wright (Camden Society, 1839), 170, cf. 162–6. For other striking examples: E. L. G. Stones, 'English Chroniclers and the Affairs of Scotland 1286–96', *The writing of history in the Middle Ages: essays presented to Richard William Southern* (Oxford, 1981), 337; for Scottish lampoons of the English: *The Brut*, ed. F. W. D. Brie (Early English Text Society, 1906), 249.

[35] Quoted by J. A. Watt in *A New History of Ireland. II, 1169–1534*, 343.

[36] Giraldus Cambrensis, 'De Invectionibus', ed. W. S. Davies, *Y Cymmrodor* XXX (1920), 141–2.

later English legislators in Ireland issued the Statutes of Kilkenny in an attempt to bolster the differences between the English and the Irish in Ireland and to halt the process known as degeneracy. Among the distinguishing characteristics of Englishness which the Statutes set out to defend were language, law, name-forms, apparel and style of riding.[37] These two comments come from different centuries and different contexts; but they could be supplemented and augmented, even for the British Isles, by many other examples. The check-list of the identifying characteristics of a people was shorter in some, longer in others; but all were broadly agreed on the main features: language, law, life-style, dress, personal appearance (especially in respect of hair and moustaches), agricultural practices, code of social values and what can only be described as national character and national temperament.[38]

Such lists were not merely a matter of ethnographic curiosity; they were regarded in their aggregate as establishing the case for a distribution of political power which corresponded with ethnic identity. That did not mean that different peoples could not be ruled by a single ruler. On the contrary, it was considered a sign of political maturity and power that a ruler governed several peoples rather than one. That is doubtless what King Stephen of Hungary had in mind when he remarked that a kingdom of one language and one way of life would be weak and fragile.[39] Such a statement could be cast in a more positive light by saying that the ruler of many peoples had pretensions to imperial power and titles, redolent of those of Roman times. That is precisely the sort of claim that the Carolingians and Ottonians had made—to be kings and emperors of many peoples. The Anglo-Saxon kings followed suit in the tenth century. Quite a lot of historical mirth has been generated by the grandiloquent imperial titles that these kings from Athelstan onwards gave themselves; but we surely err in poking too much fun at them. Not only did they reflect the remarkable overlordship which kings such as Athelstan and Edgar came to exercise within Britain, but they were also a comment on the fact that they were indeed the rulers, directly or indirectly, of many peoples. When Geffrei Gaimar came to compose his remarkable *History of the English*—the title is significant—in the mid-twelfth century, he had the true

---

[37] *Statutes, Ordinances and Acts of the Parliament of Ireland, King John to Henry V*, ed. H. F. Berry (Dublin, 1907), 430–69, esp. cap.i–iv, xiii–xv. Some of the prohibitions had already been anticipated in 1297: *ibid.* 210.

[38] Examples: William of Malmesbury, *Gesta Regum*, ed. W. Stubbs (2 vols., Rolls Series, 1887–9), I, 31; Giraldus Cambrensis, *Opera*, V, 147 (*Topographia Hibernica* III vii); *The Historical Collections of Walter of Coventry*, ed. W. Stubbs (2 vols., Rolls Series, 1872–3), II, 206.

[39] Quoted in S. Reynolds, *Kingdoms and Communities in Western Europe 900–1300*, 257.

measure of King Edgar's achievement: 'he held the land as an emperor ... He alone ruled over all the kings. And over the Scots and the Welsh. Never since Arthur had any king such power.'[40]

What is important to emphasise, however, in the present context—as indeed the style of these kings frequently acknowledged—is that what Edgar ruled was a federation of peoples. Within the heartland of his empire Edgar's rule was no doubt direct and powerful, but beyond this area the individuality of the peoples he ruled—with all that implied—was in no way questioned. In other words the unitary claims of a superior power and the acknowledgement of a plurality of peoples within the loose ambit of that power stood apparently in fairly easy relationship the one to the other. It would not always be so. The lack of alignment between the units and claims of effective political power, on the one hand, and the self-perceived and self-proclaimed identities of peoples, on the other, became, remained and remains one of the most vexed issues of European and indeed world history. The great French political commentator, Claude Seyssel, put his finger unerringly on the issue in the early sixteenth century: 'all nations and reasonable men prefer to be governed by men of their own country and nation—who know their habits, laws and customs and share the same language and life-style as them—rather than by strangers'.[41] It is the irreducibility of a people as the unit of human association and solidarity, and therefore as he sees it of governance, which was at the heart of Seyssel's comment. Paradoxically, or perhaps logically, the same argument could be made from a contrasting standpoint. If a people came to share the same people-characteristics—in such matters as language, customs, economic practices and life-styles—as a neighbouring people, then it was in danger of forfeiting its claim to be a people, or at least a self-governing people. It was on that basis that pamphleteers in the sixteenth and seventeenth centuries argued for a dynastic union between England and Scotland—because by then the two peoples were 'so like in maner, forme, language and all condicions'.[42] It was the union of peoples which, according to this argument, made a political union feasible and desirable. But what needs emphasis in the present context is that these

---

[40] Geffrei Gaimar, *L'Estoire des Engleis*, ed. A. Bell (Anglo-Norman Text Society, 1960), ll.3561–7. As Janet Nelson has put it, Edgar was the 'ruler of a British Empire, tenth-century style', *Early Medieval Kingship*, ed. P. H. Sawyer and I. N. Wood (Leeds, 1977), 70.

[41] Claude Seyssel, *La Monarchie de France et deux autres fragments politiques*, ed. Jacques Poujol (Paris, 1961), 218.

[42] Quoted in Roger A. Mason, 'Scotching the Brut: Politics, History and National Myth in Sixteenth-Century Britain', *Scotland and England 1286–1815*, ed. Roger A. Mason (Edinburgh, 1987), 68. The argument was taken further by Sir Robert Cotton as quoted in J. Wormald, 'The Creation of Britain: Multiple Kingdoms or Core and Colonies?', *ante*, 6th ser., II (1992), 178.

arguments—whatever axes their authors had to grind—start from a set of presuppositions which, with the appropriate modifications which are inevitable over the passage of time, had been taken for granted in Europe for at least a thousand years: the world was a world of peoples: each people had its own individuality, manifested in a variety of ways and duly recognised by itself and, often even more sharply, by others; no amount of military might and political empire-building could, or should be expected to, undermine this truism; on the contrary, empires came and went and worldly power was evanescent; but peoples, like the word of God, were an 'enduring reality'.

Such, very broadly, are the set of assumptions about the nature and identities of peoples which prevailed in the medieval world. Against such a background what, finally and briefly, about the identities of the peoples of the British Isles and Ireland in the period 1100–1400? At the risk of gross over-simplification it may be said that we find in England a kingdom where, at the start of our period, the memory of its being composed of several peoples was still not dead: Edward the Confessor, for example, was occasionally called 'king of the English (*Anglici*) and the Northumbrians'.[43] But it is not the memory of plurality which is really striking so much as the fact that the king is the king of a people, a single people. It is as king of the English, *rex Anglorum*, that he was styled on his coins after 973; it was the same title which was now, and remained, the almost invariable royal style in his documents; and, to revert to Edward the Confessor, it was as king of the English, ruling over the English people (*Anglica gens*), that he was referred to by his near-contemporary biography.[44] It may, of course, be objected that the fact of the style 'king of the English' did not mean that the inhabitants of England saw themselves as one people and indeed that the *gens Anglorum* was the creation of the metropolitan ambitions of Canterbury, the wistful day-dreaming of historians from Bede onwards, and the military might and political power of pre-Conquest kings.[45] That may well be so; but the fact remains that the unit over which the king ruled was a people, a people created by being recurrently called such, a people which largely acquired its identity by being subject to one king

[43] Frank Barlow, *Edward the Confessor* (1970), 166.

[44] *Vita Edwardi Regis (The Life of King Edward)*, ed. F. Barlow (1962), 3, 11, 22, 54.

[45] For the role of Bede in the 'making' of the English people, see esp. H. E. J. Cowdrey, 'Bede and "the English" People', *Journal of Religious History* XI (1981), 501–23 and Patrick Wormald, 'Bede, Beowulf and the conversion of the Anglo-Saxon aristocracy', *Bede and Anglo-Saxon England*. ed. R. T. Farrell (British Archaeological Reports no.46, 1978). On the rôle of the tenth-century monatic reformers in bolstering the notion of the unity of England: N. Bainton, 'Monastic Reform and the Unification of Tenth-Century England', *Religion and National Identity. Studies in Church History*, XVIII (1982), 71–85.

and the instruments of his authority, but a people even so. How much this was so became evident quickly after the Norman Conquest. The new dynasty claimed, of course, that its title was one by right and divine favour, not by conquest; it paraded its claims to continuity and legitimacy by rather ostentatiously adopting the title king of the English, *rex Anglorum*. But for the next few generations there were two peoples in England, legally and substantively, the French or Normans and the English.[46] It was, of course, in part a distinction between victors and vanquished and it was a distinction of gross oversimplification. But the legal distinction and the greeting clauses of charters registered the basic fact that England was now formally a country of two peoples.

The situation across the border in Scotland is not without a measure of similarity. The king's title was normally that of king of Scots (*rex Scottorum*) and this was the style also used on his seal; in other words his perception of himself is that of a king who was ruler of a people, a single people; he might refer to them indeed as 'our people' (*gens nostra*).[47] But the address clauses of some of the writs of the kings in the twelfth century tell a different story: several of them greet French, English and Scots individually and some add Gallovidians and Welsh for good measure.[48] The chroniclers could be even more prolific in their identifications.[49] Nor do modern historians dissent from their view of Scotland as a land of several peoples, acknowledging that there were four or five disparate peoples in the area north of Tweed and Solway.[50]

Wales and Ireland were countries of such fragmented and kaleidoscopic patterns of authority that it is by no means always clear when one is crossing from regional to dynastic and thence to ethnic identities or in what proportions these various identities are intermixed and overlaid. Our Welsh sources, for example, refer not infrequently

[46] George Garnett, ' "Franci et Angli": The Legal Distinctions between peoples after the Conquest', *Anglo-Norman Studies*. VIII. *Proceedings of the Battle Conference 1985*, 109–37: cf. H. R. Loyn, *Society and Peoples. Studies in the History of England and Wales, c.600–1200* (1992), 422–3.

[47] For early examples: *Early Scottish Charters prior to 1153*, ed. A. C. Lawrie (Glasgow, 1905), nos.xviii *et seq*; for discussion of the royal style: *Regesta Regum Scottorum*, I *The Acts of Malcolm IV*, ed. G. W. S. Barrow (Edinburgh, 1960), 69–72; II *The Acts of William I*, ed. G. W. S. Barrow (Edinburgh, 1971), 75–7; '*gens nostra*': Eadmer, *Historia Novorum*, ed. M. Rule (Rolls Series, 1884), 236.

[48] *Early Scottish Charters*, nos.xciv, cxix, cxxv, cxli, cxcix; *Regesta Regum Scottorum*, I, 74, no.258; II, 77.

[49] For examples from the chronicles: *Scottish Annals from English Chroniclers A.D.500 to 1286*, ed. A. O. Anderson (1908), 181 (Richard of Hexham); 193, 199–200 (Ailred of Rievaulx); *Early Sources of Scottish History A.D.500 to 1286*, ed. A. O. Anderson (1922), II, 173 (Annals of Ulster), 420 (Chronicle of Melrose, *s.a.* 1217).

[50] A. A. M. Duncan, *Scotland, The Making of the Kingdom* (Edinburgh, 1975), 102–4, 111; *idem* in *Who were the Scots?*, ed. G. Menzies (Edinburgh, 1971), 127–8; G. W. S. Barrow, *Kingship and Unity, Scotland 1000–1306* (1981), 7, 11–12.

to the men of Powys; these men certainly had their own jealously-protected privileges, their own particular saints and their own genealogies; but whether they constituted a self-conscious and regularly identified people is another matter.[51] What is clear in both Wales and Ireland is that after the invasion of the Normans and the English these were now countries of multiple peoples. When Robert earl of Gloucester and the bishop of Llandaff came to an agreement in 1126, the Welsh of the earl and the bishop were grouped together and so were their Normans and English, just as Gerald of Wales on his crusading tour of 1188 found the English and the Welsh arrayed in two distinct groups to listen to his address.[52] Land transactions might be warranted against 'all our justiciable men, French, Flemish, English and Welsh' (the order, one suspects, not being accidental), and in both Wales and Ireland greeting clauses addressed to between three and five different peoples—French, Flemish, English, Irish, Welsh—were commonplace.[53]

We must, of course, not jump from such evidence to the conclusion that there were great, impermeable ethnic blocks in these countries. Many of the groupings that we come across in the evidence are doubtless largely geographical or regional (not that we should underestimate such bonds in creating identities). Such, for example, may be the references to the men of Argyll, Hebrides, Lothian and Teviotdale or the frequent distinction drawn between the men of north and south Wales.[54] Peculiarities of custom, language, dialect and character might, paradoxically, come into sharper focus as governmental power advanced and societies became more closely textured. John Bromyard in the fourteenth century, for example, came to detect and deplore a mutual hostility between northerners and southerners in England; and it was in the later middle ages that John Fordun gave his memorable description of the profound divide between Highlanders and Lowland Scots.[55]

[51] *Brut y Tywysogyon or The Chronicle of the Princes, Peniarth Ms 20 version*, ed. T. Jones (Cardiff, 1952), 37, 47; *Breudwyt Ronabwy*, ed. M. Richards (Cardiff, 1948), 1; *Gwaith Cynddelw Brydydd Mawr*, I, eds. Nerys Ann Jones and Ann Parry Owen (Cardiff, 1991), 15–51, 113–42.

[52] *Earldom of Gloucester Charters ... to A.D. 1217*, ed. R. B. Patterson (Oxford, 1973), no.109; Giraldus Cambrensis, *Opera*, VI, 67.

[53] Welsh examples: *Cartularium Prioratus St Johannis Baptiste de Carmarthen* (Cheltenham, 1865), no.33; G. Owen, *The Description of Pembrokeshire*, ed. H. Owen (Cymmrodorion Record Series, 1902–36), I, 177–8; *Monasticon Anglicanum*, ed. W. Dugdale (Rev. edn. by J. Cayley *et al*, 1817–30), V, 267 (1223); Irish examples: *The Red Book of the Earls of Kildare*, ed. G. Mac Niocaill (Dublin, 1964), no.183 (1293); *Register of the Abbey of St Thomas, Dublin*, ed. J. T. Gilbert (Rolls Series, 1869), 202–3, 214–15, 226–7.

[54] *Early Sources of Scottish History*, II, 254; *Scottish Annals from the English Chroniclers*, 171, 199–200, 203; *Annales Cambrie*, ed. J. Williams ab Ithel (Rolls Series, 1860), 50, 71.

[55] G. R. Owst, *Literature and Pulpit in Medieval England* (Cambridge, 1933), 563. Fordun, *Chronica Gentis Scotorum*, I, 42 (II, 38).

These, however, were what we may call regional or provincial identities within what were increasingly unified polities. If we return to the late eleventh century we find a world where ethnic solidarities could be more prominent and of more consequence. John of Salisbury in his *Policraticus* conjured up some of their force when he claimed that king Harold had enacted a law that any Welshman (*Britonis*) found east of Offa's Dyke carrying a spear should lose his right hand.[56] Welsh perceptions, rather appropriately, relied on divine intervention rather than royal decree to sort out the English from the Welsh; but the assumptions were much the same. The life of St Beuno recorded that if an Englishman passed between the branch and the trunk of a holy tree he would immediately die, whereas a Welshman emerged unscathed from the experience.[57] In short, there was of course much that was grossly oversimplified and fossilised about the characterisation and assumption of Britain as an island of identifiable and separate ethnic labels, but at least such labels constructed the world as contemporaries saw it.

If we move from the late eleventh to the late fourteenth century, we find a world which is still in many respects a world of peoples and yet one which is palpably different from that of three centuries earlier. Putting it too simply, the number of identifiable peoples in the British Isles and Ireland had been considerably reduced and, in the most prominent cases, their identities were more clearly aligned, shaped and manifested through regnal solidarities and governmental control and categorisation. One change is particularly obvious in both England and Scotland: in both countries the distinction between different peoples, as expressed in legal practices and greeting clauses, which was so prominent around 1100 had disappeared by the end of the twelfth century.[58] In both kingdoms people and kingship had become formally unitary—the kingdoms of the English and the Scots; and once they were unitary they could become territorialised as the kingdoms of England and Scotland. That could not happen in Wales or Ireland, for those countries were still politically and governmentally fragmented and were still patently, even painfully, countries of two peoples. In both of them multiple forms of address survived, significantly, longer than in England or Scotland; but in both countries as the thirteenth century progressed the multiple was replaced by the dual: English and Welsh or English and Irish.[59]

[56] John of Salisbury, *Policraticus*, ed. C.C.J. Webb (Oxford, 1909), II, 19–20 (Bk.VI, cap.VI).

[57] *Vitae Sanctorum Britanniae et Genealogiae*, ed. A.W. Wade-Evans (Cardiff, 1944), 17.

[58] G. Garnett, ' "Franci et Angli" ' (as above, n.46); R.C. van Caenegem, *The Birth of the English Common Law* (Cambridge, 1973), 95–6, 139–40; *Regesta Regum Scottorum*, II, 77.

[59] R.R. Davies, *Conquest, Coexistence and Change. Wales 1063–1415* (Oxford, 1987), 214–5;

That is indeed a second change that is obvious in the terminology of peoples in the British Isles and Ireland across these three centuries. In those countries which were not fully part of the two unitary kingdoms which now dominated the political landscape of these islands there was now a much starker and clear-cut confrontation of peoples. 'Since the conquest', so commented an Irish petition of the 1350s, 'there have been two kinds of people in Ireland and there still are, the English and the Irish'.[60] The petition was, of course, deliberately and provocatively partisan in its language; but its basic claim does not, at least governmentally and administratively, admit of doubt. A basic fault-line between two peoples—natives and settlers, vanquished and victors—now ran across the face of Wales and Ireland. It informed the assumptions and practices of governance in church and society—be it in the common division between Welshries and Englishries in Wales, in the co-existence of two different legal, administrative, judicial and tenurial systems in both countries, or in the division of ecclesiastical provinces and religious orders into areas or communities 'inter Anglicos' and those 'inter Hibernicos'.[61] As Professor Robin Frame remarked in a recent paper to this Society, 'overwhelmingly the image presented is of division along ethnic lines, as the English gathered, within the setting of their own institutions, to arrange their protection against the Irish'.[62] However artificial and unreal many of these classifications were on the ground, they bespeak a mentality where governance and life were being constructed on ethnic lines. In such a world tension and conflict between peoples was now more ethnically vicious: it was 'the war of

---

idem, *Domination and Conquest, The experience of Ireland, Scotland and Wales 1100–1300* (Cambridge, 1990), 116–18. In the Welsh chronicles the Welsh/English (no longer French) duality becomes more marked from c.1215 and especially in the 1250s; in Ireland, *The Song of Dermot and the Earl*, ed. G. H. Orpen (Oxford, 1892), composed in its present form 1200–1225, sees the struggle in Ireland from the outset as between 'les engleis' and 'les yrreis'. For a full discussion of the terminology used to describe the invaders of Ireland, see John Gillingham, 'The English Invasion of Ireland'. *Representing Ireland: Literature and the Origins of Conflict*, eds. B. Bradshaw *et al* (Cambridge, 1993), 24–42.

[60] Quoted in G.J. Hand, 'English Law in Ireland. 1172–1351'. *Northern Ireland Legal Quarterly*, XXIII (1972). I have adopted the dating suggested by R. Frame, *English Lordship in Ireland 1318–1361* (Oxford, 1982), 4,n.12

[61] For Wales: R. R. Davies, 'Race Relations in Post-Conquest Wales', *Transactions of the Cymmrodorion Society, 1974–5*, 32–56; *idem, Lordship and Society in the March of Wales 1282–1400*, chap.14; for Ireland: A.J. Otway-Ruthven, *A History of Medieval Ireland* (1968), 338–4; R. Frame, *Colonial Ireland 1169–1369* (Dublin, 1981), 105–10; J.A. Watt, *The Church and the Two Nations in Medieval Ireland* (Cambridge, 1970); *idem.*, 'The Church and the Two Nations in Late Medieval Armagh', *The Churches, Ireland and the Irish, Studies in Church History*, XXV, ed. W.J. Sheils and D. Wood (1989), 37–54.

[62] R. Frame, 'Les Engleys Nées en Irlande: The English Political Identity in Medieval ireland', *ante* 6th ser.3 (1993), 93.

the English and the Welsh', as it was said in the 1270s.[63] And in that kind of cross-fire it was crucial to know one's friend, one's enemy and therefore one's ethnic identity. That is why it distressed the burgesses of Llan-faes in Anglesey that they had the status neither of Englishmen nor even of Welshmen, but the worse of both,[64] that is why the English in Ireland, a people in danger of becoming trapped in the ethnic no-man's-land of being a 'middle nation', were so raucous in the cultivation of their Englishness in the fourteenth century.[65]

By 1400 it was clear—clearer, surely, than it was in 1100—that these islands could now be claimed to be the home of four major peoples, two of which had attained a match between their perceived identity as a people and the regnal authority, political structures and state institutions which served, upheld and fostered that identity; and two had not. The oldest and most closely-textured of those peoples was the English people, the *gens Anglorum*, it was also the one best served by the remarkable precociousness and ubiquitousness of its common institutions and law. Its identity as a people across these three centuries was further underpinned by the common experience of a single law and single taxation, by a popularised version of its continuous history as a people, and by the growing awareness of a specifically English self-identity in the thirteenth century, the century (as Stubbs put it) when England was reclaimed for the English.[66] As for the Scots, neither their name nor the name of their country had the same connotations in 1100 as they had in 1400. That was a measure of the transformation that had taken place. Historians will probably always disagree as to the measure of unity and identity that both the kingdom and the people of what we call Scotland had in the eleventh century; but by the fourteenth century there can really be no argument. Nothing epitomises the transformation better, perhaps, than the two inscriptions on the seal engraved for the Guardians in 1286 after Alexander III's death: 'the seal of Scotland appointed for the government of the kingdom'

[63] *Littere Wallie*, ed. J. G. Edwards (Cardiff, 1940), 1, 116; *Calendar of Ancient Correspondence concerning Wales*, ed. J. G. Edwards (Cardiff, 1935), 110.

[64] *Calendar of Ancient Petitions relating to Wales*, ed. W. Rees (Cardiff, 1975), 82 (printed in the original Lati in *Select Cases in the Court of King's Bench under Edward I*, ed. G. O. Sayles (3 vols., Selden Society, 1936-9), III, cxxiii). That their complaint was not an idle one is shown by the demand made of a litigant to show by the next court whether he was English or Welsh: Public Record Office, Court Rolls (S.C.2) 218/6 m.6v (1358).

[65] See R. Frame as in n.62 and *idem*, 'England and Ireland, 1171-1399', *England and Her Neighbours* (as in n.11), 139-55; J. F. Lydon, 'The Middle Nation', *The English in Medieval Ireland* (as in n.13 above).

[66] W. Stubbs, *The Constitutional History of England* (3 vols., 1906 edn.), II, 4. for England's growing sense of seld-identity in the thirteenth century, see in particular M. T. Clanchy, *England and its Rulers 1066-1272* (1983), chap.10.

and 'Saint Andrew be the leader of the compatriot Scots'.[67] What these inscriptions proclaim is that kingdom and people were now one; the Scots as a people were also the subjects of the king of Scotland. That sense of solidarity was, of course, to be hugely enhanced and deepened by the experience of the Wars of Independence. It found its most eloquent vindication in the remarkable Declaration of Arbroath of 1320. For our purposes the outstanding feature of the Declaration was its affirmation of the unity of the nation of the Scots across the ages and of their distinctiveness as a people and, above all, its defiant proclamation that it was their right to be a people and to enjoy the freedom to be such, not the defence of a particular king, which was at issue. People and king could and should be as one; but ultimately a people was anterior and superior to its kingship.

The match between people and polity which had been achieved in England and Scotland was not replicated in Ireland and Wales. That should not, however, lead us to underestimate the awareness of the inhabitants of those countries that they were, both of them, individual peoples. The concept of *fir Erenn*, the men of Ireland, was a very old one; so was the notion that the story of the island had been that of the successive wars of the Irish against the foreigners.[68] Three years or so before the Declaration of Arbroath, a Remonstrance was addressed to the Pope in the name of 'Donald O'Neill, king of Ulster and by hereditary right the true heir of the whole of Ireland, the underkings and magnates of that land and the Irish people'. Though not as polished or well-constructed a document as the Declaration, the Remonstrance was likewise an affirmation of the unbroken historical continuity of the Irish, especially through their kings, and of the individuality of their laws, way of life and speech, and a catalogue of the tribulations they had suffered at the hands of the English settlers in Ireland.[69] As for the Welsh their very name *Cymry*, compatriots, proclaimed their sense of solidarity, and was strengthened by their pride in their language, laws and historical mythology. During the thirteenth century this sense of being a people was vigorously cultivated by the princess of Gwynedd in the service both of their own expansionary ambitions and as a propaganda ploy in their attempt to withstand the smothering embrace of the English king.[70] Llywelyn ap Gruffudd, the first and last formally

---

[67] G. W. S. Barrow, *Robert Bruce and The Community of the Realm of Scotland* (third edition, Edinburgh, 1988), 17.

[68] D. Ó. Corráin, 'Nationality and Kingship' (as in n.14 above), 8; F. J. Byrne in *A New History of Ireland. II 1169–1534*, 6–7.

[69] For what is probably the earliest surviving copy of the Remonstrance and for notes (by J. R. S. Phillips) on it: Walter Bower, *Scotichronicon*, ed. D. E. R. Watt (Aberdeen, 1987–), vol.6. xxi–xxiv, 384–403 (Book, XII caps.26–32), 465–81.

[70] R. R. Davies, 'Law and National Identity in Thirteenth-Century Wales', *Welsh Society*

acknowledged native prince of Wales, harped on the threat to 'our people', 'our rights' and 'our nation'; he did all in his power to appropriate the term Wales (*Wallia*) for himself and for his princely title.[71] When in the desperate closing months of 1282 'the people of Snowdonia' asserted that 'even if their prince should transfer seisin of them to the king (of England), they themselves would refuse to do homage to any foreigner, of whose language, customs and laws they were thoroughly ignorant', they were proclaiming themselves in their hour of defeat and on the eve of the annihilation of their political independence to be a people, and to be so regardless of any political compromise their prince might be tempted to strike.[72]

For a Welshman there could be no more appropriate point at which to bring this lecture to a close than with such a patriotic affirmation ringing in your ears. In Wales as in Ireland declarations of being a people were not matched by political power and institutions; Claude Seyssel's formula was not achieved. Both remained fractured societies; in both there were two peoples: the English community of Ireland and Wales on the one hand, the native Welsh and the *meri Hibernici* on the other. Both countries and both native peoples remained formally and substantively outside the regnal and ethnic solidarity that was the kingdom of England and the English people. Attempts might be made to build bridges by the grants of English liberty (in terms of law, land-succession and tenure) and later by formal letters of denizenship.[73] But the integrative processes which had welded the peoples of England, including the Normans, into one and which had forged a remarkable sense of common Scottishness out of the very disparate peoples north of Solway and Tweed failed to operate in Ireland and Wales. In 1400 the British Isles and Ireland were still a collection of peoples, albeit now much more clearly of four peoples than had been the case in 1100. What constituted some of the identifying features of these four peoples will be the theme of the remaining three addresses.

---

and Nationhood, Historical Essays presented to Glanmor Williams, ed. R. R. Davies *et al* (Cardiff, 1984), 51–70.

[71] *Royal and other Historical Letters illustrative of the Reign of Henry III*, ed. W. W. Shirley (2 vols., Rolls Series, 1862–6), II, 312–14; *Registrum Epistolarum fratris Johannis Peckham*, ed. C. T. Martin (Rolls Series, 1882–5), II, 437.

[72] *Reg. Johannis Peckham*, II, 471.

[73] For an early Irish example: R. Frame *ante* (as in n.62), 88; for fines 'to have English liberty' in Wales: R. R. Davies, 'The Twilight of Welsh Law, 1284–1536', *History* LI (1966), 153: for more general developments: R. A. Griffiths, 'The English Realm and Dominions and the King's Subjects in the Later Middle Ages', *Aspects of Late Medieval Government and Society*, ed. J. G. Rowe (Toronto, 1986), 83–105.

GENERAL FRANCO AS MILITARY LEADER

By Paul Preston

READ 22 JANUARY 1993 AT THE UNIVERSITY OF WALES COLLEGE OF CARDIFF

BOTH during his lifetime, and after his death, General Franco was reviled by his enemies on the left and subjected to the most absurd adulation by his admirers on the right. As the victor in a bloody civil war which inflamed passions throughout the world, that is hardly surprising. Leaving aside his personal political success in remaining in power for nearly four decades, his victory in the Spanish Civil War was his greatest and most glorious achievement, something reflected in the judgements of detractors and hagiographers alike. For the left, Franco the general was a slow-witted mediocrity whose battlefield triumphs were owed entirely to the unstinting military assistance of Hitler and Mussolini. For the right, Franco the general was the twentieth-century incarnation of Alexander the Great, of Napoleon and of the great warrior hero of Spanish legend, El Cid.

Beyond the propagandistic excesses of the Caudillo's wilder syco-phants, however, what is altogether more remarkable is that both his wartime allies and the most sober judges from his own side have concurred in a generally critical view of his prowess as a military leader. The views of both Führer and Duce, for instance, could barely have been more hostile. Hitler commented at a dinner in 1942, 'Franco and company can consider themselves very lucky to have received the help of Fascist Italy and National Socialist Germany in their first civil war ... The intervention of the German General von Richthofen and the bombs his squadrons rained from the heavens decided the issue'.[1] During the Civil War, Hitler's first diplomatic envoy General Wilhelm Faupel was frequently scathing in his dispatches about the painful slowness of Franco's military leadership.[2] The Italians were equally critical. In December 1937, outraged at Franco's apparent inability to press home the advantage of his superior forces, the Italian Foreign Minister Count Ciano wrote in his diary 'Franco has no idea of synthesis in war.'[3] During the battle of the Ebro in 1938, the Duce himself protested about Franco's 'flabby conduct of the war', telling Ciano, 'Put on record in your diary that today, 29 August, I prophesy

---

[1] [Adolf Hitler], *Hitler's Table Talk 1941–1944* (1953), 569.
[2] See, for instance, *Documents on German Foreign Policy* Series D, III (1951), 408–10.
[3] Galeazzo Ciano, *Ciano's Diary 1937–1938* (1952), 46.

the defeat of Franco. Either the man doesn't know how to make war or he doesn't want to. The reds are fighters, Franco is not.'[4]

The views of Franco's German and Italian allies might be dismissed as ill-founded on the grounds of distance and lack of familiarity with Spanish conditions. However, equally negative, albeit more cautiously expressed, criticisms came from within the Generalisimo's own military establishment. Two such assessments of Franco as strategist emanated from the heart of the Nationalist high command—General Alfredo Kindelán Duany, the Chief of Franco's Air Force, and Colonel (later General) Jorge Vigón Suerodiaz, Chief of Staff first to the Army of the North and then to Franco himself. During the early stages of the war, Vigón wrote several letters to Kindelán, urging him to use his influence with the Generalisimo to bring about a change of strategy and an acceleration of operations. Kindelán wrote memoirs in the immediate aftermath of the war in which he revealed his own and Vigón's reservations about Franco's overall conduct of the war. Permission for their publication was withheld until 1945 and even then the criticisms of Franco as a strategist were cut from the text and not restored until the second edition which was published seven years after the Caudillo's death.

In relation, for example, to Franco's failure to seize the opportunity opened up by the fall of Bilbao in July 1937 for a rapid sweep through the north, Kindelán wrote: 'the enemy was defeated but was not pursued; the success was not exploited, the withdrawal was not turned into a disaster. *This was due to the fact that while the tactical conception of the operation was masterly, as was its execution, the strategic conception on the other hand was much more modest.*' The italicised passage was suppressed along with many others.[5] In his own diaries, not published until 1970, it is possible to discern Vigón's frustration with those of Franco's military decisions which delayed major advances.[6] Subsequently, the Francoist army's most distinguished official historians have also been discreetly critical of their Commander-in-Chief.[7]

What all these criticisms, whether German, Italian or Spanish, have in common is the belief that Franco could have speeded up the progress

---

[4] Ciano, *Diary 37–38*, 148.

[5] Compare Alfredo Kindelán, *Mis cuadernos de guerra 1936–1939* (Madrid, n.d. [1945], 86 and *Mis cuadernos de guerra 1936–1939* 2ᵃ edición (Barcelona, 1982), 9, 127. All subsequent references are to the 2nd edition.

[6] Jorge Vigón Suerodiaz, *Cuadernos de guerra y notas de paz* (Oviedo, 1970), 149–50, 212.

[7] It is remarkable, for instance, that Franco is a shadowy figure in the seventeen-volume set of *Monografias de la guerra de España* produced by the Spanish Army's Servicio Histórico Militar under the direction of Colonel José Manuel Martinez Bande, (Madrid, 1968–1985). See also the critical comments on Franco's generalship to be found throughout Generals Ramón & Jesús Salas Larrazábal, *Historia general de la guerra de España* (Madrid, 1987).

of his war effort at several crucial moments. The basis of this view was Franco's dilatory decision-making style in general and his readiness, at Brunete and Teruel in 1937 and at the Ebro in 1938, to divert large numbers of troops to the strategically meaningless and usually costly task of recovering territory captured by the Republic in diversionary attacks. The Generalisimo's apparent propensity to lose sight of major strategic goals on these occasions, together with his readiness to ignore several opportunities to conquer a poorly defended Catalonia, has led to the conclusion that he was lacking in vision. Certainly, it cannot be denied that, as his one-time superior officer, General José Sanjurjo, commented in 1931 'he is no Napoleon'.[8] It is probably an understatement to suggest, with Hitler and Mussolini, with Kindelán and Vigón, that he was deficient as a military strategist. However, it is the contention of this paper that to judge Franco in terms of his capacity to elaborate elegant and incisive strategy is to miss the point. He won the Spanish Civil War in the way in which he wanted to win it and in the time within which he wanted to win it. Most importantly of all, he derived from his victory that which he most wanted, the political power to remake Spain in his own image, unimpeded either by enemies on the left or rivals on the right.

In both form and content, Franco's strategy pursued a long-term political agenda rather than immediate battlefield objectives. That this should have been the case derives in part from a personality in which instinctive caution coexisted with almost unlimited ambition. Even more crucial was his military education and training between 1907 and 1910 at the antiquated Infantry Academy in Toledo and his formative experiences in Spain's savage colonial wars in Morocco. In one important respect, his personal experiences and the ethos of the Toledo Academy were to come together and determine the central plank of Franco's military style during the Spanish Civil War. Deeply traumatised as a child by the infidelities of his pleasure-loving and free-thinking father, he identified with his pious and conservative mother. Throughout his life, he would reject all those things which he associated with his father, from sexual dalliance and alcoholic drink to the ideas of the left. His childhood coincided with the lowest ebb of Spain's political fortunes, and, over time, he came to associate his personal difficulties with those of his country. In 1898, Spain suffered humiliating defeat at the hands of the United States and lost the last remnants of her empire. When the fourteen-year-old Franco entered the military academy in 1907, he found an atmosphere of fetid hostility to liberal politicians who were held responsible for the imperial disaster of 1898. Throughout

[8] In a conversation with the Minister of War, Manuel Azaña, on 20 July 1931—
Manuel Azaña, *Obras completas* 4 vols (Mexico D.F., 1966–1968), IV, 35.

his life, he would blame his nation's disasters on men who were uncannily like his father.[9] During the Civil War, his objective was not speedy victory but the long-term eradication from Spain of such men and their influence.

The Infantry Academy taught Franco little by way of contemporary strategic thinking or of technological developments in warfare since the Franco-Prussian war. No lessons were drawn from the guerrilla struggle in Cuba. The emphasis was on rigid discipline, an idealised military history of Spain's past glories and a set of moral virtues of which unthinking bravery and unquestioning obedience were the highest. Spain's current international difficulties were blamed on the poisons of liberalism and leftism. By way of compensation for the battlefield failures of the military, great stress was placed on the army's position as moral and political guardian of the nation. It was axiomatic that the army had the right to rise up against any government which tolerated either social disorder or the activities of the regional autonomy movements which challenged national unity. Franco left the Academy with little applicable military science but thoroughly imbued with these assumptions.[10]

In practical terms, the formative experience for Franco the soldier was as a junior officer in Spain's Moroccan protectorate. Arriving in Morocco in 1912, he spent ten and a half of the next fourteen years there and learnt much about warfare against hostile civilians. As he told the journalist Manuel Aznar in 1938, 'My years in Africa live within me with indescribable force. There was born the possibility of rescuing a great Spain. There was founded the idea which today redeems us. Without Africa, I can scarcely explain myself to myself, nor can I explain myself properly to my comrades in arms.'[11] By dint of cold-blooded bravery and an assiduous attention to the detail of logistics and map-making, he began his meteoric rise through the ranks which would take him from Second Lieutenant in 1912 to Brigadier General a mere fourteen years later. A war concerned with the pacification of bitterly hostile warrior tribes could hardly have been more brutal. However, the savagery of the occupying forces reached new heights in August 1920 with the formation of the Spanish Foreign Legion or *Tercio de Extranjeros*, a mercenary force in which Franco would serve as second-in-command. As a matter of policy, the Legion would commit atrocities against the Moorish villages which they attacked.

[9] On the relationship between Franco's personal life and his political ideas, see Paul Preston, *Franco: A Biography* (1993), 3–9, 72.

[10] On Franco's time at the Toledo Academy, see Preston, *Franco*, 8–13.

[11] 'Declaraciones de S.E. a Manuel Aznar', 31 December 1938, *Palabras del Caudillo 19 abril 1937—31 diciembre 1938* (Barcelona, 1939), 314.

The decapitation of prisoners and the exhibition of severed heads as trophies was common.[12] Franco encouraged the brutal violence of his men in the knowledge that their grim reputation was itself a useful weapon in terrorising the colonial population.

By the time that Franco returned to the Peninsula in 1926, he had fully developed two of the central features of his war effort during the three years of Civil War—an unflinching ruthlessness in the use of terror against civilian populations and an unwavering belief in the army's right to impose its political views. By 1936, he would also have acquired the conviction that he was the best person to define those views. His growing belief to his own patriotic mission was confirmed by his period from December 1927 to June 1931 as director of the Academia General Militar in Zaragoza. There, assisted by a staff chosen from among his *Africanista* comrades, he educated a generation of officers, who would fight by his side during the Civil War, in the brutal arrogance of the Foreign Legion and the idea of the army's right to determine the nation's political destinies.[13]

The coming of the democratic Second Republic in 1931 was something of a set-back for Franco. To his intense chagrin, the Zaragoza Academy was closed and he was left for eight months without a posting until, in February 1932, he was made military governor of La Coruña. Neither that posting, nor his promotion one year later to be military commander of the Balearic Islands, diminished his hostility to the democratic regime. His fortunes changed, however, with the coming to power of the increasingly conservative Radical Party backed by the votes of the Catholic authoritarian party, the Confederación Española de Derechas Autónomas (CEDA). The Radical Minister of War, Diego Hidalgo, not only promoted him to Major General but also chose to use him as his unofficial personal adviser on military matters. In October 1934, convinced that fascism was about to be imposed in Spain, the workers of the northern mining districts of Asturias rose in protest at the entry of the CEDA into the government. Diego Hidalgo informally placed Franco in charge of the repression of the uprising. The declaration of martial law effectively transferred to the Ministry of War the responsibilities for law and order normally under the jurisdiction of the Ministry of the Interior. Diego Hidalgo's total reliance on Franco effectively gave him control of the functions of both

[12] José Martin Blázquez, *I Helped to Build an Army: Civil War Memoirs of a Spanish Staff Officer* (1939), 302; Herbert R. Southworth, *Antifalange: estudio crítico de < Falange en la guerra de España: la Unificación y Hedilla>* de *Maximiano Garcia Venero* (Paris, 1967), xxxi–xxii; Guillermo Cabanellas, *La guerra de los mil días*, 2 vols, (Buenos Aires, 1973), II, 792.

[13] On Franco's time at the Zaragoza Academy, see Carlos Blanco Escolá, *La Academia General Militar de Zaragoza (1928–1931)* (Barcelona, 1989) *passim*; Preston, *Franco*, 56–61.

Ministries, a control which he exercised with notable ruthlessness.[14] It was an intoxicating and addictive taste of real politico-military power for Franco, confirmation of the central ideas on the role of the military in politics which he had absorbed as a cadet in the Toledo Academy. It was a profoundly formative experience, deepening his messianic conviction that he was born to rule and to command Spain's armed forces in the battle against the pernicious ideologies of liberalism and the left.

Despite such inflated views of his own importance, Franco was slow to commit himself to the military uprising plotted in the course of the spring and early summer of 1936. When he finally did so, a mere five days before the Civil War broke out, it was to take over the most efficacious units on the rebel side—the Spanish Moroccan Army. He found a depressing situation when he flew into Morocco from the Canary Islands where he had been military commander since March. The Moroccan Army was trapped on the wrong side of the Straits of Gibraltar, blockaded by the Spanish fleet whose crews had mutinied against their right-wing officers and declared for the Republic. In response to this daunting problem, Franco displayed what were probably his most valuable and inspirational qualities as a military leader—his glacial *sang froid* under pressure, his unshakeable resolve and his infectious optimism. In speeches, harangues and broadcasts, he repeated his catch-phrase 'blind faith in victory' and his mere presence with the rebels was a boost to their morale.[15]

Franco's optimism and his ruthless determination to win were reflected in an historic interview which he gave to the American reporter Jay Allen in Tetuán on 27 July. Asked how long the killing would continue now that the coup had failed, Franco replied 'there can be no compromise, no truce. I shall go on preparing my advance to Madrid. I shall advance. I shall take the capital. I shall save Spain from marxism at whatever cost ... Shortly, very shortly, my troops will have pacified the country and all of this will soon seem like a nightmare.' When Allen responded 'that means that you will have to shoot half Spain?', a smiling Franco said 'I repeat, at whatever cost.'[16]

In the meanwhile, he had to resolve the problem of the Republican

[14] Diego Hidalgo Durán, *¿Por qué fui lanzado del Ministerio de la Guerra? Diez meses de actuación ministerial* (Madrid, 1934), 79–81; Manuel Ballbé, *Orden público y militarismo en la España constitucional (1812–1983)* (Madrid, 1983), 371–2; General López Ochoa, *Campaña militar de Asturias en octubre de 1934 (Narración táctico-episódica)* (Madrid, 1936), 11–12, 26–9; José Maria Gil Robles, *No fue posible la paz* (Barcelona, 1968), 140–1; César Jalón, *Memorias políticas: periodista. ministro. presidiario.* (Madrid, 1973), 128–31; Juan-Simeón Vidarte, *El bienio negro y la insurrección de Asturias* (Barcelona, 1978), 358–9.

[15] Joaquin Arrarás, *Historia de la Cruzada española*, 8 vols, 36 tomos, (Madrid, 1939–43), III, 80–2; Francisco Franco Salgado-Araujo, *Mi vida junto a Franco* (Barcelona, 1977), 165; José Antonio Vaca de Osma, *Paisajes con Franco al fondo* (Barcelona, 1987), 35–6.

[16] *News Chronicle*, 29 July, 1 August 1936.

blockade. He examined both the then revolutionary idea of getting his army across the Straits by air and, despite advice to the contrary from his staff, the bold notion of a convoy to break through the blockade.[17] He believed contemptuously that the Republican sailors, without trained officers to navigate, oversee the engine rooms or direct the guns, would present little danger. The crossing on 5 August was an audacious risk which consolidated his standing on the Nationalist side. In the meanwhile, the few aircraft at his disposal ceaselessly carried troops across the Straits. This was converted into a full-scale airlift when both Hitler and Mussolini separately decided to help the Spanish Nationalists. Their decisions to do so were ultimately determined by considerations of their own interests. However, that they should both decide to target their assistance on Franco was a reflection not only of his manifest efficacy but also of the force of conviction with which he persuaded the representatives of both Fascist Italy and the Nazi *Auslandorganization* that he was the rebel to back. His rivals, General Emilio Mola in the north and General Gonzalo Queipo de Llano in the south could not match Franco's ability to secure foreign backing.[18]

Once he had his troops in Southern Spain, Franco's first operations drew on his experiences in Africa. The terrain, the arid scrublands of Andalusia, and the fact that his opponents were poorly armed civilians, recalled the colonial wars. Franco had already demonstrated his readiness to use Moroccan mercenaries in mainland Spain in October 1934. From early August, his African columns set out from Seville, initially making rapid progress on the first step of a hard-fought journey to Madrid. With Franco's knowledge and permission, the Legion and the Moroccan mercenaries of the *Regulares Indigenas* (indigenous regulars) functioned with terrible efficacy during their advance. Franco conducted the early stages of his war effort against the Spanish left as if it were a colonial war against a racially contemptible enemy. The Moors and Legionaries spread terror wherever they went, looted the villages they captured, raped the women they found, killed their prisoners and sexually mutilated the corpses.[19] The use of terror, both immediate and

---

[17] Kindelán's son claimed that the ideas both for the airlift and for a blockade-breaking convoy emanated from his father, 'Prólogo', Kindelán, *Mis cuadernos*, 45.

[18] On Franco's role in securing Italian and German aid, see Renzo de Felice, *Mussolini il duce: lo stato totalitario 1936–1940* (Turin, 1981), 363; John F. Coverdale, *Italian Intervention in the Spanish Civil War*, (Princeton, 1975), 69–74; Ismael Saz Campos, *Mussolini contra la II República: hostilidad, conspiraciones, intervención (1931–1936)* (Valencia, 1986), 181–5; Angel Viñas, *La Alemania nazi y el 18 de julio* 2ª edición (Madrid, 1977), 264–342.

[19] *The Times*, 26 August 1926; John Whitaker, 'Prelude to World War: A Witness from Spain', *Foreign Affairs*, XXI, 1, October 1942, 105–6; Maria Rosa de Madariaga, 'Imagen del moro en la memoria colectiva del pueblo español y retorno del moro en la guerra civil de 1936', *Revista Internacional de Sociologia* XLVI, 4, October–December 1988, 590–6; Mijail Koltsov, *Diario de la guerra de España* (Paris, 1963), 88–9.

as a long-term investment, was to be an essential part of Franco's repertoire both as a general and as a dictator. During, and long after the Civil War, those of his enemies not physically eliminated would be broken by terror and forced to seek survival in apathy.

Under the overall field command of Lieutenant-Colonel Juan Yagüe, Franco's columns advanced out of the province of Seville and into Extremadura. They took town after town, advancing 200 kilometres in a little over a week. The accumulated terror generated after each minor victory, together with the skill of the African Army in open scrub, explains why Franco's troops were initially so successful. The scratch Republican militia would fight desperately so long as they enjoyed the cover of buildings or trees. However, even the rumoured threat of being outflanked by the Moors would send them fleeing, abandoning their equipment as they ran. Franco planned his operations accordingly. Intimidation and the use of terror, euphemistically described as *castigo* (punishment), were specified in written orders.[20] The most extensive slaughter took place in the days following the capture of Badajoz on 14 August, when two thousand prisoners were massacred. Franco's decision to turn back to Badajoz, a sixty kilometre detour for his columns, was typical of his obsession with the annihilation of all opposition, irrespective of the time lost or casualties incurred. If his forces had pressed on to Madrid, the Badajoz garrison could not seriously have threatened them from the rear. The decision contributed to the delay which allowed the Republic to organise its defences.

Just three days earlier, on 11 August, Franco had written Mola a letter in which he revealed this obsession with the thorough purging of captured territory. It was a strategic vision which would not change substantially in the course of the war and one that was deeply imbued with an essentially 'colonial' mentality. He made it clear that, for him, the cumulative conquest of ground and the subsequent annihilation of all resistance in the 'occupied zones' meant more than rapid victory. Nonetheless, he agreed that the ultimate objective must be the capture of Madrid. Significantly, noting that the fortress of the Alcázar in Toledo was besieged by Republican militiamen, he commented that the advance of his troops on the capital would 'take the pressure off' and relieve Toledo without diverting forces which might be needed'.[21]

After the capture of Badajoz, the African columns advanced rapidly up the roads to the north east in the direction of the capital. On 27 August, they reached the last town of importance on the way to Madrid,

[20] José Manuel Martinez Bande, *La marcha sobre Madrid* (Madrid, 1968), 165–70.
[21] José Manuel Martinez Bande, 'Del alzamiento a la guerra civil verano de 1936: correspondencia Franco/Mola', *Historia y Vida*, XCIII, 1975, 22–3.

Talavera de la Reina, which fell one week later.[22] Another savage and systematic massacre ensued. The main road to Madrid was now open and Franco took it. However, in the light of subsequent decisions to be discussed below, there is room for speculation that Franco was not especially interested in an early capture of Madrid. With resistance intensifying, his troops took more than fifteen days to reach the town of Maqueda, where the road divided to go either north-east to Madrid or south-east to Toledo.[23]

Maqueda fell to Yagüe on 21 September and from that moment on, the nature of Franco's war altered dramatically. Earlier in the month, the Republic had reorganised its government under the leadership of the Socialist Francisco Largo Caballero. That move towards central authority increased a feeling among the Nationalist commanders that they too needed a unified command. Franco had long since expressed ambitions in that direction, telling the Germans in Morocco that he wanted to be seen 'not only as the saviour of Spain but also as the saviour of Europe from the spread of Communism'.[24] That was not something which could be achieved by means of a swift military victory over the Republic and a subsequent armistice. Franco's long-term political ambitions and immediate military decisions came together in a remarkable fashion in the immediate aftermath of Yagüe's capture of Maqueda. On the same day, at a meeting of the senior rebel generals held at an airfield near Salamanca, Franco was elected Generalísimo of the Nationalist forces by his comrades-in-arms. However, behind a near-unanimous vote and rhetoric of support, there was a discernible reluctance. Three days passed and nothing was done about publicising or implementing the decision to name Franco Generalísimo. Accordingly, Franco sought a way of clinching their support.

This took the form of the strategically bizarre decision to divert his troops away from Madrid towards Toledo. He thereby lost an unrepeatable opportunity to reach the capital while it was poorly defended and demoralised. Yagüe, Kindelán and Franco's Chief of Operations, Lieutenant-Colonel Antonio Barroso, all warned him that a diversion to relieve the Alcázar would cost him Madrid. He later admitted that 'we committed a military error and we committed it deliberately'.[25] Franco was choosing to give a higher priority to the inflation of his own political position by securing the emotional victory and propagandistic coup of the liberation of the Alcázar on 27 September.

[22] Martinez Bande, *La marcha sobre Madrid*, 45–56.
[23] Martinez Bande, *La marcha sobre Madrid*, 56–71; Ramón Garriga, *El general Juan Yagüe* (Barcelona, 1985), 111–12.
[24] *Documents on German Foreign Policy*, D, III, 28.
[25] Armando Boaventura, *Madrid-Moscovo de ditadura à República e à guerra civil de Espanha* (Lisbon, 1937), 212.

On the following day, the Nationalist high command met again at the airfield near Salamanca and Franco was both confirmed at Generalisimo and elected as 'Head of the Government of the Spanish State'. Thereafter, he simply arrogated to himself the powers of the Headship of State.[26] As a consequence of his decision, there was a delay between the fall of Maqueda on 21 September and 7 October, when the advance on Madrid was renewed.

From the moment of his political elevation, the rhythm and style of Franco's war effort changed. The lightning war of the columns now gave way to a far more deliberate process wherein the gradual destruction of the enemy took precedence over grand strategic objectives. In line with his grandiose plans for permanently eradicating the left from Spain, Franco began to prolong the war both in order to crush his Republican enemies and to eliminate his rivals on the right. Visiting the ruins of the Alcázar after the Civil War, Franco said to the official historian of his military triumphs, Manuel Aznar, 'When I entered the Alcázar, I was convinced that I had won the war. From then on it was just a question of time. I was no longer interested in a lightning victory but in a total victory, on every front, as a result of the exhaustion of the enemy.'[27]

On 7 October, the Nationalist forces tentatively resumed operations against Madrid. After frequent consultations with Franco, Mola had developed a two-part final strategy to take the capital which was already surrounded on the west from due north to due south. The idea was first for Nationalist forces to reduce the semi-circle by closing in on the capital, and then for the Army of Africa, now under the command of the impetuous General Varela, to make a frontal assault through the north western suburbs. The forward defences of the city were demoralised by Nationalist bombing and then brushed aside by motorised columns armed with fast Italian 'whippet' tanks.[28] However, there was little real urgency about the attack and Franco himself was curiously absent from the front until 23 November when he came to order the cessation of the attack. He was altogether more concerned with the less important battle to relieve the Asturian capital Oviedo, for which he sent valuable troops from the Madrid front. However, when Barroso suggested that the Nationalist forces were insufficient to justify the risks involved in attacking a city which could be defended street by street and house by house, Franco replied 'let Varela have a go. He has always been lucky.' Such frivolity suggests that Franco was distancing

[26] On the machinations behind the political elevation of Franco, see Preston, *Franco*, 174–85.

[27] José Antonio Vaca de Osma, *La larga guerra de Francisco Franco* (Madrid, 1991), 209.

[28] Martinez Bande, *La marcha*, 81–95.

himself from the attack on Madrid. Varela's plan to attack the northern suburbs, a natural fortress girded by the River Manzanares, was suicidal. There were acrimonious debates within the Nationalist high command over the wisdom of an uphill advance through narrow streets, yet Franco ultimately did nothing to prevent Varela's attack. The Generalisimo could not call off the attack on Madrid when there was widespread conviction in the Nationalist ranks that the capital was about to fall. However, if Varela were to fail, there could be no opposition to his preference for a long war.[29]

By 22 November, the people of Madrid, assisted by the International Brigades, defending the city with their backs to its walls, had repulsed the Nationalist attack.[30] On the following day, Franco travelled from Salamanca to Leganés on the outskirts of Madrid and informed his generals that there was no choice but to abandon the attack. He was fortunate that the Republican forces in the capital were too exhausted to mount an immediate counter-offensive. If they had, the tide might well have turned decisively in their favour. Before the Republic could rally its forces, Franco's battered columns would receive massive reinforcements from Fascist Italy. Mussolini harboured increasing doubts about the Generalisimo's strategic vision but he was already too committed to the Nationalist cause to permit Franco to be defeated.[31] The Germans were also 'faced with the decision either to leave Spain to herself or to throw in additional forces.'[32] This was a situation which Franco would exploit with some skill.

The failure of the assault on Madrid left Franco indecisive in the face of a complex war of manoeuvre. In the judgement of General Faupel, 'his military training and experience do not fit him for the direction of operations on their present scale.'[33] Eventually, after considerable hesitation, he moved forward from the deadlock by adopting an encircling strategy against the Madrid-La Coruña road to the North West.[34] In appalling weather, bloody battles were fought for small villages. The Italian commander in Spain, General Mario Roatta, also complained to Rome that the Generalisimo's staff was incapable of

---

[29]Vaca de Osma, *La larga guerra*, 233–4; George Hills, *Franco: The Man and his Nation* (New York, 1967), 263.

[30]Vicente Rojo, *Así fue la defensa de Madrid* (Mexico D.F., 1967), 55–103; Robert F. Colodny, *The Struggle for Madrid* (New York, 1958), 52–91; Hugh Thomas, *The Spanish Civil War* (3rd ed, 1977), 82.

[31]*Documents on German Foreign Policy*, D, III, 139; *Fascistas en España: la intervención italiana en al guerra civil a través de los telegramas de la 'Missione Militare Italiana in Spagna' (15 diciembre 1936–31 marzo 1937)*, Ismael Saz & Javier Tusell, eds, (Madrid/Rome, 1981), 25. (Henceforth *MMIS*.)

[32]*Documents on German Foreign Policy*, D, III, 155.

[33]*Documents on German Foreign Policy*, D, III, 159–62.

[34]José Manuel Martinez Bande, *La lucha en torno a Madrid* (Madrid, 1968), 37.

mounting an operation appropriate to a large-scale war.[35] When the fronts had stabilised by 15 January, each side had lost about 15,000 men.[36] The various efforts to take Madrid had severely depleted Franco's forces. The Republicans were now solidly dug in and Franco was doubly fortunate that they were unable to launch a counter-attack to break through his severely overstretched lines and that substantial reinforcements would soon arrive from Italy.

Partly out of contempt for Franco's generalship and partly out of a desire to monopolise the anticipated triumph for Fascism, Mussolini insisted that Italian troops must be used as an independent force under an Italian general only nominally responsible to Franco's overall command. Rejecting the Duce's more ambitious plans to cut off Catalonia from the rest of Spain, Franco agreed to an assault on Malaga to provide a seaport nearer to Italy and a launching pad for an attack on Valencia from the south west.[37] Mussolini considered that he could send instructions to Franco as to a subordinate and the attack on Malaga seems to have been his personal idea.[38] Franco was not much interested in the Italian tactic of *guerra celere* (lightning war) and the possibility of victories for Mussolini which might end the war before his own leadership was consolidated. He visited the southern front only once and was furious that Italian troops were first to enter Malaga and mortified by a telegram from Roatta which read 'Troops under my command have the honour to hand over the city of Malaga to Your Excellency'.[39] In fact, given the massive numerical and logistical superiority of the attackers, the triumph was less of an achievement than it seemed at the time.

While the Italians attacked in the south, and heartened by the availability of the crack German Condor Legion, Franco had renewed his efforts to take Madrid, launching on 6 February 1937 a major attack through the Jarama valley towards the Madrid-Valencia highway to the east of the capital. Still convinced that he could capture the capital, Franco took a special interest in the Jarama campaign.[40] However, when Colonel Emilio Faldella, Roatta's Chief of Staff, offered the Generalisimo the opportunity to use the Italian forces to close the circle around Madrid, he responded negatively: 'This is a war of a special kind, that has to be fought with exceptional methods so that such a numerous mass cannot be used all at once, but spread out over several

[35] MMIS, *Telegramas*, 79.

[36] Carlos de Arce, *Los generales de Franco* (Barcelona, 1984) 186; Martinez Bande, *La lucha en torno a Madrid*, 51–69.

[37] De Felice, *Mussolini il Duce*, 389–90.

[38] Mussolini to Roatta, 18 December 1936, MMIS, *Telegramas*, 69.

[39] Roatta to Ufficio Spagna, 8 February 1937, MMIS, *Telegramas*, 130.

[40] Franco Salgado-Araujo, *Mi vida*, 220.

fronts it would be more useful.'[41] He thereby revealed not just his resentment of the victory at Malaga, but also the narrowness of his own strategic vision. His preference for piecemeal actions over a wide area reflected both his own practical military experiences in a small-scale colonial war and his desire to conquer Spain slowly and so consolidate his political supremacy.[42] Franco would not be shaken from his preference for the gradual and thorough occupation of Republican territory, telling Faldella: 'In a civil war, a systematic occupation of territory accompanied by the necessary purge (*limpieza*) is preferable to a rapid rout of the enemy armies which leaves the country still infested with enemies'.[43]

However, when the Nationalist attack in the Jarama was blunted by the determined resistance of Republican troops reinforced by the International Brigades, Franco was forced to eat his words and beg Faldella for a diversion to relieve his exhausted forces. The Generalisimo perceived an Italian attack on Guadalajara, forty miles north-east of Madrid, to be an ideal way to divert Republican troops away from the Jarama. The Italians, however, were not thinking in terms of a supplementary action but rather of a bold and decisive initiative. The way in which Franco resolved in his own interests the contradiction between his own and the Italians' strategic conception was to reveal his political ruthlessness. More significantly, it was also to underline the extent to which he had gained in confidence and developed his notion of how the war should be fought since the débâcle at Madrid had occasioned the contemptuous remarks of Faupel and Roatta.

Anxious to get the Italians to relieve the pressure on his exhausted forces in the Jarama, on 1 March, Franco agreed to Faldella's proposal to close the circle around Madrid, with a joint attack south west by the Italians from Sigüenza towards Guadalajara backed up by a north eastern push by Nationalist troops from the Jarama towards Alcalá de Henares. On 8 March, the Italians under General Amerigo Coppi initially broke through the Republican defences. However, it became clear by the evening that Franco's promised attack from the Jarama had not materialised. The Republicans were thus permitted to withdraw forces from that front and concentrate reinforcements to the north of Guadalajara. The Italians were further disadvantaged by the weather. Equipped for African operations, they were unprepared for heavy snow and sleet. Their aircraft were grounded while the Republican air force

[41] Olao Conforti, *Guadalajara: la prima sconfitta del fascismo* (Milan, 1967), 30–2; Coverdale, *Italian Intervention*, 215.

[42] Cantalupo to Ciano, 17 February 1937, Archivio Storico del Ministero degli Affari Esteri, Spagna Fondo di Guerra, b.38, no.287/137.

[43] Conforti, *Guadalajara*, 33.

operated almost normally. Their light tanks with fixed machine guns were vulnerable to the Republic's Russian T-26 with revolving turret-mounted cannon. As Roatta desperately called for the promised supporting attack from the south, Franco feigned powerlessness. While he prevaricated before an apoplectic Roatta, the Italian forces were routed. The defeat of Guadalajara had many components—the weather, the poor morale and inappropriate equipment of the Italians and the skill of the Republican operations. Nevertheless, if Franco's attack had taken place as promised, the outcome might have been very different. The Generalisimo's refusal to commit his own troops and his readiness to let the Italians exhaust themselves in a bloodbath with the Republicans makes it difficult to avoid the conclusion that he had decided to use the Italians as cannon fodder in his strategy of defeating the Republic by gradual attrition. He let the Italians bear the weight of the fighting while his own units regrouped.[44]

Franco could take comfort from the fact that Guadalajara was a defeat which cost the Republic dearly in terms of casualties. However, it obliged him fundamentally to reconsider his strategic options. The unmistakable conclusion offered by the easy victory at Malaga and the bloodbaths at the Jarama and Guadalajara was that the Republic was concentrating its best units around the capital and neglecting other fronts. Accordingly, albeit reluctantly, Franco accepted the possibility of destroying the Republic by instalments far from the centre. Throughout March, Franco was subjected to pressure from Colonel Vigón, Chief of Mola's General Staff, via Kindelán, and General Hugo Sperrle, commander of the German Condor Legion, to intensify the war in the north in order to seize the heavy industrial resources of the Basque provinces. It took Guadalajara to change Franco's mind.[45] Franco made the decision with uncharacteristic rapidity, persuaded by promises from Sperrle and his Chief of Staff, Colonel Wolfram von Richthofen, about the likely impact of 'close air support' in smashing the morale of opposing troops.[46] The Condor Legion was theoretically responsible directly to Franco.[47] However, given the difficulties of hour-by-hour liaison, Franco gave Sperrle a free hand to deal directly with Mola and Vigón. Accordingly, with Franco's acquiescence, the Germans had the

---

[44] On the battle of Guadalajara, see Preston, *Franco*, 229-37; MMIS, *Telegrams*, 161-83; Emilio Faldella, *Venti mesi di guerra in Spagna* (Florence, 1939), 255-66; Conforti, *Guadalajara*, 51-178; Martinez Bande, *La lucha en torno a Madrid*, 133-46; Alberto Rovighi & Filippo Stefani, *La partecipazione italiana alla guerra civile spagnola (1936-1939)* 4 vols (Rome, 1993) I, 232-333.

[45] Kindelán, *Mis cuadernos*, 120-3; General Jorge Vigón, *General Mola (el cospirador)* (Barcelona, 1957), 303-4; Franco Salgado-Araujo, *Mi vida*, 225.

[46] Williamson Murray, *German Military Effectiveness* (Baltimore, 1992), 104-5.

[47] *DGFP*, D, III, 125-6.

decisive voice in the campaign. While the advance was being planned, von Richthofen wrote in his diary, 'we are practically in charge of the entire business without any of the responsibility'.[48]

Although Franco was delighted to bask in the sensation of having the Condor Legion at his orders, its novel use of ultra-modern technology was some distance from his strategic world. Indeed, to the consternation of Sperrle, he weakened the Basque offensive (Bilbao did not fall until 19 June) by keeping substantial forces near Madrid and requested, unsuccessfully, that the Condor Legion be split up among his units in central Spain. Nevertheless, German ground attack methods, exemplified by atrocities such as the bombing of undefended civilian targets like Durango on 31 March and Guernica on 26 April, fitted well with his notion of a war effort which would terrorise the enemy into defeat.

He explained his thinking in this regard to the Italian Ambassador Roberto Cantalupo on 4 April 1937. He dismissed the idea of swift strategic strikes as appropriate only for war against a foreign enemy. Speaking of 'the cities and in the countryside which I have already occupied but which are still not redeemed', he declared ominously that 'we must carry out the necessarily slow task of redemption and pacification, without which the military occupation will be largely useless. The moral redemption of the occupied zones will be long and difficult because in Spain the roots of anarchism are old and deep.' Redemption meant bloody political purges such as those which had followed the capture of Badajoz and Malaga: 'I will occupy Spain town by town, village by village, railway by railway ... Nothing will make me abandon this gradual programme. It will bring me less glory but greater internal peace. That being the case, this civil war could still last another year, two, perhaps three. Dear ambassador, I can assure that I am not interested in territory but in inhabitants. The reconquest of the territory is the means, the redemption of the inhabitants the end.' With a tone of helpless regret, he went on, 'I cannot shorten the war by even one day ... It could even be dangerous for me to reach Madrid with a stylish military operation. I will take the capital not an hour before it is necessary: first I must have the certainty of being able to found a regime.'[49] There can be no doubting that Franco placed the greatest important on the consolidation of his political power. That had been shown throughout September and October 1936 and it was

[48] Wolfram von Richthofen, 'Spanien-Tagebuch', in Maier, Klaus A. *Guernica 26.4.1937. Die deutsche Intervention in Spanien und der 'Fall Guernica'* (Freiburg, 1975) diary entries for 24, 28 March 1937, on pages 79, 82.

[49] Cantalupo to Mussolini, 29 March 1937, ASMAE, SFG, b.38, T.709/345; Roberto Cantalupo, *Fu la Spagna. Ambasciata presso Franco* (Milan, 1948), 230–3.

to lead, concurrently with the Basque campaign, to his devoting considerable time, effort and cunning to creating a single party under his undisputed leadership.[50]

By the summer of 1937, with the Basques defeated and a further assault about to be launched on Santander, Franco was confident of ultimate victory, though with a calender marked in years rather than months. His Axis allies, however, found it difficult to accept his long term view of the political benefits of a plodding war of attrition. This led to talk of a negotiated settlement, something which the Caudillo dismissed out of hand—he wanted a war to the death. Nonetheless, he moved with crab-like slowness and this enabled the Republican Chief of Staff, General Vicente Rojo, to try to halt the attack on the north by a diversionary attack on 6 July at the village of Brunete, in arid scrubland fifteen miles west of Madrid. As he was later to show at Teruel and the Ebro, Franco's notion of a war of moral redemption by terror did not permit him to give up an inch of once captured territory nor to turn aside from any opportunity to hammer home to Republican Spain the message of his invincibility—whatever the human cost. By responding to the attack at Brunete, Franco delayed the far more important campaign in the north because he believed that he could destroy large numbers of Republican troops on the Madrid front.[51]

Franco's decision to accept the challenge of Brunete has widely been considered a strategic error. In fact, it ensured that, in one of the bloodiest slogging matches of the war, the Republic, in delaying the fall of Santander only by about five weeks, would lose twenty thousand of its best troops, an objective on which Franco always placed the highest value.[52] More remarkable than the decision to abandon the northern campaign in order to fight at Brunete was Franco's response to the success of his troops. General Varela was convinced that, with the Republican forces in disarray, he could take Madrid. Franco now had no interest either in the early capture of Madrid nor in risking his advance in the north and ordered a flabbergasted Varela to dig in.[53] The collapse of Madrid would probably have ended the war. Franco, however, did not want victory until every square inch of Spain had

[50] On the process of the so-called unification of all right-wing parties under Franco, see Maximiano Garcia Venero, *Falange en la guerra de España: la Unificación y Hedilla* (Paris, 1967) *passim*; Southworth, *Antifalange*; Preston, *Franco*, 248–74.

[51] Kindelán, *Cuadernos*, 131–7.

[52] On the battle and its strategic significance, see Faldella, *Venti mesi*, 357; Vicente Rojo, *España heroica: diez bocetos de la guerra española* 3ª edición (Barcelona, 1975) 91–101; Thomas, *The Spanish Civil War*, 710–16.

[53] Kindelán, *Mis cuadernos*, 136–7; Manuel Aznar, *Historia militar de la guerra de España* (Madrid, 1940), 460; José Ignacio Luca de Tena, *Mis amigos muertos* (Barcelona, 1971), 205–6; Vaca de Osma, *La larga guerra*, 294–7.

been cleansed of leftists and liberals.

The campaign in the north became something of a walk-over. On 24 August 1937, two days before the fall of Santander, Rojo launched another diversionary offensive along a broad front westwards from Catalonia aimed at encircling Zaragoza. The small town of Belchite fell and Franco gave long consideration to a response. However, given the low strategic value of the ground lost and the likely impact on both Nationalist and Republican morale of delaying the attack on Asturias, this time he did not take the bait.[54] Belchite hardly interrupted the Nationalist conquest of Asturias during September and October. In terms of control of industrial production and population, the balance of power had now shifted dramatically in the Generalisimo's favour. His lines shortened and his commitments diminished, Franco now had powerful and well-equipped army available for use in the centre and the east.

After nearly two months reorganising his forces into six army corps, Franco hesitated over the direction of his next great offensive. After lengthy consideration of a great push through Aragón and then either an attack on Valencia or else a sweep through Catalonia to cut off the Republic from the French frontier, he decided, in early December, to launch his next attack against Madrid.[55] He hoped to complete the encirclement of the capital with a push towards Alcalá de Henares. However, Rojo pre-empted the operation by another diversionary offensive on 15 December against the bleak city of Teruel in Aragón. The Republican forces quickly captured one thousand square kilometres and, for the first time, entered an enemy-held provincial capital.[56] Franco abandoned his Guadalajara offensive despite the firm, not to say frantic, advice of his own staff and of the senior German and Italian officers to abandon Teruel. His goal of the total, humiliating annihilation of the Republic did not admit of allowing the enemy such successes. With Rojo having thrown everything into the Teruel offensive, the capture of Madrid was a realistic possibility but Franco was not inclined to end the war before he had thoroughly 'redeemed' more territory. In that sense, the attraction of confronting Rojo at Teruel was that it provided the opportunity to destroy a large body of the Republic's best forces.[57]

[54] Rojo, *España heroica*, 103–15; Servicio Histórico Militar (Coronel José Manuel Martinez Bande), *La gran ofensiva sobre Zaragoza* (Madrid, 1973), 78–167; Aznar, *Historia militar*, 499–516; Thomas, *Civil War*, 722–8; Franco Salgado-Araujo, *Mi vida*, 241–2.

[55] José Manuel Martinez Bande, *La batalla de Teruel* 2ª edición (Madrid, 1990), 16–26.

[56] Rojo, *España heroica*, 117–125; José Manuel Martinez Bande, *La batalla de Teruel* (Madrid, 1990), 52–64; Aznar, *Historia militar*, 543–54.

[57] Claude Martin, *Franco soldado y estadista* (Madrid, 1965), 293; Aznar, *Historia militar*, 551, 622; Garriga, *Yagüe*, 139–40.

When Franco pulled troops towards Teruel, an outraged Ciano commented 'Our generals are restless, quite rightly. Franco has no idea of synthesis in war. His operations are those of a magnificent battalion commander. His objective is always ground, never the enemy. And he doesn't realise that it is by the destruction of the enemy that you win a war'.[58] Ciano was wrong. Franco's obsession with 'ground' was a deliberate quest for great battles of attrition which could, and did, destroy vast numbers of the enemy's troops. Teruel would be just such a conflict. Conducted in freezing conditions and at enormous cost to both sides, the battle was eventually won by Franco's forces on 22 February.[59] The Republican army was shattered and the Nationalists were now poised to sweep through Aragón at their leisure. Franco now had a twenty per cent advantage in terms of men and an overwhelming one in terms of aircraft, artillery and other equipment.[60] The destruction of the best Republican units at Teruel made it the military turning point of the Civil War. The battle also coincided with a further step forward in the institutionalisation of Franco's political power, with the formation of his first government on 30 January 1938.[61]

The triumph at Teruel opened up vistas of uninterrupted victories against an exhausted Republic and, over the next five months, Franco made good use of his opportunities. His concern with the physical annihilation of the enemy precluded stylish strategic operations to finish off the Republic quickly. Nevertheless, he was now to show some skill in handling a large army of several hundreds of thousands of men across a huge front and should therefore be seen as more than the petty-minded battalion commander so often derided by Hitler and Faupel, Mussolini and Ciano. In early March, six army corps totalling 200,000 men began an advance across a 260 kilometre wide front in the direction of the Ebro valley. The objective was to destroy more Republican forces and to reach the point where the River Segre, which ran north to south through eastern Catalonia, met the Ebro running west to east near Lérida. So spectacular was its success that, by 15 March, Franco decided to push on to the sea and cut off Catalonia from Valencia and the central Republican zone.

However, when Lérida fell on 4 April to Yagüe, he along with Kindelán, Vigón and the new commander of the Condor Legion, General Hellmuth Volkmann, advocated the occupation of a badly

[58] Ciano, *Diary 37–38*, 46.

[59] Martinez Bande, *Teruel*, 165–209; Lojendio, *Operaciones militares*, 380–95; Aznar, *Historia militar*, 569–85; Salas Larrazábal, *Ejército*, II, 1672–1704.

[60] *DGFP*, D, III, 556–7; Gerald Howson, *Aircraft of the Spanish Civil War 1936–1939* (1990), 20–8.

[61] *The Times*, 4 March 1938; *DGFP*, D, III, 613–14; Ramón Serrano Suñer, *Entre Hendaya y Gibraltar* (Madrid, 1947), 60–4.

defended Catalonia. It seemed to be the moment to finish off the Republic.[62] If he had followed all this advice, Franco could probably have brought the war to a speedier conclusion. There were no significant Republican forces between Lérida and Barcelona. The loss of Catalonia, with the Republic's remaining war industry and the seat of government, would be a devastating blow to Republican morale. Franco rejected such a move partly because of fears of French intervention on behalf of the Republic.[63] However, he seems to have been motivated rather more by concern than a sudden Republican collapse in the wake of the fall of Barcelona would still have left a substantial number of armed Republicans in central and southern Spain. His goal remained the total annihilation of the Republic and its supporters. Accordingly, to the astonishment of Rojo as well as of Yagüe, Kindelán and Vigón, he decided to divert his troops south for an attack on Valencia. He wanted further destruction and demoralisation of the Republic's human resources before the war was over.[64]

After reaching the Mediterranean on 15 April 1938, Franco's forces set off on a slow and bloody advance towards Valencia through the difficult terrain of the Maestrazgo. Kindelán begged Franco to desist from an operation which was incurring high casualties for the Nationalists as well as for the Republicans but he refused.[65] By 23 July 1938, however, his forces were less than forty kilometres from Valencia. In an attempt to restore contact between Catalonia and the rest of the Republican zone, a desperate diversionary assault across the River Ebro was launched by General Rojo on 24 July. With the advantage of surprise, by 1 August, the Republicans had advanced forty kilometres to Gandesa. Although his staff were dismayed by the Ebro crossing, Franco himself welcomed the opportunity to encircle the Republicans with their backs to the river. He poured troops into the area and began a merciless four-month battle of attrition in order, at no little cost in Nationalist lives, to smash the Republican forces. Valencia was abandoned and a strategically meaningless battle which would involve a bloodbath worse even than those of the Jarama, Brunete and Teruel. But Franco thought the losses a reasonable price to pay for the annihilation of the Republican army.[66]

[62] Kindelán, *Mis cuadernos*, 157–63; *DGFP*, D, III, 628.

[63] Jaime Martinez Parrilla, *La fuerzas armadas francesas ante la guerra civil española (1936–1939)* (Madrid, 1987), 184–92; David Wingeate Pike, *Les français et la guerre d'Espagne 1936–1939* (Paris, 1975), 296–7; *DGFP*, D, III, 620–2.

[64] José Manuel Martinez Bande, *La ofensiva sobre Valencia* (Madrid, 1977), 16–18; Garriga, *Yagüe*, 145–6; Vicente Rojo, *¡Alerta los pueblos! estudio politico-militar del periodo final de la guerra española* 2ª edición (Barcelona, 1974), 40, 46–50, 54–5.

[65] Martinez Bande, *La ofensiva*, 69–96.

[66] Franco Salgado-Araujo, *Mi vida*, 264; Aznar, *Historia militar*, 739–70.

Once more, his own staff and his German and Italian advisers were dismayed. They pointed out to him that it would be easy to contain the Republican advance and attack a now virtually undefended Barcelona.[67] He was not interested, much preferring to convert Gandesa into the cemetery of the Republican army than to seek a swift and imaginative victory.[68] The cost was horrendous on both sides. It was not until the end of October, after he had secured substantial supplies of German weaponry in return for mining concessions, that Franco could launch his decisive counter-offensive. By mid-November, he had recovered the territory lost in July. He had side-stepped another chance of quick victory and secured what he most wanted—the annihilation of the Republican army. There would be no negotiated truces, no conditions, no peace with honour. It was effectively the end for the Republic. The last push against Catalonia began on 23 December. Barcelona fell on 26 January 1939. In Madrid, on 4 March, the commander of the Republican Army of the Centre, Colonel Segismundo Casado revolted against the Republican government in the hope of stopping increasingly senseless slaughter. His hopes of a negotiated peace were rebuffed by Franco and, after a minor civil war within the civil war, troops all along the line began to surrender. The Nationalists entered an eerily silent Madrid on 27 March. On 1 April 1939, Franco issued his final victory communiqué.

Franco had fought a political war. He had not set out to emulate Napoleon. Indeed, he stated often enough his conviction that 'stylish military operations' did not serve his purpose. He was almost certainly lacking in the vision and the capacity to conceive such operations. His talents lay in other directions. He had a remarkable capacity to raise the morale of those around him simply by his imperturbability under pressure. No reverse affected his equanimity. His ability as a rebel general to secure the logistical support of Germany and Italy was crucial to the success of his war effort. His success in domesticating and unifying the disparate political forces in his coalition was hardly less remarkable. These were achievements which outweighed his deficiencies as a stylish strategist. In the last resort, his primordial concern as a military leader had been to ensure a long future as dictator, and his war effort successfully traumatised the defeated into long years of apathy. Many of Franco's strategic decisions—Toledo, Brunete, Teruel, the Maestrazgo, the Ebro—confirm that he was not a great military thinker. Yet each of those decisions brought him nearer to his goal. He can hardly be considered a military failure. His strategy

[67] Kindelán, *Mis cuadernos*, 173.
[68] Manuel Tagüeña Lacorte, *Testimonio de dos guerras* (México D. F., 1973), 230; José Manuel Martinez Bande, *La batalla del Ebro* 2ª edición (Madrid, 1988), 168.

was based on an assumption of the primacy of political concerns. His war effort was the first and bloodiest stage in a political repression that would maintain an intense rhythm of killing until 1943 and never be entirely relaxed. Throughout the years following his victory, he rejected any thought of amnesty or reconciliation with the defeated. Over four hundred thousand Republicans were forced into exile. As many again were sentenced to periods in prison, concentration camps or labour battalions. Until he died, Franco's regime deliberately kept alive the memory of the Civil War and maintained the division between victors and vanquished as an instrument of policy.[69] His long war was the pillar on which his long dictatorship rested.

[69] Paul Preston, *The Politics of Revenge: Fascism and the Military in Twentieth Century Spain* (1990), 30–47.

SYMBOLIC MEANINGS OF HAIR IN THE MIDDLE AGES

By Robert Bartlett

READ 5 MARCH 1993

BEATNIKS, hippies, punks; marines, convicts, monks—it does not need much reflection to see that styles of head and facial hair in our own society convey meanings about status, attitude and role. The same is equally true of other societies, including those of the past, and the purpose of this paper is to explore some of those meanings as found in medieval Europe.[1]

Hair is a particularly fertile and powerful bearer of meaning for three basic reasons. First, hair is an exceptionally malleable body part. It has almost the same range of possibilities of treatment as clothing—it can be shaped, dyed, removed—but it emerges from the body and is thus organic in a way that clothes are not. Second, head and facial hair surrounds the face, the part of the body with the most concentrated and diverse communicative functions. Here are grouped the organs of sight, smell, taste and hearing; here speech originates and eye contact focuses. The treatment of hair is thus a pre-eminently socially visible act. Indeed, those theorists who see hair treatment as primarily sexually expressive would argue that the social visibility of head and facial hair is a prerequisite for its effective role as an open bearer of otherwise hidden messages.[2] Third, hair gives a few pieces of biological information, but only a few. Thus it starts with some inherent associations but is not tightly structured into a whole system of meanings. In the populations discussed here, those of medieval Europe, the most important biological differentia were that adults and not children had body hair and that only adult males had facial hair. The beard was thus of

---

[1] Special acknowledgement is due to two scholars who kindly provided the author with offprints of their publications that have been of enormous help: Giles Constable, 'Introduction' (on beards in the Middle Ages), to Burchard of Bellevaux, *Apologia de Barbis*, ed. R. B. C. Huygens, in *Apologiae duae (Corpus Christianorum, continuatio mediaevalis*, LXII, Turnhout, 1985), 47–130; William Sayers, 'Early Irish Attitudes toward Hair and Beards, Baldness and Tonsure', *Zeitschrift für celtische Philologie*, XLIV (1991), 154–89. Many years ago Keith Thomas supplied a helpful introductory bibliography which was an encouragement to think further in this area.

[2] See the discussion in E. R. Leach, 'Magical Hair', *Journal of the Royal Anthropological Institute of Great Britain and Ireland*, LXXXVIII (1958), 147–64, and C. R. Hallpike, 'Social Hair', *Man: The Journal of the Royal Anthropological Institute*, IV (1969), 256–64.

general importance as a biological marker and body hair was also occasionally significant, as in the passage in the thirteenth-century law-book, the *Sachsenspiegel*, which prescribes as a proof of age for a man 'if he has hair in his beard and down below and beneath each arm, then one will know that he is of age'.[3]

This innate sex and age differentiation gave a few basic structures to the symbolic grammar of hair in the Middle Ages, but left plenty of room for elaboration. Much more important than what hair did was what was done to hair. It could be combed or left unkempt, it could be grown long, trimmed or removed entirely, it could be bound or loosed. These actions and treatments conveyed social meanings.

A very fundamental distinction is that between hair that is cut and hair that is grown long. This contrast was used to mark status, ethnic identity, age and sex. In the case of status, an equation of long hair with high birth is found in many medieval societies. In early medieval Ireland cropped hair was a sign of a servant. Hence when Irish-speaking devotees of a saint took names expressing their devotion, they might chose to signal their subordination through the word *mael*, 'cropped one', the personal name Mael Patraic, 'cropped one of Patrick', thus being a precise parallel to the name Gilla Patraic, 'servant of Patrick'.[4] The long hair of the early Germanic free men is fairly well attested and in Italy the free Gothic warriors were known as *capillati*, 'the long-haired men'.[5] Perhaps the most famous case of the connection between high birth and long hair is that of the Merovingian kings, 'the long-haired kings' as they have been called. When a wicked Merovingian uncle offered his nephews a choice between the scissors and the sword, he was saying 'do you wish to live non-regally or to die?'[6] This association of aristocracy and long hair continued well into the High Middle Ages. The thirteenth-century satirical poem *Meier Helmbrecht* portrays a young peasant with ideas above his station. Amongst his other affectations is the wearing of his hair: 'it flowed long and full

---

[3] *Sachsenspiegel, Landrecht* I. xlii, ed. Karl Eckhardt (Göttingen, 1955), 104.

[4] *(Contributions to a) Dictionary of the Irish Language* (Royal Irish Academy, Dublin, 1913–76), *s. vv. gilla* (e), *mael* II c; Sayers, 'Early Irish Attitudes', 177.

[5] Herwig Wolfram, *History of the Goths* (Eng. transl., Berkeley and Los Angeles, 1988), 301–2.

[6] Gregory of Tours, *Libri Historiarum X* III. xviii, ed. B. Krusch and W. Levison, *Monumenta Germaniae historica, Scriptores rerum Merovingicarum* I, i (1951), 118. See J. M. Wallace-Hadrill, *The Long-haired Kings* (1962), 156–7, 232–3, 245–6; Averil Cameron, 'How Did the Merovingian Kings Wear Their Hair?', *Revue belge de philologie et d'histoire*, XLIII (1965), 1203–16; Conrad Leyser, 'Long-haired Kings and Short-haired Nuns: Power and Gender in Merovingian Gaul', *Medieval World* (March–April 1992), 37–42 (R. I. Moore kindly provided the last reference).

over his shoulders'.[7] At the very time and in the very place where this
poem was composed—mid-thirteenth century Bavaria—sumptuary laws
prescribed 'peasants and their sons shall cut their hair to the ears'.[8] In
the poem Helmbrecht suffers the consequences of his insubordination.
He joins a band of robber knights and is eventually killed by the
ordinary country people who have been victimised by the knights'
plundering raids. Before they finish him off they tear out his hair and
scatter it on the ground.[9] In this one violent act the peasants express
their class hatred of the plundering knight by ripping out his aristocratic
hair and, simultaneously, the poet reaffirms his belief in the proper
stations of society, as marked by hair, for this particular knight is an
upstart whose hair pretensions are being brutally rectified.

One of the oldest and most general functions of hair treatment was
to distinguish ethnic groups. Tacitus described the knotted hair of the
Germanic Suevi as 'a mark of that people' (*insigne gentis*)[10] and when the
Byzantines were first confronted with a new group of barbarians, such
as the Avars, their hair-style was amongst the first things that they
noticed and remarked upon: 'they wore their hair very long at the
back, tied with bands and braided'.[11] The distinction between the short-
haired, shaven Normans and the long-haired, whiskered Anglo-Saxons
is memorably conveyed by the story of how King Harold's scouts
returned with the report that the Norman army consisted almost
entirely of priests.[12] Even as late as the 1190s some Englishmen were
supposedly still maintaining a tradition of wearing beards to express
their hostility to the Normans.[13]

The significance of hairstyle as a mark of ethnic differentiation was,
of course, particularly great in those areas where different populations
lived side by side. In Ireland, for example, after the settlement of a
sizeable English population in the island in the twelfth and thirteenth
centuries, hair became one of the signs distinguishing the English
settlers, 'the king's loyal subjects', from 'the wild Irish', the king's
enemies. Indeed, one aspect of the cultural assimilation, or gaelicisation,

[7] Werner der Gartenaere, *Helmbrecht*, lines 10–13, ed. Ulrich Seelbach, tr. Linda Parshall
(New York and London, 1987), 2.

[8] *Pax Bawarica* LXXI, ed. Ludwig Weiland, *Monumenta Germaniae historica, Constitutiones
et acta publica imperatorum et regum*, II (1896), no. 427, 577 (1244).

[9] *Helmbrecht*, lines 1896–1900, ed. Seelbach, 124.

[10] *Germania* XXXVIII.

[11] Theophanes Confessor, *Chronographia*, ed. Karl de Boor (Leipzig, 1883) sect. 6050,
232; Walter Pohl, *Die Awaren* (Munich, 1988), 18.

[12] William of Malmesbury, *Gesta regum* III, ed. William Stubbs (2 vols., Rolls Series,
1887–9) II, 301; the passage was borrowed by Pseudo-Alanus, *Commentary on the Prophecies
of Merlin* (Frankfurt, 1603), 62.

[13] Mathew Paris, *Chronica majora*, ed. Henry R. Luard (7 vols., Rolls Series, 1872–84),
II, 418.

of some members of the settler population was their adoption of Irish hair fashions, a kind of apostasy in matters of style that became the subject of restrictive legislation as early as 1297, when there was a condemnation of 'the degenerate English of modern times who wear Irish clothes, have their heads half shaved and grow their hair long at the back, calling this *culan* [a word derived from *cul*, the back of the head], making themselves like the Irish in clothing and appearance.' The problem, as this legislation goes on to say, was that Englishmen were being mistaken for Irishmen and killed as Irishmen, even though the killing of an Englishman and the killing of an Irishman required quite different punishments. Therefore the English settlers were required to maintain English *mores* and *tonsura* on pain of distraint of their property or imprisonment.[14] Hair style was thus one of the most patent outward markers of the pervasive judicial dualism of colonial Ireland.[15] Conversely, Irishmen who were admitted to the privilege of English law were required to mark this change by the same visible indicator. When, in 1333, Dermot O'Dwyer was permitted 'to enjoy all the liberties that the English have in Ireland', it was noted 'and he has had his *culan* hair cut, to have English law'.[16] The politics of hair continued in Ireland well into the Tudor period, when we can find an act of Henry VIII repeating hair prescriptions very like those of 1297 and, from the opposite side, a Gaelic poet reproaching the native Irish 'who follow English ways, who cut short your curling hair...'[17]

A situation not dissimilar from that in Ireland existed in Reconquest Spain where the Muslim subjects of Christian kings formed a distinct quasi-ethnic group within the population. Here too legislative prescription relating to hair was issued by the dominant people, not, in this instance, attempting to prevent their own members becoming 'degenerate', but rather enforcing a distinctive style for the alien group. By the middle of the thirteenth century most of the Iberian peninsula was in the hands of Christian kings and in some areas the subject Muslim population was very large. It was a situation that prompted the promulgation of identifying rules. In the 1250s Castilian legislation

---

[14] *Statutes and Ordinances and Acts of the Parliament of Ireland: King John to Henry V*, ed. Henry F. Berry (Dublin, 1907), 210; for *culan* and *cul, Dictionary of the Irish Language, s. v.*.

[15] For the general context see the present writer's *The Making of Europe: Conquest Colonization and Cultural Change 950–1350* (1993), 214–20, and Robin Frame, '"Les Engleys nées en Irlande": The English Political Identity in Medieval Ireland', *ante*, 6th ser., III (1993), 83–103.

[16] *Parliaments and Councils of Mediaeval Ireland*, I, ed. H. G. Richardson and G. O. Sayles (Irish Manuscripts Commission, Dublin, 1947), no. 13, 17.

[17] Constantia Maxwell (ed.), *Irish History from Contemporary Sources (1509–1610)* (London, 1923), 113; Kenneth H. Jackson (ed.), *A Celtic Miscellany* (rev. ed., Harmondsworth, 1971), 218; see also David B. Quinn, *The Elizabethans and the Irish* (Ithaca, 1966), 92, 126, 151, 169.

required 'that the Moors who live in towns settled by Christians should go about with their hair cut in a circle and parted without a forelock and that they should wear long beards as their law commands'.[18] The *cortes* of Catalonia adopted identical rules in 1301, specifying monetary and physical punishments for infringement and pithily setting out the rationale for the law: 'so that he [the Moor] may be recognised among Christians'.[19] Such provisions were frequently repeated in the fourteenth century.[20] They are part of a series of rules regulating Muslim-Christian interaction and are clearly akin to those prescriptions which demanded distinctive clothing for Jews and Muslims. Indeed, some light may be thrown on laws regulating the hair styles of Spanish Muslims by the wording of the canon of the Fourth Lateran Council of 1215 which introduced distinctive dress for Jews and Muslims. 'In many regions,' it reads, 'Jews and Saracens are distinguished from Christians by their dress but in some areas there is confusion and no differences can be remarked between them.' On this occasion the explicit anxiety that prompted discriminatory legislation was the occurrence of sexual relations between Christians and non-Christians[21] and it might be reasonable to suspect a similar issue lurking behind the Spanish examples too. In these Irish and Iberian cases, we find an insistence that ethnic groups be identified by clear hair markers. Inter-ethnic violence in Ireland and, probably, sexual activity in Spain were to be canalised by the patent symbolism of hairstyle.

Age categories could also be identified in the versatile code of hair treatment. A classic rite of passage practised in early medieval Europe was the first cutting of a boy's hair as a mark of his transition to the age group beyond infants and the very young. There were classical antecedents to this tradition but it may well also have been indigenous to the Germanic peoples and the Church very soon recognised it with liturgical forms 'for the first hair cut' (*ad capillaturam incidendam*).[22] Frankish law equated a boy's *capillaturia* (an alternative spelling) with a girl's wedding as an occasion for endowment and prescribed a heavy monetary penalty for 'anyone presuming to cut the hair of a long-haired boy (*puer crinitus*)

---

[18] *Córtes de los antiguos reinos de Leon y Castilla*, I (Real Academia de Historia, Madrid, 1861), 59 (cl. 27); *cf.* Francisco Fernández y González, *Estado social y político de los mudéjares de Castilla* (Madrid, 1866), 130 n. 2.

[19] *Cortes de los antiguos reinos de Aragón y de Valencia y principado de Cataluña*, I/i (Real Academia de Historia, Madrid, 1896), 190 (cl. 12).

[20] John Boswell, *The Royal Treasure: Muslim Communities under the Crown of Aragon in the Fourteenth Century* (New Haven, 1977), 331 (*cf.* 289-90).

[21] *Conciliorum oecumenicorum decreta*, ed. J. Alberigo et al. (3rd. ed., Bologna, 1973), 241-3 (can. LXVIII).

[22] Adolf Franz, *Die kirchlichen Benediktionen im Mittelalter* (2 vols., Freiburg, 1909), II, 245-52. Franz believes that this ceremony does not simply represent the tonsuring of oblates (252).

without the permission of his kindred'.[23] An important relationship was established between the boy whose hair was cut and the person who cut it. In the late 730s, Charles Martel sent his son to the Lombard king Liutprand so that the king might cut the boy's hair, 'as the custom is. Cutting his hair, he became a father to him...'[24]

This early medieval Frankish practice does not seem to have survived long into the Carolingian period, though a possible linguistic trace has been left in later French, Provençal and north Italian dialect in the term *tos* and its cognates. This means 'young man' or 'youth' and there is general agreement among philologists that it derives from *tonsus*, 'cropped' or 'shorn'. A commonly suggested interpretation is that it originally referred to boys who had already had their first ceremonial hair-cut but were not yet of full age.[25] The *Chanson de la Croisade Albigeoise* refers to Count Raymond VII of Toulouse as an *avinens tos* ('prepossessing young man') at a time when he was in fact about eighteen.[26] The mere linguistic evidence, which occurs as early as the twelfth century, does not of course mean that the custom itself was in general use in France or Italy in the High Middle Ages, although in the early fourteenth century it was stated that parish priests in Pavia received offerings 'at the blessing of the hair of male children'.[27]

There is good evidence for the ritual first hair-cut beyond Germanic and Romance Europe. In addition to some elusive Irish material, there are west Slav sources of the tenth and twelfth centuries which refer to the practice and a particularly explicit reference occurs in the founding myth of the Piast dynasty, which ruled Poland down to the fourteenth century. Here the rise of the dynasty is linked with the custom. As recounted in the pages of the Polish court chronicler of the early twelfth century, the story runs that 'there was in the city of Gniezno a duke by the name of Popel, who had two sons; he had, in the pagan way, prepared a great feast for their hair-cutting and had invited many of his great men and relatives.' Two unnamed visitors then arrive in Gniezno, but are turned away from the duke's house. They seek

[23] *Pactus legis Salicae* XXIV, LXVII, ed. Karl Eckhardt, *Monumenta Germaniae historica, Leges nationum Germanicarum*, IV, i (1962), 89–90, 238.

[24] Paul the Deacon, *Historia Langobardorum* VI. liii, ed. L. Bethmann and G. Waitz, *Monumenta Germaniae historica, Scriptores rerum Germanicarum in usum scholarum separatim editi*, XLVIII (1878), 237.

[25] Emil Levy, *Provenzalisches Supplement-Wörterbuch*, VIII (Leipzig, 1924), 327–8, s. v. 'tos', 335–6, s. v. 'toza'; Walther von Wartburg, *Französisches etymologisches Wörterbuch*, XIII/ii (Basel, 1965), 32–3, s. v. 'tonsus'; Ivan Pauli, *'Enfant', 'garçon', 'fille' dans les langues romanes* (Lund, 1919), 260–8, 'Dénominations établies d'après la coups des cheveux'.

[26] *La Chanson de la Croisade Albigeoise* XV. cxliii, line 13, ed. Eugène Martin-Chabot (3 vols., *Les classiques de l'histoire de France au Moyen Age*, Paris, 1931–61), II, 42.

[27] *Anonymus Ticensis commentarius de laudibus Papiae* XV, ed. L. A. Muratori, *Rerum italicarum scriptores*, XI (Milan, 1727), col. 31.

hospitality instead in the surrounding settlement, the *suburbium*, at the house of a poor ploughman called Piast, who receives them kindly. When the travellers ask for something to drink Piast replies 'I have a barrel of beer that I have got ready for the hair-cutting of my only son'. They command him to serve it and it miraculously refills itself. A piglet that Piast has been fattening for the same occasion is killed and provides—'mirabile dictu'—ten buckets of pork. Meanwhile up in the citadel the duke's party is not going so well, since his jars of drink are found to be empty. The ploughman Piast invites the duke and his guests to join his celebration and the duke—since, as the chronicler observes, 'in those days the ruler of the city had not yet swelled up with such great pride'—is happy to accept. The mysterious strangers then cut the hair of Piast's son and name him Semovith. Not surprisingly, as soon as he has grown up Semovith expels duke Popel and his line and establishes himself as duke in his place. His son, Miesko, was the first Christian ruler of Poland.[28]

The function of the story as a legitimising myth for the Piast dynasty is patent. More important for our purpose is the light it throws on the ritual haircut. Here one sees two fathers of very different social rank preparing lavish celebrations for this important event, the ploughman carefully nursing his beer and pig. The mysterious unnamed strangers are given the central role of cutting the hair of Piast's son and thus becoming his patrons or fictive fathers. In the eyes of the twelfth-century chronicler telling the story, a writer who was attached to the ducal court and probably non-Polish, such arrangements involve acting *more gentilitatis*—'in the pagan way'—but the practice was not ineradicably pagan. The first of the Polish ducal line to have his hair-cut as a Christian was Miesko's son Boleslaw and, according to his epitaph, when his hair was cut at the age of seven the clippings were sent to Rome,[29] thus establishing the same kind of patronal relationship as that between King Liutprand and Charles Martel's son. It is this same Miesko, the father, who, in a dramatic gesture of clientship, donated his whole dominions to the papal see, and the transmission of his son's hair-clippings to the pope is a symbolic counterpart. The hair-cutting of Piast's son in the story thus appears as a generally important social custom and rite of passage which is here given a particular political twist to point out the future success of the boy and his descendants.

Hair cutting was a mark of sex as well as age. Although there is no biological ground for the association, long hair was frequently deemed

[28] Gallus Anonymus, *Chronicon*, ed. K. Maleczynski, *Monumenta Poloniae historica*, n. s., II (Cracow, 1952), 9–12.
[29] 'Epitaphium Chabri Boleslai', ed. A. Bielowski, *Monumenta Poloniae historica*, I (Lwów, 1864), 320.

appropriate for women and shorter hair for men. Both the strength of the association and its purely conventional nature are brought out sharply in those moments when the customary patterns were transgressed. The craze for long hair among men that swept the upper classes in northern France and England in the late eleventh and early twelfth century is fairly well documented and we are in this case able to investigate a moment when contemporaries were confronted, in the words of Henri Platelle, who studied the issue in depth in an article published in 1975, with 'the problem of scandal'.[30]

The earliest evidence is from the mid 1090s. On Ash Wednesday 1094 Archbishop Anselm of Canterbury refused to give ashes or his blessing to those young men who 'grew their hair like girls' unless they had their hair cut.[31] Two years later the Council of Rouen prescribed 'that no one should grow his hair long but have it cut as befits a Christian'; the sanction was exclusion from church and from Christian burial.[32] The monastic historians Orderic Vitalis and William of Malmesbury, writing several decades later, also associated the 1090s, the reign of William Rufus, with the cult of luxuriant male hair. Orderic denounced the novelties and effeminacy of the styles of the time, such as long hair, pointed shoes and trailing clothes. 'After the deaths of Gregory VII and William the Conqueror', he wrote, 'the decent customs of our forefathers were almost completely swept away', here making an extremely apt choice of these two particular dour and domineering patriarchs as enemies of effeminacy and frivolity.[33]

According to one source the effeminacy of William Rufus' court was so pronounced that some people expressed the opinion that it would be a good thing if his brother Henry were to rule.[34] The wish was realised in 1100, but the problem of long hair seems to have continued. In 1102 the Council of Westminster ruled 'that long-haired men should have their hair cut so that part of the ears is visible and the eyes are not covered'.[35] A few years later a memorable scene occurred during the Easter service in the church of Carentan in Normandy when the bishop of Séez upbraided King Henry and his courtiers for their long hair and, at the end of his sermon, produced a pair of scissors and cut

[30] Henri Platelle, 'Le problème de scandale: les nouvelles modes masculines aux XIe et XIIe siècles', *Revue belge de philologie et d'histoire*, LIII (1975), 1071–96. There is an important discussion in Frank Barlow, *William Rufus* (1983), 101–10.

[31] Eadmer, *Historia novorum*, ed. Martin Rule (Rolls Series, 1884), 48.

[32] Orderic Vitalis, *Historia ecclesiastica* IX. iii, ed. and tr. Marjorie Chibnall (6 vols., Oxford, 1968–80), V, 22.

[33] *Ibid.* VIII. x, ed. Chibnall, IV, 186–90.

[34] William of Malmesbury, *Gesta regum* IV, ed. Stubbs, II, 370.

[35] Eadmer, *Historia novorum*, ed. Rule, 143; *Councils and Synods with Other Documents relating to the English Church 1 (871–1204)*, ed. D. Whitelock, M. Brett and C. N. L. Brooke (2 vols., Oxford, 1981), II, 677–8.

their hair on the spot (an incident vividly depicted by the appropriately named Victorian narrative painter Ernest Prater).[36] These Anglo-Norman courtiers were perhaps more fortunate than the nobles of Amiens who, in the following year, were turned away from the altar during mass by their bishop on account of their long hair. They had obviously not expected such a rebuff and had to improvise a solution: 'lacking scissors, they cut their hair with their swords or knives'.[37] Despite revivalist moments of this kind, the monk-bishops with their scissors did not win a definitive victory. Anselm's failure in this respect was acknowledged by his biographer Eadmer, who noted that after the archbishop's death in 1109 'the men with long hair whom father Anselm had banned from the threshold of holy church abound to such a degree and glory so much in their wickedly long and feminine hair that whoever is not long-haired is called as an insult "peasant" or "priest" '.[38] The battle against womanly long hair on men continued into the twelfth-century, as disapproving comments from Bernard of Clairvaux and Alan of Lille show.[39]

William of Malmesbury seems to have regarded long hair on men as a particularly striking instance of moral decadence. In his denunciation of Rufus' reign he criticised 'the flowing hair, the luxurious clothes, the shoes with curving points' of the courtiers, castigated the young men who 'tried to outdo women in the softness of their bodies' and 'were unwilling to remain what they had been born' and damned 'the crowds of effeminates' who followed the court.[40] In an anecdote that he dates to the years 1128 or 1129 he tells how 'a provincialknight who gloried in the luxuriance of his hair' had a dream in which someone was choking him with his own locks. Next day the knight had his hair trimmed and his example quickly spread throughout England 'among almost all the knights'. This moral revival was short-lived, however. 'Scarcely a year went by before all who wanted to appear courtly (*curialis*) fell back into their former vice, trying to outdo women in the length of their hair'.[41] William attached so much importance to

---

[36] Orderic Vitalis, *Historia ecclesiastica* XI. xi, ed. Chibnall, VI, 64–6.

[37] Nicholas of Soissons, *Vita Godefridi episcopi Ambianensis*, ed. Albert Poncelet, *Acta Sanctorum Novembris*, III (Brussels, 1910), 905–44, at 926.

[38] Eadmer, *Historia novorum*, ed. Rule, 214.

[39] Bernard of Clairvaux, *De laude novae militiae* II. iv, in J. Leclerq and H. M. Rochais (eds.), *Opera*, III (Rome, 1963), 205–39, at 216, 220; Alan of Lille, *Anticlaudianus* VII. iii. 32, ed. Thomas Wright, *The Anglo-Latin Satirical Poets and Epigrammatists of the Twelfth Century*, II (Rolls Series, 1872), 268–428, at 387.

[40] William of Malmesbury, *Gesta regum* IV, ed. Stubbs, II, 369–70.

[41] William of Malmesbury, *Historia novella*, ed. and tr. K. R. Potter (1955), 5–6. Gaimar has a story about hair-cropping at *Rufus'* court, but this is very difficult to interpret: Geffrei Gaimar, *L'Estoire des Engleis*, lines 6072–6104, ed. Alexander Bell (*Anglo-Norman Texts*, XIV–XVI, Oxford, 1960), 192–3.

this vice of long hair that he appears even to have regarded it as a cause of the Norman Conquest. In his *Life of Wulfstan* he depicts the saintly bishop of Worcester travelling around, in the period before 1066, with a little knife, of the kind 'used for removing dirt from the nails or blots from books'. Wulfstan used to 'cut with his own hands the wanton locks' of 'those who grew their hair long ... If anyone thought to refuse he publicly reproached them for their softness and publicly threatened evils to come: "Those who are ashamed to be what they were born and who copy women in their flowing hair will be no better than women in defending their country against overseas peoples." This was illustrated that very year by the coming of the Normans.'[42] It has recently been argued that William of Malmesbury was a crucial figure in the formation of English imperialist ideology;[43] here he appears equally central to the Roundhead tradition.

The rhetoric that monastic writers produced as part of their campaign against long hair is extensive and multi-layered. It clearly had a political side, and could, as we have seen, be shaped into an expression of support for a particular lord (Henry I) or an explanation of national political disaster (the Norman Conquest). It was buttressed by the uncompromising Pauline command, 'if a man grows his hair, it is a dishonour to him' (I Corinthians 11: 14), which these authors frequently cited. Monastic criticism identified the hated hairstyles with youth and the court. Eadmer explicitly traces the new style to 'the youth of the court' (*curialis iuventus*) and the anti-curial note in this moralism is all-pervasive. It is not at all unlikely in fact that new and extravagant fashions would be generated in lay courts, tiny centres of intense and competitive self-display. We shall return to the question of the meaning of this particular hair-style.

Hair markers for age, sex, class and race were intended to be permanent and general to all members of the relevant group. Hair treatment was also versatile enough to carry individual and temporary messages, identifying those who were in a particular phase or moment of their lives. Penitents, for example, might either grow their hair or crop it to signify their state. Sometimes this was done on the death bed, as in the case of Isabella, wife of Richard of Cornwall, who, as she lay dying in the year 1240, had 'the dark locks of her abundant hair cut and made full confession of her sins'.[44] Before battle lay knights might cut their hair as a propitiatory gesture, to signify their submission

[42] William of Malmesbury, *Vita Wulfstani* XVI, ed. R. R. Darlington (*Camden* 3rd. ser., XL, 1928), 23.

[43] John Gillingham, 'The Beginnings of English Imperialism', *Journal of Historical Sociology*, V (1992), 392–409.

[44] Mathew Paris, *Chronica majora*, ed. Luard, IV, 2.

to the deity and seek divine help.[45] Pilgrims were expected to adopt specific hair styles. When the Lombard prince Gisulf II of Salerno feigned a pilgrimage to Jerusalem but in fact went to Constantinople to plot with the Byzantine emperor, on his return 'they did not reverence him for his holiness coming from Jerusalem, but marvelled that he arrived with a big beard, as if he had been to Constantinople'.[46] In this instance the implication is that pilgrims should be shaved and Gisulf's claim was out of keeping with the witness of his hair.

Mourning was an occasion when temporary treatments of hair and beard were particularly important. Tearing or shaving off head or facial hair are extremely ancient and widespread expressions of distress and there are plenty of examples of such practices from the medieval period. In the *Song of Roland* the Muslim queen 'pulls her hair' (*trait ses chevels*) when her wounded husband is brought back, Charlemagne does likewise at the sight of Roland's corpse, tearing out hair from his beard and head with both hands, and the very last lines of the poem have him lamenting the weariness of his life, weeping and pulling his white beard.[47] Later in the twelfth century Reginald of Durham's collection of the miracles of St Cuthbert gives many similar contemporary descriptions: when the only son of a rich man fell desperately ill the household and onlookers 'poured out prayers with copious flowing tears, tore their cheeks with their nails and pulled out their hair with their own hands'; the sailors on a ship threatened by enemies beat their breasts, called out and 'pulled their hair in anguish'.[48]

Elaborate hair display in mourning for the dead was particularly women's business. In part this is simply a function of the greater latitude allowed women for emotional display on such occasions. There seems to have been fairly general agreement with the opinion expressed by Tacitus, speaking of the Germans, 'it is proper for women to lament and men to remember'.[49] The poet Hartmann von Aue, for example, in his romance *Erec*, describes the heroine Enid grieving over her wounded husband: 'she pulled out her hair and avenged herself upon her own body, in the way of women' (*nâch wîplîchen site*).[50] Manipulation

---

[45] E.g. Galbert of Bruges, ed. Henri Pirenne, *Historie du meurtre de Charles le Bon* (Paris, 1891), 162–3 (1128); *Flores historiarum*, ed. H. R. Luard (3 vols., Rolls Series, 1890), III, 256 (1265).

[46] Amatus of Montecassino, *Storia de' Normanni* IV. xlix, ed. Vincenzo de Bartholomaeis (*Fonti per la storia d'Italia*, LXXVI, Rome, 1935), 211.

[47] *La Chanson de Roland*, lines 2596, 2906, 2930–1, 2943, 2982, 4001–1, ed. F. Whitehead (Oxford, 1942), 76, 85–7, 117.

[48] Reginald of Durham, *Libellus de admirandis beati Cuthberti virtutibus* LXX, XXX, ed. James Raine (Surtees Soc., I, 1835), 142–5, 67–9.

[49] *Germania* XXVII.

[50] Hartmann von Aue, *Erec*, lines 5760–2, ed. Albert Leitzmann (*Altdeutsche Textbibliothek*, XXXIX, 5th ed., Tübingen, 1976), 150 (there is nothing corresponding to this phrase in Chretien's version, on which Hartmann's was based).

of hair was one of the most common and expressive ways that women lamented.[51] They might, like Enid, pull at their hair or pull it out. They might also let it down, and this letting down or loosing of the hair was a form of mourning exclusively the preserve of wives and widows. When married women let their hair down, they expressed a suspension of the normal social code. They were unloosing bonds, both physically and metaphorically, and they were behaving inappropriately, since long flowing hair was a sign of maidenhood. The collection of miracles written by Reginald of Durham, just mentioned, contains an incident in which a young man is injured and presumed dead, and, as the author describes the responses of the spectators, he distinguishes them explicitly according to sex: 'you could see the men running up, the wives letting their hair down in lamentation and both sexes pouring out tears and cries with copious wailing.'[52] Weeping and wailing were here common to men and women, letting the hair down particular to women, naturally enough since only women—and married women at that (these are *uxores* not *mulieres*)—wore their hair bound. The practice seems to have been an ancient one, for at a siege in the first half of the sixth century the women of the city went in procession around the battlements weeping, 'veiled in black clothes, with their hair loose and ashes on their heads, so that you would think they were performing funeral rites for their husbands'.[53]

Women with their hair loosed or women tearing their hair out were thus a common sight at a funeral. It was indeed possible for some women to make a full time profession out of this activity, since there is evidence for hired female mourners. Their practices are described in a chapter entitled 'Mourning Customs' in a rhetorical work by Boncompagno da Signa, the treatise known as the *Antiqua rhetorica* or simply the *Boncompagnus*, composed around 1200:

Certain women are hired at Rome to lament over the bodies of the dead. They are called 'reckoners' (*conputatrices*) because they reckon up the nobility, wealth, beauty, fortune and other praiseworthy aspects of the dead in a kind of chant. The 'reckoner' sometimes stands upright, sometimes leans forward with her hair spread out on her knees. Alongside the corpse, she recites praises in an undulating tone, and always at the end of a phrase utters 'ho' or 'hy' like one grieving and then all the bystanders express sounds of weeping along with her. But the reckoner produces tears for a price, not from sorrow.[54]

[51] See, for discussion of hair and mourning, Mosche Barasch, *Gestures of Despair in Medieval and Early Renaissance Art* (New York, 1976) 18, 22–7, 36, 42, 68, 78, 88, 103–23.
[52] *Libellus* XCII, ed. Raine, 201–4.
[53] Gregory of Tours, *Historia Francorum* III. xxix, ed. Krusch and Levison, 134.
[54] Ludwig Rockinger (ed.), *Briefsteller und Formelbücher des elften bis vierzehnten Jahrhunderts*

In Boncompagno's account of mourning, hair is a recurrent expressive medium. 'The Romans', he writes, 'do not deem it mourning unless you tear part of your face with your nails, pull out hair and rip your clothes to the breast or navel.' In Calabria the widow 'after removing her veil, pulls out no small amount of hair'. Tuscany also witnesses the *evulsio capillorum*. On the other hand, the English and the Slavs seem to Boncompagno to have different ways of dealing with grief: 'they mix drink with their weeping until they are drunk and thus are consoled in a particularly pleasant way.'[55]

Mourning was a time when unusual behaviour might be allowed. There was not always, however, general agreement about how far such relaxation of norms might go. From a very early period there are indications that some authorities were nervous about mourning customs and would try to control them. Hair expressiveness was one of the targets of this criticism. In late antiquity and the early Middle Ages ecclesiastics reiterated prohibitions on what they deemed extravagant mourning. The Church Fathers denounced it as pagan vanity and diabolical artifice. In the fourth century John Chrysostom, a notorious enemy of Jezebels, singled out the women of Antioch for their funerary behaviour, indeed identifying excessive mourning as 'the malady of women':

> For they make an exhibition in their dirges and laments, they bare their arms, tear their hair, make furrows in their cheeks. Some do this from sorrow, some from show and ostentation, some from wantonness, baring their arms even in the sight of men.[56]

In the early medieval West the Carolingian penitentials took up the theme: 'those who lacerate themselves over the dead man with steel or nails or pull their hair or tear their clothes shall do penance for forty days.'[57]

Later in the medieval period other voices, in a very different milieu, were also raised against the excesses of loose-haired women. From the second half of the thirteenth century some of the Italian communes enacted restrictive legislation against funerary practices, trying to curtail the numbers at the funeral and the ostentation and emotional extravagance of the mourners, in the hope, it has been argued, of controlling

---

(Quellen und Erörterungen zur bayerischen und deutschen Geschichte IX, 2 vols., Munich, 1863–4), I, 141.

[55] *Ibid.*, 141–2.

[56] John Chrysostom, *Homilies on John* LXII. iv. ed. J. P. Migne, *Patrologia graeca*, LIX (Paris, 1862), col. 346.

[57] 'St Hubert Penitential' LIII, ed. J. Schmitz, *Die Bussbücher und das kanonische Bussverfahren* (Düsseldorf, 1898), 338 (for other examples see 300, 344, 356).

noble gatherings and limiting 'manifestations of family power'.[58] Again, hair treatment was a target. Prohibitions were not directed only toward women, for both in Siena and Orvieto limits were set as to how long male mourners might forego shaving after a bereavement, but the laws clearly regard women's behaviour as demanding especial attention. In Orvieto there were financial and physical penalties for 'reckoners' (*computatrices*) and no one but the widow was allowed 'to go outside the house pulling out their hair or to remove their head bands or head coverings' beyond a certain period.[59] It may have been 'proper for women to lament', but the lamentation of loose-haired women was also disturbing and prompted restrictive rule-making.

One of the problems of dealing with a subject such as the meaning of hair in the Middle Ages, when the evidence is so sporadic and scattered in time and place, is that there is the constant danger of the exercise degenerating into the simple accumulation and classification of examples. In one sense this is unavoidable. The basic analytical point, that hair treatment serves as a social marker of various kinds, is quickly made and can be presumed to command fairly widespread acceptance. The next step is to ascertain which markers are used, when and where. To use an analogy, once one has asserted that the nouns of a particular language have three genders, it is then necessary to learn which nouns are which gender. Similarly, it is necessary to know when and where penitents grew their hair, when and where they cropped it. No analytical principles can substitute for this empirical knowledge. Once the basic point—that hair treatment expresses social ordering—is grasped, what matters, as in learning a language, is to master the vocabulary.

Is it possible, however, to go beyond this rather limited taxonomic approach? Can one make general points about the symbolic grammar of hair and is there any prospect of explaining rather than merely describing hair patterns and their significance?

Recent thinking has tended to stress the arbitrariness of signification. Signs and symbols have been viewed as having no intrinsic connection with the objects they signify. One could argue that this holds true of the symbolism of hair, for often what first strikes the eye is the importance of polarities in hair symbolism rather than the natural associations of either side of the polar opposition. In some societies,

---

[58] Diane O. Hughes, 'Sumptuary Law and Social Relations in Renaissance Italy', in *Disputes and Settlements*, ed. John Bossy (Cambridge, 1983), 69–99, at 74.

[59] *Codice diplomatico della Città d'Orvieto*, ed. Luigi Fumi (*Documenti di storia italiana*, VIII, Florence, 1884), 804.

like early medieval Europe, children grew their hair and the first hair-cut signified maturation. In others, like ancient Egypt or Crete, children were shaved and only grew their hair on reaching mature years. Medieval penitents might be commanded to crop their hair or to grow it. What mattered, it seems, was the function of hair as a marker in a system of oppositions, not any intrinsic value attached to particular treatments. If in the twelfth century the Latin priest wore shorter hair than the bulk of his parishioners and the pagan Slav priest longer hair than his,[60] this might only mean that the priestly function needed to be marked out visibly and that distinctiveness in one direction was as good as distinctiveness in the other.

What seems, at first glance, an illustration of this lack of inherent determining associations is the case of the beardedness of Christian priests, for the eastern and the western Churches associated the priestly state with absolutely opposite treatments of hair, the Latin Church insisting on clerical shaving, the Greek Church approving clerical beards. Especially revealing is the western Church's manipulation of the early canonical rulings on the subject. A fifth-century canon stated quite clearly 'Clerics should not grow their hair long nor shave their beards'. Before the ninth century western interpreters had emended this text so that it read 'Clerics should not grow their hair long but should shave their beards'.[61] This embrace of the opposite extreme of the bearded-shaven polarity could be taken to demonstrate that neither beardedness nor non-beardedness is best regarded as having an intrinsic association with priestly status. However, this very instance could be given a different interpretation. Many observers have noticed the importance of hair treatment in conveying sexual information and there is a case to be made that the usual social meaning of hair removal is sexual renunciation. One might then manage a fairly strong argument for connecting the hairlessness of the Latin clergy with the celibacy that was at least prescribed for them and viewing the hairiness of the Greek clergy as an appropriate badge for a married priesthood.

This case illuminates the difficulties of interpretative analysis of non-verbal social symbols. Hair meanings are symbolic in that their natural or biological import is limited and they are social in that they are construed by others and elicit behaviour keyed to a code. There is then the truly vexing question of where meaning in such a system of social symbolism is to be located and the closely associated problem of what status we should attach to the consciously elaborated rationale held by a subject bearing a particular hair-style. If a medieval priest explains

---

[60] Saxo Grammaticus, *Gesta Danorum* XIV. xxxix. 4, ed. J. Olrik and H. Raeder (2 vols., Copenhagen, 1931–57), I, 465.

[61] Constable, 'Introduction', 105–7.

the tonsure as a reminder of Christ's crown of thorns while a modern anthropologist looks on it as a symbolic castration, how are we to judge between them? The last part of this paper seeks angles of approach to this difficult matter.

A particularly important key in the analysis of the social meaning of hair is the point of tension—the moment when we see shifts or clashes of contemporary understanding. Much of the material already discussed in this paper consists of prescription and proscription, that is, rules about hair treatment. When we look at this evidence, we know that it proves at least two things: the proscribed practices were actually current and some authorities thought they were wrong. Such moments are especially valuable for teasing out the complexities and ambiguities of contemporaries' perceptions.

Let us return briefly to the example of the long-haired Anglo-Normans of around 1100 and 'the problem of scandal'. Scandal is an illuminating muddying of the waters since it is the clash of two different contemporary estimations of a style. We have already established fairly satisfactorily that the style in question was that of aristocratic lay youths with curial aspirations. What requires a little more reflection is the sexual significance attached to the fashion. Here we must stress that all the texts come from monastic critics and, hence, lacking a curial defence of long hair, we do not know the connotations of the fashion in the actual words of its wearers.

The critics said that long hair made men like women. It was grown by men who were not content to be what they had been born—men. When their hair was cut they resumed the form of men (thus, incidentally, announcing their innate characteristics by an entirely conventional act). The sexual code is simple and reiterated. Yet here it seems we may have something rather different from the association with youth and the court, which was a connotation accepted by the long haired youths themselves. Long hair meant youth and courtliness both to those who bore it and to those who couldn't bear it. The feminine association is, however, less likely to be one with which the long-haired would identify. There are indeed in the sources some suggestions of a connection between long hair and homosexual practice and this might then point to conscious adoption of the style of the other sex, but these suggestions are not numerous or compelling. More common is the strident tone of Wulfstan addressing the effete Anglo-Saxons or the bishop of Séez reproaching Henry I's household: 'those who ... copy women in their flowing hair will be no better than women in defending their country'; 'you all have long hair like women, which is not right for you who are made in the image of God and ought to act with manly strength.' These are images intended to shame. The monastic moralists are appealing to an image of manliness that they calculate their hearers will share. They wish to awaken this consciousness, to convince the courtly youths of the rightness of their own connotative scheme and to shame them into conformity with it. When they talk of the youthful and courtly side of male long hair they are probably sociologically accurate but when they call the young men women they are preachers. The long hair of the Anglo-Normans was a self-consciously youthful, lay, aristocratic and curial style. The attack on it by its critics recognised these features, but did not assault them directly. Instead it tried a flanking assault, by appealing to a common sexual language which would undermine the obvious attractiveness of the other connotations of long hair. An analysis of the rhetoric of hair in this instance can thus distinguish a characterisation which both bearer and critic could accept from a moralising substratum. There was conflict over meaning. Long hair could mean femininity but the monastic critics had to fight to establish that meaning and, as we have seen, had limited success.

If prescription, proscription and scandal are informative fissures or tensions in the systems of meaning, disguise is another. Since hair is such a malleable marker, it was naturally possible to change one's apparent status quickly by changing one's hair style. This could involve not only the sincere public adoption of a new role, such as that of monk or penitent, but also disguise. Disguise presents us with a crystal clear instance of meanings presumed by contemporaries and it thus gives us one avenue to interpretation. Passing oneself off as a member of another race, class or sex was sometimes desirable. Geoffrey of Monmouth tells of a Saxon leader slipping through King Arthur's lines after 'he cut his hair and beard',[62] a picture of long-haired Saxons and short-haired Britons that is not at all historically implausible. In 1190 Muslims trying to run the blockade of Acre disguised as westerners shaved their beards, as well as putting on Frankish clothes and placing pigs on deck.[63] In these instances we are located on an ethnic interface where contemporaries' manipulation of their hair makes its predominant intended meaning quite clear. Similarly, when a knight escaping from battle has his hair cut 'like a squire' to disguise himself, we know that in this critical situation a sharp hair-based status marker is being both recognised and manipulated.[64] It is in the nature of things that disguise by cutting hair is quicker to achieve than disguise by growing hair but there were sometimes ways around this problem. In the early twelfth

[62] *Historia regum Britannie* IX. i (143), ed. Neil Wright (Cambridge, 1984), 101; the implication might alternatively be that minstrels had short hair and were clean shaven.

[63] Francesco Gabrieli (ed.), *Arab Historians of the Crusades* (Eng. tr., Berkeley and London, 1969), 201 (Baha' ad-Din).

[64] Orderic Vitalis, *Historia ecclesiastica* XII. xxxix, ed. Chibnall, VI, 352.

century the pagan and short-haired Slav raiders who harried the German borderlands apparently wore the scalps of Christian captives in order to disguise themselves as long-haired German Christians when on plundering expeditions.[65]

Hair meanings are highly contextual. The same style or action could have different meanings depending on the local systems being invoked. Producing a pair of scissors, when performed by the bishop of Séez, meant 'be a man and respect the teaching of the Church'; when leading up to monastic tonsure, 'you are leaving behind the secular world to live as a servant of God'; when offered by the wicked Merovingian uncle, 'do you wish to live or die?' Since meanings were contextual, they were often ambiguous, because context needs to be construed. The present brief foray into the wide and delicate area of hair meanings concludes with a story that shows rather vividly the way hair treatment could have multiple meanings. In the year 1253 the Franciscan friar William of Rubruck set out on a mission to the court of the Mongol ruler, Möngke, grandson of Genghiz Khan. In his travels through Asia he met adherents of many religions, including Buddhist monks. These, he noted, shaved their beards and hair, wore saffron robes, lived in communities and meditated—William was unsuccessful in trying to talk to them while they did so. When their heads were covered 'they seemed to me,' he wrote, 'to be Frenchmen with their shaved beards ...' (at this time beardlessness was very general in western Europe). When preparing for an audience with Möngke Khan, William and his companions shaved off the beards they had grown during their travels 'so that we should appear before the Khan according to the custom of our own country.' The result was that the first people they encountered after their shave presumed, not that they were Frenchmen, but that they were Buddhists.[66] Here, very far from its place of origin, a method of hair treatment that was presumed by the bearers to express a national identity was immediately construed, in the terms of the locally prevalent grammar of hair, as signifying a particular religious commitment. If, even to men of the thirteenth century, there could be uncertainty whether a particular hair treatment meant 'I am a Frenchman' or 'I am a Buddhist', it is fair to conclude that, though the language of hair was highly expressive, it was, like all language, prone to many interpretations.

---

[65] Herbert Helbig and Lorenz Weinrich (eds.), *Urkunden und erzählende Quellen zur deutschen Ostsiedlung im Mittelalter (Ausgewählte Quellen zur deutschen Geschichte des Mittelalters*, XXVI, 2 vols., Darmstadt, 1968–70), I, no. 19, 98.

[66] William of Rubruck, *Itinerarium*, XXV, XXVIII, ed. Anastasius van den Wyngaert, *Sinica Franciscana I: Itinera et Relationes fratrum minorum saeculi XIII et XIV* (Quaracchi, 1929), 164–332, at 229–30, 248.

MEN'S DILEMMA: THE FUTURE OF PATRIARCHY IN ENGLAND 1560-1660

By Anthony Fletcher

READ 30 APRIL 1993

PATRIARCHY was very old when Queen Elizabeth ascended the English throne. Historians have sought its origins in the Old Testament record of the creation of Jewish monotheism and in the social conditions of Hebrew society.[1] They have explored the contributions of classical Greece and early Christian thinking to its development and evolution.[2] By the time that the Tudor dynasty ruled in England, the institutionalised male dominance over women and children in the family and the extension of that subordination to women in society in general, the scriptural patriarchy with which I am concerned, had become so deeply embedded that it has appeared immutable. Something so permanent, something that was so given, has seemed not to deserve scrutiny by the historians of early modern England. It was socialist and radical feminists who took up the notion of patriarchy in the 1960s because they needed a concept which would help them to theorise male dominance. From their contemporary perspective also, patriarchy appeared immovable and monumental. There was a tendency among them at first to study it as such: feminist historians approached the past with the premise that there has always been an undifferentiated and consistent male commitment to domination and control over women in every sphere of life. The conflation of patriarchy with misogyny, I suggest, produced an unhistorical patriarchy as the staple of women's history. It is only fairly recently that historical studies of gender have broken free from these shackles, that historians have begun to penetrate the discourses and strategies through which men have—or have not—coerced, or oppressed or subordinated women through the ages.[3] Most

---

[1] G. Lerner, *The Creation of Patriarchy* (Oxford, 1986).

[2] G. Lloyd, *The Man of Reason: Male and Female in Western Philosophy* (1984); D. H. Coole, *Women in Political Theory: From Ancient Misogyny to Contemporary Feminism*; R. Radford Ruether, *Sexism and God-talk* (Boston, Massachusetts, 1983); I. Maclean, *The Renaissance Notion of Woman: A Study in the Fortunes of Scholasticism and Medical Science in European Intellectual Life* (Cambridge, 1980).

[3] *Manful Assertions: Masculinities in Britain since 1800*, eds. M. Roper and J. Tosh, (1991), 1–24; J. Scott, 'Gender: a useful category of historical analysis', *American Historical Review* XCI (1986), 1067; D. Purkiss, 'Material girls: the seventeenth-century woman debate', in *Women, Texts and Histories 1575–1660*, eds. C. Brant and D. Purkiss, 71–2; G. Block, 'Women's history and gender history: aspects of an international debate', *Gender and*

of these studies have concentrated upon the nineteenth and twentieth centuries.[4] This is why I believe it is appropriate for me to be opening this paper on early modern patriarchy with a brief review of the infant historiography of the subject and with some comment upon the conceptual issues which it raises.

The structures of domination which sustain patriarchy, I shall argue, are not inert but adaptable, not solid but adjustable. Gender is a social system, it has been suggested recently, 'which at any time constructs the opportunities and experience of both men and women'.[5] Men, in other words, have been making and remaking patriarchy for hundreds of years. Their power has resided in their masculinity, as well as in their material advantages and their construction of theology and philosophy, law and custom in their own terms. I am particularly concerned with masculinity, or rather masculinities, since men have continually shaped and reshaped notions of their manliness as a means towards exercising social and political power. Thus gender as power, the story of sexual politics, I take it, is about personal relationship as well as about structures, institutions and practices. As a subject of historical enquiry it evidently presents formidable, some may think insurmountable, methodological problems. This paper aims to do no more than open up some questions about a period which others besides myself are saying provides irrefutable evidence of a particularly fraught sexual politics. There is no claim here that the period of a hundred years from 1560 to 1660 is marked by a cataclysmic change in the nature of English patriarchy. I would not even go so far as to maintain that we can see here a crisis of gender relations, a possibility that has been raised by David Underdown.[6] But I do think it is time for the dissection of patriarchy to be more firmly established on the early modernist agenda: a discussion of the reasons for men's fears and unease about its stability in this particular period seems a good place to begin.

The historical record which is available for the investigation of the relationships between men and women in this period has been produced almost but not quite entirely by men. What we want to know from

---

History I (1989), 7–30. See also E. P. Thompson's comments on the use of patriarchy as a historical concept in his *Customs in Common* (1991), 499–501.

[4] e.g. L. Davidoff and C. Hall, *Family Fortunes: Men and Women of the English Middle Class 1780–1850* (1987); S. Mendus and J. Rendall eds, *Sexuality and Subordination*, (1989); S. Walby, *Patriarchy at Work* (Cambridge, 1986).

[5] *Manful Assertions*, 7.

[6] D. E. Underdown, 'The taming of the scold: the enforcement of patriarchal authority in early modern England', and S. D. Amussen, 'Gender, family and the social order 1560–1725, in *Order and Disorder in Early Modern England*, eds. A. J. Fletcher and J. Stevenson (Cambridge, 1985), 116–36; J. A. Sharpe, 'Witchcraft and women in seventeenth-century England: some northern evidence', *Continuity and Change* VI (1991), 182–3.

that record, in so far as it reveals anything about the intimate aspect of people's lives, is how men and women managed their marital relationships. For, at one level, this is the crux of how patriarchy works. The kind of distinctions that need to be explored are distinctions between brutality and coercion on the one hand and varying degrees of subordination and subservience, within a companionate framework, on the other. The crucial issue is how far, in practice, love and devotion softened and modified, even perhaps subverted, the harshest prescriptions of men's God given patriarchal authority. This is as much a matter of what men thought they should require of their wives as of what women thought they should give in duty and respect. I have made nine case studies[7] of the marriages of a series of Elizabethan and Stuart gentry based upon the surviving correspondence between the spouses and their personal memoirs or those of their wives: the men concerned are Percy Freke, Sir Robert Harley, Sir Thomas Hoby, Sir Anthony Mildmay, Samuel Pepys, Richard Sackville third earl of Dorset, John Thynne and Thomas Thynne. I conclude from these studies, based on a mixture of evidence from both the men and women concerned, that there was a restless dynamic in marriage at this time, a dynamic which brought together spirited love and mutual devotion on the one hand with precepts of duty and obedience on the other. Each marriage had its own particular set of ingredients: the strength of will, besides the emotional inclinations, that the partners brought into it. But the women in these marriages, and I believe in thousands of others, were mostly not docile and passive.

I want to pursue this point using a text from contemporary drama. My assumption here is that, though they come to us as a record of contemporary performance, as texts written for a theatrical marketplace, plays can properly be employed to our purposes as historical evidence: not of realities, nor of the opinions of the author but of the imaginative and ideological constructions of the period, of its mentality.[8] Probing the opacity of a Shakespearean text—in this case *The Taming of the Shrew*—is, I contend, one proper means of seeking the meaning which the age attached to romance, love and the establishment of a successful marriage. Moreover there are times, I believe, when a new production of such a play, creatively addressing a text, can assist the historian's quest for understanding of past attitudes as fruitfully as the reading of a neglected document. Directors should not play the role of a 'failing

---

[7] These studies will appear in my forthcoming book *Transforming Gender: Men and Women in Early Modern England* (Yale University Press).

[8] M. Hattaway, 'Drama and society' in *The Cambridge Companion to English Renaissance Drama*, eds. A. R. Braunmuller and M. Hattaway, 91–6; K. McLuskie, 'The patriarchal bard: feminist criticism and Shakespeare: King Lear and Measure for Measure', in *Political Shakespeare*, eds. J. Dollimore and A. Sinfield (Manchester, 1985), 88–92.

archaeologist', Jonathan Miller has argued, for there is the possibility of actors and director 'remaking a work of art that is essentially emergent'.[9] My sources in this instance therefore include the text itself, discussions of it by literary scholars and comment by actors on their experience of playing Shakespeare as well as my own experience of live performance.

Stephen Greenblatt has argued persuasively that what the series of comedies from *Much Ado about Nothing* to *Twelfth Night* are about is the emergence of personal identity through what he calls 'the experience of erotic heat'. Rosalind and Orlando, Beatrice and Benedick, Kate and Petruchio all come together, though in their different ways, by means of sexual chafing and friction. The dance of love precedes the realisation of desire to which the plots so clearly gesture.[10] The verbal wit of these comedies celebrates the element of play in a prospective marriage relationship. The affectionate nicknaming of actual married lovers at this time indicates how playfulness could and did lighten the more burdensome aspects of people's life and work together.[11] The fact that the puritan cleric William Gouge, who found this nicknaming reprehensible, thought it necessary to comment on it disapprovingly from the pulpit at Blackfriars in London is good evidence of its popularity.[12]

Kate at the opening of the *Shrew* is a termagant and misfit, unhappy in the household of Baptista Minola where no one understands her, and playing the shrew is the only way left to express herself. She is a girl who no one is going to take on as a wife. From the moment they meet though, Petruchio likes her and has time for her. Jonathan Miller's production of this play, for the Royal Shakespeare Company in 1987, was especially instructive. The keynote for Miller, who sees the taming as a kind of therapy, comes in Petruchio's lines:

> Ay and amid this hurly I intend
> That all is done in revered care of her
> This is a way to kill a wife with kindness
> And thus I'll curb her mad and headstrong humour.[13]

Specific contemporary warrant for reading the play as a literal taming

[9] Cited in K. McLuskie, *Renaissance Dramatists* (1989), 7.

[10] S. Greenblatt, *Shakespearean Negotiations: The Circulation of Social Energy in Renaissance England* (Berkeley, 1988), 88–92.

[11] P. Collinson, *The Birthpangs of Protestant England: Religious and Cultural Change in the Sixteenth and Seventeenth Centuries* (1988), 72–3; A. D. Wall, ed., *Two Elizabethan Women: Correspondence of Joan and Maria Thynne 1575–1611* (Wiltshire Record Society, XXXVIII, 1983), 32, 36–7, 48.

[12] *As You Like It*, act 3, scene 2, 95–7; W. Gouge, *Domestical Duties* (1622), 376.

[13] *The Taming of the Shrew*, act 4, scene 1, 183–4, 188–9; J. Miller, *Subsequent Performances* (1986), 121–2.

appears in Joseph Swetnam's misogynist tract of 1615: 'as a sharp bit curbs a froward horse even so a curst woman must be used'.[14] But it is perhaps more illuminating, seeing what actually happens, to draw the parallel between Petruchio's ritual humiliation of Kate and the contemporary practices of charivari or recourse to the cucking stool. These were shaming practices not sources of outright violence.[15] Kate is left in the mud while her husband bullies a servant for letting her horse stumble on the way home; she is deprived of food and sleep; rich clothes are dangled before her eyes and then whisked away. What is the lesson of all this? Not that Petruchio means any harm to Kate: on the contrary he provokes her to show her spirit in speech and is pleased when she does so. He wants a real marriage. To achieve this he employs inversion, arriving late for his wedding dressed like a maniac so as to cock a snook at the ordered world of Paduan society.[16]

In public, Petruchio shows, they must play it by the book: Miller had Petruchio hand Kate a bible during the famous 'goods and chattles' speech, which he addressed not to her but to the crowd, thereby making it ludicrous: 'And here she stands', he ends, 'touch her whoever dare'. Fiona Shaw comments from her experience of playing Kate in this production:

> I flick through this missal and it dawns on me, this is what I have inherited as an Elizabethan woman … its a tough revelation to discover that your protection, the bible, is also your danger: a book telling you you're nothing. Grumio is standing there with a sword to keep back people who aren't coming forward; Petruchio is talking nonsense … and that's why I throw the bible down and choose to go with Petruchio.

There was great insight in this inspired piece of contemporary theatre.[17] For what Miller, his Petruchio Brian Cox and Fiona Shaw were saying is something about prescription and practice, and about the public and private worlds of Elizabethan marriage, that the puritan conduct book writers set out very clearly at the time. Patriarchal order, these writers insisted, rested upon the moral and social example of heads of households. The wife's duty was to set an example of obedience to children and servants. Petruchio, as his behaviour at his own home exemplifies, is absolutely committed to the idea that there must be rule in a

---

[14] K. U. Henderson and B. F. McManus, eds., *Half Humankind: Contexts and Texts of the Controversy about Women in England 1540–1640* (Urbana, Illinois, 1985), 209.

[15] M. Ingram, 'Ridings, Rough Music and the "Reform of Popular Culture" in Early Modern England', *Past and Present* 105 (1984), 79–113; *Cambridge Companion to English Renaissance Drama*, 111–12.

[16] C. Rutter, *Clamorous Voices: Shakespeare's Women Today* (1988), 12.

[17] Rutter, *Clamorous Voices*, 13–14.

household. He wants Kate to understand that. Yet in the private domain, behind the chamber door, he wants a mutual relationship and a richly sexual one, which is also what the puritan clerics avowed he should want.[18]

Kate's bantering early in the play leads Petruchio into some lewd punning on tongues and their sexual function; he apologises too late and she wallops him; he respects her for that.[19] Once they are married, he teaches her how they now have the freedom to mock the patriarchal imperative of obedience to male authority through play. On the way back to Padua he calls the sun the moon and insists that she do so too. She picks up the trick and hence she knows exactly what is required when he summons her in the final scene and she comes to give the company her stern and celebrated lecture on wifely duty.[20] Jonathan Miller sees this speech as 'an agreement to abide by the rules within a framework in which it is possible to enjoy a close affection'.[21] Fiona Shaw saw Kate here as falling in line with patriarchy, but at the same time handing back the challenge of that status quo: 'these two people have to rise, through their pain, above the usual territory of negotiation'. This 'very serious play' is for her 'terribly fundamental, almost transcendental.'[22] All this I find warrantable but we can take the argument further. Given the maturity of their relationship by the final scene, Kate's docility there is a genuinely subversive strategy because it represents play within the play. Petruchio's marriage with this once unhappy and unruly woman now promises to be more successful than the marriage of Bianca and Hortensio. The disobedient Bianca is the real shrew. Thus the final scene reiterates the inversion announced by Petruchio's monstrous and apparently insulting wedding garb.[23]

I have dwelt upon this Shakespearean play in order to suggest that the patriarchy of Elizabethan and early Stuart England must have been a limited patriarchy, one often lightened by a vivid sexual politics and humanised by trust.[24] Shakespeare could not have written the *Shrew* and drawn the audience that he did if it was otherwise. So in what

---

[18] A. J. Fletcher, 'The Protestant Idea of Marriage', in *Religion, Culture and Society in Early Modern Britain*, eds. A. J. Fletcher and P. R. Roberts (Cambridge, 1994), 175–9.

[19] *The Taming of the Shrew*, act 2, scene 1, 214–20; Rutter, *Clamorous Voices*, 11; L. Jardine, *Still Harping on Daughters: Women and Drama in the Age of Shakespeare* (1983), 121.

[20] *The Taming of the Shrew*, act 5, scene 2, 136–79.

[21] Miller, *Subsequent Performances*, 122.

[22] Rutter, *Clamorous Voices*, 24–5.

[23] For feminist and other readings see L. Woodbridge, *Women and the English Renaissance: Literature and the Nature of Womankind 1540–1820* (Urbana, Illinois, 1986), 206–7, 221–2; McLuskie, *Renaissance Dramatists*, 6–10.

[24] For recent statements of this view see R. Houlbrooke, *The English Family, 1450–1700* (1984) 119; J. A. Sharpe, *Early Modern England: A Social History 1550–1760* (1987), 62–9; K. Wrightson, *English Society, 1580–1680* (1982), 100.

respect did men face a dilemma at this time? Thomas Platter, who travelled through England in 1599, noted the independence of women here: they 'have far more liberty than in other lands and know just how to make good use of it', he wrote, 'for they often stroll out or drive by coach in very gorgeous clothes and the men must put up with such ways and may not punish them for it'. John Ray had something to say about the well known proverb 'England is the paradise of women', which Platter had quoted, in his *Collection of English Proverbs* published in 1670. He declared that all the world was 'therein satisfied', noting that 'if a bridge were made over the narrow seas all the women in Europe would come over hither'. 'Yet it is worth the noting', he went on, 'that though in no country of the world the men are so fond of, so much governed by, so wedded to their wives yet hath no language so many proverbial invectives against women'.[25] The work of the modern editor of a dictionary of recoverable early modern proverbs amply confirms Ray's conclusion: he lists 102 proverbs under 'woman' or 'women' almost every one derogatory.[26] So there appears to have been an ambivalence about women among Englishmen at this time. On the one hand, the popular proverb 'better a shrew than a sheep' suggests that the English liked strong women. Ray commented about this proverb that it was held true 'for commonly shrews are good housewives'.[27] On the other hand many of the literary genres of the period from the 1560s to 1660s are marked by an obsession with the dangers ascribed to womanhood and are inhabited by fear of women's intentions and behaviour. Their principle vices, identified over and over again, were a voracious sexuality, a loquacity which made women into scolds and shrews and a wilful pride and vanity that deprived men of the just fruits of their livelihood. We find these vices being consistently portrayed in the drama of the period, which is characterised by a series of powerful and subversive women like Cleopatra, Gertrude, Lady Macbeth, Vittoria in *The White Devil* and Beatrice-Joanna in *The Changeling*. They are also prominent in ballads and other forms of popular literature, including the virulent misogynist tracts of James I's reign.[28]

[25] C. Williamms, tr. *Thomas Platter's Travels in England 1599* 1937), 181–2; J. Ray *A Collection of English Proverbs* (1670), 54. For citation of the proverb in social descriptions see S. D. Amussen, *An Ordered Society: Gender and Class in Early Modern England* 1988), 48.

[26] M. P. Tilley, *A Dictionary of the Proverbs in England in the Sixteenth and Seventeenth Centuries* (Ann Arbor, 1950), 741–9.

[27] Ray, *Collection of English Proverbs*, 50.

[28] For a short discussion of these and other demonic women in the drama see C. Belsey, *The Subject of Tragedy: Identity and Difference in Renaissance Drama* (1985), 183–8. See also McLuskie in *Political Shakespeare*, 98–106; D. Callaghan, *Women and Gender in Renaissance Tragedy: A study of King Lear, Othello, The Duchess of Malfie and The White Devil* (1989), especially 49–73.

Women's vices were perceived to flow directly from their bodily constitution. Their cold and moist honours, which made them the 'weaker vessel', were seen as the root cause of their lasciviousness as well as of their loose tongues.[29] Numerous proverbs refer to the instability of mind which these humours were believed to make ineradicable: 'a women is a weather cock', 'a woman's mind and winter wind change oft', 'a woman's mind is always mutable', 'a woman, like a German clock, is ever repairing' or 'never goes true'. A strong vein of oral tradition painted women as scatty, empty-headed and unreliable.[30] They were seen as being at the mercy of their wombs which could wander dangerously through the body causing hysteria and other maladies.[31] Women, more proverbs declared, were fickle, irresponsible and slippery. Above all they lacked self control, which was what made them sexually insatiable.[32] Protestantism seems to have heightened men's fears in this respect. Lyndal Roper argues, in her study of Reformation Augsburg, that the period saw a 'strengthening of the belief that women's lusts were to be feared as unbridled and demonic'.[33] Thus the unruly wife who turned from berating her husband to cuckolding him became an emblematic representation of men's worst fears about womankind. Numerous ballads pursued variations on the theme, touching in one way or another on the raw nerve of men's potency, their ability to satisfy their wives sexually and their control over them. For the uneasy male listener or reader the threat implicit in the bawdy chorus line of the ballad *The Discontented Married Man*, 'she cannot keep her lips together', made the connection explicit and went to the heart of the matter.[34] Tertullian had believed women had open mouths and were hence garrulous; Ambrose thought only the ears of virgins rightly opened that they might be instructed, Sartre wrote that 'the obscenity of the feminine sex is that of everything which gapes open'.[35] There was nothing new in all this projection of male fears; it is deeply embedded in the misogynistic tradition. What seems incontrovertible is

---

[29] L. M. Beir, *Sufferers and Healers: The Experience of Illness in Seventeenth-Century England* (1987), 213–5; Jardine, *Still Harping on Daughters*, 104; Maclean, *Renaissance Notion of Woman*, 41. I explore this issue fully in my forthcoming book *Transforming Gender*.

[30] Tilley, *Dictionary of Proverbs*, nos, W653, W658, W673, W674.

[31] H. Smith, 'Gynaecology and ideology in seventeenth-century England', in *Liberating Women's History*, ed. B. A. Carroll (Urbana, 1976), 97–114; Beier, *Sufferers and Healers*, 126.

[32] Tilley, *Dictionary of Proverbs*, nos W638, W649, W659, W710, W713, W720.

[33] L. Roper, *The Holy Household: Women and Morals in Reformation Augsburg* (Oxford, 1989), 131.

[34] *The Discontented Married Man: or a merry new song that was pen'd in foul weather, of a scold that could not keep her lips together*, in W. Chappell, ed. *The Roxburghe Ballads* (1871), I, 295–9. The editor dates the printing to the reign of Charles I.

[35] Citations from a review by Daphne Hampson in *The Times Higher Education Supplement*, 24 May 1991, 18.

the scale and intensity of unease about women and about the security
of men's hold on their actions and conduct around the period from
1560 to 1660. How we should account for this historical phenomenon
is deeply problematic. Whether women were being made scapegoats
for men's sense of a general social and political instability or were in
large numbers actually becoming more assertive it is hard to say. I shall
concentrate here on one aspect of the matter, the debate about
transvestism, where there is some reliable information about what
happened besides much hysterical commentary.

The question of how men and women dressed was of vital importance
at a time when gender was not rooted in sexual difference. For gender
was still according to the legacy of the ancients a cosmological principle,
a matter of heat and cold, of greater and lesser degrees of physical
perfection. Genital distinctions, obvious as they were, did not come
into the matter.[36] The Elizabethan fashion for the codpiece declared a
difference of status, tremblingly obtained with the rites of separation
from the female world of childbirth and childhood nurture, not membership of a stable and fixed category of males who were entirely
distinct and opposite from females. Gender in this mental world was
terrifyingly unstable; it was built upon shifting sands. The Elizabethan
audiences watching *As You Like It* could enjoy the spectacle of boy
playing girl playing boy, as Rosalind, dressed as Ganymede, comforted
his maid Aliena, because 'doublet and hose ought to show itself
courageous to petticoat'.[37] It was a very different matter when some
women started appearing in public in Elizabethan London in partially
masculine attire.

The sources are not fully adequate to establish how much female
transvestism occurred in Elizabethan and Jacobean London but the
chronology of the affair can be roughly established by inference from
the pattern of contemporary comment. George Gascoigne was the first
to note female transvestism on the streets in a satire on women in
1576.[38] Philip Stubbes, in *The Anatomy of Abuses* published in 1583,
produced the first shrill denunciation of women's audacity in public.
He quoted Deutoronomy chapter twenty-two and insisted:

Our apparel was given us as a sign distinctive to discern betwixt sex
and sex and therefore one to wear the apparel of another sex is to
participate with the same and to adulterate the verity of his own

[36] T. Laqueur, *Making Sex: Body and Gender from the Greeks to Freud* (Cambridge, Masachussetts, 1990).

[37] *As You Like It*, act 2, scene 4, 3–7.

[38] Woodbridge, *Women and the English Renaissance*, 139.

kind. Wherefore these women may not improperly be called her-maphrodites, that is monsters of both kinds, half women, half men.[39]

Publications by William Harrison and William Averell made passing references to the fashion later in the same decade. It may have been less virulent during the 1590s, when the critics went silent, but there was more comment by Henry Parrot, Richard Nicols and Thomas Adams between 1606 and 1615. Preachers began to inveigh against the fashion. John Williams, in *A Sermon of Apparel* in 1619, protested that women were even attending church in masculine dress. In a marriage sermon the same year, Thomas Gataker paralleled 'a mankind woman' with a 'masterly wife': both were monsters in nature.[40] Thomas Middle-ton's play *A Mad World My Masters*, written around 1608, contains a comic scene in which the young gallant Follywit prepares for a prank by having his comrades cover his breeches with the lower part of a gentlewoman's gown, making him half man and half woman. This aped the normal pattern of the transvestite fashion as it had been adopted in the 1570s and continued since then. Follywit laughingly points the moral to his puzzled companions:

Why the doublet serves as well as the best and is most in fashion. We're all male to th' middle, mankind from the beaver to the bum. 'Tis an Amazonian time; you shall have women shortly tread their husbands.[41]

Gascoigne's 1576 pamphlet had identified precisely how women transformed the upper part of their bodies: they wore doublets in place of gowns, the latest styles of ruffs from Spain and France and high 'copt' hats flaunting a feather in place of coifs or kerchiefs.[42] The account given of the masculine woman who was to be seen on the London streets more than forty years later, in pamphlets published in 1620, differs only in a few details. Short hair had become de rigueur; daggers, swords or pistols were often worn and sometimes boots as well; hats became broad-brimmed and retained the 'wanton' feather; the long padded doublet of Stubbes's day was replaced by an indecently short French one; petticoats were abandoned for knee length skirts. We should note that, although there were references on the stage at this time which implied that some women wore breeches as well, they

---

[39] Deuteronomy, chapter 22, verse 5: 'A woman must not wear men's clothes nor a man put on women's dress; anyone who does this is detestable to Yahweh your God'. P. Stubbes, *The Anatomy of Abuses* (1583), sig F5.

[40] Woodbridge, *Women and the English Renaissance*, 141–3; S. C. Shapiro, 'Feminists in Elizabethan England', *History Today* 1977, 704.

[41] D. L. Frost, ed. *The Selected Plays of Thomas Middleton* (Cambridge, 1978), 53–4.

[42] Woodbridge, *Women and the English Renaissance*, 139.

invariably refer to people like tavern hostesses rather than to the middling sort and gentry.[43] The resonances of all this are obvious: transvestism of this kind, displayed at the playhouse and on the London social scene, blatantly challenged the gender order and put men's patriarchal authority on the line.[44] How many women practised it is much less important than the fact that it occurred at all and the reaction that it provoked. The misogynist critics accused the transvestite women of flaunting their sexuality. The fashion was alleged to include bared breasts or short doublets 'all unbuttoned to entice'.[45] We need to be careful though about how we interpret women's motives in this aping of male dress. It is likely that for many of them modishness in the competitive social circles of the London merchant community was what this was about rather than assertiveness or sexual inducement. These women were no early feminists.

The transvestite vogue seems to have been effectively checked in 1620 by a combination of official and spontaneous action. What happened provides an instructive case study in the politics of male action to combat threats to patriarchal order. On 24 January 1620, the bishop of London passed on to his clergy an express command from James I 'to inveigh vehemently and bitterly in their sermons against the insolvency of our women and their wearing of broad brimmed hats, pointed doublets, their hair cut short or shorn and some of them stilettos or poinards'. The pamphlet *Hic Mulier or The Man Woman: Being a Medicine to cure the Coltish Disease of the Staggers in the Masculine-Feminines of our Times* was entered at the Stationers Company on 9 February. The wood cut on the title page shows one woman being fitted with a man's plumed hat while another waits for the shearing of her locks. Within a week *Hic-Mulier* was answered by *Haec-Vir or the Womanish Man*, a comical dialogue between a female transvestite and a foppish young gentleman. In the meanwhile, John Chamberlain reported to the English ambassador at the Hague in one of his regular newsletters that

> our pulpits ring continually of the insolence and impudence of women and to help the matter forward the players have likewise taken them to task and so too the ballads and ballad singers, so that they can come nowhere but their ears tingle

The responsiveness of the clergy to the King's lead and the sensitivity of the purveyors of popular print to the issue of the moment are both

[43] Henderson and McManus, eds, *Half Humankind*, 266–8, 279–80; Woodbridge, *Women and the English Renaissance*, 217.
[44] Jardine, *Still Harping on Daughters*, 154–6.
[45] Henderson and McManus, eds, *Half Humankind*, 267, 271.

evident. But London's male heads of households knew of course that the actual remedy lay with themselves. *Hic Mulier* was quite explicit about this: they controlled or should do the purse strings and they were supposed, according to the patriarchal model, to take account of how their wives went out and about. Chamberlain reported that 'the King threatens to fall upon husbands, parents and friends that have or should have power' over the transvestites 'and make them pay for it' if they failed to enforce their authority.[46] It rather seems they managed to do so, though this cannot actually be documented with certainty, since the controversy died down. Or, it could be argued, the fashion simply passed, as fashions do.

I have left on one side until now the most remarkable literary manifestation of this affair, the play *The Roaring Girl*, a collaboration between Thomas Dekker and Thomas Middleton which was performed at the Fortune by Prince Henry's company in 1611. The male fantasy of female domination and role reversal is here taken to its logical and devastating conclusion. Whereas the transvestites on the streets stopped short of adopting complete male attire, Moll the Roaring Girl is to be seen early in the play fitting herself with a pair of breeches in the latest fashion. The conversation between Moll and her tailor is full of innuendo:

> *Taylor:* Your breeches then will take up a yard more
> *Moll:* Well pray look it be put in then
> *Taylor:* It shall stand round and full I warrant you
> *Moll:* Pray make em easy enough
> *Taylor:* I know my fault now, t'other was somewhat stiff between the
> legs, i'le make these open enough I warrant you.

Moll is intent on actually being a man. In the next scene, an assignation set up in Grays Inn Felds with the randy gallant Laxton who wants to treat her as a prostitute, she is one, entering in full male dress, challenging the bemused rake by drawing her sword, and fighting him till he pleads for his life. Middleton wrote a signed preface to the play in which he recommended its sixpence worth of 'venery and laughter' as good reading 'to keep you in an afternoon from dice'.[47] Seen or read, *The Roaring Girl* offered the respectable London householder a cathartic experience: the low life of the city's taverns might really have its Moll Cutpurse, a woman with no master, but the daring dress

---

[46] N. E. McClure, ed., *The Letters of John Chamberlain*, (Philadelphia, 1939), II, pp. 286–7, 289; Woodbridge, *Women and the English Renaissance*, 143–4; Henderson and McManus, eds., *Half Humankind*, 275.

[47] F. Bowers, ed. *The Dramatic Works of Thomas Dekker* (Cambridge, 1958), III, 11, 39, 43–6; Woodbridge, *Women and the English Renaissance*, 254–5.

sported by modish dames in his own social circles had nothing to do with that wholly illicit world. *The Roaring Girl*, especially when experienced in the safety of the playhouse, forcibly illustrated the gap between patriarchy tested by a fashion adopted by some city wives and the spectre of its actual collapse.

Men's dilemma then was that in various ways a good many of them felt threatened by women. They were acutely sensitive to assertive female behaviour, whether it was real or imagined. So how could they combat it? The central argument of my paper is that, in one way and another, they worked hard to do so. The transvestite phenomenon was local and specific, a visible and public manifestation of the fragility of patriarchy, a modishness though that was relatively easy for men to stamp upon. More broadly, I want to consider four ways in which men offered each other support and the possibility of action when there was a felt need to defend the gender order. I shall look at prescriptive literature, satirical literature, community action, and some relevant legislation and its enforcement.

In everything they wrote and in the sermons they preached, the puritan clergy of these decades were not only the stormtroopers of evangelisation but also the propagandists of patriarchal order. Lyndal Roper's conclusion that a 'politics of women's role in marriage and the household' was a key to the successful implementation of the German Reformation can be applied equally to the English Reformation.[48] The conduct books, written by clerics like William Gouge, John Dod and Robert Cleaver, William Whateley and Daniel Rogers, sold well because puritan householders thirsted for the kind of supportive advice they gave, advice which, while advocating mutuality in the private and sexual domain of marriage, maintained that the display of patriarchal authority was absolutely essential to the proper government of a household.[49] Around 1622 Nehemiah Wallington, that quintessential puritan artisan, recently married and feeling the weight of 'the charge of so many souls', went and bought his copy of Gouge's *Domestical Duties*. 'Every one of us', he noted in his diary, 'may learn and know our duties and honour God every one in his place where God has set them'. He had the articles he drew up for reform and order in his household signed by his three servants and his apprentice as well as by his wife.[50]

[48] Roper, *Holy Household*, 5.

[49] W. Gouge, *Domestical Duties* (1622); J. Dod and R. Cleaver, *A Godly Form of Household Government* (1614); W. Whateley, *A Bride Bush* (1623); D. Rogers, *Matrimonial Honour* (1642).

[50] P. S. Seaver, *Wallington's World: A Puritan Artisan in Seventeenth-Century London* (London, 1985), 79.

The fracas that had occurred between William Gouge and his congregation at Blackfriars is specific evidence that patriarchy was actively contested by some of the city dames when a cleric tried to push things too far. He was in trouble with them for expecting formal rituals of reverence and obeisance by wives to husbands and for his demand for them to show complete submission, in a humble and cheerful manner, even when a husbandly reproof was manifestly unjust. Gouge's protestations about this affair, in the published version of the sermon in which he first uttered his domestic precepts, shows how sensitive he was to the charge, heard on some London streets, that he was a 'hater of women'.[51] But such personal business apart, the general message of the conduct books was a reassuring one for men who had any doubts about how far they should play a stern and authoritative role in their households.[52]

Women's vices, I have suggested, were held up to ridicule in a series of popular literary genres of the time. Feminine friendships were satirised in a way which suggests that there was a strong masculine suspicion of women meeting together. The two best examples of the genre, which Linda Woodbridge has dubbed 'the gossips meeting', are the pamphlets by Samuel Rowlands *Tis Merry when Gossips meet* and *A Whole Crew of Kind Gossips*, which went through several editions after their first publication in 1602 and 1609 respectively. They are in a tradition which goes back at least as far as the Chester Mystery Cycle which has Mrs Noah drinking malmsey wine with her friends.[53] But the etymology of the word 'gossip' suggests that the notion of female conviviality as a serious threat to male dominance had become considerably more obsessive since the fifteenth century. Whereas the *Oxford English Dictionary* has numerous medieval references for the word in its original sense of godparent or sponsor, the first citations in the sense that Rowlands is using the word are Elizabethan. By 1600 a gossip has become, to the uneasy male, a woman 'of light and trifling character especially one who delights in idle talk'.[54] The briefest analysis of Rowland's satires makes plain the nature of the fears he is seeking to neutralise. In the brilliantly realised *Tis Merry* a widow, a wife and a maid, meeting at a tavern door, discuss what men are really like and how they can be managed. Their conversation is punctuated by debates about which wine they should choose, whether they should order sausages and whether they should go home or have another round.

[51] Gouge, *Domestical Duties*, xxx. For accounts of this episode see Collinson, *The Birthpangs of Protestant England*, 71 and Amussen, *An Ordered Society*, 44–7.
[52] *Religion, Culture and Society in Early Modern Britain*, eds. Fletcher and Roberts, 161–81.
[53] Woodbridge, *Women and the English Renaissance*, 225–35.
[54] *OED*, gossip 3.

This is a piece of instruction literature, showing the wicked tricks women allegedly learnt from each other and illustrating the contagiousness of female insubordination.[55]

A Whole Crew of Kind Gossips, addressed to the maids of London, is intended as a warning about the unfair abuse men can suffer by being wronged behind their backs. The point is made six times over as six wives present their complaints and are duly put in their place by the replies of their husbands. The men are painted as mean or brutal, as gamesters, drunkards or womanisers. But their treatment of their wives emerges, predictably, as a necessary recourse to discipline for women who are idle spendthrifts, scolds and shrews. The double standard is very evident: a drunkard husband, the smell of whose tobacco nauseates his wife, declares his drinking is mere good fellowship and he is anyway seldom too drunk to stand up. His virility accused, he makes 'a solemn vow':

> The chiefest art I have I will bestow
> About a work called taming of the shrew.[56]

Women's demands and expectations are unreasonable; they must be checked by the firm exercise of household discipline; once out of the house they can never be trusted. The precepts of this literature hold no surprises. 'A rouk-town's seldom a good housewife at home', they said in Yorkshire in the seventeenth century: 'rouk-town' was dialect for a 'gossiping woman who loved to go from house to house'.[57] Another more generally current proverb put the issue explicitly: 'women and hens are lost by gadding'.[58]

The satirical lecture was a favourite format for exposing women's wiles and bringing them down for their shrewishness. John Taylor's *Juniper Lecture* of 1639 advertised itself on the title page as including 'the description of all sorts of women, good and bad: from the modest to the maddest, from the most civil to the scold rampant'.[59] Bedtime was believed to be the crux of domestic guerilla warfare. Thus Desdemona, who one hardly thinks of as a domineering shrew, made her promise to further Cassio's suit with Othello:

> I'll watch him, tame and talk him out of patience
> His bed shall seem a school, his board a shrift.[60]

Richard Braithwaite's *Art Asleep Husband: A Bolster Lecture*, which runs to

---

[55] S. Rowlands, *Well Met Gossip* (1619).
[56] S. Rowlands, *A Crew of Kind Gossips all met to be Merry* (1613) sig D 3 v.
[57] Ray, *A Collection of English Proverbs*, 52.
[58] Tilley, *Dictionary of Proverbs*, no W 695.
[59] Henderson and McManus, eds. *Half Humankind*, 290.
[60] *Othello*, act 3, scene 3, 23–4.

318 pages, shows on the frontispiece a loquacious woman hectoring a husband who can get no sleep while the words, as an accompanying rhyme indicates, go in one ear and out the other. Thomas Heywood's *A Curtain Lecture* is another lengthy diatribe containing lots of good stories. There was always a moral in them. A country fellow, for example, exasperated to find he had married 'an arch scold', and convinced by manifest proofs that she was 'very lascivious and unchaste', went for advice to his father-in-law. Her mother, he was told, had been just the same but he had been patient and there was now 'not a more quiet and chaste matron amongst all her neighbours'.[61]

The broadside ballads which the ballad-monger sang in the market place and which were the staple of the chapmen's packs, as they travelled from village to village, were much cheaper than conduct books or satirical pamphlet literature and so reached a wider audience. They are only just beginning to be studied as a historical source.[62] A good many of them, predictably, deal with marital discord, providing insight into fears about the 'imagined horns' which often haunted men's minds. Scolding and cuckolding, I have argued, were seen as going together: public knowledge of a man's suffering either from his wife threatened his reputation. A curious ballad entitled *A Banquet for Sovereign Husbands* describes the ritualistic roasting of a ram at St Giles in the Fields in London in 1629.[63] It seems that the men present believed that if they gathered the courage to eat some of the ram, whose horns so powerfully symbolised cuckolding, they would be given strength to control their wives and escape the ridicule which cuckoldry could bring. The story may be apocryphal. What matters is that it's publication tells us something about how tense this issue was for men.

The significance of the scolding and cuckolding ballads, Elizabeth Foyster has suggested, lies in the laughter they provoked, a laughter which mixed the pleasure of learning of someone else's plight with the pain of sharing his discomfiture. Hearing the ballads sung or reading them aloud to each other enabled men to reconfirm shared attitudes and values. The experience was cathartic, neutralising men's fears, strengthening their determination to be masters in their houses. Control of the pursestrings often emerges as a crucial recommended tactic. It is notable that the trigger for action in these ballads is usually embarrassment at the behaviour of wives in public. In *The Scolding Wife* the husband eventually ties his wife down and labels her a lunatic with the

---

[61] R. Braithwaite, *Art Asleep Husband* (1640); T. Heywood, *A Curtain Lecture* (1637), 183–4.

[62] N. Wurzbach, *The Rise of the English Street Ballad 1550–1650* (Cambridge, 1990); T. Watt, *Cheap Print and Popular Piety 1550–1640* (Cambridge, 1991), 11–130.

[63] 'A Banquet for Sovereign Husbands', in H. E. Rollins, ed. *A Pepysian Garland: Black Letter Broadside Ballads of the Years 1595–1639* (Cambridge, Massachusetts, 1971), 328–31. I am grateful to Elizabeth Foyster for drawing this ballad to my attention.

support of friends. In *A Caution for Scolds* the husband finally summons a doctor, who sets about correcting the woman's humoral imbalance by bleeding her and cutting her hair. The woman relents just before he adopts the ultimate remedy of cutting her tongue.[64]

The realities of scoffing and disgrace that some men suffered can be documented from the local records of the period. We know of written libels circulated, reunited in alehouses or attached to church doors. Much ingenuity was used in the derisive display of horns. In a Norfolk village in 1591 they were made out of the branches used to decorate the church and attached to the victim's pew; in another case they were tied to the necks of a neighbour's geese. The Somerset man William Swarfe had his mare led round the village in 1611 amid, we are told, 'great laughter and derision, with great clamours, shouts and outcries': the mare was apparently wearing horns and a paper attached to her tail summoning Swarfe to a 'court of cuckolds'. No wonder that men who felt their reputations for control over their wives was insecure readily accepted the procedure of ducking them as scolds on the see-saw-like contraption, the cucking stool, which some towns and villages had available for this means of discipline. Checking a sharp tongue might halt the woman's slide into sexual infidelity. David Underdown has assembled an impressive range of evidence to show that an intense preoccupation with scolding can be detected in many local communities between the 1560s and the civil war. Not that ducking was new. But, whereas in the fourteenth and fifteenth centuries it had been used for men as well as women and for a range of offences, by Elizabeth's reign it seems to have become a gender-specific punishment reserved for scolds. Town corporations acquired cucking stools in many parts of England at this time: Norwich by 1562, Bridport by 1566, Shrewsbury in 1572, Marlborough in 1578, Devizes in 1583, Clitheroe, Thornbury and Great Yarmouth by 1600. They were less common in villages, not surprisingly given the effort and expense of building one, so here scolding women were sometimes fined instead. This campaign to enforce the ritual immersion of unruly women, making a spectacle of them in the process, provides some of the most telling evidence there is that strained gender relations were very widespread.[65]

The worst that could happen for a man of course was the humiliation and contempt of the charivari, the village ritual of riding a couple with neighbours acting their parts to the accompaniment of noise and festivity, which we know occurred at intervals in many parts of England

---

[64] E. A. Foyster, 'A Laughing Matter? Marital Discord and Gender Control in Seventeenth-Century England', *Rural History* IV (1993), 1–17.

[65] This paragraph is based on Underdown in *Order and Disorder in Early Modern England*, 119–28.

during this period. Charivari was usually directed at the shrew who had been unfaithful and her cuckolded husband, but it was the husband, for abdicating his household authority, who took the brunt of the ridicule. E. P. Thompson has argued that rough music of this kind usually attached to the victim a lasting stigma: it was 'a public naming of what has been named before only in private'.[66] For the community charivari was fun. 'If you beat cuckold your husband again about the horns,' a Norfolk woman told a neighbour in 1615, the village would have an even better riding than the last one. With her jumbled words she had managed a remarkably succinct summary of the mixture of seriousness and excitement that charivari was all about.[67] The difficulty is that there is no means of knowing how much it was used, where or when, since unless it led to disorder that came to the notice of local authorities, or was useful evidence for someone in a court case about feud, there was no particular reason for anyone to record a village riding. What is now well established, through the work of David Underdown and Martin Ingram, is the function of charivari. It provided a cathartic release for communal tensions, when gossip had identified personal behaviour that went beyond accepted boundaries; it drew the line between the tolerable and the intolerable; it was a means of reasserting the gender order.[68]

Finally we can consider some new legislation of these decades against illicit sexual behaviour and evidence about its local enforcement. Puritan gentry in parliament defined and addressed sexuality across the polarity of the ordered patriarchal household, outlined in the conduct books, and the libidinous festive communities of rural England where the 'toyish censures' of the ecclesiastical courts counted for little.[69] The young female poor were, to their minds, the nation's most dangerous people. In the contemporary notion of the body the female adolescent past the menarche was seen as ready for and needing sex; she might even suffer greensickness without it.[70] So, outside the strict control of parents and masters, she was an enormous liability. Hence the ferocious bastardy legislation of 1576 and 1610 to catch those who could be proved to have fallen, legislation that was punitive as well as administrative. Following the 1576 act, JPs could have the parents of a bastard

---

[66] Thompson, *Customs in Common*, 488.

[67] Cited in Amussen, *An Ordered Society*, 118.

[68] Underdown in *Order and Disorder in Early Modern England*, 127–36; *Past and Present* 105 (1984), 79–113.

[69] For this theme see D. E. Underdown, *Revel, Riot and Rebellion* (Oxford, (1985), 44–72 and *Fire Under Heaven* (1992), 90–129.

[70] P. Crawford, 'The Construction and experience of maternity in seventeenth-century England' in *Women as Mothers in Pre-Industrial England*, ed. V. Fildes, (1990), 6.

child that might prove chargeable to the parish whipped.[71] In practice, partly because magistrates often found it hard to be sure they had caught the right father, it was by and large the women who suffered. The Essex bench moved from stocking mothers before 1580, to moderate whipping in 1588 and whipping until their backs were bloody in 1600.[72] The 1610 statute, which followed a period of high illegitimacy rates, was openly gender-specific: 'every lewd woman which shall have any bastard which may be chargeable to the parish, the justices of the peace shall commit such women to the house of correction, to be punished and set on work during the term of one whole year'. We know from quarter sessions records that in several counties, Essex, Lancashire and Warwickshire for example, the new policy was at once adopted in full.[73]

At the same time the House of Commons was turning its attention to the killing of base children, an even more heinous aspect, as MPs saw it, of unbridled female sexuality. According to the notorious infanticide act of 1624, which followed abortive bills on the subject in 1606–7 and 1610, any mother of a bastard child who concealed its death was to be presumed guilty of murder unless she could prove by the oath of a witness that the child was born dead. Uniquely in this period, the principle of English justice that the innocent were taken to be so until proved guilty was abandoned.[74] The only investigation so far as the enforcement of this act, based on the Essex assize files, shows that twenty-nine women were hanged for the offence there between 1601 and 1665 and twenty were acquitted. Keith Wrightson's view is that many of the accused mothers were innocent of any offence other than concealment and that even among those subject as domestic servants to acute emotional strain the actual crime was infrequent.[75] The statute suggests a moral panic among certain gentry, in which a particular social group became the target for vituperative action, rather than a rash of infanticidal mothers in rural England.[76] It must have been a very reassuring business pushing this legislation through parliament. Anxiety about sin and sex, about social and gender order, made it immensely plausible.

[71] 18 Elizabeth c.3.

[72] W. Hunt, *The Puritan Moment* (Cambridge, Masachussetts, 1983), 75–6.

[73] 7 James I c.4; A.J. Fletcher, *Reform in the Provinces: The Government of Stuart England* (1986), 252–7.

[74] 21 James I, c. 27; J.R. Kent, 'Attitudes of members of the House of Commons to the regulation of personal conduct in late Elizabethan and Early Stuart England', *Bulletin of the Institute of Historical Research XLV* (1972), 69.

[75] K. Wrightson, 'Infanticide in earlier seventeenth-century England', *Local Population Studies* XV (1975), 10–22.

[76] For an interesting parallel in the Victorian period see L. Nead, *Myths of Sexuality* (Oxford, 1988), 80–118.

I hope I have said enough to demonstrate that a considerable number of Englishmen of the period between 1560 and 1660 felt there was a problem about their control of women. The cumulative evidence of literary genres, parliamentary legislation and local action seems to me to point strongly to this conclusion. There was nervousness, anxiety, fear. What could be done? This form of patriarchy in the end rested on force and during this period there was no legal check on a man's beating his wife:

> A spaniel, a woman and a walnut tree
> The more they're beaten the better they be

John Ray included the old proverb as one still current in 1670.[77] But whereas early sixteenth century advice book writers had accepted that wife beating was legal and passed no further comment, the puritan ones almost all emphatically rejected it.[78] In 1609 an Oxford scholar, William Heale, published a lengthy tract arguing that the closeness of the marriage relationship made nonsense of beating wives and that it represented a 'public example dangerous unto the commonwealth'.[79] When Benezer, the husband of Xantip the scold, argued he should be allowed to beat her, in a satire by Robert Snawsel, he was taken to task by the pious evangelical Abigail who said love and correction were incompatible. Moreover, she declares, 'the wife would be made more unruly and outrageous by beating. We are women and have some experience of these things'.[80] Abigail's warning was the lesson that Thomas Heywood drew when, in his *Curtain Lecture*, he unravelled the meaning of an old proverb with a reading of it as a story of revenge. The proverb ran 'if I should be so foolish as to yield unto you where in the meantime can you find a fit tree to which to tie the sow'. A rustic, he explained, who had beaten his wife 'for reading a lecture to him somewhat too loud' sent her to market next day to sell their sow. Her chance to avenge herself for the beating came on the way when a young man, who had long wooed her unsuccessfully, met her just before she left the path through a thick wood for the open fields ahead.[81] It is hard to tell what impact the puritan campaign against wife beating made on the general populace or how people took tales like this one. The practice certainly remained endemic well beyond this period. But there probably was some growing understanding during

[77] Ray, *A Collection of English Proverbs*, 50.
[78] K. M. Davies, 'Change and continuity in literary advice on marriate' in *Marriage and Society*, ed. R. B. Outhwaite, (1981), 68; Gouge, *Domestical Duties*, 394–7; Whateley, *Bride Bush*, 96–116, 123–5, 210–16; Amussen, *An Ordered Society*, 42–3.
[79] W. Heale, *An Apology for Women* (1609), 18–19.
[80] R. Snawsel, *A Looking Glass for Married Folks* (1631), 109–12.
[81] Heywood, *A Curtain Lecture*, 189–92.

the seventeenth century, at least among the better educated, that force was usually counter productive and that patriarchal authority had to be exercised by persuasion and negotiation. A new framework for gender relationships was needed, a framework which rested on something more than, or something different from, God's word in scripture and a tradition which condoned male power and the use of force.

This paper has concentrated upon some of the dynamics of the sexual politics of the period from 1560 to 1660. But there were other dimensions to the question of the future of patriarchy in early modern England. Scientific advances were shaking the foundations of the old cosmology. Woman could not be dismissed for ever, as this process continued, simply as a creature inferior to but not different from man, distinguished by her lesser heat. Perhaps even more fundamentally, a huge epistemological shift had begun to alter the basic premises of the old mental world, a shift which was removing the body from its protected status as a microcosm of some larger order, unknowable except in terms of the signs that God had laid down in things. The victory at the Restoration of the Baconian vision of knowledge had enormous implications for thinking about gender.[82] So did the triumph of the mechanical world view associated with Descartes and Newton.[83] This is the context in which the subject must be further investigated. I have been concerned with some of the English manifestations of the woman-on-top, a historical phenomenon of the early modern period in Europe as a whole which Natalie Davis first brought to our attention nearly twenty years ago. I have tried to show how as an immediate tactic, in the drama, in satire and in village ritual, the age played constantly with the notion of inversion. But 'the woman-on-top', Davis argued, not only 'renewed old systems', it also 'helped change them into something different'.[84] So where did the dilemma men felt about enforcing patriarchy on its old scriptural basis lead them? Was there a new kind of future for patriarchy? That, as they say, has to be regarded as another story.

---

[82] E. F. Keller, *Reflections on Gender and Science* (New Haven and London, 1985), 6–8, 33–42.

[83] D. Zohar, *The Quantum Self* (1990), 38, 74–6.

[84] Davis, *Society and Culture in Early Modern France*, 151.

EDWARD III AND THE DIALECTICS OF STRATEGY,
1327–1360
The Alexander Prize Essay
By Clifford J. Rogers
READ 28 MAY 1993

He that will fraunce wynne, must with Scotland first beginne.[1]

WHEN I tell people that I'm studying English strategy in the Hundred Years War, the response is very often something to the effect of 'did they really have "strategy" in the middle ages?' This idea, that strategy was absent from the medieval period, remains deeply embedded in the historiography of the subject. Sir Charles Oman, probably still the best-known historian of medieval warfare, wrote of the middle ages that 'the minor operations of war were badly understood, [and] strategy— the higher branch of the military art—was absolutely nonexistent.[2] Professor Ferdinand Lot said much the same. Other scholars have argued that the medieval commander 'had not the slightest notion of strategy,' or that 'never was the art of war so imperfect or so primitive.'[3] But the truth is that most medieval commanders did not show 'a total scorn for the intellectual side of war' nor ignore 'the most elementary principles of strategy'[4]; nor is it fair to say that ' "generalship" and- "planning" are concepts one can doubtfully apply to medieval warfare.'[5]

If medieval commanders have in general received little credit for their strategic understanding, Edward III in particular has been singled out as, in Oman's words, 'a very competent tactician, but a very unskilful strategist'. Oman argued, indeed, that 'the details of the campaign which led up to the battle of Creçcy are as discreditable to

---

[1] 'the old auncient proverbe used by our forfathers,' according to Edward Halle. *The Union of the Two Noble Families of Lancaster and York* (1548), sub Henry V, folio 39v.

[2] He first made this comment in 1885, but as late as 1953 John Beeler, then among the foremost medieval military historians, wrote that 'this is still the generally accepted view of the medieval concept of war.' C. W. C. Oman, *The Art of War in the Middle Ages* revised and edited by J. H. Beeler (1953), 61, 61n.

[3] Ferdinand Lot, *L'art militaire et les armées au moyen age* (1946), II, 449: 'la grande stratégie est inexistante' in the Middle Ages. Napoleon III and I. Favé, *Études sur le passé et l'avenir de l'Artillerie*, (1846), 31; R. Van Overstraeten, *Des principes de la guerre à travers les âges* (1926), quoted in Philippe Contamine, *War in the Middle Ages* (Oxford, 1987), 209.

[4] Lynn Montross, *War Through the Ages* (New York, 1960), 135.

[5] John Keegan, *The Face of Battle* (New York, 1984), 336. Cf. Sir Michael Howard, *War in European History* (Oxford, 1977), 27.

his generalship as those of the actual engagement are favourable'.[6] J. F. C. Fuller agreed that 'what his strategic aim was, it is impossible to fathom ... Edward's conduct of the campaign of Crécy shows no proof of any rational scheme'. Major-General George Wrottesley, an amateur historian of some distinction, wrote that the campaign was conceived 'against every principle of the military art'.[7]

H. J. Hewitt's study of the organisation of war under Edward III, which appeared in 1966, put forward a new interpretation of the strategic rationale for Edward's campaigns of devastation in France.[8] He argued that these great English *chevauchées* of the fourteenth century served two purposes: to undermine the political support of the Valois monarchy by showing its military weakness in comparison with English might; and, as part of a war of attrition, to destroy the resources with which the Valois fought the war. Hewitt argued further than the aim of the *chevauchée* 'was not, as might have been supposed, to seek out the enemy and bring him to decisive combat'; indeed, according to his analysis, the English actively sought to avoid battle.[9]

This new interpretation of the *chevauchée* has become the dominant one, adopted by C. T. Allmand, Kenneth Fowler, Michael Prestwich, and Maurice Keen, among others.[10] It comes much closer to the truth than the older ideas of Oman and his school; but it still misses the mark in important ways which have led to serious misinterpretations of some of the English campaigns, notably the 1346 'Crécy' *chevauchée*. The most important error made by Hewitt and his followers is to portray the *chevauchée* as a battle-*avoiding* rather than a battle-*seeking*

---

[6] C. W. C. Oman, *A History of the Art of War in the Middle Ages* (1924) II, 111, 126; cf. 160. This view remains pervasive: the best general textbook on medieval history, Brian Tierney and Sidney Painter's *Western Europe in the Middle Ages, 300–1475* (New York, 1983), 495, claims that Edward 'had too little grasp of reality to be a competent strategist'.

[7] J. F. C. Fuller, *The Decisive Battles of the Western World and their Influence upon History*, ed. J. Terraine, (1970), 311. G. Wrottesley, *Crecy and Calais from the Public Records* (1898), iii; cf. Michael Powicke, 'The English Aristocracy and the War', in *The Hundred Years War*, Kenneth Fowler (ed.) (1971), 127.

[8] Although Hewitt himself was unwilling to acknowledge it as such—he considered it part of the 'practice of war' as distinct from the 'art of war', thus separating it from the realm of strategy. H. J. Hewitt, *The Organization of War Under Edward III, 1338–62* (Manchester, 1966), 111. Cf. H. J. Hewitt, *The Black Prince's Expedition of 1355–1357*, (Manchester, 1958), 13, 105.

[9] Hewitt, *Organization*, 99; H. J. Hewitt, 'The Organisation of War' in *The Hundred Years War* (ed.) Kenneth Fowler (1971), 86–7. Cf. Christopher Allmand, *The Hundred Years War*, (Cambridge, 1988), 54–5.

[10] C. T. Allmand, 'The War and the Non-Combatant' in *The Hundred Years War* (ed.) Fowler, 166; Allmand, *The Hundred Years War*, 54–5. Kenneth Fowler, *The Age of Plantagenet and Valois* (New York, 1967), 152. Michael Prestwich, *The Three Edwards* (1980), 177–8, 180, 186. Maurice H. Keen, *England in the Later Middle Ages* (1973), 135. Scott L. Waugh, *England in the Reign of Edward III* (Cambridge, 1991), 17.

strategy. In this paper, using the Crécy *chevauchée* as my primary example, I will put forward the opposite case. I will then proceed to a deeper analysis of what Hewitt correctly perceived to be the other important components of the *chevauchée* strategy: political destabilisation and economic attrition. First, though, I will address the origins of the English version of the *chevauchée* in the Scottish campaigns of the earlier fourteenth century, and also the tactical basis on which the English method of war rested: for without the 'Halidon' tactics, there could have been no strategy of *chevauchée*.

Historians now generally accept that Edward's war-aims in 1337 were first and foremost to secure sovereignty over his continental possessions, and so to put an end to the interference of the French royal bureaucracy in his government of Guienne.[11] Doubtless, Edward would have preferred to have made good his claim to the French throne, but he was realistic enough to know—even after his triumphs in the 'year of miracles', 1346, that this was practically beyond his reach. Still, it did remain a secondary goal, to be pursued if opportunity arose, as his negotiations with Burgundy in the course of the 1359–60 Reims campaign show.[12]

It is striking that Edward, when he began the war, had already seen equivalent goals accomplished by others. In 1326–7, his mother Isabella and her lover Roger Mortimer succeeded in defeating and deposing Edward II, and replacing him on the throne with the young Edward III himself. Then, just a year later, Robert Bruce of Scotland wrested from the English exactly what Edward himself would later seek for his duchy of Aquitaine: *de jure* acknowledgement of long-held *de facto* sovereignty. A smaller, weaker, poorer country had forced its larger, richer, more populous neighbor to renounce its claim to feudal superiority in order to put an end to devastating mounted raids. If this sounds familiar, it is for good reason: there is more than a coincidental relationship between the 'Shameful Peace' of Northampton (1328) and the Treaty of Brétigny which Edward imposed on the French in 1360. Edward won that latter treaty precisely by doing unto the French as the Scots had done unto him in 1327.

The experiences of the English in their Scottish wars, especially from Bannockburn to Halidon Hill, led Edward III and his advisors to develop new tactical and strategic conceptions that decisively shaped

[11] But see J. Le Patourel, 'Edward III and the Kingdom of France', *History*, XLIII (1958).

[12] For a concise but informed treatment, see Kenneth Fowler, *The King's Lieutenant* (New York, 1969), 205–6.

the first half of the Hundred Years War. Tracing Edward's military evolution through these Scottish campaigns serves two important purposes: it enhances our understanding of English strategy during the first phase of the Hundred Years War; and it provides a valuable paradigm of the dialectical process by which a commander's understanding of the craft of war develops.

In 1314, not long after Edward's birth, his father, Edward II, led a large English army to the relief of Stirling castle, which was under siege by the Scots. The English were attacked under unfavourable circumstances near Bannockburn and decisively defeated. The military reputation of the English sunk so low as a result that, as Knighton commented, 'two Englishmen were hardly a match for one feeble Scot'.[13] Bannockburn, by far the most important battle fought during Edward III's childhood, showed clearly the difficulty of disrupting a tight infantry formation by cavalry charges alone, a lesson Edward was later to use to good effect.

Over the succeeding years, the triumphant Scots used the threat of further devastating raids to extort large sums of money from the northern counties, in the process almost totally eliminating the revenues which the Exchequer received from the region.[14] In 1327, the year of Edward III's coronation, with England weakened by internal dissension arising from the deposition of Edward II, Robert Bruce decided to try to extort a much greater prize from the English: acknowledgement of his independent sovereignty over Scotland.

A large group of Scottish mounted infantry (soldiers who rode from place to place, but fought on foot in pike phalanxes called 'schiltrons') raided deep into English territory that year 'with a strong hand, and laid it waste with fire and sword'.[15] An English army under Edward III's nominal command set out after them, but could not match the speed of the highly mobile Scots. Eventually the English abandoned all their excess baggage and tried to outmanoeuvre the Scots instead of out-marching them. Their intention, explains Jean le Bel (who took part in the campaign on the English side), was to pin the Scots against the Tyne and force them 'to fight at a disadvantage (*à meschief*) or to remain in England, caught in the trap'.[16] But they failed, and in the

[13] Knighton, I, 452. Cf. Petrarch's comment to the same effect, quoted in R. Boutruche, 'The Devastation of Rural Areas During the Hundred Years War and the Agricultural Recovery of France', in *The Recovery of France in the Fifteenth Century*, ed. P. S. Lewis, (New York, 1972), 26.

[14] For tax revenues, see Public Record Office, London: E359/14 mm 13, 13d. For extortion, see J. Stevenson (ed.), *Chronicon de Lanercost*, (Edinburgh, 1839), 222, and *Calendar of Close Rolls, 1318–23*, 274.

[15] John of Fordun, *Chronica Gentis Scotorum* ed. W. F. Skene, (Edinburgh 1871), 351.

[16] Jean le Bel, *Chronique de Jean le Bel* ed. Jules Viard & Eugene Deprez. (Paris, 1904), I, 55.

end were only able to find the Scots because the raiders sent a captured English esquire to inform the English of their location. The Scots were quite eager to give battle, so long as they could do so on their own terms.[17] The English host found the Scottish schiltrons deployed in an unassailable defensive position, across a swift river (the Wear) and atop a steep hill, without enough room between the water and the slope for the English to form up.[18] The English tried to persuade the Scots to fight on a more even field, but the raiders declined. 'The king and his council saw well,' they replied, 'that they were in his kingdom, and had burnt and devastated it; if this annoyed the King, he might come and amend it, for they would stay there as long as they liked.'[19]

This left the English in a lose-lose situation. To attack would be to invite a repetition of Bannockburn, which is clearly what the Scots hoped for; on the other hand, not to attack would be to allow the enemy to escape unpunished; the massive effort and expense put into mounting the English expedition dissipated without result; and the royal government's prestige once again sent to rock bottom. Opting for the lesser of the two evils, the English declined the assault. As a result, their enemies escaped—Scot free, as it were—after having committed such destruction that, because of it, for the Twentieth granted in the fall of 1327, Cumberland, Westmoreland, and Northumberland contributed nothing at all, and even Yorkshire and Lancashire contributed only about 40 per cent of their 'peacetime' levels.[20] The young king returned to England 'in great desolation and sorrow because things hadn't gone better for him at the beginning of his reign; and, stricken with shame, he grieved much,'[21] as Knighton tells us. The Brut adds that 'when the Kyng wist that the Scottes were ascapede, he was wonder' sory, and ful hertly wepte with his yonge eyne.'[22] Murimuth describes him as returning to York 'sorrowing and without honor'.[23] The point I want to make here is that this expedition was deeply engraved on the consciousness of the young king, and did much to shape his understanding of the craft of war. The moreso, since the end result of his military failure was the *turpis pax*, or 'shameful peace' of

[17] le Bel, *Chronique*, I, 63.

[18] This was just what the English Council had anticipated. See *ibid.*, I, 54.

[19] *Ibid.*, 66.

[20] J. F. Willard, 'The Scotch Raids and the Fourteenth-Century Taxation of Northern England' *University of Colorado Studes* V, no. 4 (1908), 238–40. Cf. *Rotuli Parliamentorum*, II, 176.

[21] Henrici Knighton, *Chronicon*, ed. J. R. Lumby. (Rolls Series, 1895), I, 445.

[22] *The Brut, or The Chronicles of England*, ed. F. W. D. Brie (1906), 251. Cf. Thomas Gray, *Scalacronica* ed. Joseph Stevenson (Edinburgh, 1836), 155: 'Le roy, vn innocent, plora dez oils'. The *Chronicon de Lanercost*, ed. J. Stevenson (Edinburgh, 1836), 260, also supports the story.

[23] Adam Murimuth, *Continuatio Chronicarum* ed. E. M. Thompson (1889), 53.

1328, which required Edward to renounce his suzerainty over Scotland.[24] However, he learned well the lesson of the power of a mobile raiding force relying on the tactical defensive when brought to battle. In his later conflicts with France, he would use this lesson extremely well.

First, though, England had to quell the menace to the north. When Robert Bruce died in 1329, leaving an infant son to be king after him, the opportunity soon presented itself. In 1332 Edward Balliol, a pretender to the Scottish throne, mounted an invasion of Scotland with an army composed largely of English men-at-arms and archers. Balliol's tiny army defeated two larger Scottish forces in succession, the second one probably ten times the size of his own.[25] He then had himself crowned as king of Scots at Scone—another important precedent showing Edward III the political potential of a battlefield victory.

Balliol's successes encouraged Edward III to grant him more overt support, and in 1333 the English king led a large army into Scotland. The Plantagenet monarch forced his opponents into open battle by threatening Berwick, much as the Scots had drawn Edward II to battle by besieging Stirling in 1314, and as Edward later sought to draw the French into battle by besieging Cambrai in 1339. The Scottish army of 1333, which far outnumbered the English force, was pressured into taking the tactical offensive, even though Edward had the advantage of a powerful defensive position atop Halidon Hill, one not utterly unlike the site held by the Scots in 1327. Using the same tactical formation as he was later to employ at Crécy, with dismounted men-at-arms in the center flanked by archers equipped with the immensely powerful yew longbow, Edward utterly routed the attacking Scots, inflicting outrageously unequal casualties.[26] For the moment, at least, Balliol was restored to power in Scotland and the 'Shameful Peace' of 1328 completely overturned.

*   *   *

Let us briefly consider the tactical system which made this dramatic turn of events possible. Strategy is the art of using available military means to achieve desired political goals, and the strengths and limi

---

[24] It is worth noting that Edward personally objected to the Treaty of Northampton, agreeing to its terms only under pressure from Mortimer and Isabella. Ranald Nicholson, *Edward III and the Scots* (Oxford, 1965), 51.

[25] Bridlington Chronicler, *Gesta Edwardi Tertii Auctore Canonico Bridlingtonensi* in *Chronicles of the Reigns of Edward I and Edward II*, ed. W. Stubbs (1883), II, 102–3, 106; *Scalacronica*, 159; *Lanercost*, 267; Andrew of Wyntoun, *Orygynale Chronykil of Scotland*, ed. D. Lang (Edinburgh, 1872), II, 383–5.

[26] For Halidon hill, see Bridlington, *Gesta Edwards*, 114–16; Wyntoun, *Orygynale Cronykil*, II, 401–2; *Lanercost*, 273–4; *Brut* I, 283–9; Walter of Hemingburgh, *Chronicon* (1849), II, 308–9; Thomas Burton, *Chronica Monasterii de Melsa* (1867), II, 369–70.

tations of the tactical means employed by a commander can have a powerful effect on shaping his strategy. The precise formation employed by the English is not entirely clear, and varied slightly from battle to battle, but its basic characteristics remained constant from Dupplin Muir to Agincourt and beyond. The English men-at-arms, using their lances like pikes, drew themselves up on foot in a dense phalanx, often subdivided into three divisions or 'battles', one of which might be held back in reserve. On the flanks of this core of dismounted men-at-arms were ranged the English archers, protected by such natural barriers or improvised field works as could be prepared before a battle. The archers' arrows, coming 'thicker than rain', wounded or killed men and horses before they could close with their enemy, throwing an attacker's formation into disarray and driving it onto the lance-points of the men-at-arms.[27] An immobile formation of pikemen is difficult to disrupt under the best of situations,[28] and by the time the attacker reached the English men-at-arms, his situation would be very far from the best.

The key point about this tactical system is that it proved extra-ordinarily effective so long as the enemy could be provoked to attack, but it was not well suited to taking the tactical initiative, especially against the heavy cavalry for which the French were renowned. The strategic implications of this fact will become clear, I hope, in the forthcoming examination of the Crécy *chevauchée*.

Edward's original objectives in launching the Hundred Years War in 1337 were to establish full sovereignty over his Continental duchy of Aquitaine, and put an end to French interference in Scotland, though his goals later grew with his successes. The first strategy employed by Edward to this end, initiated in 1339, was to attempt to do to the French what he had already done to the Scots in 1333: ravage the lands of the French king, besiege an important city, and thus draw his enemy into battle[29] where he could be decisively defeated. Of course, France was a far greater enemy than Scotland, so Edward prepared for this initial expedition by securing substantial Imperial and mercenary contingents to supplement his own forces. Indeed, English supporters of the Continental alliances claimed that Edward 'need not bring

---

[27] For an explanation of the effectiveness of the longbow, and an analysis of the broader social implications of the English infantry-based style of war, see Clifford J. Rogers, 'The Military Revolutions of the Hundred Years' War', *Journal of Military History*, LVII (1993), 249–57.

[28] Except by an enemy with missile superiority.

[29] *Chronica Monasterii de Melsa*, III, 73; cf. 41, 50, and John of Reading, *Chronica Johannis de Reading et anonymi Cantuariensis, 1346–1367* ed. J. Tait (Manchester, 1914), 122.

anyone with him except [his chamber servant], as he would be strong enough with his allies over there alone to conquer his heritage of France'.[30] The plan did not work, however: the two hosts met at Vironfosse, but Philip VI, as Edward had at Stanhope Park in 1327, chose the lesser of two evils and declined to initiate a battle, despite the '*trop grant blasme*' this occasioned.[31] Much the same happened the next year when, despite Edward's siege of Tournai, Philip refused to give battle.

Edward had made his bid for a decisive confrontation, but without success. In the wake of the 1339 and 1340 campaigns, his finances in complete disarray, he fell back on a less costly war of opportunity in Guienne and Brittany, where he enjoyed substantial success. At the conference of Avignon in the fall of 1344, Edward tried to turn these military successes into the political result he desired: the cession to him of Guienne in full sovereignty. Philip was willing to return the duchy as a fief, but not as an independent territory. Edward began to realise that France was too big for his gradualist strategy to be successful, given the limited resources of manpower, money and time available to him; he needed a big victory to force the peace terms he desired. The means he employed to this end was the *chevauchée*.

Beginning with the campaign of 1346, Edward sought to put Philip of Valois into the same position Edward himself had been in after 1327. He would ride through Philip's territory as Robert Bruce had ridden through England, destroying and burning as he went. This destruction, which Hewitt has effectively described, did not result from the indiscipline or poor pay of the English troops,[32] nor from the need to live off the land: none of those factors could account for the degree of devastation reported in chronicles and records of the period. Houses, windmills, orchards, ships, fields, vineyards: all were plundered, destroyed, and burnt in this 'werre cruelle and sharpe'.[33] This was

---

[30] *Scalacronica*, 168. Cf. Froissart, *Oeuvres*, II, 353 and III, 16.

[31] Froissart, *Oeuvres*, III, 44.

[32] Allmand, 'The War and the Non-Combatant,' 169–70, attributes the destruction to lack of regular pay, although this seems to be inconsistent with his overall argument. But if the lack of regular pay were the reason for the devastation, then we would expect to see little or no destruction at the outset of a campaign, since most indentures specified that one quarter or more of the total wages be paid in advance; yet there is no evidence for an increase in the amount of destruction inflicted as the campaign went on. Furthermore, le Bel comments repeatedly on how well paid Edward's armies were.

[33] The phrase is from Sir John Fastolf's 1435 report advocating a return to the *chevauchée* strategy, in *Letters and Papers Illustrative of the Wars of the English in France during the Reign of Henry the Sixth, King of England* ed. J. Stevenson (1861–4), II, 581.

clearly an intentional element of Edward's military policy:[34] the destruction would damage Philip's tax revenues, just as the Scottish raids of 1327 had eliminated Edward's revenues from the northernmost counties of England; it would threaten Philip with the same kind of popular and baronial discontent that had made possible the deposition of Edward II; and, most importantly, it would place strong political pressure on Philip to attack Edward's army and thus give Edward the chance to win a decisive victory like the one he had gained at Halidon Hill but been denied at Vironfosse. Philip would thus be faced, as Edward had been in 1327, with the choice of either forcing a battle under unfavorable conditions, or accepting the dishonour and political destabilisation—as well as the loss of taxation revenue—that would result from his failure to defend his vassals and subjects. Edward, as we shall see, was hoping that Philip would choose the former alternative—battle. The Plantagenet king knew, however, that even if his enemy declined battle it would be a major political victory for England, and it would be the Valois monarch left 'sorrowing and without honor'. During the Middle Ages, perhaps more than at any other time, war was intimately intertwined with politics. It could not be otherwise when the men who formed the most important part of every army also composed the political élite. Since the nobility and gentry who provided the king with his men-at-arms were directly tied to their land, to such an extent that they usually took their names from it, an attack on the land was equally a political, economic, and military assault.

The feudal system, even in its 'declined' form of the fourteenth century, rested on the contract of homage, whereby a vassal pledged support and military service to his lord in exchange for land (theoretically) and protection and 'good lordship' (practically). This contract was replicated down the social ladder from king to magnates to simple knights and gentry to (implicitly if not literally) the peasants themselves, who provided their lords with food and labor service in exchange for tenure on the land and protection. The king who willingly failed to provide protection to his vassals, rear-vassals, and subjects violated the contract which enabled him to demand taxes and military service from them, and seriously undermined the basis for his claim to legitimacy.[35] As the Count of Foix put it, 'all landed lords are duty-

---

[34] Despite Hewitt's contention, which I find quite mystifying considering the overall direction of his argument, that 'looting arose neither from military policy nor from military necessity' ('Organisation', 37; cf. *Organisation*, 96). Compare Fastolf's suggestions on military policy of 1435, in *Letters and Papers*, ed. Stevenson, II, 581.

[35] John Fortescue, *De Laudibus Legum Anglie* ed. and tr. S. B. Chrimes (Cambridge 1942), 33: 'a king ... is obliged to protect the law, the subjects, and their bodies and goods, and he has the power to this end issuing from the people, so that it is not permissible for him to rule his people with any other power.' Cf. 35, 89.

bound to guard their people; it is for that that they hold their lordships.'[36]

So in 1346 Edward landed in Normandy and began a *chevauchée*—a destructive mounted raid designed to ravage rather than to conquer, 'burning, devastating and driving away the people; then did the French greatly sorrow, and loudly cried: where is Philip, our king?'—in that poorly defended land.[37]

Up to now, it has been unclear whether Edward III wanted to do battle with the French in 1346, or whether he was forced to do so when caught by Philip. Despite the claims of Edward himself and his contemporaries to the contrary, those modern authors who give their position on the matter, including Edouard Perroy, Philippe Contamine, Michael Prestwich, Richard Barber, Barbara Emerson, Jim Bradbury and Maurice Keen, unanimously agree that, in Perroy's words, 'Edward did not dream of measuring himself against this imposing enemy, too numerous for him.'[38] Most descriptions of the campaign interpret all of Edward's actions with this assumed, and when this does not fit the English actions, merely comment that 'at this point Edward's tactics seem obscure'[39] or that they are 'surprising'.[40] Statements of those involved which contradict this assumption are considered to be jokes,[41] propaganda for distribution in England,[42] or attempts at deceit[43] which 'cannot be taken seriously'.[44]

The conviction that Edward was unwilling to risk a general engagement seems to come from two sources: the 'inherent military probability' idea that no commander so outnumbered would wish to fight; and the fact that Edward was moving rapidly northwards, towards Flanders, before Philip 'overtook' him. Before we turn to the primary source evidence which suggests that the English were indeed willing, even anxious, to do battle, these contrary arguments must be addressed. Neither is convincing when subjected to close examination.

---

[36] Froissart, *Oeuvres*, XII, 109. Philip's repeated failure to prevent the English from ravaging his realm led Jean le Bel to denounce him as unworthy of the apellation 'noble'—in contrast with Edward III, who 'cannot be too much honored'. *Chronique*, II, 65.

[37] Chandos Herald, *Life of the Black Prince*, eds. M. K. Pope and E. C. Lodge (Oxford, 1910), 7.

[38] Edouard Perroy, *The Hundred Years War* (New York, 1965), 119. Cf. Philippe Contamine, *La Guerre de Cent Ans* (1972), 29; Prestwich, *The Three Edwards*, 177–8, 186; Jim Bradbury, *The Medieval Archer* (Woodbridge, 1985), 105, 111; Maurice Keen, *England in the Later Middle Ages* (1973), 135, and citations to other authors named, below.

[39] Richard Barber, *Edward, Prince of Wales and Aquitaine* (1978), 58, re. Edward III's decision to wait for Philip at Poissy.

[40] *Ibid.*, 62, re. his not attempting to escape Philip after the crossing of the Somme.

[41] Barbara Emerson, *The Black Prince* (1976), 34.

[42] *The Life and Campaigns of the Black Prince*, ed., Richard Barber (1979), 13.

[43] A. H. Burne, *The Crecy War* (1955), 154.

[44] Barber, *Edward, Prince of Wales and Aquitaine*, 59.

The 'inherent military probability' idea, always risky, necessitates particular caution when applied to the mind of the medieval commander. Edward probably believed—and indeed had many good reasons to believe, since his earlier successes from Halidon Hill to Sluys had been phenomenal, and his claim to the French crown was a strong one—that God was on his side.[45] Both this belief and the complementary secular ethos of chivalry, which held that a good knight should *'fais ce que dois, adviegne que peut'*[46] would have discouraged him from placing too much emphasis on the smaller size of his army. Furthermore, deficiency in numbers can be compensated for by superiority in tactics, equipment, discipline, leadership and morale. The English soldiers and captains were largely experienced veterans, many of whom had participated in the glorious victories of Halidon Hill, Morlaix, or Dupplin Muir. At Halidon Hill they had overcome odds of, perhaps, 3:1; at Dupplin Muir, they won against odds of about 10:1. Clearly the victors of such engagements would not see a disadvantage in numbers as an insurmountable obstacle.[47] As Froissart says, the English 'never worried about it if they were not in great numbers'.[48] To paraphrase a contemporary poem on the battle of Halidon Hill, if the French outnumbered them by 3:1 it would be like 'fifteen sheep against wolves five'.[49]

Edward was in a much better position than are we to evaluate his own army in comparison with that of his enemy. The Valois host was

---

[45] See his letter to Clement VI, in Robert of Avesbury, *De Gestis Mirabilibus Regis Edwardi Tertii* ed. E. M. Thompson (1889), 380–81; his earlier letter to Simon Boccanegra, quoted in Jonathan Sumption, *The Hundred Years War: Trial by Battle*, (1990), 380; and also his letters cited in notes 63 and 68, below.

[46] That is the version of the saying, which translates roughly as 'do the right thing, come what may,' in Guillaume de Machaut's *Le confort d'ami*, a near-contemporary text on chivalry. Françcois de Montebelluna also gives the same admonition. See Françoise Autrand, 'La déconfiture. La bataille de Poitiers (1356) à travers quelques textes français des XIVe et XVe siècles', in *Guerre et société en France, en Angleterre et en Bourgogne. XIVe–XVe Siècle*, eds. Philippe Contamine et. al. (Lille, 1991), 95–96. Edward's personal character was well in accord with this motto, for 'he dred neurer of none myshappes, ne harmes ne evyll fortune, that myght falle a noble warryour'. *The Brut or the Chronicle of England* ed. F. W. Brie (1906–8), II, 333.

[47] Among the leaders of the English army at Crécy, for example, Richard Talbot, Ralph Stafford and Fulk Fitzwarren had fought at Dupplin Muir, while Edward III, Bartholomew Burghersh, Ralph Basset, John Willoughby and the earls of Warwick, Oxford, Arundel and Suffolk had fought at Halidon Hill. The earl of Northampton had been the commander at Morlaix, where lord Stafford and Reginald Cobham also fought. It is significant that the four veteran soldiers assigned to choose the ground for the English formations at Crécy—Warwick, Stafford, Cobham and Godfrey d'Harcourt— thus included at least one of the leaders from each of these three battles.

[48] Froissart, *Oeuvres*, VII, 333: 'ne n'ont pas ressongné pour ce se il n'estoient point moult grant fusion'.

[49] *The Brut*, I, 288.

relatively incohesive, lacking in missile capability, and had no tactical doctrine to match that of the English. Edward could not have expected to win as overwhelming and total a victory as we know with hindsight that he did; yet it seems equally unlikely that victory *per se* came as any great surprise to him. Philip's reluctance to force battle early on in the campaign indicates that he, too, was less than certain of a French victory. Indeed, Jean le Bel specifically states that the Valois monarch 'had neither the boldness nor the courage to fight'.[50] With God and his veteran army fighting for him, Edward was confident enough to risk battle, at least if he could fight it on his own terms.

The English movement towards Flanders may at first appear to be an attempt to slip away northwards, hoping to reach the coast before being overtaken, and thus to avoid battle,[51] in fact, however, this movement was intended to help keep the army fed and to secure the best possible situation before the sought-after confrontation. Edward had hoped to link up with his Flemish allies, who were supposed to be marching to meet him, to counter the endless stream of reinforcements to the Valois host, and also wanted to fight with his back to friendly territory in case of defeat.[52] Furthermore, Calais had been his destination from early in the campaign, so his path would have been sensible even if Philip had not had any army in the field at all.[53] But most important of all, Edward had to avoid the trap which Philip was trying to set for him, a trap precisely similar to the one the English had tried to set for the Scots in 1327. Philip wanted to pin his enemy in place against an impassable barrier—the sea, the Seine or the Somme—just as Edward had earlier sought to trap the Scots against the Tyne.[54] Edward would then presumably do what he had done at Vironfosse, and what he indeed did do at Crécy: draw up his army in a Halidon-style array.

[50] *Chronique*, II, 86–7. See Sumption, *Trial by Battle*, 514 for the concessions offered by Philip early in the campaign in hopes of avoiding battle.

[51] This is the interpretation in Perroy, *The Hundred Years War*, 119, for example.

[52] For Edward's desire to meet his allies, and the English army's need for food, see the *Chronique et Annales de Gilles le Muisit, Abbé de Saint-Martin de Tournai* ed. H. Lemaître (1906), 158–9. The northward movement after crossing the Somme led to the capture '*graunt plente du vitailles*' on the eve of the battle of Crécy. Avesbury, *Gestis Mirabilibus*, 368.

[53] Jean le Bel's statement that Edward, after crossing the Seine and reaching Beauvais, 'did not want to stop to drive out the local people nor for any other reason, because he had no other intention but to besiege the strong city of Calais, since he could not be attacked [estre combastu] by king Philip, as he desired' (*Chronique*, II, 89), like Froissart's indication that Edward had already decided to march to Calais before his capture of Caen (*Oeuvres*, IV, 412) would seem to be distortions of hindsight, were it not for the support offered by PRO C81/314/17803, in which Edward orders from Caen that supplies be sent to Le Crotoy, which is north of the Somme on the way to Calais. Edward probably hoped that a siege of Calais would be enough to provoke Philip into an attack if the ravages of his *chevauchée* proved insufficient.

[54] Froissart, *Oeuvres*, V, 3, 7, makes this explicit.

But, as you will remember from the above discussion of the tactical strengths and limitations of this formation, it was a purely defensive one. If the English were pinned between the French army and a natural barrier, however, Philip would have no need to take the tactical offensive. Earlier, at Vironfosse, after waiting for the French to attack, Edward had run out of food and been forced to move off back towards his base.[55] In 1346, too, he would have been unable to stand on the defensive for long without supplies. Then Edward would have had his battle—but on Philip's terms, not on his own.[56] Given that the French army was much larger and, indeed, better prepared for such an 'open' battle, the outcome would not have been a Crécy or a Poitiers, except perhaps in reverse. But Edward managed to avoid this trap by crossing the ford at Blachetacque. When he had, thus, secured his line of retreat, he quickly found a good defensive position and halted to wait for Philip's army.

In addition to these negative arguments, there are three positive reasons to believe that Edward wanted an engagement. First, Parliament had advised him to seek battle. Second, he claimed at the time that he had actively sought to engage the Valois forces, and those with him said the same. Third, and most important, some of his actions, which are difficult to explain otherwise, support his words.

The Parliament of 1344, the last before the battle, was requested by Edward to advise him concerning the war. They responded by requesting that he 'make an end of this war, either by battle or a proper peace, if such might be had';[57] indeed, they made the collection of the second year of the subsidy they voted conditional on his going in person to France with that aim.[58]

The taxpayers of England, 'that with their chattels and their goods/maintained the war both first and last',[59] as a contemporary poem had it, were nearly exhausted, and wanted the king to end the war quickly. He had tried to secure 'a proper peace,' at the 1344 Conference of Avignon and failed: battle was the remaining alternative for a rapid settlement—or so he thought.

Now to the second point. None of the seven surviving English campaign letters from 1346 indicate that the English wished to avoid

---

[55] *Scalacronica*, 169.

[56] Just as the English tried to do to the Scots along the Wear in 1327. Froissart, *Oeuvres*, II, 166–7.

[57] *Rotuli Parliamentorum*, II, 148.

[58] G. L. Harris, *King, Parliament, and Public Finance in Medieval England to 1369* (Oxford, 1975), 320. The writs of summons for the expedition specified that it was being undertaken 'to make an end of the war'. Wrottesley, *Crecy and Calais*, 53.

[59] John Barnie, *War in Medieval English Society: Social Values in the Hundred Years War 1337–99* (Ithaca, New York, 1974), 21.

battle. Froissart says that Edward 'desired nothing more than to meet his enemies in arms.'[60] Geoffrey le Baker, one of our best sources for the campaign, describes the king as 'always ready for a battle'.[61] Edward III himself, in his letter to Thomas Lucy, says that after leaving Caen

> because we were assured that our enemy had come to Rouen, we made our way directly to him; and as soon as he knew this, he had the bridge at Rouen broken so that we could not cross ... We found all the bridges broken or strengthened and defended, so that in no way could we cross over to our adversary; nor would he approach us, although he paced us from day to day along the other bank, greatly annoying us ... So we stayed for three days at Poissy, as much to await our enemy in case he wanted to give battle as to repair the [broken] bridge ... And when we saw that our enemy did not want to come to give battle, we therefore (*sy*) had the country burnt and devastated all around ... And to better draw our enemy to battle, we headed towards Picardy.[62]

Nor can these accounts be dismissed as mere propaganda for public consumption, since another private letter by the King to his Council in London, outlining his plans after leaving Caen, states that he intended to 'hasten towards our adversary, as well as we can, wherever he may be from day to day, with firm hope in God that He will give us a good and honourable outcome to our emprise'.[63]

The *Acts of War of Edward III*, written from a campaign diary, notes that after crossing the border of Normandy the vanguard of the army 'drew themselves up in battle array against a possible enemy attack which, *they hoped*, was imminent'; that after leaving Cormolain 'they burnt the town and the surrounding country *so that the enemy should know of their coming*', and that since 'although the enemy were opposite the English army, and could have chosen various places at which to cross the river, they never showed themselves nor offered battle ... the English armed themselves and raised fire-signals everywhere *to encourage the enemy to attack*.' 'On the 14th,' continues the account, 'rumours ran through the army that the enemy were lurking in the very strong city

---

[60] *Oeuvres*, IV, 381–2: 'ne désiroit fors à trouver les armes et ses ennemis'.

[61] Geoffrey le Baker, *Chonicon Galfridi le Baker de Swynebroke*, ed. E. M. Thompson (1889), 82.

[62] Printed in the notes to the Roxburgh Club edition of Chandos Herald's *The Black Prince* (1842), 351–5, here at 352–3. An English translation of the letter is easily available in Barber, *Life and Campaigns*, but it should be used with caution, because the (usually reliable) editor has at one point left out four lines of text. Cf. the *Anonimalle Chronicle, 1333–1381* ed. V. H. Galbraith (1927), 21, and *Chronica Monasterii de Melsa*, III, 57.

[63] PRO, C81/314/17803; Cf. Froissart, *Oeuvres*, XVIII, 287. Compare the letter of Bartholomew Burghersh to Archbishop Stratford, written at the time: 'et [le roi] pense de sui trere tot dreit devers soun adversere, de faire tiel fyn coom Dieu luy ad ordeyne'. Murimuth, *Continuatio Chronicarum*, 203.

of Paris, and the king remained where he was on that day and the next waiting for the appearance of the enemy, which *he heartily hoped to see*..[64] Indeed, he did more than just wait: according to the *Chronica Monasterii de Melsa*, Edward 'in particular burnt the manor of Montjoye, the most pleasant of all the manors of the king of France, *in order better to provoke Philip to fight*'.[65] Then, explains Jean le Bel, he advanced towards Calais, intending to besiege the town 'since he could not be attacked [estre combatu] by king Philip, as he desired'.[66]

The famous letter sent by Edward to Philip just before the English crossed the Seine has been described as 'disingenuous' and intended 'chiefly for consumption in [Edward's] own army',[67] but I believe that it is a serious and important statement of Edward's aims in 1346:

we have come without pride or presumption into our realm of France, *making our way to you to make an end to war by battle*. But although you could thus have had a battle, you broke down the bridges between you and us, so that we could not come near you nor cross the river Seine. When we came to Poissy and had the bridge there which you had broken repaired, and stayed there for three days, waiting for you and the army which you have assembled, you could have approached from one side [of the river] or the other, as you wished. Because we could not get you to give battle, we decided to continue further into our realm, to comfort our faithful friends and punish rebels, whom you falsely claim as your subjects; and so we will remain in the realm without leaving to carry on the war as best we can, to our advantage and the loss of our enemies. Therefore if you wish, as your letters purport, to do battle with us and protect those whom you claim as your subjects, let it now be known that at whatever hour you approach you will find us ready to meet you in the field, with God's help, which thing *we desire above all else* for the common good of Christendom, since you will not deign to tender or accept any reasonable terms for peace. But we would not be well advised to [allow ourselves to] be cut off by you, nor to let you choose the place and day of battle.[68]

[64] I use here the readable translation of Richard Barber, in *Life and Campaigns*, with emphasis added. The relevant pages in Barber are 30, 31, 37. The original Latin can be found in J. Moisant, *Le Prince Noir en Aquitaine* (1894), 162–3, 163, 168–9. On the use of fire and smoke to provoke the enemy, see also le Bel, *Chronique*, II, 85–6.

[65] *Chronica Monasterii de Melsa*, III, 57 (Emphasis added). Cf. II, 73, and the *Anonimalle Chronicle*, 21.

[66] *Chronique*, II, 89.

[67] Sumption, *Trial by Battle*, 520.

[68] Emphasis added. *Calendar of Patent Rolls (1345–48)*, 516–17; dated August 15, (the day before Edward crossed the Seine) at Autes(?). It is quite possible, however, that 'Autes' is Auteuil, which Edward did not reach until the 17th.

The more often used version given in the *Acts of War of Edward III* (Moisant, *Le Prince*

Once again the parallel with the Weardale campaign of 1327 is striking. When Edward requested that the Scots descend from their position and give battle on a fair field, they declined and told him that they would tarry in his kingdom as long as they liked, unless he dared to do something about it. Nineteen years later, Edward responded to Philip's similar offer with a more elaborate but essentially equivalent response.[69]

Richard Wynkeley's campaign letter, and indeed all the sources, agree with Edward's challenge that Philip 'neither wished nor dared to cross the Seine, as he could have, in defense of his people and his realm, even though all the land was wasted and burnt for twenty miles around, and to within a mile of his position'.[70] Moreover, Philip did break or strengthen all the bridges along the Seine to prevent the English from crossing, showing his equal unwillingness to fight on the northern side of the river either. Even Jean de Venette, a loyal Frenchman and particularly well-disposed towards Philip, remarks that even when flames from the raiders' fires could be seen from Paris itself, 'no one interfered with what the English were doing, and King Philip of France passively awaited their withdrawal'.[71] According to the *Valenciennes Chronicle*, 'all the people of Paris wondered greatly that ... [Philip] did not hasten against (*courir sur*) the King of England, who was camped in the middle of France, with so few men that the King of France had five men for his one'.[72] These testimonies hardly support the contention that Philip was the hunter and Edward a fugitive. Quite on the contrary, they present a clear portrait of the Plantagenet's eagerness for an engagement, provided he could provoke Philip into assuming the tactical offensive; and of the Valois' desire to avoid doing so.

This portrait of words is supported by the louder voice of actions. Philip *did not* cross the Seine to engage Edward. The English *did* burn as they went to make it easy for the enemy to find them and to

---

Noir, 171–2; reprinted in Froissart, *Oeuvres*, IV, 497, and in English translation in Barber, *Life and Campaigns*, 38) is nearly identical to the enrolled form of the letter (which I have checked), but misses out one key phrase in the first sentence of the text given above: it has 'to make an end to the war' omitting the 'by battle' immediately following.

[69] Cf. le Bel, *Chronique*, II, 106, 212.

[70] Avesbury, *Gestis Mirabilibus*, 363. The author of the *Grandes Chroniques* considered it a great marvel that 'the nobles [of France] sank the boats and broke the bridges everywhere the king of England passed, when they should, quite the opposite, have used the boats and bridges to cross over against him in order to defend the country.' *Grandes Chroniques de France*, ed. J. Viard (1937), IX, 276.

[71] This version, from *The Chronicle of Jean de Venette* tr. J. Birdsall, ed. R. A. Newhall (New York, 1953), 41, is more complete than the Latin version in the *Société de l'histoire de France*'s 1843 edition, 199, which omits the adverb 'taciter'.

[72] In Froissart, *Oeuvres*, IV, 495. Cf. the *Grandes Chroniques*, IX, 276.

encourage him to attack.[73] The English *did* linger and await their adversaries at Poissy—if we believe the *Acts of War of Edward III*, which is probably our single best source for the campaign, Edward stayed there three days even though the bridge could be crossed with horse and cart by the end of the first day[74]—and then again at Crécy after crossing the Somme, just as the Scots had awaited the English on the Wear in 1327. Indeed, Edward reportedly even offered the Valois army free and peaceful passage over the Somme so that Philip could choose a fitting place for a battle.[75]

Those who hold to the theory that, in 1346, Philip was the pursuer and Edward the prey, find many of these actions difficult to explain. A. H. Burne, in his book *The Crecy War*, remarks that the French failure to attack at Poissy is 'hard to understand', and that the slowness of the English retreat (they continued to burn and plunder all the way up to Crécy) at times 'reminds one of a hunted fox stopping in the course of its flight to rob a hen roost'.[76] Barber comments that the English tactics at Poissy 'seem obscure', and that it is 'surprising' that, though in the two days following the English crossing of the Somme Edward could have easily outdistanced his French pursuers, he did not.[77] All of these puzzles come clear at once if we abandon the assumption that Edward was simply trying to escape, and Philip attempting to catch him.

The English strategy of 1346 was a battle-seeking one, and battle they got. Surprisingly, to the French at least, the battle resulted in a total victory for the English. The reasons for the English success are beyond the scope of a paper on strategy; suffice it to say that they benefitted from superior organisation, cohesion, and leadership; from a good defensive position and an extraordinarily effective tactical doctrine; from the presence of a large contingent of longbowmen, by far the most effective missile troops of their day; and from the indiscipline of the French. In any case, the English strategy was proven as valid as their tactics.

So much for the campaign of 1346. It is only one specimen of the genre I am analysing here: to what extent, then, do the other great *chevauchées* of Edward's reign share its characteristics? All of them were essentially the same in operational terms—they moved fast, with troops spread out usually in three parallel columns so as to devastate a broad swathe of territory along their march, and inflicted maximum damage as they passed to fields, other elements of the economic infrastructure

---

[73] Cf. le Bel, *Chronique*, I, 53, for the English using the smoke from fires set by the Scots in 1327 to find their enemy.

[74] In Moisant, *Le Prince Noir*, 170–171.

[75] According to le Baker, *Chronicon*, 82.

[76] Burne, *The Crecy War*, 152, 157.

[77] Barber, *Edward, Prince of Wales and Aquitaine*, 58, 62.

and—when these could be taken without long investments—castles and towns. Let us consider in somewhat more detail the Black Prince's *grand chevauchée* of 1355. In Edward III's 1346 response to Philip of Valois' challenge to do battle at an appointed place, Edward said that he was continuing his *chevauchée* 'to comfort our faithful friends and punish rebels, whom you wrongly claim as your subjects; and ... to carry on the war as best we can, to our advantage and to the loss of our adversaries'. It is clear that the Black Prince, in his great expedition of 1355, had these same four objectives in mind.

First, 'to comfort our faithful friends'. The initial target of attack was the territory of the count of Armagnac, the general who had led the French forces in assaults on English supporters in Guienne. 'He had more harmed and damaged the liegemen and land of our most honoured lord and father the King,' said Prince Edward in his letter to the Bishop of Winchester, 'than anyone else in those parts ... So we rode through the country of Armagnac, ruining and destroying the land, which much comforted the liegemen of our most honoured lord'.[78]

Second, 'to punish rebels'. Having acted to support his father's vassals on the borders of Guienne, the prince reinforced his message by contrasting treatment at Carcassone of those who held to King John. The inhabitants of the *bourg* of that city offered him 250,000 gold *écus*, a very substantial sum indeed, to spare it from the flames. 'Offered the gold,' says Geoffrey le Baker's chronicle, 'the Prince responded that he had come to seek justice, not gold; to take cities, not sell them. Since the citizens remained in fear of the French king (*coronati*), did not wish to obey their natural lord, and indeed would not listen to him because they feared the revenge of the aforesaid French king, the Prince therefore ordered that the town be burnt.'[79]

Third, 'to carry on the war to our advantage'. 'They seized' le Baker tells us, 'no small wealth from the land of the enemy, enriching their own country.'[80] Froissart agrees that the Black Prince and his men secured a 'very great profit' from the expedition, acquiring 'so many goods, fine supplies, and so much good wine, that they didn't know what to do with it all'.[81] According to Jean le Bel, they found an unbelievable amount of wealth, so that even the common troops paid no attention to silver coins, goblets, tankards or furs, being interested only in gold florins, brooches and jewels.[82]

Fourth, and most interesting of all: 'to the loss of our adversaries'.

[78] Avesbury, *Gestis Mirabilibus*, 434.
[79] le Baker, *Chronicon*, 133. There is a similar story concerning Périgueux (for the 1356 *chevauchée*) in Avesbury, *Gestis Mirabilibus*, 457.
[80] le Baker, *Chronicon*, 138-9.
[81] Froissart, *Oeuvres*, V, 353, 351. Cf. 347.
[82] *Chronique*, II, 221-2.

The key document for this aspect of the *chevauchée* is the letter written by Sir John Wingfield to the bishop of Winchester, who, significantly, was then Treasurer of England. It is worth quoting at length:

> I am certain that since the beginning of this war against the king of France, there has never been such destruction in any region as on this *chevauchée*. For the countryside and good towns which were destroyed in this *chevauchée* found more money each year for the king of France in support of his wars than did half his kingdom (excluding the annual devaluation of the money and the profits and customs which he takes from Poitou), as I could show you from good records found in various towns in the tax-collectors' houses. For Carcassone and Limoux, which is as large as Carcassonne, and two other towns besides Carcassone, find each year for the king of France the wages of a thousand men-at-arms and, in addition, 100,000 old crowns, in support of the war. And I know, by the records we found, that the towns which we destroyed around Toulouse and Carcassone, along with Narbonne and the Narbonnais, found each year an additional 400,000 old crowns in aid of his wars, as the citizens of the large towns and other men from the area, who should be familiar with the matter, have told us.[83]

Note that the prince and his advisers were so concerned with this aspect of the *chevauchée* that they went to the effort of confirming the tax records they collected with a second source—the testimony of influential citizens. And Wingfield's figures are not as incredible as they might seem. In 1329 the king of France had a document prepared to estimate how much a war in Gascony would cost him, and where he could find the necessary money. The clerks who prepared that document expected to get more money from Carcassone alone than from Champagne, Anjou, Maine, Touraine, Valois, Chartres, Senlis, Vermandois, Amiens, Bourges, Sens, and Tours combined. Toulouse was expected to provide even more than Carcassone,[84] and then there was Narbonne, which Wingfield described as 'only a little smaller than London'!

From all of that, it is clear that the importance of the economic attrition aspect of the *chevauchée* can hardly be exaggerated. And what about the third aspect I emphasise in my analysis of the *chevauchée*: the desire to bring the enemy to battle? That, too, is borne out by the testimony of the participants of the 1355 *chevauchée*. Wingfield writes:

[83] Avesbury, *Gestis Mirabilibus*, 442. The *Anonimalle Chronicle*'s claim (page 35) that the English destroyed eleven *bonnes villes* and 3,700 villages on this *chevauchée* is doubtless an exaggeration, but it is certainly evocative.

[84] M. Jusselin, 'Comment la France se préparait à la guerre de cent ans' *Bibliothèque de l'école des chartes*, LXXIII, (1912), doc. II (Touraine and Sens in doc. III). Froissart (*Oeuvres*, V, 344) points out that Toulouse was not much smaller than Paris.

'my lord had news that the French forces had come out of Toulouse towards Carcassonne, and he wanted to turn back on them suddenly; and so he did. And the third day, when we should have come upon them, they had news of us before dawn; and they retreated and disappeared ...'[85] Prince Edward himself wrote much the same to the bishop of Winchester: how the English repeatedly sought to come up with the French forces, 'intending to have a battle,' and then returned to their own lands only after it became clear that the French did not want to fight.[86] The *Anonimalle* chronicler, similarly, writes that when Prince Edward encountered a French army under the Count of Armagnac and the Constable of France, 'he eagerly prepared to encounter them and to give battle ... [But] they fled without giving or taking a blow of the lance or the sword'.[87] Geoffrey le Baker writes that the French were in effect defeated, since they 'fled from their adversary in terror', when the English had 'made a long and hard journey in search of them'.[88]

So at every point, the 1355 *chevauchée* fits my model exactly. If space allowed, I could provide similar evidence for the 1356 Poitiers campaign and for the 1359–60 Reims campaign, when for nine months the English traversed as much of France as they were able 'seeking battle to maintain the right of their lord, but not finding any takers anywhere'.[89]

It took those two latter *chevauchées*, along with the battle of Poitiers, to fully drive the message home. Then, with the 1360 treaty of Brétigny, the English strategy faithfully pursued since the Crécy campaign bore full fruit, and Edward gained territories comprising a full third of France, to be held in full sovereignty, along with a huge ransom for the captive King John—his original war aims and much more. His effective use of a sophisticated strategy involving political destabilisation, economic attrition, and open battle, shows that Edward III, far from being the general of 'scant strategical skill' described in the standard reference work of military history,[90] was probably the finest commander of his day.

[85] Avesbury, *Gestis Mirabilibus*, 441–2.

[86] Avesbury, *Gestis Mirabilibus*, 435–6.

[87] *Anonimalle Chronicle*, 35.

[88] le Baker, *Chronicon*, 137.

[89] *Scalacronica*, 196 ('ne troucrount nul part countenaunce a ceo faire.') Cf. 194. I intend to argue this case more fully in a book to be entitled *Werre Cruelle and Sharpe: English Strategy under Edward III, 1327–1360*.

[90] R. Ernest Dupuy and Trevor Dupuy, *The Encyclopedia of Military History* (New York, 1970), 357.

MONASTERIES AND THEIR PATRONS AT FOUNDATION AND DISSOLUTION*

By Benjamin Thompson

The Alexander Prize Essay, Proxime Accessit

IN June 1536 Thomas Starkey, a royal chaplain, humanist, and 'commonwealth man', wrote to Henry VIII concerning the Act passed in the spring of that year suppressing monasteries worth less than £200:[1]

> many ther be wyche are mouyd to iuge playnly thys acte of suppressyon of certayn abbays bothe to be agayne the ordur of charyte & iniuryous to them wych be dede bycause the foundarys therof & the soulys departyd seme therby to be defraudyd of the benefyte of prayer & almys dede ther appoyntyd to be done for theyr releyffe...

—to which he argued that the common weal of all took precedence over arrangements made for the private weal of the individual. Moreover, in answering those who would argue for 'rather a just reformatyon then thys vthur ruynose suppressyon', he went on,[2]

> for though hyt be so that prayer & almys dede be much to the comfort of them wych be departyd, & though god delyte much in our charytabul myndys thereby declaryd, yet to conuerte ouer much possessyon to that end & purpos, & to appoynt ouer many personys to such offyce & exercyse, can not be wythout grete detryment & hurt to the chrystian commynwele ... & though hyt be a gud thyng & much relygyouse to pray for them wych be departyd out of thys mysery, yet we may not gyue al our possessyonys to nurysch idul men in contynual prayer for them...

Starkey was certain that the possessions of monasteries had been given to the 'end and purpose' of providing spiritual benefits for the 'founders', to help the passage of their souls through Purgatory.

In the history of the Dissolution, however, the question of the interest

*I am grateful to Dr Christine Carpenter for her valuable suggestions and comments on this paper, which attempts to summarise different parts of my work in order to apply some conclusions in a new field. The deficiencies and errors are entirely my own.

[1] *Starkey's Life and Letters*, ed. S.J. Herrtage (Early English Text Society, extra ser., 32, 1878), lv; cited in Joyce Youings, *The Dissolution of the Monasteries* (1971), 168–9 (no. 14).

[2] *Starkey's Life and Letters*, lvi.

of these founders has not often been to the fore.[3] If the monasteries existed to serve the spiritual needs of founders, how far did they and their successors exert themselves to defend the houses when it was proposed to do away with them? A complete answer to this question would examine both the role of founders in the counsels of the kingdom which produced the Acts of Suppression, and the extent of local resistance as the religious houses were suppressed one by one by the visiting commissioners. My purpose here is to suggest the framework of an answer through an analysis not of Tudor high politics, but of the relationship between the monasteries of Norfolk and their 'founders'. If that word sometimes denoted all 'benefactors' who expected spiritual benefits in return for their gifts, here the initial focus will be upon the main class of benefactors, those who 'instytute & foundyd' the religious houses, the first founders. Further, the relationship established at foundation must be traced through the subsequent generations of the founders' heirs and successors, the tenurial lords of these perpetual institutions. It will be possible thereby to establish not only what was the intended function of monasteries in the eyes of their founders, but also how far such expectations changed and were fulfilled in the succeeding centuries. This is therefore primarily an essay in medieval history, within which one aspect of the cataclysm of the 1530s may be understood.

The most convenient way of introducing the *dramatis personae* of this story is to use the order provided by the monasteries' date of foundation.[4] This provides a hierarchy of religious houses which is reinforced by three other criteria, their wealth (measured in the ecclesiastical taxations of 1291 and 1535),[5] their affiliations to other religious houses and orders,[6] and, most significantly here, the status of their founders: for not only

---

[3] An exception is Youings, *Dissolution*.

[4] See Table on pages 124–5. The houses, their histories, and patrons are described in the following, heavily interdependent, works, most conveniently *The Victoria History of the Counties of England* (1900–) *[VCH]*, *Norfolk*, ii, and David Knowles & R. N. Hadcock, *Medieval Religious Houses: England and Wales* (2nd edn., 1971). Francis Blomefield, *An Essay towards a Topographical History of Norfolk* (1805–10, originally King's Lynn, 1739–75) [Blomefield]; Thomas Tanner, *Notitia Monastica* (3rd edn., Cambridge, 1787) which gives valuable source references; William Dugdale, *Monastico Anglicanum* (2nd edn. ed. J. Caley, H. Ellis, B. Bandinel, 6 vols. in 8, 1817–30). For patrons see also GEC, *The Complete Peerage* (ed. V. Gibbs et al., 12 vols. in 13, 1910–59) *[CP]*; I. J. Sanders, *English Baronies: a Study of their Origin and Descent, 1086–1327* (Oxford, 1960).

[5] *Taxatio Ecclesiastica Angliae et Walliae auctoritate papae Nicholai IV, circa A. D. 1291* (Record Commission, 1802); *Valor Ecclesiasticus* (6 vols., Record Commission, 1810–34), vol. iii; see also the notes in the works above.

[6] David Knowles, *The Monastic Order in England* (2nd edn., Cambridge, 1963) is the classic study.

was the wealth of a religious house commonly dictated by the wealth of its first founder, but also monasteries in post-conquest England were understood to be the tenants of their founders and one step below them in the landholding hierarchy. The history of foundation presents a chronological succession of different religious orders, but also a gradual decline in the status of founders and the wealth of their monasteries.

The assumption of all lordship by the conqueror in 1066 created a group of ecclesiastical tenants-in-chief which comprised the abbeys then in existence and the bishoprics. The only monastic representative of this group in Norfolk was the abbey of St Benet at Holme.[7] But it was joined at the top of the monastic hierarchy by the cathedral priory, carved from the bishopric when it finally settled at Norwich before 1100. These were the two richest houses in the county, and they were independent Benedictine convents. Following the conquest, the Norman aristocracy naturally used their newly-won lands for monastic endowment, in part by augmenting the resources of their native French abbeys. These properties were farmed out or run by bailiffs, sometimes monks in small cells, in order to transmit the bulk of their profits to houses across the Channel.[8] But it was also necessary to bring the church in England into the main stream of continental reformed practice, so that not only were the older abbeys taken over by French superiors, but also new convents were founded. In Norfolk, the latter form a group of seven houses founded between 1085 and 1113. Six of them were broadly Benedictine, but each was made dependent upon a mother-abbey which provided the first monks (and sometimes appointed the prior), and whose customs the new convent adopted. So Thetford was subjected to Cluny, Castleacre to Lewes (itself also subject to Cluny), and Bromholm to Castleacre; two houses, Binham and Wymondham, were colonised from St Alban's.[9] In terms of status, these houses were all in effect founded by tenants-in-chief, most of them the first holders of the honours on which the houses were founded, and they remained amongst the wealthier monasteries of the county right up to the Dissolution.[10] They were often located near the castles or residences

---

[7] *Domesday Book: Norfolk*, ed. Philippa Brown (2 vols., Chichester, 1984); landholders nos. X, XVII.

[8] D.J.A. Matthew, *The Norman Monasteries and their English Possessions* (Oxford, 1962); Marjorie M. Morgan, *The English Lands of the Abbey of Bec* (Oxford, 1946).

[9] Also Horsham St Faith to Conques. The seventh, Westacre, does not belong to this group ecclesiastically, since it was a secular college which became Augustinian later, Nicholas Vincent, 'The Foundation of Westacre Priory, 1102–26', *Norfolk Archaeology*, XLI (1993), 490–4.

[10] Sanders, *English Baronies*, 12, 43, 46–7, 70, 117, 128; *CP, ad loc.*; Blomefield, x. 433, xi. 17; *Monasticon*, iii. 635, v. 59: Horsham St Faith and Bromholm were possibly founded by sub-tenants of the honour of Eye when it was vacant, 1105–13.

of their founders at the centres of new baronies, as with the two greatest Domesday landowners in Norfolk, the Warennes at Castleacre, and Roger Bigod at the heart of his East Anglian power at Thetford.[11]

No further convents of black monks were added after the middle of Henry I's reign: canons of the new orders and nuns became the foci for lay patronage. Between 1115 and 1265, five nunneries, seventeen houses of Augustinian canons and three of Premonstratensian, and one Gilbertine double-house were established.[12] The later they were founded, the more likely were their founders to be of lesser status and they themselves to be poorly endowed: sixteen out of the twenty-six were founded by sub-tenants or below—some of whom were of highly localised substance—and a further three by lesser tenants-in-chief. Moreover those established by greater tenants-in-chief and their wives and heiresses were additional to (and always smaller than) the central houses of their honours, such as the Warennes' canons at Thetford and nuns at Marham, and the Bigods' canons at Weybridge. The ten houses founded after 1199, including the latter two, were all at the bottom of the hierarchy of endowment, and add weight to the impression that Norfolk was a county of poor canonries and nunneries, often staffed by only half a dozen religious. Moreover, the decline into smaller and poorer institutions extended into the arrival of the friars in the thirteenth century: since they accepted no endowments beyond a site in a town, the patron was of small importance and they were often established by townspeople in a collective manner. The history of monastic foundation was completed by the later-medieval secular colleges, which probably resembled some of the canonries in that they were to be staffed by half-a-dozen secular chantry-priests living a life in common; they were founded by gentry families or burgesses, and most were towards the bottom of the hierarchy of wealth.[13] They therefore form a coda to this history. The majority of the thirty-five endowed monasteries which are the main focus here were small, locally-based houses towards the bottom end of landowning society. Whereas two kings and ten earls or ecclesiastical tenants-in-chief founded one-third of them, seven lesser barons and fifteen sub-tenants or below founded the other two thirds, a configuration reinforced by the addition of the gentry founders of the fourteenth century.

*   *   *

[11] Also Wymondham near the Albinis' Buckenham Castle, and Horsham and Brom-holm, see n. above.

[12] See Table. There were no Cistercian monks in Norfolk. See J. C. Dickinson, *The Origins of the Austin Canons* (1950); H. M. Colvin, *The White Canons in England* (Oxford, 1951); Rose Graham, *St Gilbert of Sempringham and the Gilbertines* (1901). Full bibliographies are to be found in Knowles & Hadcock, *Medieval Religious Houses.*

[13] The friars and colleges are at *VCH Norfolk*, ii. 425–38, 453–62.

At the heart of the relationship between patrons and their monasteries was the exchange of temporal support for the spiritual benefits which would secure or ease the path of the lords in the after-life. Founders and benefactors described their gifts as alms, or given in free alms which, although it became a technical term, nevertheless described the nature of the grant.[14] First, these were simple gifts to poor religious: the grant itself constituted a meritorious act, since the monks were pursuing a path of holiness, whether through the continual liturgy of Cluniac houses, the eremitism of the new orders of monks, or the pastoral emphasis of the canons. Gifts of alms brought direct benefits in accordance with the biblical injunction to give alms, for 'as water extinguishes fire so alms remove sin'.[15]

Second, the grants of property supported the holy lives of the religious, and therefore brought the donors some share in the spiritual benefits accruing from the monks' activities. 'Confraternity' was the least which a monastic founder would expect from the house he founded.[16] Founders did not, however, define what the monks were to do for their souls, or how they were to procure their salvation, a matter which was in any case still being worked out in the twelfth century and was not in the ken of the laity: the religious were professionals in whatever spiritual way they had chosen to pursue and the founder had chosen to support. Free alms tenure was held by later lawyers to be an indefinite tenure, providing no specific services enforceable by the lord.[17] It was the religious recipients who had control over the spiritual services they offered, not any layman or secular jurisdiction: they performed their various works of piety and charity, and could not formally be compelled, except by an ecclesiastical superior, to perform any particular act for a benefactor. A grant in alms was, however, held to have created some form of tenure between the lord—founder or patron in succeeding

---

[14] F. Pollock & F. W. Maitland, *The History of English Law before the time of Edward I* (2nd edn., Cambridge 1898, reprinted 1968), i. 240–51; *Littleton's Tenures*, bk. II, ch. vi, §§ 133–8 (ed. Eugene Wambaugh, Washington, D. C., 1903, 66–70). Foundation charters are conveniently found in *Monasticon*; e.g. iii. 345 (Binham), referring to the grant as 'elemosinam'; vi. 974–5 (Shouldham), developed free alms formula. The arguments in this section are elaborated in more detail now in my 'Free alms tenure in the twelfth century', *Anglo-Norman Studies*, XVI (1994), 221–43; see also 'From "alms" to "spiritual services": the function and status of monastic property in medieval England', in *Monastic Studies*, II, ed. J. Loades (Bangor, 1991), 227–61.

[15] Ecclesiasticus, iii. 33; quoted by the bishop of Norwich to his monks c. 1100: *The Life, Letters, and Sermons of Bishop Herbert de Losinga*, ed. E. M. Goulbourn & Henry Symonds (Oxford & London, 1878), ii. 26–8.

[16] H. E. J. Cowdrey, 'Unions and confraternity with Cluny', *Journal of Ecclesiastical History*, XVI (1965), 152–62; Emma Mason, 'The Mauduits and their Chamberlainship of the Exchequer', *Bulletin of the Institute of Historical Research*, XLIX (1976), 21–2.

[17] Pollock & Maitland, i. 240; *Littleton's Tenures*, II. vi, § 136.

generations—and the monastery, the tenant.[18] Despite the fact that free alms tenure lacked content and was intended to exempt the religious from tenurial burdens, it did reflect the relationship between the founding lineage and the perpetual institution in that it provided a framework for the informal connection between them stretching into the future: the exchange of benefits occurred within tenure, but in a loose and flexible form quite different from secular tenure, which increasingly became a vehicle for contractual exchange. It provided the context for a cycle of gift-exchange extended through time, as succeeding generations of lords continued to support their monks, and the religious prayed for the souls of heirs and successors as well as for the first founders and their ancestors.[19] The founder and his successors could not claim to be owed any tenurial services in the form of specific acts; rather, they expected their endowments to be the medium of their salvation both through the intrinsic merit of the gifts, and through the confraternity with the religious which they brought.

These expectations of the return on ecclesiastical endowments changed in the course of the thirteenth century, so that later generations of founding families would neither have founded similar institutions, nor done so on the same terms. The succession of different forms and orders in monastic endowment by which new monasteries became progressively cheaper and smaller, culminated in the late-medieval secular colleges which were the tip of a large iceberg of chantries. The foundation charters of late-medieval institutions were not phrased in the earlier form 'dono pro anima mea', which implied that the act of giving was itself a primary source of spiritual benefit. The phrase was transformed by two words into 'dono ad celebrandum pro anima mea': the gift was in return for a specific act, a daily mass or other form of spiritual service, as in the typical case of Elizabeth de Burgh's chantry at Dereham Abbey in 1336.[20] It could be costed not only according to how much was needed to support a mass-priest, but also as a commodity in itself purchasable in various quantities from ecclesiastical institutions

---

[18] E.g. *Tractatus de legibus et consuetudinibus regni Anglie qui Glanvilla vocatur*, ed. G. D. G. Hall (1965), xii. 3, p. 137.

[19] For gift-exchange, see references in Miri Rubin, *Charity and Community in Medieval Cambridge* (Cambridge, 1987), 1–2.

[20] 'ad inveniendum quemdam capellanum divina in capella sancti Winwaloei pro anima Gilberti de Clare quondam comitis Gloucestrie et animabus ipsius Elizabethae ac antecessorum ac heredum suorum ac omnium fidelium defunctorum singulis diebus celebraturum imperpetuum'; G. H. Dashwood, 'Some early deeds relating to the priory of St Winwaloe in Wirham and lands there', *Norfolk Archaeology*, V (1859), 301: the chantry was in fact a re-use of an alien cell, ibid., 301–3; *Calendar of Patent Rolls, 1334–8*, (1891–), 252–3; Norfolk Record Office, Hare MSS 4114–17; BL Add. MS 6041, fo. 86 (nos. i–vi).

or clergy.[21] The contractual nature of late-medieval grants is explicit in the foundation charter for Rushworth College, founded by Edmund Gonville in 1342, which annexed the statutes for the fellows to the 'habendum et tenendum' clause, the part of the charter which dictated the terms on which conveyed property was to be held.[22] The same was true of the next college to be founded, Raveningham in 1343, where the land was granted 'faciendum prout in regula domus plenius continetur'.[23] Unlike the spiritual activities performed by twelfth-century religious, sanctions could be applied legally to enforce statutory services of prayers and masses where they were neglected, either by distraint on land or by resumption of it—the same sanctions as were applied to secular services.[24] Moreover the contractual element was accentuated after 1290 by the fact there could, by the statute *Quia emptores*, no longer be tenure between the parties after 1290:[25] the removal of the donor from the tenurial chain forced the parties to do a commercial deal as contracting equals, rather than to create a formal tenurial relationship open to the flexible operation of gift-exchange. Furthermore, the secular clergy who received most late-medieval endowments were no longer professionals in the spiritual life, monastic craftsmen whose particular path in the 'vita apostolica' was bought by founders as a package: they were hired labourers, different from lay donors in their ability to say mass, but otherwise directed by them in their way of life. The colleges and chantries were much more the creations of their founders, since the chaplains were subject to no external monastic discipline or supervision other than that of the bishop, who in partnership with the founder drew up the statutes and took responsibility for supervising the operation of the institution.[26]

The contract in which late-medieval donors bought spiritual services also specified the beneficiaries of the services more closely: this was partly inherent in the fact that the services themselves were now defined and were no longer left to the discretion of the religious. Chantries were institutions more obviously suited to the needs of individuals rather than families; of eighty mortmain licences to establish chantries in fourteenth-century Norfolk, ancestors of some sort were mentioned

---

[21] E.g. *Statutes of the Realm* (Rec. Comm. 1810–28), i. 373–4, ii. 188. Most wills prove the point.

[22] E. K. Bennet, 'Notes on the original statutes of the college of St John Evangelist of Rushworth, co. Norfolk, founded by Edmund Gonville A.D. 1342', *Norfolk Archaeology*, X (1888), 51–2.

[23] BL Stowe MS 939, fo. 5v (no. 13).

[24] *Statutes*, i. 82–3, 91–2; Norfolk Record Office, FLI 65.

[25] *Statutes*, i. 106.

[26] E.g. Gonville's statutes in n. 22, and Stapleton's in n. 28.

in one half, heirs in only one sixth.[27] Their spiritual benefits were conceived as being focused on the founder and perhaps others in the same generation, as could also be true of colleges.[28] But even the colleges, which might also be institutions for a lineage in the old mode, were subject to a greater awareness of the increasing individualisation of spiritual services in time. The late-fifteenth-century heiress to the Gonville estate granted the two main family manors to Rushworth College; but these were to support two 'Dame Annys prestes' and five 'Dame Annys childeryn', who were to pray primarily for her through separate statutory provisions and were clearly distinguished from the main foundation. She separated her own suffrages from the benefits enjoyed by Edmund Gonville and the lineage.[29] Where chantries were founded in monasteries, patrons were conscious that it would be to diminish the spiritual benefits for the founders of both, were the institutions not to remain distinct from one another: so Edmund Mortimer, in confirming Elizabeth de Burgh's chantry within Dereham abbey (also in his patronage) insisted that the chaplain be secular not regular, and that the number of canons or the accustomed suffrages of the abbey be not attenuated by the chantry.[30]

The peculiarity of this contractual relationship was that its currency was not subject to the ordinary temporal limits which constrain secular exchange. Even if the relationship between the lineages of lords and tenants was in principle perpetual, each party to a secular tenure could only enjoy the benefits of the tenurial contract during his lifetime. Spiritual benefits, on the other hand, broke the barriers of time because the perpetual suffrages done here on earth were capable of being enjoyed by the dead, to speed their way towards the goal of eternity through Purgatory. On the one hand, the members of a patronal lineage—both alive and dead—could all benefit from a suffrage performed at a single moment in time. On the other, any individual in the lineage was capable of enjoying all the benefits which had ever been done and ever would be done in the house. Thomas Aquinas

[27] *CPR, passim*; Benjamin Thompson, 'The church and the aristocracy: lay and ecclesiastical landowning society in fourteenth-century Norfolk' (unpublished Ph.D. dissertation, Cambridge, 1990), 112, n. 171.

[28] See the long list of beneficiaries at Ingham priory/college, Norwich Episcopal Registers, v. fo. 3.

[29] Bennet, 'The college of St John Evangelist of Rushworth, co. Norfolk', *Norfolk Archaeology*, X (1888), 368–73. See also the argument at Raveningham in which the emphasis of the services between generations was an element: BL Stow MSS 939, fos. 23–5; 934, fos. 171–2; *Calendar of Papal Registers: Papal Letters* (1893–), v. 260–1; Thompson, '*Habendum et Tenendum*: lay and ecclesiastical attitudes to the property of the church', in *Religious Belief and Ecclesiastical Careers in Late Medieval England*, ed. Christopher Harper-Bill (Woodbridge, 1991), 236.

[30] Dashwood, 'Wereham', 306.

expounded the spiritual calculus according to which benefits were distributed, which emphasised the primary position of the named beneficiaries, followed by the general categories specified, and extending, as most late-medieval grants did, to 'all the faithful departed'.[31]

These ideas had different effects on the two different modes of ecclesiastical foundation characteristic of the high and later middle ages. In the latter case, it meant that resources on this earth could be devoted to the benefit of persons no longer here, with the concomitant danger that no-one alive might have an interest in preserving those institutions. Commercialisation had been applied in a context quite unsuited to it because of the absence of the constraints of time which govern ordinary commerce. The combination of perpetual property and a religion based on the after-life gave benefactors the opportunity to bind the future by tying up resources to provide for their souls long after they had died.[32] On the other hand, the older relationships between patrons and monasteries had the potential for great flexibility. Since spiritual benefits were under the control of the religious, patrons in each generation had to earn their benefits by themselves becoming benefactors to the monks; the most general meaning of the word 'founder' was indeed 'benefactor'.[33] The weak tenurial relationship had to be kept alive by the continuing process of gift-exchange: the monks were not automatically obliged to do anything specific for the heirs of the patrons, unless they had ingratiated themselves with the monks by giving them protection and additional benefits. Indeed, if the religious were neglected they could, and had to, take their benefits elsewhere in the 'bastard feudal' world of the late-medieval locality, and offer prayers and confraternity in return for the protection and support which were essential to them. As a matter of fact, monks usually remembered their first founder, who might be mentioned daily at high mass, as would have satisfied a late-medieval benefactor.[34] But if he was the only one to be remembered, the monastery was in the same position as the later chantries: it was devoted to suffrages for one long dead. Monasteries used the spare capacity available through the non-specification of services by their first founders to offer benefits to the living. Therefore each succeeding patron, who had the incentive to nurture an ancient

---

[31] See n. 20. Jacques le Goff, *The Birth of Purgatory* (trans. Arthur Goldhammer, 1984), 276.

[32] Starkey's theme, above, 1.

[33] E.g. 'Register of Crabhouse Nunnery', ed. M. Bateson, *Norfolk Archaeology*, XI (1892), no. 89.

[34] The evidence as to whether this was common practice is thin; see *Monasticon*, vi. 1572–3; and *Valor Ecclesiasticus*, iii, where the sections including alms have some first founders in a context which suggests they were performing the norm. Thompson, 'Church and the Aristocracy', 95–6.

institution on his doorstep because it reflected his family's antiquity and local lordship as well being responsible for the souls of his forebears, had the opportunity to earn these benefits by continuing such support.

The late-medieval expectations of gifts to the church have been outlined here because it was through these that the later patrons of earlier monasteries understood, albeit sometimes anachronistically, their relationships with their houses. Indeed in the Statute of Carlisle of 1307 they articulated the general assumption that monasteries were founded and endowed in order to perform alms and works of piety for the souls of the founders and their heirs for ever, and they applied this assumption to the whole church in the same parliament in a petition which became the preamble to the statute of Provisors:[35]

the Holy church in England was founded by kings and their progenitors, and by the earls, barons and other nobles of the said realm and their ancestors, to teach them and the people the law of God and to perform prayers and alms in the places where the churches were founded, for the souls of the founders, their heirs, and all Christians; and certain possessions were granted by the founders to sustain such charges...

Moreover this principle was coupled with a threat to the pope that misuse of such endowments might lead to their being resumed by the founders whose ancestors had originally granted them: this was to apply on a national scale the statute of 1285 which allowed resumption of lands from the church for non-performance of services.[36] The role of such attitudes and the practical effect of such threats at local level is less easily ascertainable; it can only emerge from an examination of the relationship between patrons and monasteries in the locality.

Where the patron was a male heir of the founder, and especially if he kept up a residence at the same place, he would almost certainly continue the gift-exchange relationship and give support in the form of grants or other benefits to his house: the feudal lord continued as the bastard feudal patron. So, the connections between the Warennes and Castleacre (and Lewes too), and the Bigods and Thetford, continued into the fourteenth century. Indeed, patronal action was the more urgent for these houses because their foreign affiliations rendered them

---

[35] *Statutes*, i. 150, 316; *Councils and Synods with Other Documents relating to the English Church, II, 1205–1313*, ed. F. M. Powicke & C. R. Cheney (Oxford, 1964), ii. 1233.

[36] Ibid., 1239–40; see above n. 24.

vulnerable to royal seizure during periods of war with France.[37] The last two Warennes secured the removal of Castleacre from royal custody in 1296, 1325, and 1337, and of Lewes in 1340.[38] Equally Roger Bigod tried to remove Thetford from the jurisdiction of Cluny in 1300.[39] Under less pressure, other patrons continued to support the monasteries which adorned their residences, as the lesser-noble Scales did at Blackborough, the Plays at Bromehill, and the gentry Gyneys for the small canonry of Mountjoy on their home manor.[40] Where a lordship of which a house was a part was inherited through an heiress, or it escheated and was re-granted by the king to a new lord, the same often applied, especially in the case of the larger houses at the centre of the old Anglo-Norman honours. These were inherited by or granted to members of the nobility, or people who thereby joined the nobility, and the monasteries had plenty to offer new lords in terms of both worldly presence and spiritual benefits. The Bardolfs took over Wormegay Priory when they inherited the eponymous honour in 1243, and they treated it thereafter as their own.[41] The Fitzalan successors of Warenne, although not resident, continued supporting Lewes and Castleacre, confirmation of whose denization was secured from Edward III in 1373.[42] The countesses Marshall and the patron of Thetford by courtesy, William Ufford, helped get Thetford out of royal hands in 1376 and procure free election of the prior from Cluny.[43]

These alien convents are instructive for our purposes, because the process of saving them from royal exploitation in the Hundred Years' War transformed them not only in form, by the introduction of English monks and the cutting of ties to foreign abbeys, but also in the emphasis of their spiritual function and its beneficiaries. The clearest example is that of Stoke-by-Clare priory in Suffolk (subject to Bec) which suffered from two successive minorities in the Mortimer

---

[37] See Matthew, *Norman Monasteries*, chs. iii–iv; and for what follows now my 'The laity, the alien priories and the redistribution of ecclasiastical property', in *England in the Fifteenth Century*, Harlaxton Medieval Studies V, ed. Nicholas Rogers (Stamford, 1994) 19–41.

[38] *Calendar of Close Rolls* (1892–), *1288–96*, 470, *1323–7*, 251–2, *1337–9*, 151; *Monasticon*, v. 54; *CPR 1338–40*, 505.

[39] *Registrum Roberti Winchelsey*, ed. Rose Graham (Canterbury & York Society, 1952–6, ii. 703–4, 792; *Cal. Papal Lett.*, i. 594–5; *CPR 1307–13*, 140.

[40] E.g. BL Egerton MS 3137, fos. 62v, 125v–6v, 198–201; *CPR 1348–50*, 20, 349, *1358–61*, 195, *1374–7*, 13, *1391–6*, 62; Blomefield, ii. 154, 244, viii. 474–5; *Cal. Papal Lett.*, iv. 519; *Catalogue of Ancient Deeds*, (1890–1915), ii. A 2781–4, 2788, 2879, 3056–7. See Thompson, 'Church and the aristocracy', ch. 5.

[41] Sanders, *English Baronies*, 101; *CPR 1334–8*, 157; PRO C 143/139/9.

[42] *CPR 1370–4*, 286; *CP*, i. 244; Lambeth Palace, Register of Simon Sudbury, fos. 92v–3v, 102.

[43] *Calendar of Fine Rolls* (1911–), v. 227, ix. 129–30; *CPR 1374–7*, 301; *Calendar of Inquisitions Post Mortem* (1904–), xv. 249; *Monasticon*, v. 153.

family, inheritor of the honour of Clare. Denization was secured in 1395, but the minority between 1398 and 1413 halted the process of restoring the dilapidated monastery and introducing English monks.[44] On reaching his majority in 1413, Edmund Mortimer petitioned to re-found the priory as a secular college in a text which encapsulates the patronal view of monastic foundation: Mortimer outlined the role of various ancestors in founding the first college at Clare, its subsequent transformation into a monastery subject to Bec, its removal from Clare to Stoke, and its recent denization, of which story his own translation back to a secular college was therefore a natural development.[45] It was for laymen, and particularly heirs, to take in hand the reform of ecclesiastical institutions where this was necessary. Moreover, the actual statutes of the college failed to fulfil his original inclusion of those ancestors in the spiritual benefits of the college: rather, these were to be narrowly focused upon Edmund himself, the first dean, and the bishop of Lincoln, and they were in the modern specific form of daily requiem masses as well as anniversaries.[46] This process both transformed an older house into a modern one, and concomitantly updated the previously flexible spiritual services into fixed forms focused on particular individuals. Such a transformation could only happen once: the paradoxical freedom to bind the future was a card which, like an entail, could only be played by one member of a lineage.

The fate of the alien cells is equally instructive.[47] Since their function was to send English revenue abroad in order to support monastic life in French abbeys, it is not surprising that fourteenth-century political society did not see them as performing a useful role. Even if they had been praying for the original donors of the land (as they claimed to be), the loss of the local connection between patronal family and monastery after 1204 was crucial to the attitude of English patrons: they were no longer present to continue the cycle of reciprocal exchange and so to continue to benefit from the abbeys' suffrages—now directed towards contemporary French lords who could actually provide support. No-one was found to defend such properties, and the crown and Commons found they could seize the revenues with little opposition.[48] The institutions which anyone cared about, on the other hand, most of which were convents, were saved by local patronal action, and thereby transformed—as

[44] CP, viii. 448–51; CPR 1391–6, 640; Monasticon, vi. 1415–16.
[45] CPR 1413–16, 291–2; Cal. Papal Lett., vi. 456; Monasticon vi. 1416–17.
[46] Monasticon, vi. 1417–23, esp. 1421.
[47] See Matthew, Norman Monasteries, ch. iv; Thompson, 'Laity and the alien priories'.
[48] E.g. Rotuli Parliamentorum (1783), iv. 22.

in the case of Elizabeth de Burgh and the cell at Wereham—into something useful to contemporaries.[49]

The alien houses were not the only ones to suffer resumption and transformation before 1535.[50] Less deliberate was the failure of some smaller houses from the mid-fifteenth century through economic weakness, presumably exacerbated by lack of local support. With one exception these were all among the later foundations of Augustinian canons which littered the Norfolk landscape.[51] Thus, Molycourt and Peterstone priories were united to Ely and Walsingham respectively in 1449; it is significant that we do not know who were patrons, and probable that they did not know either.[52] Two houses in crown patronage were transformed: Massingham was united to Westacre in 1475, and when Creake escheated in 1506 through the death of all the canons by plague, Henry VII granted it to his mother, who used it for her Cambridge foundation of God's House.[53] A further two were in lay patronage: perhaps the failure of the Bardolf line left Wormegay without active support, for in 1468 the priory was united to Pentney with the consent of the then (non-resident) patron, John Nevill, earl of Northumberland: he stipulated that the canons of Pentney were to pray for ever for himself and his ancestors and heirs, the patrons of the house.[54] On the eve of the Dissolution something similar happened at Flitcham, when it became a cell to Walsingham: again the patron (the Lutrell lord of Dunster Castle in Somerset) consented and reserved the masses and prayers of two canons of Walsingham for himself.[55] In both cases the transformation was accompanied by a re-focusing of spiritual benefits onto the current patrons. The patronal role is also seen in two of Wolsey's dissolutions for his colleges, Bromehill and Mountjoy in 1528: in the former case the patron, the earl of Oxford, consented,[56]

---

[49] See n. 20; the third Norfolk alien house was Horsham, saved in a process involving the patrons, *Cal. Fine Rolls*, ix, 261; *CPR 1388–92*, 366.

[50] See the dissolution of the Maison Dieu hospital at Thetford by Warenne in 1335 and confirmed by Lancaster in 1347: but in doing so the latter added himself to the new spiritual services and dropped Warenne's name; *CPR 1334–8*, 158, *1348–50*, 19; Thomas Martin, *The History of the Town of Thetford* (1779), 93–4. Also the re-foundation of West Somerton hospital by Richard II and Henry IV, *CPR 1399–1401*, 114. Also the Calthorpe take-over of a chantry at Anmer, *CPR 1370–4*, 156; Historical Manuscripts Commission, *Various Collections*, iv. 316.

[51] The exception, Molycourt Benedictine priory, is the sort which proves a rule, for it was so obscure that we know almost nothing about it.

[52] *VCH Norfolk*, ii. 349, 391, and the works in n. 4: *Monasticon*, iv. 588; Tanner, *Notitia Monastica*, Norfolk, *ad loc.*; Blomefield, vii. 24, 476–7.

[53] *VCH Norfolk*, ii. 386, 371–2; Blomefield, vii. 77; *A Cartulary of Creake Abbey*, ed. A. L. Bedingfeld (Norfolk Record Society, 1966), xvi, xxii–xxiii.

[54] Blomefield, vii. 500.

[55] H. Maxwell-Lyte, *A History of Duster* (1909), i. 138; Blomefield, viii. 418–19.

[56] Blomefield, ii. 165–6; *VCH Norfolk*, ii. 375.

but in the latter, William Hales, successor of the Gyneys and therefore the resident lord of the manor, pre-empted Wolsey by seizing the priory into his own hands as a patronal resumption or escheat:[57] since the monastery was no longer doing services for him or anybody, he ought to have the land back instead.

These examples are a useful preamble to the Dissolution proper. Where there was no patron to defend a priory—or even none at all as far as anyone knew—it was easy for a house to be resumed for other purposes. The crown as patron was unlikely to care for the spiritual services of all but the greatest houses actually founded by royal forebears, so that its houses also fell easily. If the patron was not local, he might be willing to accept a dissolution (and his neglect might be responsible for the weakness which made it necessary), although he might also be tenacious of his rights and extract some compensation. Alternatively, the patron—the king or another—might take the land as an escheat and re-use it for his own purposes rather than trying to support or transform the institution: like all lordship, escheat depended upon feudal rights which might no longer reflect real relationships but were exploitable, as the Tudors were so expert at doing, for what they could yield in terms of current material benefit.

All these cases, as well as the fading out of many chantries and the drifting of the smaller houses into lacklustre obscurity in the later middle ages, show the importance of locality, both of space and of time. At the time of foundation, monasteries were intended to pray for those who lived both in the present and in physical proximity to them. Moreover, since the temporal well-being of endowed churches depended, like that of any landowner, upon local support, it would be essential to continue in each generation the exchange with those living nearby of temporal support for spiritual services. The passage of time had two effects, however: first, the monasteries' obligation, general or specified, to pray for past generations increased, and thereby reduced their capacity to offer prayers for the living. Second, unlike monasteries, lineages did not continue perpetually and in the same place, but died out and moved away. They might therefore not be present to continue to give support, might stop minding about the services, and might even forget about the houses in their patronage. The disjunction between monasteries' obligations and their needs was therefore bound to increase with the passage of time. On the one hand the monasteries were obliged to remember a growing number of past generations, who could not help them in the present; on the other hand they had to attract support from those immediately around them in both time and space. To hold fast to their original function was to risk decay and decline

---

[57] Blomefield, viii. 231; Tanner, *ad loc.*

through lack of support; but to abandon such obligations was equally to lay themselves open to transformation by the laity, since it was an admission that their original function might be forgotten and they might be put to better uses—and these might come to be defined as not only different beneficiaries, but also different activities. As a matter of fact, monasteries tended towards the former danger of inertia, and continued to define themselves by their original function of praying for dead generations; certainly that is what Starkey thought they were there to do, and it is that which provides the context for the cataclysm which befell the monasteries in the 1530s.

In that it was initiated from above, by the crown and probably with the support of the Commons looking for more land on the market, the Dissolution was not dissimilar to the removal of the alien priories.[58] But in the 1530s the scope for patronal action either to preserve or to exploit ecclesiastical property was much more limited, since the suppression was carried out and tightly controlled by Thomas Cromwell and his small group of ministers. Our final task here is to discern, in the light of the medieval background, what role the patronal relationship played in these events, and how much this contributes to our understanding of the whole.

That founders were a live issue in the 1530s is already clear, as well from Wolsey's suppressions as from Starkey.[59] Henry VIII himself wrote to Chapuys that he was determined 'to reunite to the crown the goods which churchmen held of it, which his predecessors could not alienate to his prejudice', a reference both to the coronation oath's promise not to alienate too much of the crown's substance, and to the assumption that much ecclesiastical land was in fact held of the king.[60] It would fit with the Tudor exploitation of feudal rights if Henry was envisaging a resumption of such land, and there is evidence that even Cromwell thought of proceeding by way of escheat and persuading the monks to 'render their possessions to your majesty, by whose progenitors they were first created'.[61] High up in the articles for the visitations of 1535 was the question of who was the first founder, and who was then patron; and the *comperta* for the dioceses of York and Coventry and

[58] Youings, *Dissolution of the Monasteries*, is a useful supplement to David Knowles, *The Religious Orders in England* iii (Cambridge, 1959), part three.

[59] For Wolsey, see also *Letters and Papers, Foreign and Domestic, of the reign of Henry VIII*, ed. J. S. Brewer, J. Gairdner, & R. H. Brodie (1862–1910), [*LP*], iv/2. 3538.

[60] Youings, 32. See the statutes in nn. 24, 35 above, which assume that much of the land was given by the king, as does the Act in Restraint of Appeals, 24 Henry VIII, c. 12, *Statutes*, iii. 427. See below for crown patronage.

[61] Youings, 40–1; Knowles, iii. 291.

Lichfield reported this information.[62] The 1535 visitors thought that they were entitled to suppress houses in royal patronage, and did so.[63] Moreover, one draft set of visitation injunctions even included a provision to enforce prayers for the founders' souls. But it is significant that this was soon amended to an order to each monk-priest to pray in his daily mass 'for the most happy and prosperous state of our sovereign lord the King and his most noble and lawful wife, queen Anne'.[64] The problem of proceeding by way of escheat was that other founders might assert their own rights, and much would be lost to the crown.[65] When, therefore, it was decided to proceed by statute, the rights of founders had to be comprehensively excluded. The Act of 1536, in its desire to suppress the lesser houses 'for better uses', not only gave title to their property to the Crown forever, but also excluded the rights of founders so comprehensively as to leave them in a worse position than others with regard to material rights in the monasteries.[66] Even when an addition provided a remedy to this imbalance, it clearly excluded the possibility of claims to escheats of the property of dissolved houses.[67] As a result, the instructions to the Commissioners for suppression made no mention of the identity of the founders of the houses, nor do their returns.[68] Yet the fact that the Suppression Act of 1539 had to mention the exclusion of the interests of founders no less than four times suggests that the issue was not yet dead, even if there was now no question of patrons converting their spiritual services into material rights.[69]

The reaction of patrons to this position at local level to some extent follows the lines which the medieval background suggests. Thomas Howard, duke of Norfolk, did precisely what we should expect of a nobleman rooted in a tradition of family lordship; he tried to persuade the king at least to convert Thetford priory into a secular college.[70] He urged the king to remember that his father and other relatives and

---

[62] *LP*, viii. 76; x. 364 (pp. 137–43); Youings, 38; see also much of the *Valor* for Suffolk, iii. 412–47.

[63] Knowles, iii. 289–90.

[64] *LP*, viii. 76 [3]; also Youings, 152.

[65] Some of the applications for monastic property in early 1536 were from founders: Knowles, iii. 292–3 and references to *LP*, e.g. x. 531; Youings, 41–2.

[66] 27 Henry VIII, c. 28 (*Statutes*, iii. 575 ff): section iii.

[67] Ibid., sec. xvi.

[68] Youings, 160–3; A. Jessopp, 'The Norfolk monasteries at the time of the suppression by Henry VIII', *Norfolk Antiquarian Miscellany* ii. (ed. W. Rye, Norwich, 1883), prints the returns at 450–63.

[69] 31 Henry VIII, c. 13 (*Statutes*, iii. 733 ff.).

[70] *LP*, xiv/2. 430, 815–16; *VCH Norfolk*, ii. 368; Blomefield, ii. 106–7. For similar requests see J.J. Scarisbrick, *The Reformation and the English People* (Oxford, 1984), 70–2; Helen Miller, *Henry VIII and the English Nobility* (Oxford, 1986), 227–8; *LP*, x. 552.

ancestors were buried in the priory, as was the king's natural son Richmond, for whom, as for himself, Norfolk was constructing a tomb at great expense. His draft set of articles for the college emphasised its continuity from its predecessor, the Cluniac monastery, and the duke's position as founder. This was to be a traditional re-foundation, continuing the tradition of the earls and dukes of Norfolk dominating East Anglia from its centre, now to be reflected not only in the old mausoleum of Thetford updated for the Howards, but also in Norfolk's new and great palace of Kenninghall nearby.[71] When, however, Norfolk's project was finally refused by the king, he did at least secure the property of the priory instead.[72] A few founders had been able to take their monasteries by escheat before the Act prevented them;[73] but even afterwards, when they had to apply to purchase monastic lands through the court of Augmentations, they still hoped that their position would give them an advantage in the scramble for the pickings, as in lord Morley's request for Beeston, 'whereof I was sometime founder'.[74] Among various patronal applications for lands,[75] one curious failure shows what patrons expected. In 1534 the canons of Ingham had allegedly offered their patrons first refusal on a sale of the priory by themselves, but had then sold the property elsewhere and disappeared with the proceeds. Despite the fact that the patron made his complaint in 1537, he clearly expected some sympathy for his position from Cromwell.[76]

The patrons' awareness of their position in reacting to the Dissolution makes it even more difficult to explain why they allowed it to happen at all. But a plausible answer emerges from a survey of who the patrons of the religious houses were in 1535.[77] Since advowsons of religious houses were integral to landed inheritances, they descended in the same way as them, and they were held by landowners distinguished by

[71] J. Weever, *Ancient Funerall Monuments* (1631 edn.), 828–30; D. MacCulloch, *Suffolk and the Tudors* (Oxford, 1986), 60, 69; Blomefield, i. 215.

[72] Martin, *Thetford*, 145–6, 159–60 & 54–8*; Blomefield, ii. 107, 116. The claimants in n. 70 equally bought the lands.

[73] See n. 57; Norfolk himself had Bungay (Suffolk) in 1535 when the nuns fled, and Woodbridge by surrender, MacCulloch, *Suffolk*, 66; *LP*, x. 599.

[74] *VCH Norfolk*, ii. 373.

[75] Anne, countess of Oxford/Blackborough: *VCH Norfolk*, ii. 351, *Valor*, iii. 395; Rutland/Pentney: *VCH Norfolk*, ii. 390, *CP*, xi. 97–108; Knyvet/Buckenham: *VCH Norfolk*, ii. 378; Calthorpe/Burnham friars; *VCH Norfolk*, ii. 425–6; earl of Sussex/Attleborough: Blomefield, i. 516, 540–1; for Suffolk picking from his own houses, MacCulloch, *Suffolk*, 66–7 f. Less direct connections may be found between patrons and grantees; e.g. the grantee of Crabhouse, father-in-law of the half brother of the patron, Blomefield, ix. 169, 174–5, *CP*, ix. 92, 93 n. 'i', 97, xii/i. 118, 122 n. 'a'.

[76] *LP*, ix. 785, 849; *VCH Norfolk*, ii. 411–12.

[77] See the Table below. Information on patronal descents is mostly drawn from Blomefield, Sanders, *English Baronies*, and *CP*.

contemporary notions of status into titled and lesser nobility and gentry, as well as various ranks within these.[78] A comparison between the 1535 patrons of the thirty-four religious houses whose founders are identifiable with the status of their first founders suggests an accumulation of property at the top of the scale by an increasingly restricted group of nobles through the later middle ages.[79] The effect of entails and escheat, and even of transmission through heiresses, tended to make the rich richer: families which survived tended to rise in status and accumulate, and those which did not tended to pass their land on to those which did. There was therefore a striking upward mobility of advowsons: whereas the crown and greater tenants-in-chief founded only one-third of the houses, by the 1530s two-thirds of them were in the patronage of the crown or higher nobility; the gentry and lesser nobility, therefore, whose earlier equivalents founded two-thirds of the houses, in 1535 held only one-third of the advowsons (seven and four respectively).[80] Moreover, a decisive shift had taken place during the fifteenth century, for even in 1400 the crown and the titled held only just over half the advowsons. The crown in the 1530s was lord of ten houses, and the titled nobility thirteen, including seven in the hands of the Howards and the de Veres. Not only could most of these, like the crown, not be resident (the earls of Oxford, for example), neither were many of the lesser patronal families, for instance the Luttrells of Dunster in Somerset, patrons of Flitcham.[81] Perhaps even more significant is the fact that no monastery was in the hands of the lineage which founded it. Of the thirty houses founded by lay landowners, only twelve were in the hands of the same lineage by 1300, and the two of these which were left in 1400 did not survive half the remaining distance to the Dissolution.[82]

If none of the houses had been founded by the family which held the patronage in 1535, there was no direct duty incumbent on patrons to support the prayers for the first founders. The locality of time between lords and spiritual beneficiaries had been lost. It might be regained by the process of updating or continuing the cycle of gift-exchange, but this link depended on the preservation of proximity in space. Non-resident patrons were unlikely to be willing or able to

---

[78] See the listing of monatic advowsons amongst the perquisites of land in the inquisitions *post mortem*, eg n.43.

[79] K. B. McFarlane suspected this, *The Nobility of Later Medieval England*, (Oxford, 1973), 59, 136–41, 151–3, 155–6, 172–6.

[80] See the Table. The trend is all the more striking because statistical bias would go the other way, because of the 'fall of the gentry from the nobility' in the fourteenth century, McFarlane, 122–5, 142, 268–9.

[81] See above, n. 55.

[82] The most long-lived in Norfolk, apart from the Plantagenets, were the Scales (c. 1150–1460); *CP*, xi. 496–7–507.

become the main supporters of their houses. If some patrons were absent gentry families based elsewhere, many more were nobles whose interests, albeit wide, were not primarily based in East Anglia, such as the earls of Oxford, Arundel, Rutland and soon even Suffolk. Norfolk's attempts to save Thetford showed what the local link might mean for ecclesiastical institutions; but it is an isolated example amongst the general neglect of his fellow non-resident nobles. Even when it came to gaining possession of the lands, these lords focused their major efforts on their central houses, as the de Veres did in securing their Essex priories of Earl's Colne (their mausoleum) and Hedingham (at the residence).[83] The same applies *a fortiori* to the crown: it could not possibly mind about most of the spiritual services done by the quarter or third of monasteries in its patronage. Moreover, these were often the most valuable houses, including as they did the old pre-conquest abbeys: of the eight Norfolk houses exempt from the Act of 1536, four were in royal patronage, and the king probably was lord of half the monastic wealth of England. Patrons had probably lost interest, therefore, in most of the monasteries by the 1530s; and once the smaller (and less spiritually justifiable) houses had been swept away in 1536, it was even easier to remove the larger because their patrons were usually the crown or the higher nobility. The Norfolk rising of 1537 was not supported by the landowning orders at all.[84]

It is therefore not hard to see why there was no outcry from the patrons in the lords or commons when the first dissolutions were proposed at the end of the Reformation Parliament. Most monasteries had no resident local patron prepared to support suffrages for forebears, so that the link of locality between lineage and religious was lost. It was also lost in time, because none of the founding lineages survived to support their houses into the sixteenth century. In point of fact, the lesser monasteries were caught in a vicious circle in which their own poverty made them less able to attract contemporary lay patronage through the quality of their spiritual services, which lack of support further weakened them. It is not surprising that Cromwell first picked on the myriad small and poor institutions which littered the Norfolk landscape; even if they were not as corrupt as he claimed, they were often not seen to be performing a useful contemporary function for the living. All perpetual institutions run the risk of becoming outmoded if

[83] *VCH Essex*, ii. 104, 122–3.
[84] T. H. Swales, 'Opposition to the suppression of the Norfolk monasteries', *Norfolk Archaeology*, XXXIII (1962–5), 254–65; G. R. Elton, *Policy and Police* (Cambridge, 1972), 144–51.

they do not continually update their function to suit contemporary needs, or indeed to mould those needs. The currency in which the monasteries dealt, suffrages which could be enjoyed by the dead, left them particularly vulnerable to becoming out of date in the eyes of contemporaries. They were left behind by the simple passage of generations, as a result of which they seemed not to be devoted to the welfare of the living. Moreover monasteries were also being left behind by demands for different types of suffrage in the later middle ages (large numbers of masses and charitable provision), quite apart from the new demands of the Reformation: it is not even necessary to invoke Protestantism to explain the Dissolution. This is to re-state Starkey's misapplication argument, which featured not only in the preamble of the Act of 1536, with its emphasis on corruption, but also in the Act for bishoprics of 1539, with its talk of better, and different, uses to which the resources would be put.[85] The Dissolution was to be one great updating to re-employ resources according to contemporary perceptions of need and utility, just as previous updatings had emphasised the forms and functions demanded by the generations which enacted them.

The fact that the resources were not in fact adequately re-deployed leaves a sting in the tail of this story. Laymen had always been able to exercise physical power over the clergy, a fact which the medieval church from the eleventh century onwards tried to obscure, with its mirage of clerical independence. But lay control was just as liable to bring with it abuse of that power, as it was wise reform—'secularisation' in medieval terminology. Perhaps this is nowhere more obviously seen than in the patronage of churches, in which laymen, who provided the resources, proceeded also to lay down the terms; they created a new start in religion, but insisted on retaining some control of it. This model, seen *a fortiori* in the more commercialised foundations of the later middle ages, was also re-imposed on older foundations by later patrons. So, the function of monasteries was perceived to be less the spiritual welfare of the religious themselves (the ideal of so many religious movements), than the provision of vicarious perpetual benefits for their benefactors. But to support suffrages with perpetual property was to encase religion in a framework of temporal exchange inappropriate to benefits which could be enjoyed out of time. The result was monasteries doing nothing useful to living contemporaries, and thereby becoming even less able to do what they did; and this was even truer of the new foundations, which became outdated even more quickly. The laity then had the perfect excuse to turn round and reform, or resume, the institutions which they had created to fulfil their

[85] Above, n. 66; 31 Henry VIII, c. 9, *Statutes*, iii. 728.

own impossible expectations. They forced secularisation on the church, and then reformed it for its lack of spirituality.

The Dissolution, therefore, ought not to appear to medievalists as a gloomy termination to a great episode in religious history. The seeds of the 1530s were sown in the very foundation of the monasteries, in the very attempt to devote perpetual resources to the welfare of the dead. Historians above most others are aware of the changes and chances of this fleeting world: the circumstances of temporal existence are always changing, always in time. A religion based on an incarnation, on the injunction to be 'in' the world,[86] is no less subject to such a law. Even the monasteries, in origin the separate, world-rejecting, parts of the church *par excellence*, could not avoid their subjection to the passage of time and of history.

[86] John, xvii. 11, 18.

THE MONASTERIES OF NORFOLK, 1066–1540

Date	Name	Order	Founder	Status[87]	INCOME 1291	1535	Patron 1535	Status[87]
1066	ST BENET, HULME	Benedictine	[Crown]	1	326	583	Crown	1
1096	NORWICH CATHEDRAL	Benedictine	Bishop	2	489	1061	Bishop	2
1085	CASTLEACRE	Cluny (Lewes)	Warenne	2	235	306	Arundel	2
1091	BINHAM	Ben (St Alban's)	Valoines	3	103	140	King/St Alban's	1/2
–1100	WESTACRE	Coll→Aug Cans	Tony	3	140	260	Crown	1
1104	THETFORD BVM	Cluny	Bigod	2	123	312	Norfolk	2
1105	HORSHAM St Faith	Ben (Conques)	FitzWalter	3	78	162	Dacre	3
1107	WYMONDHAM	Ben (St Alban's)	Albini	2	153	211	Knyvet	4
1113	BROMHOLM	Cluny (CAcre)	Glanville	3	110	100	Suffolk	2
tHI	HEMPTON	Aug	St Martin	4	29	32	King/Oxford	1/2
1130	PENTNEY	Aug	Vaux	4	68	170	Rutland	2
1140	THETFORD Canons	Aug	Warenne	2	20	39	Crown	1
1146	CARROW	Ben nuns	K Stephen	1	69	64	Crown	1
1146	BUCKENHAM	Aug	Albini	2	52	108	Knyvet	4
1150	COXFORD	Aug	Cheney	4	144	121	Clinton	3
1150	CRABHOUSE	Aug nuns	Lisewis	4	—	30	Fitzwilliam	4(2)
1153	WALSINGHAM	Aug	Faverches	4	79	390	Crown	1
1150	BLACKBOROUGH	Ben nuns	Scales	4	36	42	Oxford	2
1160	THETFORD nuns	Ben nuns	Bury abbey	2	72	40	Bury	2
1185	HICKLING	Aug	Valoines	4	15	101	Tyndall	4
1188	W DEREHAM	Premonstratens.	Hubert Walter	4	170	228	Crown/ABC	1/2
1190	SHOULDHAM	Gilbertine	FitzPeter	2	207	138	Crown	1
1190	WORMEGAY	Aug	Wormegay	3	37	38	Oxford/King	1/2

[87] Status categories are: 1, Crown; 2, Titled nobility; 3, Lesser tenants-in-chief/lesser nobility; 4, Sub-tenants/gentry.
[88] These figures include four houses whose status is uncertain between the crown and the titled nobility: so 10 actually represents a minimum of 8, a maximum of 12.

Date	House	Order	Founder	St.		Patron		St.
C12	PETERSTONE	Aug	?		23	?	47	3
1195	LANGLEY	Prem	FitzRoger	3	178	Dacre	104	4
1199	MOUNTJOY	Aug	Gyney	4	9	Hales	30	1
1206	CREAKE	Aug	Narford	4	60	Crown	–	2
e-C13	WEYBOURNE	Aug	Manwaring	4	16	Oxford	28	3
1216	BEESTON	Aug	Beaufoe	3	28	Morley	43	4
1216	FLITCHAM	Aug	Aguillon	4	28	Lutrell	55	2
1225	WEYBRIDGE	Aug	Bigod	2	8	Norfolk	7	2
1249	MARHAM	Cist nuns	Warenne	2	27	Arundel	39	2
1250	BROMEHILL	Aug	Plays	4	25	Oxford	–	
1260	MASSINGHAM	Aug	le Sire	4	18	Crown	24	1
1265	WENDLING	Prem	Wendling	4	38	Hastings	56	4

STATISTICS

STATUS[87]

	FOUNDATION		1300		1400		DISSOLUTION	
	/34	%	/34	%	/34	%	/34	%
1	2	6	4	12	5	15	10[88]	29
2	10	29	12	35	13	38	13[88]	38
3	7	21	12	35	8	24	4	12
4	15	44	6	18	8	24	7	21

PRINCE AND STATES GENERAL: CHARLES V AND THE NETHERLANDS (1506–1555)

The Prothero Lecture

By H. G. Koenigsberger

READ 7 JULY 1993

ON the 18th June 1902 the viceroy of India, Lord Curzon, wrote to his government in London:

> The fact is that your Political Committee and the Foreign Office have gone completely off the rails ... Now, why could not the India Office trust me ...? You send me out to India as an expert and you treat my advice as though it were that of an impertinent schoolboy.[1]

In another letter, about the same time, Curzon put the point more generally:

> It is not against the exercise of superior authority that I have any complaint to make. It is against the assertion of an interference ... conducted in a spirit not of confidence or helpfulness, but of distrust and suspicion.[2]

Such interference, Curzon explained in a third letter, came from

> your old veterans ..., many of whom have left India for a decade or more, (and who) are as dogmatic about the subjects that they have ceased to understand as a young curate in a pulpit is about those he has not yet commenced to know.[3]

Some 350 years earlier, Juan de Vega, outgoing viceroy of Sicily, wrote to Philip II that the ministers at home,

> however wise and sufficient they were (for their offices), ... are motivated differently from what is due to the king's service and authority ... and their interference is as if a body interposed itself between the sun and the moon and eclipsed their brightness.

---

[1] Lord Curzon to Sir A. Godley. Quoted in the earl of Ronaldshay, *The Life of Lord Curzon*, II (1928), 239.

[2] Curzon to Lady Curzon, 19 June 1902. *Ibid.*, 238.

[3] Curzon to Godley, 24 June 1902. *Ibid.*, 238. I wish to thank Prof. P. J. Marshall for finding the quotations from Lord Curzon for me.

For these ministers in Madrid were mostly ambitious men of low birth who thought they could treat the viceroys of Sicily and Naples as if they were the mayors of Salamanca or Avila.

> They do not know what it is to be a king, nor wherein lies the greatness and authority of monarchy, nor of the provinces of the world and the quality of their peoples; nor (do they know) of chivalry and honour, nor what manner of man a viceroy has to be.[4]

Two years before Juan de Vega wrote this explosive letter, of which soon many copies circulated in Europe,[5] Mary of Hungary wrote a letter of resignation from her regency of the Netherlands to her brother, the emperor Charles V, on the occasion of his abdication, in 1555:

> All states under the obedience of a prince should desire above all that he should be most wise and virtuous ... Yet I would say that a person who governs under a prince must be wiser than the prince himself who, governing for himself, has to render account only to God ... But he who governs under another must not only render account to God but also to the prince and to his subjects ... Apart from the consultations all governors have to engage in, here in the Netherlands one has to gain everyone's good will, nobles as well as commons; for this country does not render the obedience which is due to a monarchy, nor to an oligarchic regime, nor even to a republic; and a woman, especially a widow, finds this very difficult to cope with ...; for a woman, whatever her status, is never respected and feared like a man. [If things went wrong in war], one is given the fault; for people hate to have to give from their property, as is necessary in such times ... I could write a volume, listing all the difficulties ... I would not desire to go on governing, even if I were a man ... for, as God is my witness, governing is so abhorrent to me that, sooner than continue with it, I would earn my living.[6]

Evidently, a regent's or a viceroy's lot is not a happy one, whether in the sixteenth or in the twentieth century. But before suggesting that we all take out our handkerchiefs, or that we make quick generalisations about the systemic or contingent nature of this unhappy gubernatorial lot of viceroys, regents, governors-general, lords-lieutenant, Statthalter, wielkorzdcas and all other species of satraps, I want to look at the problem from different points of view, those of the prince who is a ruler of a multiple kingdom and those of his subjects. Charles V and

[4] Ch. Weiss, ed., *Papiers d'État du Cardinal de Granvelle*, V, (Paris, 1844), 142–66.

[5] A. Saitta, ed., *Avvertimenti di Don Scipio di Castro a Marco Antonio Colonna*, (Rome, 1950), 45. First publication in *Thesoro Politico*, II (Milan, 1601).

[6] *Papiers d'État*, IV, 469–80.

the Netherlands make a particularly good case study; for the Netherlands were not only one of the constituent parts of his huge multiple
monarchy, but they were themselves a composite state.

Let me quickly recapitulate the history of the Netherlands. In the
late fourteenth and in the fifteenth centuries the Valois dukes of
Burgundy brought a number of duchies and counties in northwestern
Europe together under their rule. This apparently ramshackle polity,
with its contrasting economic and social structures, its several different
languages and with its local privileges defended by long-established
provincial estates and by solemnly sworn princely charters, known as
joyeuses entrées—this composite state survived a revolution against the
autocratic and centralising policies of Charles the Bold, in 1477, and
fifteen years of intermittent civil wars during the regency of Maximilian
of Austria for his and his wife Mary of Burgundy's infant children.[7]

In 1493 Maximilian, by this time King of the Romans and effectively
Holy Roman Emperor, gave up his regency. The Netherlands were
now governed again by a native prince, Maximilian's son, Philip the
Handsome, and by a council dominated by the Netherlands nobility,
notably the rich Walloon clan of the Croy, led by the Seigneur de
Chièvres. In a deliberate reaction to Charles the Bold's and Maximilian's
attempted autocracies, Philips's government ruled by consent, summoning the States General on average twice a year to discuss monetary
and currency matters, taxation and even foreign policy. It was the
States General, the combined assembly of the provincial estates, which
had come out of the civil wars with most credit.

As against the personal policies of the regent, the self-serving
ambitions of many of the high nobility and the narrow-minded city
imperialism and ferocious guild dictatorship of Ghent, the States
General had appeared to many as the only player who represented the
interests of the country as a whole. Here, therefore, was the regime
which, following Fortescue's famous description of England, I have
characterised as a *dominium politicum et regale*, a regime which contrasted
itself quite consciously with the *dominium regale* of France. It was the
regime which, fifty years later, Philip's daughter, Mary of Hungary,
was to describe as 'not rendering the obedience which is due to a
monarchy, nor to an oligarchic regime, nor even to a republic'.

And yet, even during the reign of Philip the Handsome, the Netherlands were sliding into dependence of a wider political constellation.
Maximilian sought to build up a grandiose system of dynastic alliances,
ranging from the Yorkists in England to the Jagiellons of Hungary,
including the Sforzas of Milan and either the Valois of France or the

---

[7] H. G. Koenigsberger, 'Fürst und Generalstaaten: Maximilian I in den Niederlanden
(1477–1493), *Historische Zeitschrift*, Bd. 242. No. 3., 557–79.

Trastámara of Spain, depending on the political circumstances of the moment. Philip the Handsome was never free from his father's influence. The Venetian ambassador wrote of him as being, between the love for his father and his loyalty to his councillors, in a 'great labyrinth'.[8] It was Maximilian who proposed Philip's marriage with Ferdinand and Isabella's daughter, Juana. Not that the Netherlanders in Philip's government objected to this plan. Like most of the European nobility, they were only too keen to see their prince acquire new titles and more patronage. When Isabella died, in 1504, the Netherlands seigneurs enthusiastically supported Philip's claim to the throne of Castile. The States General also supported Philip's claim, although with rather less enthusiasm, for they had to find the money for Philip's two expeditions to Spain.

On 3 October 1506 the news of Philip's sudden death in Spain arrived in the Netherlands. Chièvres summoned the States General for the 15th. Here was a typical early modern succession crisis; for the legitimate heir, Philip's eldest son, Charles, was only six. But unlike 1477 when, on the sudden death of Charles the Bold, the country was clearly on the verge of revolution, no one in 1506 seems to have felt a great sense of urgency. The Chancellor, addressing the States General, admitted that his own and every ducal official's office had legally terminated with the duke's death. The States General was therefore the only body which could legally function on its own authority. But this was so only by implication. Everyone simply expected the States General to take the necessary decisions, without drawing any constitutional conclusions from this situation. The deputies immediately agreed to confirm the position of the councillors and of the judges of the duke's courts, though there was some argument whether this should be done for four or only two months, and the Brabanters, very reasonably, wanted the Treasury officials first to present their accounts.

All other matters proceeded in slow motion. Everyone was agreed that young Charles was the rightful heir and that the provinces had to remain united, and they hardly needed an unctuous letter from Henry VII to tell them so. Henry VII, after all, was the king who had only recently taken advantage of Philip's forced landing in England to blackmail him into accepting the *malus intercursus*, a trade treaty very unfavourable to the Netherlands. The States General faced two practical problems. The first was the tutorship and regency for young Charles; the second was defence against France and Guelders. Maximilian claimed tutorship and regency for his grandson as of right. No one remembered his previous regency with pleasure; but all wanted to act

---

[8] C. R. von Höfler, 'Depeschen des venetianischen Botschafters bei Erzherzog Philip, Dr Vincenzo Quirino, 1505–1506,' *Archiv für österreichische Geschichte*. LXVI (1885), 148.

legally. Flanders and Artois were fiefs of the French crown, and Louis XII had forty days in which legally to claim the regency for these provinces. But memories of the French occupation of Artois were not in his favour. Louis XI had, at one point, forced all the citizens of Arras to leave their city and their property—an example of ethnic cleansing which did not generally find favour in the fifteenth century, even when, as in this case, it was disguised as punishment for rebellion. In the event, in 1506, Louis XII was more interested in Milan than in Flanders and allowed the forty days to pass without action.

The deputies of the States General talked and negotiated with each other for nearly a month and, at times, returned to their provinces for further instructions. While France did not pose an immediate problem, Guelders did. Charles the Bold had dispossessed its duke, on very dubious grounds. The emperor Frederick III had invested Maximilian with the duchy, and Maximilian, in his turn, had invested his son Philip and his heirs. Understandably, the old Gueldrian duke's son, Charles of Egmont, would have none of this. In 1492 he returned from enforced exile to a welcoming duchy. From then on, neither side would give up its claims, and intermittent warfare escalated from Gueldrian cattle raids to open military confrontation, not only over the duchy itself but over the control of Utrecht, Overjissel, Drenthe and Groningen, the whole of the northeastern border of the Netherlands, right up to the North Sea. The States General would have dearly loved an accommodation; but there was no squaring of the circle of the conflicting Habsburg and Egmont claims. In 1506 the States General managed to scale down Chièvres' proposals for a defensive force by half. Only gradually and reluctantly, as Gueldrian raids reached The Hague and the very walls of Antwerp, did the estates of even the most directly threatened provinces, Holland and Brabant, come to see the Gueldrian wars as a concern not only of the ruling house but of their own safety.

In the succession crisis of 1506 it did not prove easy to get Maximilian to act. The States General's delegation, sent to offer him the regency, found that he ran away from them. They did not manage to catch up with him until January 1507, in Innsbruck. He was preoccupied with typically Maximilianesque projects for a regency of his own in Castile, a regency which was to be camouflaged by a crusade against the North-African Muslims. When the Venetians would not allow him to march an army over the Alpine passes, Maximilian switched to a plan for an alliance with Ferdinand of Aragon (whom he had wanted to displace in Castile), even offering him the imperial crown if he agreed to accept Charles, their mutual grandson, as his heir.[9] In contrast to 1482, when

[9] R. Wellens, 'Les États Généraux et la succession de Philippe le Beau dans les Pays-Bas,' *Anciens Pays et Assemblées d'États*, XVI (1972), 123–59. H. Wiesflecker, *Maximilian I*,

his wife Mary of Burgundy had died, Maximilian was not worried about his own position in the Netherlands. Immediately, of course, he needed an acting regent. He appointed his daughter Margaret, widow of the Castilian Infante Juan and also of duke Philibert II of Savoy. The Netherlanders were pleased to have a native princess as regent and, in April 1507, the States General accepted her without difficulty.

In the crisis of 1506, the beginning of Charles V's reign, everyone had behaved true to character. Maximilian, who believed that French agents had poisoned his son, veered from deepest depression to the exaltation of grandiose visions for himself and his house and regarded the Netherlands as no more than a means to these ends. The king of England remained on the sidelines, giving moral advice. The king of France made threatening noises but failed to move decisively because he was more interested in Italy than in the Netherlands. The duke of Guelders took the opportunity to recapture a few towns. The Netherlands council, dominated by the Croy family, was diffident about its own authority but tried to preserve the smooth working of the government. The estates were anxious to preserve legality and the union of the provinces. The constitutional problems which the crisis threw up were barely recognised and none of the parties was anxious to pursue them. The balance of *dominium politicum et regale* was functioning effectively, with the States General recognised as an indispensable part of the political regime of the Netherlands.

But two problems became immediately apparent. The first was the question of who took ultimate decisions on foreign policy and with what end in view. The second was who controlled government patronage: appointments to ministerial, judicial and military posts, to provincial governorships, to all types of profitable minor administrative positions and to ecclesiastical benefices. In practice, the two problems were closely linked. Since the major internal political issues had been resolved, at least for the time being, foreign policy and defence became the key issues in the relations between the government and the States General; for it was the estates who had to provide the funds for defence. And the practical handling of relations with the States General depended, in its turn, on the control of patronage. It remained to be seen whether these problems could be solved in the context of the now enormously enlarged and still growing composite monarchy of the Habsburgs.

Immediately after her appointment Margaret broke the ascendancy of the Croy in the council, balancing their francophile policy with the appointment of Jean de Berghes and other seigneurs with estates in

---

(Vienna and Munich, 1991), 152–3. Not surprisingly, Ferdinand the Catholic did not go along with any of these schemes and he only accepted his grandson as his heir in Spain when his son from his second marriage died in infancy.

Brabant. These seigneurs derived much of their income from lordship over small manufacturing towns or from leases of local tolls. In this way they could cream off some of the profits of the Antwerp trade in English cloth and of the Brabant finishing industries. Naturally, they were more inclined towards a pro-English policy than the Walloon nobility. Such an inclination coincided with Margaret's own preferences. Having spent much of her childhood in France, as the fiancée of the dauphin, later Charles VIII, she did not readily forgive the French monarchy for her being jilted in favour of the heiress of Brittany.

With a divided council, Margaret came to rely, more than any previous ruler of the Netherlands, on professional lawyers and administrators. Most of these came from Franche-Comté which Maximilian had given her as a personal possession for life. The county was French speaking but not French and, while part of the Holy Roman Empire, certainly not German. Here, and notably at the law school of the university of Dôle, the international traditions of the Carolingian Empire were still alive and were interpreted in classical and Roman Law terms. The Dôle graduates tended to look for their careers outside their small and relatively poor country. In the fifteenth century the Valois dukes of Burgundy had brought some of them to the Netherlands. In the sixteenth century, with the widening of the house of Burgundy's political horizons, the Franche-Comtois lawyers found a natural home in the Netherlands council and became eager supporters of Burgundian-Habsburg imperial policy.[10]

Margaret had appointed her own council; yet, less than a year later, she complained to her father that she was not fully in control of her government and that she could not rely on the primary loyalty of her ministers and servants. Maximilian's correspondence with his very intelligent and strong-minded daughter was sometimes humorous, often acrimonious when they did not see eye to eye, and sometimes downright vicious.[11] On this occasion he wrote soothingly that she should make appointments under his seal, 'for it seems to me that, as grandfather and guardian of our children, I should retain some authority to rule you, both for the sake of my own reputation and for yours which derives from it'.[12] In practice this formula did not work as smoothly as Maximilian suggested. Those who disagreed with the regent's policies intrigued against her at the emperor's court. By 1511 Margaret told

[10] A. Walther, *Die Anfänge Karls V,* (Leipzig, 1911), 15–26.
[11] A. Le Glay, *Correspondance de l'empereur Maximilien Ier et de Marguerite d'Autriche,* 2 vols. (Paris, 1839), *passim.* H. Kreiten, 'Der Briefwechsel Kaiser Maximilians I mit seiner Tochter Margareta,' *Archiv für österreichische Geschichte,* XCVI, pt. 2, (1907). Critique and extensive corrections of Kreiten's publication by A. Walther in *Göttingische gelehrte Anzeigen,* CLXX (1908).
[12] Le Glay, *Correspondance,* I, 122.

Maximilian that she could find hardly any help in her council. By this time her relations with her father had deteriorated sharply, mainly over foreign policy. This was the field Margaret was particularly good at. It was she who played a major role in bringing together the League of Cambrai, which lined up the emperor, Ferdinand the Catholic, Louis XII, Pope Julius II and a clutch of smaller vultures against Venice. For Margaret and the Netherlands this otherwise disreputable alliance had the advantage of producing a temporary stand-off with France and the consequent isolation of Charles of Guelders who therefore had to negotiate at least a temporary peace.

There was, however, no way of actually solving the problem of Guelders, and time, and again Margaret had to ask money from the States General for this minor but destructive war. Maximilian himself appealed to the reluctant States General: 'What touches the king or prince of the country', he wrote to the in August 1508, 'touches all his subjects and, conversely, everything that touches the subjects touches the king or prince.' They should all go to the assistance of Holland which the Gueldrian bands were ravaging, for they were all his subjects and allied together. Moreover, at the last meeting of the States General, they had all promised to help when one was attacked.[13]

The States General was not impressed. Five years earlier Maximilian had told them that it was their simple duty to support their prince's policy over Guelders without argument.[14] The estates knew very well that Maximilian was pursuing his private aims, even if they had not yet heard of the most bizarre of even Maximilian's ideas, that of having himself elected pope. (He wrote to Margaret that then he would become a saint and she would have to adore him, which would give him great satisfaction). In the States General the Walloon provinces argued that they were the frontier and bulwark against France, a much more powerful enemy than Charles of Egmont, and that their own defence expenditure had gone on for much longer and had been much higher than that of Holland.[15] Even in Holland itself it took time for the estates, oriented as they were towards the sea, to see the Guelders war as a concern for the whole province and not just the frontier towns. The estates of Brabant were quite definite that defence should be left to the endangered cities, 's Hertogenbosch and Antwerp.[16]

[13] L. P. Gachard, *Lettres inédites de Maximilien d'Autriche sur les affaires des Pays-Bas (1478–1508)*, Compte rendu de la Commission Royale d'Histoire, ser. 2, vol. 2/3, pt. 2, 310–311. A. Henne, *Histoire du règne de Charles Quint en Belgique*, I, (Brussels, 1858), 177–86.

[14] R. Wellens, *Les États-Généraux des Pays-Bas des origines à la fin du règne de Philippe le Beau (1464–1506)*, Anciens Pays et Assemblées d'États, LXIV (Heule, 1974), 261.

[15] Archives Générales du Royaume à Bruxelles, *Copies du Régistre aux Mémoriaux de Béthune*, B.B.5, fos. 26r–31r.

[16] J. D. Tracy, *Holland under Habsburg Rule 1506–1566: The Formation of a Body Politic*, (Berkeley, 1990), 64–89.

By February 1512 Margaret was so hard pressed over defence expenditure that she had to put a direct question to the States General: should the war with Guelders be continued in the spring? In that case she would need money for at least 6000 foot and 1200 horse. Alternatively, should she negotiate peace? Obviously it would not be a favourable peace, not to speak of Maximilian's reaction. Even with peace, the government would need 200,000 florins to pay off the troops and to keep the usual garrisons going. Unsurprisingly, the States General insisted on peace. Brabant would not even pay for its own frontier guards, and the deputies of 's Hertogenbosch suggested to the deputies of the other towns that they should treat directly with Guelders. In fact, the war went on. Only when Gueldrian troops actually threatened Brabant seriously did the province agree to an *aide* of 150,000 florins and persuaded the reluctant Flemish deputies to agree.[17]

In the autumn of 1512, Margaret's letters to her father became more and more desperate. The estates were recalcitrant and the people full of malicious talk. She was doing her best, and she begged him to have pity on her, for she had lent the government all she herself possessed. 'I assure you, Monseigneur,' she ended one letter, 'I feel so bad about all this that I am in danger of falling ill and many times I have wished I were still in my mother's belly.' Her Secretary, as a good civil servant, would not let her send this last sentence from her draft.[18] Maximilian, for his part, could not suggest anything more than that she continue her negotiations with the States General.

Apparently as a purely tactical device, Margaret's government proposed to the States General a procedure that, in the long run, was to have far-reaching political and constitutional implications. The deputies had complained that money which they had voted for defence was not used for this purpose, or not efficiently, or paid to non-existent soldiers. The immediate reaction of Margaret's ministers seems to have been irritation. Those who wanted to know how the money had been spent should go to the War Treasurer, they said. And anyway, if anything had gone wrong, it was because the States General had not provided enough money in time. But then the ministers went much further. Madame had agreed, they told the States General, that in future her council and representatives of the estates should jointly appoint the officers of the *gendarmerie*. Or, if they knew of any better way, Madame would listen to them; for the young prince had no one to turn to but his loyal subjects.[19]

[17] Henne, *Histoire ... de Charles Quint*, I, 287–94. *Régistre ... de Béthune*, B.B.5, fos. 26r–31r.

[18] A. Walther, 'Hubert Kreiten, Briefwechsel,' *cit.*, 266.

[19] *Régistre de Béthune*, B.B.5., fos. 26r–31r.

At the time, the estates were less interested in this offer than they were in peace, although in the summer of 1513 the estates of Flanders insisted that, in return for a vote of 120,000 écus, the garrison troops should be under the orders of their provincial governor and of four commissioners appointed by the four 'members' of Flanders, Ghent, Bruges, Ypres and the group of small towns and castelries known as the Franc de Bruges.[20] It is likely that the Flemings remembered a similar arrangement they had insisted on in 1488, when Maximilian was their prisoner in Ghent,[21] and perhaps this was the reason why Margaret did not mention the details of her proposal to her father. During her second regency, in the 1520s, estates control over finances and a role for them in military appointments was to become a serious political issue. Nothing of this was foreseen or foreseeable in 1513. A weak and divided government, in military and financial straits, had quite naturally turned for help to the States General. This body responded in a traditional manner. It proclaimed its willingness to help, stressed the present inability of the provinces to do more, urged the regent to make peace with France and Guelders and, after long negotiations, granted some financial aid, but much less than the government said it needed. No one sought to exploit this situation to change the political relationship between monarchy and States General. But it was also clear that this body did more than defend the privileges of the provincial estates. It was the body to which, it was agreed, the prince should turn in periods of crisis and danger. It was a conviction which the Netherlanders would never forget.

Relief from the crisis of 1512/13 came with the formation of the self-styled Holy League: Julius II, Maximilian, Ferdinand, Henry VIII and, hopefully, the Swiss were to turn on France. Again Margaret played a leading part in the diplomacy, and this time she achieved a special coup, the neutrality of the Netherlands in the forthcoming war. For a short time it was the best of all possible worlds. The more adventurous Netherlands seigneurs could indulge their love of fighting by taking service under Henry VIII and help the English capture Tournai from the French (21 September 1513). The rest of the country made 'a million in gold', as Margaret gleefully wrote to her father.[22]

Nevertheless, Margaret's position in the Netherlands was getting weaker. Since 1508 Chièvres had been responsible for the upbringing of the young archduke Charles. Perhaps to weaken his influence, and

---

[20] Henne, *Histoire ... de Charles Quint*, II, 10. See also Tracy, *Holland under Habsburg Rule*, 74.

[21] I. L. A. Diegerick, *Correspondence des Magistrats d'Ypres ... pendant les troubles de Flandre sous Maximilien*, (Bruges, 1853), 4 and Annexe 7.

[22] Quoted in F. W. N. Hugenholtz, 'Filips de Schone en Maximiliaans tweede regentschap, 1493–1515,' *Algemene Geschiedenis der Nederlanden*, IV, (Utrecht, 1952), 47–48.

certainly to please a large number of the nobility, Margaret set up a separate household for the prince, in October 1513. The effect was to add a third centre of loyalty and intrigue to the already confusing polarity between herself and her father. The Netherlands government was effectively paralysed. In December 1514 the States General offered Maximilian 100,000 florins if he agreed to have Charles declared of age. Just as with Philip, in 1493, Maximilian was happy to be bought off. On the 15th January 1515 Charles appeared before the States General as ruler in his own right, and Margaret's first regency came to an end.[23]

Like many political leaders, before and after her, Margaret of Austria blamed her fall on a conspiracy. The States General had been led astray by evil spirits, she wrote to Maximilian. She meant Chièvres and his francophile friends and there she was correct; for it was Chièvres who now became the effective head of government. Charles made the rounds of the provinces and swore to observe their *joyeuses entrées*, their charters and privileges. In return, the estates granted him handsome *aides*.

Nevertheless, because of the accumulated debts of the Guelders war, the government's financial position remained precarious. In February 1516 news arrived of Ferdinand the Catholic's death. Just as he had done for Philip the Handsome, Chières immediately set about organising his prince's journey to Spain. This time, however, it was not only for the crown of Castile but also for that of Aragon with its Italian dependencies. Charles would therefore also inherit the Aragonese tradition of competition with France over Italy and its enmity to the Ottoman Turks, just then on the eve of their greatest conquests in the Middle East, the Mediterranean and the Balkans. Relations with France and the Turks, and soon also the problems of Germany and the Reformation, were to be the principal and inescapable concerns of Charles V. By the very efficiency with which Chièvres had organised the diplomatic and financial conditions of the Spanish succession he had effectively manoeuvred the Netherlands into the backwater of a huge composite polity. And this time, the gods, having granted the Netherlanders a second chance to choose their destiny, did not rescue them again from their own pride by the premature death of their prince.

The choice had been that of the court and the nobility, with the States General showing rather less enthusiasm. But while they haggled over the taxes they did not really oppose Charles's Spanish expedition, any more than they had opposed, or even been critical of, those of his father. Erasmus wrote to Sir Thomas More, lamenting the condition of a country overrun by soldiers and in which the nobles and prelates had agreed enormous sums in taxes which the ordinary people had to pay.[24]

In June 1517 the States General was informed of the arrangement for the government of the Netherlands while Charles and Chièvres were in Spain. There was no viable alternative but to bring back Margaret of Austria. Once again she found herself heading a government, with responsibility for the safety of the country and the reputation of the monarchy, but without the power to take final decisions. Unfortunately, we do not have a publication of her correspondence with her nephew, as we have it of her correspondence with her father. But the nature of their relationship is clear enough. In some ways it was better than with Maximilian. Margaret was now the older and more experienced partner. Charles's chief adviser, after the death of Chièvres in 1521, was the grand-chancellor Gattinara, a Piedmontese who owed his career to her. Charles himself, a cold fish compared with his grandfather, was not given to writing nasty personal letters. But he was just as ruthless in harnessing his family members to the interests of the house of Austria, as he saw them, and he was much more consistent. In place of Maximilian' fitful interference Charles tried to exercise continuous control.

Since there were no institutions spanning the whole of Charles V's composite monarchy, there were only two ways in which such continuous control could be exercised: the first was by reserving to himself all important decisions on foreign and defence policy; the second was by an even more rigorous personal control over government patronage than Maximilian had exercised. The first great test over control of foreign policy came with the imperial election of 1519, while Charles was still in Spain. Margaret suggested that both the pope and the German electors would more readily accept Charles's younger brother, Ferdinand, than the man who already ruled the Netherlands, Spain and half of Italy. Charles, characteristically going for the grandest prize—and here he resembled his grandfather—rejected Margaret's prudent advice outright. His success in the election, even though it was bought by massive bribes, confirmed him in the belief in his God-given imperial destiny. And this meant that the interests of the separate parts of his composite monarchy would always be subordinated to the interests of the whole polity as he perceived it.

Of course, this was not the way it was put. Within the Habsburg family, to his aunt, he argued that her plan smacked of a French intrigue to divide him from his brother—again the sort of argument his

[24] Quoted in Henne, *Histoire ... de Charles Quint*, II, 157, and in J. D. Tracy, *The Politics of Erasmus*, (Toronto, 1978), 92.

grandfather would have produced. And Maximilian, he told Margaret, virtuous and victorious prince that he had been, had always been hard put to preserve his imperial rights. Ferdinand would be in no better position. By contrast, he himself, with all his great dominions, would be feared and esteemed by all and would be able to defeat the enemies of the faith.[25] This declaration was a manifest relegation of the specific interests of the Netherlands to a subordinate role. In terms of personalities it meant new Gattinara succeeded Chières as Charles's chief adviser on international affairs.

Gattinara, who had probably drafted Charles's letter to Margaret, put the point more decorously to the States General in Brussels, in June 1520. It was a grand affair, with Charles sitting between Margaret and Ferdinand, while the grand-chancellor harangued the deputies in his long-winded lawyer's style.[26] He compared Charles with Alexander, Caesar and Hadrian; he desired to preserve the Netherlands in peace and tranquillity, and if he was corporeally absent, his heart would always be with them. He had accepted the imperial dignity not from worldly ambition but to serve all his dominions and work for the union of all Christian princes, for the sake of the Catholic faith and the whole Christian commonwealth. For this purpose he had raised troops to fight the Turks and he had sent ships to the New World to lead its inhabitants to the knowledge of God, as well as to draw from the New World spices, to the great profit of himself and of his subjects. In these efforts he had spent more than a million in gold. 'All these matters', Gattinara concluded, 'His Majesty has willingly imparted to you because of the entire confidence he has in your loyalty, so that you should know the complete state and disposition of his affairs.' Thus you can aid him with your goods and persons, 'for you are those who reap greater fruits from the grandeur of your prince ... and in future he will help and support you better and trouble you less with *aides* and impositions ... By participating in the great good and grandeur which will ensue for the service of God and of the whole of Christendom, you will recognise clearly that the hand of God is with His Majesty.'[27]

One does not start an argument at a photo opportunity. At the time, none of the deputies of the States General voiced any doubts about the splendid prospects which their prince's composite monarchy,

[25] K. Brandi, *Kaiser Karl V,* (Munich, 1937/1959), 88–89. H. G. Koenigsberger, 'The empire of Charles V in Europe,' *New Cambridge Modern History,* II, (2nd ed., Cambridge, 1990) 344.
[26] Brussels, Bibliotèque Royale, *Root Boeck behelsende het sommier van de Consenten ... rackende de Staeten van Brabant ... 1503 tot de Jaere 1578.* MSS 16955–57, fos. 44r–v. (Eighteenth-century copy).
[27] Archives Générales du Royaume, *Recueil de Propositions faites aux États Généraux des Pays-Bas,* I, fos. 9–13.

through the workings of divine providence, would bestow on his subjects, nor of the way he was graciously taking them into his confidence and promising government by consensus. No one mentioned that, only two months earlier, similar harangues had left the deputies of the Castilian cortes, at Coruña, quite unmoved, that Gattinara's parliamentary tactics had badly backfired on that occasion and that, even now, Castile was rapidly sliding into open rebellion and civil war.[28]

In the Netherlands there was, as yet, no rebellion. But the reality of Charles V's regime was very different from the glorious picture Gattinara had painted. Already in April 1519, and quite probably prompted by Gattinara, Charles had commended Margaret for refusing the request of the estates of Brabant to summon the States General, for fear that they might form a league or confederation in diminution of his prerogatives.[29] In the session of June 1520 the government followed the grand-chancellor's address with separate discussions of its tax demands with the estates of the individual provinces. Previously it had been customary to ask the States General for a global sum which was then divided between the provinces in a fixed ratio. Nor did the government take very seriously Gattinara's remark that the emperor had 'entire confidence' in his Netherlands subjects. At a States General in Brussels, in April 1522, Gattinara outlined the apparently favourable political situation. The emperor had conquered Milan and acquired Tournai, and his alliance with Henry VIII would safeguard the Netherlands in his absence.[30] He did not, however, mention the disreputable secret agenda in the Anglo-Imperial alliance, the complete conquest and partition of France.

It could, of course, be said, that strategic plans could not be divulged. It should certainly be said that there does not seem to have been any objection, at least at this time, by the provincial estates at the reduction of the States General to little more than a ceremonial role. They had their own misgivings about common discussions in the States General, especially about financial matters, in which they were always afraid of being made to accept majority rule. And yet, discussions between the delegates from the different provinces did take place, about taxation as well as other matters, and sometimes the delegates were specifically instructed to have such discussions and to exercise their discretion.[31]

[28] H. G. Koenigsberger, *Estates and Revolutions*, (Ithaca, 1971), 185–87. M. Fernández Alvarez, *Charles V,* (1975), 26.

[29] Charles to Margaret, 9 April 1519. L. Ph. C. van den Bergh, *Gedenkstukken tot Opheldering der Nederlandsche Geschiedenis*, III, (Utrecht, 1849), 219.

[30] Henne, *Histoire de … Charles Quint*, II, 248–50.

[31] Aert van der Goes, *Register van alle de Dachvaerden by deselve Staten* [i.e. the estates of Holland] *gehouden … 1524–1543*, I, (Amsterdam, 1772), 350. L. Wils, 'De Werking van de Staten van Brabant omstreks 1550–1650,' *Anciens Pays et Assemblées d'États*, V, (1953), 11ff.

The smaller towns of Holland said, very reasonably, that if others ran, they could not stand still.[32]

The government, for its part, had an equally ambiguous attitude towards joint discussions. Negotiating with the individual provinces, often even with individual towns, over grants was a time-consuming and distasteful business. 'The emperor is not a merchant' who will haggle with the towns, the governor of Holland, the Count of Hoochstraten, quoting a widely rehearsed classical tag, grandly told the deputies of Amsterdam.[33] But that was precisely what he had to do, and the government had to bribe the towns, that is, give tax rebates called *gracien*, to get them to agree to grant the ordinary *aide*. Dordrecht and Haarlem negotiated as much as sixty-six per cent *gracien* on their *aides*, and when the other towns of Holland tumbled to this ploy they naturally demanded similar advantages.[34] The government therefore constantly urged cooperation and mutual help on the provinces. In practice this meant co-operation in the States General which, therefore, could not be permanently restricted to ceremonial functions. Joint or separate discussion remained an open question and, by itself, it did not lead to a constitutional confrontation, nor was it likely to do so. What worried the estates much more were the increasing financial demands of the government for causes which did not seem to have much to do with the subjects' interests. Worse still, this happened on two levels, the international and the local, Netherlands, level.

The 1522 campaign against France did not go well. By June of that year the regent was writing letters to her nephew as dramatic as those she had written, ten years earlier, to her father. The financial situation was desperate. Government credit on the Antwerp money market was exhausted. A bad harvest was in prospect, and there could easily arise a conspiracy or a rebellion. If all were to be lost for the lack of 10,000 florins, these could not be found. She ended on an even more caustic note than anything she had used with Maximilian: 'To leave great debts behind and few revenues, in a country such as this one, is not conducive to keeping it in such security, obedience and peace as one would wish.'[35]

If the emperor made life difficult for his regent by reserving decisions on foreign policy for himself, the same could be said for his other method of governing his multiple monarchy: his personal control of

[32] A. Jacobszoon, *Protocolle van alle de Reysen ... gedaen zedert ick de Stede Aemstelredamme gedient heb gehadt ...*, Amsterdam, Gemeente Archief, MS., 31 May 1524.

[33] *Ibid.*, fo. 107.

[34] Tracy, *Holland under Habsburg Rule*, 53–54.

[35] Instructions to the Secretary Jehan de la Sauch, 11 June 1522, quoted in Henne, *Histoire ... de Charles Quint*, III, 266–67.

government patronage. Margaret's relations with Charles over patron-age were a re-run of those with Maximilian, except that Charles kept government appointments and patronage much more rigidly and consistently in his own hands than his grandfather had done. Once again, those who opposed Margaret's policies or whom she had disappointed took their grudges to the emperor; and he was willing to listen to them. Some members of the nobility, he wrote to Margaret in March 1527, had complained that she had shown them no confidence nor appreciation for their faithful service. She had given preference to low class persons ('petits gens') and that these enjoyed her exclusive favour. Would she, 'with her great prudence and experience,' look at these complaints and deal with them?[36]

The attack was the more wounding as it came not in a personal letter but in a memorandum delivered by a third person. Margaret reacted sharply, and also in a memorandum, rather than a letter. She had been misrepresented, she wrote, and in consequence had fallen into great disrespect and loss of reputation with the Netherlanders; for they had observed that the emperor had, for trivial reasons, revoked appointments she had made according to the powers he had actually given her. A governor or regent of a country, who did not have authority to punish the bad and reward the good, would not be highly regarded by the prince's subjects. The prince himself would then lose authority. The regent would not be able to obtain money from the estates or get their support in other matters if she could not sometimes bestow some office or benefice, nor would the great lords be willing to negotiate with the estates for her. Several of them were already reproaching her that she could do them harm and disfavour but that she had no power to do them any good. His Majesty should therefore allow her to make urgent appointments with the advice of the council and, if he was approached directly by some Netherlanders, he should not lightly give them anything without first informing her.[37]

No doubt, Juan de Vega and lord Curzon would have approved of Margaret of Austria's sentiments. Her last point would have meant that the traditional roles of prince and regent in the control of patronage would have been reversed. Charles V showed no sign of accepting it. In July 1530, and still with the aura of her greatest diplomatic triumph, the 'Ladies Peace' of Cambrai, shedding lustre on her reputation, Margaret once more raised the question of patronage, and again in

---

[36] 'Instructions à ... le Seigneur de Praet ... devers Madame,' Valladolid, 6 March 1527. *Recueil concernant le gouwernement de Marguerite d'Autriche 1515–1530*, Brussels, Bibliotèque Royale, MSS 16068–72, fos. 189v–190r.

[37] 'Instructions ... de par madame ... donné à Messire de Rosimboz ... en ce present voiage d'Espagne ...' *Ibid.* fos. 24r–27r.

terms of the management of the estates: His Majesty had left her with
a list for the filling of Church benefices and had given her discretion
over only twelve, and none of these had fallen vacant for a long time.
Yet she needed such favours for the relatives of the governors of
important cities. Would the emperor allow her the disposal of every
third benefice in his gift?[38]

The emperor, busy with the Reichstag of Augsburg, did not answer.
It seems unlikely that he would have granted the regent's request since
it would have abrogated from his personal authority. But he would
certainly have taken her advice in individual cases when, as he planned,
he visited the Netherlands later in the year, and especially when it was
a matter of managing the States General. He approved of his aunt's
liking for autocratic action. In 1526 he had declared that his subjects
had the right to petition himself or the regent and her ministers over
grievances; but if such petitions were rejected, a further petition to the
estates would be regarded as sedition.[39] The ploy of sanitising whistle-
blowers by forcing them to use official channels was well developed in
the sixteenth century. But, for Margaret and Charles, it was just as
much a move to limit the competence of the estates. In 1530 the regent
went a step further and suggested to the emperor that the States
General should not be allowed to make requests before agreeing to an
aide, and that this rule should be imposed by edict when the emperor
was in the country or by special deals with the separate provinces.[40]

It seems quite likely that Charles would have dealt with this proposal.
In the autumn of 1530 he travelled to the Netherlands. On the way he
received the news of Margaret's sudden death, on 1 December, at the
relatively young age of fifty. It was time to rethink the whole position
of the government of the Netherlands within the multiple monarchy of
the Habsburgs.

The first task was the systematising of the councils, in much the
same way as Gattinara had done this for Charles in Spain in the
1520s.[41] The unwieldy old council of the Netherlands was divided into
a Council of Finance, a Privy or Secret Council for administrative,
judicial and legislative matters, and a Council of State for general

[38] 'Articles proposez à l'Empereur ... de par Madame,' *Ibid.*, fos. 140r–141r.

[39] 'Extrait de la minute des apostilles sur la declaration des affaires de flandre apportée
par Mre. Guillaume des Barres,' Brussels, Bibliotèque Royale, MS II 358, I, file
Correspondence de l'Empereur avec Madame Marguerite de l'an 1526 fo. 385.

[40] 'Articles proposez à l'Empereur ... de par Madame,' July 1530. *Ibid.*, MSS 16068–
72, fo. 136. Partly printed in G. Griffiths, *Representative Government in Western Europe in the
Sixteenth Century*, (Oxford, 1968), 354. See also H. G. Koenigsberger, 'Why did the States
General of the Netherlands become revolutionary in the sixteenth Century?' in *Politicians
and Virtuosi*, (1968), 64 and n.3.

[41] F. Walser, *Die spanischen Zentralbehörden und der Staatsrat Karls V*, ed. and completed by
R. Wohlfeil, (Göttingen, 1959), pt. 4.

policy and especially defence and all military matters. As was the case in the Spanish Council of State, its membership was not fixed. Charles himself appointed twelve councillors and one of these was also a member of the Spanish Council of State. All members of the emperor's own council were given the formal right to attend the regent's Council of State whenever they happened to be in the Netherlands.[42]

This reorganisation did not give the emperor as much control over the Netherlands as he had hoped. Only a year later we find him complaining that he was not being kept informed about a riot in Brussels.[43] Nor did his efforts to control patronage work more smoothly than they had before. He had appointed as the new regent his younger sister Mary, widow of the unfortunate Louis II of Hungary who had perished at Mohács. Mary turned out to be at least as strong-minded as her aunt had been. She insisted immediately on having the countess of Salm, a childhood friend, as one of her ladies of honour. Charles did his best to block this appointment. He would have much preferred 'a good and honest old lady from the Netherlands'. But his preferred ladies had refused because of age or bad health. Reluctantly he gave in. The countess was German, 'but at least not a Lutheran,' he wrote to his brother Ferdinand.[44] Mostly, however, Charles got his way. When in 1538 Mary complained to him that he had reversed some of her appointments, he wrote to her in his own hand, but firmly and patronisingly, that she should look again at her instructions and that his authority was more important than hers. He had to keep appointments in his own hands; for otherwise those who served him in his court would lose all hope of reward.[45]

After the reorganisation of the councils, the emperor's next move was to try to rationalise the defence of the Netherlands. The provinces had all too often failed to help each other when one was attacked. They had allowed foreign powers to play them off against each other by granting commercial privileges to some but not to others. They had even pursued their own foreign policy, as Holland had done in the Baltic. At a States General at Malines, in July 1534, Mary therefore proposed a defensive union of all the provinces. The proposal had been

---

[42] M. Baelde, 'De Collaterale Raden onder Karel V en Filips II (1531–1578),' *Verhandelingen van de Koninglijke Vlaamse Academie voor Wetenschappen, Letteren en Schone Kunsten van België*, Klasse der Letteren, XXVIII No. 60, (Brussels, 1965), chapt. 3. *Idem.*, 'Monarchie in Opbouw: de eerste Instructie voor de Raad van State (1531),' *Miscellanea Roger Petit*, (Brussels, 1990), 314 and 327.

[43] M. Baelde, 'De Collaterale Raden,' 58.

[44] Charles V to Ferdinand, Brussels, 29 July 1531. H. Wolfram and C. Thomas, *Die Korrespondenz Ferdinands I*, III, *Die Familienkorrespondenz 1531 und 1532*, (Vienna, 1989), 228–29.

[45] Charles to Mary, Toledo, 22 Dec. 1538. Brussels, Archives Générales du Royaume, *Papiers d'État et de l'Audience*, vol. 50, fos. 124v–125v.

discussed at length by the regent's council and by the great lords of the Order of the Golden Fleece. The provinces should agree to treat any attack on any one of them as an attack on all. This could best be done by regular contributions to a standing army. A great point was made that none of this should interfere with the individual privileges of the separate provinces.

For a year negotiations between the government and the estates continued. Most of the smaller provinces were in favour, hoping for military and financial aid from the bigger ones. The estates of Malines, the seat of the supreme court of the Netherlands, and evidently reflecting the views of the legal establishment, were the most enthusiastic and suggested the transformation of the provinces into a kingdom.[46] But the bigger provinces, Flanders, Brabant and Holland, opposed the union, even when the government made concessions over the proposed inclusion of the newly-acquired provinces, Friesland, Utrecht and Groningen, which did not regularly send deputies to the States General. It was over the role of the States General in the proposed union that negotiations eventually broke down. The emperor would not accept the demand of the Holland deputies that the States General should have the power to decide whether a war was just or not. The regent's council replied curtly to this proposal that, firstly, the union was meant to be defensive, anyway, and that, secondly, the emperor recognised no earthly superior and that his subjects were not allowed to examine such points as the justification of his wars. It was a classic point at issue between princes and estates in western Europe. In July 1535 the States General flatly rejected a standing army and refused all regular monthly payments. 'If we accept this project,' they said, 'we would undoubtedly be more united—and we would be treated *à la mode de France*.'[47] Charles V decided to drop the project.

It was certainly not the time to have a lengthy dispute with the States General over a controversial proposal. In 1536 the war with France broke out again. The government's financial situation was calamitous, and Mary's letters to Charles, with warnings of imminent disaster in the Netherlands, began to read more and more like those of her predecessor, except that where Margaret had wished to be in her mother's belly, Mary wished to be a thousand leagues away.[48] Nevertheless, the States General granted the government substantial sums for defence, while, however, insisting on strict appropriation, with

[46] *Ibid.*, vol. 1228, fo. 15v.

[47] *Ibid.*, fos. 15–46. L. van der Essen, 'Les États Généraux de 1534–1535 et le projet de confédération défensive des provinces des Pays-Bas,' *Mélanges d'Histoire offerts à Ch. Moeller*, II (Louvain—Paris, 1914), 122–39.

[48] Mary to Charles, Brussels, 4 Jan. 1536, Brussels, Archives Générales du Royaume, *Papiers d'État*, vol. 49, fos. 1–7.

their own representatives present at the pay parades.

Only Ghent refused, offering instead to raise troops. The reason for this refusal, as the government knew perfectly well, was the fear of the city councillors of popular revolt. But the issues were not a simple class conflict. Patricians and populace in Ghent were at one in resenting the government's attempt to bypass the city's traditional domination of its surrounding countryside in negotiating directly with the smaller towns in the Quarter of Ghent over the proposed taxes. The distrust between the monarchy and Ghent had a long history, stretching back to the fourteenth century. Right at the beginning of this particular dispute Mary wrote to Charles that she would try to avoid observing Ghent's *joyeuse entrée* as far as she could.[49] The usual Habsburg tactics of moving against the lower classes when there was any sort of trouble in an individual city and then confirming patrician dominance after the imposition of a stiff fine—these tactics did not work in the case of Ghent. For three years Mary and Ghent negotiated, without conclusion and with increasing bitterness.

From my specific point of view, that of analysing the relations between prince and estates in a composite monarchy, two aspects of this dispute stand out. The first is the reliance of the patricians of Ghent on their written privileges and their trust in the emperor's succession oath to uphold these privileges. They stuck to this belief even when the regent and Charles's special envoy, the Comte de Roeulx, assured them that the emperor would not accept their interpretation of their privileges. As late as the summer of 1539 the Ghenters organised an elaborate and expensive public festival of the Chambers of Rhetoric to demonstrate their own view that they were entirely loyal and pacific. In the autumn of 1539, however, there occurred a real popular revolution, organised by several of the guilds. In good Ghenter tradition they set up a kind of popular dictatorship and executed several patrician councillors for allegedly having betrayed the city and its privileges. This was open defiance of the prince, though even then many Ghenters do not seem to have realised that he would react by using force.

The second outstanding aspect is the helplessness of the regency government in the face of Ghent's refusal to contribute to the taxes which all the other provinces, and even the rest of Flanders, had agreed to in the States General. Mary and her council did not have the military means, and perhaps not even the political will, to coerce the country's second largest city. Nor, as far as I can see from Mary's correspondence, did the emperor empower her, let alone provide her with the means, to use force. He reserved this action for himself. In 1540, during a lull in international conflict, Francis I allowed him to

<hr />

[49] Mary to Charles, Brussels, 27 May 1536. *Ibid.* fo. 58.

march some troops through France to the Netherlands. He occupied Ghent without meeting the sort of resistance which Maximilian had met in similar circumstances in the 1480s, and he could without difficulty execute his vengeance on the leaders of the revolt, pocket the usual fines from the patricians and exclude the last vestiges of guild representation from the city council.[50]

While the revolt of Ghent demonstrated the weakness of regency government in a composite monarchy, it also demonstrated the inherent strength of a *dominium politicum et regale* regime. By keeping cool; by sticking to the point of principle that the States General was supporting their tax demands for the reasonable cause of the defence of the Netherlands, while only Ghent stood out, Mary and her council were able to keep the city isolated—again very much in contrast to the 1480s, when Ghent had been able to mobilise the rest of Flanders and a considerable party in the States General against the then regent, Maximilian. Already in his lifetime a myth was growing up that Charles V, the native Netherlander, could be trusted in a way that Maximilian had not been and that Philip II would not be. Yet Charles V tried to restrict the privileges of his cities and provinces wherever and whenever he could. In this policy he could be quite ruthless and machiavellian and, at times, thought of asking the pope to release him from some of the articles of his coronation oath. But he did not think it possible to make a frontal, wholesale attack on the laws and privileges of any of his dominions in the way Philip II and the duke of Alba were to attempt this in the 1560s. 'One must make a virtue of necessity and take what one can graciously,' Charles had advised Margaret, in 1525,[51] and he stuck to this principle, at least until the last few years of his reign.

Such a principle, however, still left plenty of room for dynastic, princely manoeuvring. In 1544 Charles V considered two alternative policies for obtaining a lasting peace with France in order to free his hands against the two most important enemies he claimed to have, the Muslims and the heretics. The first option was to marry his daughter to Francis I's second son, the duke of Orleans, with the whole of the Netherlands and Franche-Comté as their dowry, to rule in full sovereignty after his own death. The second was to marry his niece,

---

[50] L. P. Gachard published an extensive but not complete collection of documents: *Relation des Troubles de Gand sous Charles-Quint* ..., (Brussels, 1846). The most recent work on the subject is the composite volume *Keizer tussen stropdragers: Karel V 1500–1558*, eds. J. Decavele et al., (Louvain, 1990). I wish to thank Dr Alastair Duke for drawing my attention to this book.

[51] Apostille by Charles V to a memorandum from Margaret, presented by the Seigneur de Praet, Toledo, 9 July 1525. Brussels, Bibliotèque Royale, MSS 16068–72, fo. 158. The emperor's remark was later quoted by Nicolas Perrenot to Margaret, Toledo, 27 Oct.

Ferdinand's daughter, to the French prince, with Milan as dowry. This 'alternativa' was discussed at length in the Habsburg family and the two proposals were submitted to the Order of the Golden Fleece[52] and the Council of State, in Spain.[53] As far as I know, the States General was not consulted in a matter so vital for the Netherlands and one about which States Generals normally expected to be consulted.[54] There was no confrontation; perhaps because Charles was most unlikely to have opted for giving up his native country and first inheritance. Only the duke of Alba and other military experts preferred keeping Milan. They argued that the Netherlands, in the absence of its prince, was strategically not defensible. Events were to show that Alba was right, although this selfsame Alba did his ferocious and obstinate best to prove himself wrong—and very nearly succeeded.[55] In 1544 the 'alternativa' was resolved by the convenient death of the duke of Orleans.

The relief felt by the emperor's court was probably shared by the Netherlanders; but it did not resolve the fundamental problem which the 'alternativa' had been meant to solve: the cost of being part of a composite monarchy which was one of three competing superpowers, the other two being the kingdom of France and the Ottoman Empire. The other European powers had little choice but to group themselves around the hostilities of these three. Even the temporary change of this pattern, when the emperor attacked the Protestants in Germany, did not exempt the Netherlands from being almost permanently involved in warfare and required to bear a large part of its costs. Mary's government therefore proposed a number of tax reforms to the States General. They were meant to raise more revenue but they were also meant to distribute the tax burden more fairly. The two most important proposals were the imposition of excise duties for the whole country, without the traditional exemptions for nobles, clergy and government

---

1525. Le Glay, ed., *Négotiations Diplomatique entre la France et l'Autriche*, II (Paris, 1845), 629. I wish to thank Dr J. M. Rodríguez-Salgado for drawing my attention to this letter.

[52] At least, I assume he did, since he certainly did so when the matter was mooted in October 1540. Archives Générales du Royaume, *Papiers d'État*, vol. 52, fos. 252r–53r.

[53] Philip (II) to Charles V, Valladolid, 13 Jan. 1544. M. Fernández Alvarez, ed., *Corpus Documental de Carlos V*, II (Salamanca, 1975), 306–9. F. Chabod, '¿Milan o las Paises Bajos? Las Discusiones en España sobre la "alternativa" de 1544,' *Carlos V (1500–1558)*. *Homenaje de la Universidad de Granada*, (Granada, 1958), 367–70.

[54] As far as I know, there has been no specific study of the Netherlands side of the 'alternativa'.

[55] This last is the judgment of the most recent and most knowledgeable historian of Alba's governor-generaliship of the Netherlands. See G. Parker, 'Philip II, Paul Kennedy and the Revolt of the Netherlands 1572–76: a Case of Strategic Overstretch?' *Clashes of Cultures: Essays in Honour of Niels Steensgaard*, eds. J. C. V. Johansen et al., (Odense, 1992), 50–79.

officials, and secondly various forms of income tax, both on income from land and from commerce. None of these proposals was accepted for more than short periods by the States General. The deputies voiced all the usual arguments against income tax, including the accusation that the government was tempting people to commit perjury, when they were required to declare their income, and thus would lead them to eternal perdition. In the end the government chose the line of least resistance when the estates offered to raise taxes in the traditional manner or according to their own choice.

The one really effective financial innovation of the period was a purely practical development, arrived at without political argument. Governments in western Europe had for a long time raised funds by selling annuities (*rentes, renten*). But when revenues could not keep pace with expenditure, these governments had found it increasingly difficult to pay the annuities and to pay back the capital. After 1540 the provincial estates of Flanders, Brabant and Holland stepped into the breach. Buyers of *renten* found they could trust the estates, where they could no longer trust the government. But such trust could only be assured if the estates themselves controlled and audited their own revenues, so that taxes and funds allocated for the payment of annuities would really be used for this purpose and not diverted for other government expenditure, however pressing. The result was that the estates now greatly expanded their own financial administration—at the expense of that of the central government.

The advantages for the Habsburg monarchy were both financial and political, very much as with the sale of *juros* in Spain. It became possible to raise much larger sums than before and to do so more quickly. One could also, of course, raise bank loans on the Antwerp money market with the prospect of the estates' sale of *renten* as collateral. Without all this the increasing military expenditure of the 1550s could not have taken place. At the same time the system bound the ruling and moneyed classes of the provinces more closely to the regime; for many of the purchasers of the *renten* were the local nobility, the magistrates of the cities and the deputies of the provincial estates. On the negative side for the government, the new system (which historians have called the novel expedients, *de nieuwe middelen*) meant not only a retreat from central control over parliamentary finance but the development of administrative expertise, experience and self-confidence by the estates. It has been plausibly argued that this development played an important, perhaps a crucial, role in the success of the provincial estates and the States General in the course of the revolt of the Netherlands.[56]

---

[56] Cf. M. Baelde, 'Fianciële politiek en domaniale evolutie in de Nederlanden onder Karel V en Filips II (1530–1560),' *Tijdschrift voor Geschiedenis*, LXXVI (1963), 14–33. N.

But it was not a direct cause of the revolt nor of the breakdown of the regime of *dominium politicum et regale* in the Netherlands. What the system did do, by the deceptive ease with which apparently larger and larger sums could be raised, was to help lure the Habsburgs into vastly overstretching all their resources in the final round of their war with the Valois. We know about this policy from the magisterial books of the late Heinrich Lutz and of Mia Rodríguez-Salgado, the one based on the Italian and German and the other on the Spanish archives.[57] This was the fratricidal strife of the two greatest Catholic Christian princes in which all earlier idealism, the defence of Christendom against Turk and heretic, had been lost sight of in the quest for power and princely reputation. Contemporaries spoke of an afflicted Christendom, and the Netherlanders in particular felt they had been made to pay for the Spanish conquest of Italy, while the Castilians felt they had been made to pay for the defence of the Netherlands against France.

Peace, when it finally came with the Treaty of Cateau-Cambrésis in 1559, dissolved the familiar pattern of bi-polar great-power rivalry in western Europe and allowed local problems to blossom into full-blown crises. France collapsed into civil war. Its *dominium regale* regime could not cope with the coincidence of wartime debts and the spread of Calvinism during royal minorities. In the Netherlands there was a similar coincidence of the spread of heresy and of unmanageable wartime debts, in a period when the economic expansion of western Europe had come to a halt. Even so, it seems quite likely that its flexible *dominium politicum et regale* regime could have survived. What tilted the balance was the position of the Netherlands in the composite Habsburg monarchy, with a regency government which could not take vital decisions about its own most pressing problems on the basis of local knowledge. It was Philip II's and the duke of Alba's frontal attack on the political traditions and the public law of all the Netherlands provinces which produced a degree of co-operation among all those opposed to royal policy that, for all the fears expressed by Margaret of Austria and Mary of Hungary, was always most unlikely during the

---

Maddens, 'De Invoering van de "Nieuwe Middelen" in het Graafschap Vlaanderen tijdens de regering van Keizer Karel V,' *Revue Belge de Philologie et d'Histoire*, LVII (1979), 342–63 and 861–91. J. D. Tracy, 'The Taxation System of the County of Holland during the Reigns of Charles V and Philip II, 1519–1566,' *Economisch- en Sociaal-Historisch Jaarboek*, 48 (1985), 72–117; *Idem., A Financial Revolution in the Habsburg Netherlands: Renten and Renteniers in the County of Holland, 1515–1565*, (Berkeley, 1985), *passim*.

[57] H. Lutz, *Christianitas Afflicta. Europa, das Reich und die päpstliche Politik im Niedergang der Hegemonie Kaiser Kaqrls V (1552–1556)*, (Göttingen, 1964). M.J. Rodríguez-Salgado, *The Changing Face of Empire: Charles Philip II and Habsburg Authority, 1551–1559*, (Cambridge, 1988).

reign of Charles V. And, unlike France, the Netherlands had in the States General an alternative focus of loyalty to the monarchy. Its eventual victory in the northern provinces of the Netherlands destroyed the Carolinian balance of *dominium politicum et regale* and created the first truly parliamentary regime in European history.

THE FAILURE OF SOCIALIST UNITY IN BRITAIN
c. 1893–1914
By Keith Laybourn
READ 25 SEPTEMBER 1993 AT THE UNIVERSITY OF SHEFFIELD

SOCIALIST unity became an issue for the British left within a year of the formation of the Social Democratic Federation (SDF) in 1884. The secession of William Morris and his supporters from the SDF and the formation of the Socialist League in reaction to the autocratic leadership of Henry Mayers Hyndman brought about a fundamental division within British socialism. Subsequently the creation of other socialist parties, most particularly the Independent Labour Party (ILP) led to further disunity within the British socialist movement. Nevertheless, notwithstanding the proliferation of British socialist societies with their distinctive socialist credentials, there were several attempts to form a united socialist party between 1893 and 1914. They were normally encouraged, on the one hand, by advocates of the 'religion of socialism' such as William Morris, Robert Blatchford and Victor Grayson, and, on the other, by Hyndman and the SDF. The aim of these efforts was to strengthen socialist organisation in times of both political failure and success, but in every instance they failed due to the intractable problem of bringing together socialists of distinctively different persuasions under the umbrella of one party. These failures have led recent historians to debate two major questions connected with socialist unity. First, they have asked at what point did socialist unity cease to be a viable alternative to the Labour Alliance between the ILP and the trade unions? Stephen Yeo feels that socialist unity became impossible after the mid 1890s, David Howell suggests that this 'suppressed alternative' became unlikely about five to ten years later, as the leaders of the Independent Labour Party opted for the trade union rather than socialist alliance, whilst Martin Crick feels that socialist unity was still a viable alternative to at least 1911, if not 1914, when a determined effort was made to form the British Socialist Party, the one socialist party and forerunner of the Communist Part of Great Britain.[1] Thus

[1] D. Howell, *British Workers and the Independent Labour Party 1888–1906* (1984), 389–97; S. Yeo, 'A New Life; The Religion of Socialism in Britain, 1883–1896', *History Workshops Journal*, IV (Autumn, 1977), 5–56; M. Crick, 'A Call to Arms'; the Struggle for Socialist Unity in Britain, 1883–1914', in *The Centennial History of the Independent Labour Party* (eds.) D. James, T. Jowitt and K. Laybourn (1992), 181–204.

the dates of 1895, 1900 to 1906 or 1911 are offered as the alternative years when the prospects of socialist unity in Britain reached a watershed. Historians have been equally divided on the second, and related, question of why was socialist unity not achieved? In particular, they have focused upon two subsidiary questions. First, why did the Independent Labour Party choose the Alliance with trade unions and parliamentary-route way to power rather than socialist unity? Secondly, how important was the intransigence and narrowness of the Social Democratic Federation in thwarting moves towards socialist unity? Some writers have noted the steadfast opposition of the ILP leadership as the main problem whilst others have focused upon the inflexible and domineering nature of Henry Mayers Hyndman and the quasi-Marxist Social Democratic Federation, offering the 'image of the Social Democratic Federation as a narrow and dogmatic sect unsuited to the rigours of British politics'.[2]

This paper will argue that there was little real prospect of socialist unity being achieved in Britain after the mid 1890s and that the reason for the failure of socialist unity campaigns is to be found in the diverse and compromising nature of the ILP and the continued intransigence of the SDF, or Social Democratic Party as it became in 1907. Even if the domineering influence of Hyndman has been blown up out of proportion into a marvellous myth, it is clear that even in 1912 his antipathy towards industrial action, amongst other issues, still prevented the newly-formed British Socialist Party, the 'one united socialist party', from presenting any type of common front for British socialism. If anyone doubts the inflexibility of the leadership of SDF/SDP then they have to explain away the conflicts and tensions evident in the failure of the BSP between 1911 and 1914, particularly with regard to syndicalism, strike action, defence and foreign policy.

As Yeo suggests, by the mid 1890s, with the political failure of the ILP in the general election of 1895 which Beatrice Webb dubbed 'the most expensive funeral since Napoleon'[3], Keir Hardie and other ILP leaders were forced to choose between the business of 'making socialists' and the need to make a political party. Up the 1890s socialism was in the business of 'making socialists' and it did not matter which socialist organisation an individual belonged to. Yeo argues that, after the 1895 general election and the death of William Morris on 1896, the ILP and other socialist groups chose to become entrenched in a trade-union

[2] Howell, *British Workers and the ILP*, 389. This is a view which Martin Crick challenges in his article 'A Call to Arms'.
[3] R. Moore, *The Labour Party 1880–1924* (1978), 53, quoting Beatrice Webb's Diary, 10 July 1895.

alliance that focused upon parliamentary and local political organisation. The need to win elections, and electioneering, replaced the
ethical aspects of socialism which had focused upon leading the moral
and ethical life of a socialist. The general drift of Yeo's argument does
not seem unfair, although some of the fine detail has proved contentious.
Indeed, Yeo has emphasised that party connection became much more
important to socialists towards the end of the 1890s. David Howell
accepts much of what Yeo says although he dates the rise of electioneering and its impact upon the prospects for socialist unity to the
early years of the ILP and trade unions alliance: 'The ILP pursuit of
trade union influence rendered socialist unity a still viable but less likely
option.'[4] This view seems plausible but what is difficult to accept is the
argument of Martin Crick, who, looking from the point of view of the
SDF, seeks to extend the socialist unity debate to at least 1911, and
possibly 1914. His argument is that many socialists were unattached,
that the ILP and the SDF worked closely together in Lancashire, and
that the socialist revival of the 1904 to 1909 period ensured that there
was an alternative to the trade-union alliance on the eve of the First
World War and that the SDF was far more flexible and less sectarian
than is often supposed. Nevertheless, his argument and supporting
evidence could be interpreted in another way. As Jeff Hill has noted,
the SDF in Lancashire appeared to be detached from the policies of
its parent organisation and its success may have been despite the actions
of its national body.[5] It is also possible that the vibrancy of socialism
was just as likely to produce sectarian rigidity as it was likely to engender
a desire for social unity, as each organisation viewed its own individual
successes as confirmation of the correctness of its policies. In the final
analysis, the intransigence of both the ILP and the SDF, and the success
of the ILP-trade union alliance in 1906 made socialist unity a highly
unlikely proposition and confirmed the experience of the previous
twenty years that socialism in Britain was to be characterised more by
schism than unity. Indeed, there was little prospect of socialist unity
being achieved in the 1890s and none after 1906 when the Labour
Representation Committee/Labour Party had established its trade
union credentials and parliamentary achievements.

In August 1911, Victor Grayson, a controversial figure whose parliamentary by-election victory at Colne Valley in 1907 had been an
inspiration to British socialists, wrote that 'The time for the formation

---

[4] Howell, *British Workers and the Independent Labour Party*, 393–7.
[5] J. Hill, 'Social Democracy and the Labour Movement: the Social Democratic
Federation in Lancashire', *North West Labour History Society*, Bulletin 8, 1982–83.

of the BRITISH SOCIALIST PARTY had definitely come.'[6] He then called for others to follow his example and to withdraw from the Independent Labour Party, vowing never to join another socialist organisation until the BSP, the 'one socialist party', had been formed. Grayson's appeal worked briefly. There was a period of ecstatic enthusiasm leading up to the Socialist Unity conference in Manchester in September 1911, when a clamour of support emerged. Within a week of his appeal Grayson was writing that 'The British Socialist Party is practically an accomplished fact ... the response has been extraordinary.'[7] After the Unity Conference, Grayson wrote that it 'was the most harmonious and unanimous Conference of the kind that has ever been held'.[8] Throughout the autumn and winter months of 1911, hundreds of members of the ILP wrote to Grayson and the *Clarion* expressed their disgust at the recent policies of the Party and extending a warm welcome to the BSP.'[9] It seemed that the dream of uniting socialists of all persuasions under the umbrella of one organisation was about to become reality. The attempt had been made several times previously but this moment seemed propitious for Britain was experiencing a period of serious industrial unrest and both the ILP and the Labour Party were under attack because of their failure to lead in the fight for socialism. Yet support for the BSP seemed to evaporate almost as quickly as it had emerged. The vast majority of ILP members were not attracted to it and the new party, the BSP, was soon little more than the old Social Democratic Federation, then the Social Democratic Party, in a new form. Yet for a brief moment, carried forward by the impetus of Grayson's enthusiasm and changes within the SDF, the BSP promised to be something more. Some ILP members and their branches went over to the new organisation. Yet, in the end, the BSP left the ILP remarkably unscathed. The British Socialist Party was eventually undermined and destroyed by the bitter disagreements that had blighted earlier moves towards socialist unity and had made earlier efforts untenable.

The idea of forming a united socialist party was, clearly, not new in 1911 and, indeed, it was fitting that Grayson should begin his campaign in the *Clarion* for it was Robert Blatchford, its editor, who had set the precedent by his staunch advocacy of the ideal during the 1890s. In 1894, Robert Blatchford had called for the formation of 'One Socialist Party' maintaining that

[6] *Clarion*, 4 August 1911.
[7] *Ibid.*, 11 August 1911.
[8] *Ibid.*, 6 October 1911.
[9] *Ibid.*, 18 August 1911.

The only hope of the emancipation of Labour lies in Democratic
Socialism

A true Labour Party should therefore be a Socialist Party.

A true Socialist Party should consist of Socialists, and of none others
but Socialists.

Now, the Independent Labour Party does not consist wholly of
Socialists.

It has in its ranks very many men who are not Socialists. These men
are a source of danger and weakness.

I am perfectly convinced myself that the only men likely to fight
victoriously for Socialism are Socialists, and that the first and greatest
work of all true Socialists to undertake is the formation of a united
Socialist party ... I desire to see the one party, and I shall continue
to advocate the formation of one party, but if it is formed it must be
formed by the action of the members of the various existing bodies.[10]

Blatchford's clarion call was loud and clear; it was a demand that the
ILP, the SDF and the Clarion Scouts should submerge their differences
and unite all genuine socialists into one party. It was an extension to
the provinces, and to the whole of the socialist movement, of the
concept of unity amongst socialist organisations. Moves in that direction
had already occurred in London in 1892 and 1893. William Morris and
his Hammersmith Socialist Society, had promoted an agreement on
aspects of socialist thought which was carried to the SDF and the
Fabians. Yet, this movement aimed at seeking agreement upon points
of socialist theory rather than of building unity of action around issues
of common importance to all socialists.[11] The result was the rather
vague and imprecise, although too revolutionary for the Fabians,
Manifesto of English Socialists issued on May Day 1893. Apart from the
fact that it attempted to present a common ground between the Fabians
and the SDF, the main weakness of the document was that it was
agreed without reference to the newly-formed national ILP. Blatchford's
appeal was something of an attempt to rectify this omission and to
obtain unity of action among all socialist parties. Nevertheless, the
campaign proved to be mistimed and misplaced, and Blatchford's faith
was unfounded.

Blatchford's readers were being urged to form some type of socialist
fellowship, without regard to party affiliation, but hopefully with the
support of the ILP and the SDF leadership. In other words, he envisaged
the possibility of a mass socialist party, or fellowship, coming into
existence. Such support was not forthcoming, Hyndman was reluctant,

---

[10] *Ibid.*, 22 December 1894.
[11] E. P. Thompson, *William Morris, Romantic and Revolutionary* (1971), 605–10.

Keir Hardie positively hostile, and even Tom Mann, more favourably inclined than most to Blatchford's suggestions, was cautious.[12] The ILP was particularly concerned to present a clear and unclouded image to the electorate at the coming general election, and the National Administrative Council made it clear that it did not wish to confuse the electorate by changing the name of the party or by 'diverting the attention of the part from the main issues'. It had set its course, and socialist unity was to be no part of its strategy.[13]

Nevertheless, the failures of socialist and ILP candidates in the 1895 general election revived the prospects of socialist unity. The defeat of 29 ILP candidates, including Keir Hardie, stirred doubts about the wisdom of the ILP's policy. When its membership fell from 35,000 to 20,000 between 1895 and 1896, some members began to campaign to unify the ILP with the SDF. At this point, it is essential to understand the respective positions of the ILP and the SDF, the two main socialist organisations in Britain.

There were marked divisions within the ILP both between the leadership and the rank and file, and also within the rank and file based upon geographical differences. The ILP leadership was adamantly opposed to any moves towards unity with the SDF. The 1895 general election defeats had convinced the 'big four'—Keir Hardie, J. Bruce Glasier, Philip Snowden and J. Ramsay MacDonald—of the need to form a progressive alliance with the trade unions in order to win parliamentary seats. To them it thus became more important to win trade-union support than to rush headlong into socialism, and socialism was to be delayed, possibly until 1953 according to Hardie reflecting upon the 1,953 votes he had received in his unsuccessful parliamentary by-election contest at Bradford East in November 1896.[14] In any case, socialism became a long-term rather an immediate objective. As David Howell has suggested, the ILP leaders now became 'subject to con-servative influences'.[15] In contrast, some of the rank and file began to advocate a return to the business of 'making socialists' in the way that William Morris, Robert Blatchford and others advocated. This was a move towards the idea being put forward by Robert Blatchford, to whom Hardie was personally opposed.[16]

Nevertheless, faced with electoral defeats and a loss of membership

---

[12] *Clarion*, 22 December 1894 and subsequent issues indicate the nature of the response.

[13] NAC of the ILP, minute book M.890/1/1, Coll. Misc. 464, meetings for 1894, deposited in the British Library of Political Science.

[14] *Bradford Observer*, 12 November 1896.

[15] Howell, *British Workers and the ILP*, 118.

[16] Their hostility had been nurtured further in 1895 when Hardie supported John Lister, Treasurer of the ILP, against the local criticism of the Halifax ILP which had been nurtured by both Montague and Robert Blatchford.

Keir Hardie agreed to support the idea of a conference of all Socialist organisations, trade unions and co-operative bodies, and the ILP's Easter Conference of 1896 instructed the NAC to organise such a conference, an 'Informal Conference', which was held on 29 July 1897, after some preliminary meetings.

Initially, the SDF leadership was unwilling to respond to these overtures but appears to have changed its mind when a combination of financial difficulties, due to expenditure on the Southampton parliamentary by-election and internal pressure within the party, forced its leaders to think anew.[17] As a result it decided to send five delegates to the 'Informal Conference' where it was agreed that a joint committee would be set up until decisions were made about the nature and name of the new arrangement. An additional committee was formed to deal with arbitration in electoral disputes. Subsequently, H. W. Lee, secretary of the SDF, gave his support to attempts for 'real unity of people anxious and willing to work together for a common object' of socialist unity.[18] There was then a referendum of the joint membership of the ILP and the SDF which voted 5,158 to 886 in favour of fusion. Yet that decision was never implemented.

Keir Hardie immediately intervened to inform the ILP that less than one-third of its paying membership had in fact voted, and a decision on the ballot was postponed until the next annual conference. In the meantime, Hardie campaigned strongly against fusion, expressing his views through the pages of the *Labour Leader* and the *ILP News*. He maintained that 'Rigidity is fatal to growth as I think our SDF friends are finding out', and reflected upon the possible loss of trade-union support for the two organisations if they merged. His attitude was neatly presented in the *ILP News*:

> It may be that there is something in the methods of propaganda, if not in the principle,, of the SDF that not only renders it somewhat antipathetic to our members, but out of touch and harmony with the feelings and ideals of the mass of our people. If, too, it be the case that the SDF, even if not decaying, is not growing in membership, the indication would seem to be that it has not proceeded on the lines of British industrial evolution. It might be, therefore, that the introduction of its spirit and methods of attack would check rather than help forward our movement.[19]

Political expediency was clearly more important than socialist unity as Hardie began to campaign for federation. His leading spokesman of

[17] M. Crick, 'A Call to Arms', 184.
[18] *Justice*, 7 August 1897.
[19] *ILP News*, August 1897.

this strategy was J. Bruce Glasier, whose paper at the ILP Conference in Birmingham, of April 1897, maintained that federation and continued separate existence would be advantageous to the ILP. The crux of his argument was that

> the ways of the SDF are not our ways. If I may say so, the ways of the SDF are more doctrinaire, more Calvinistic, more aggressively sectarian than the ILP. The SDF has failed to touch the hearts of the people. Its strange disregard of the religious, moral and aesthetic sentiments of the people is an overwhelming defect. The ILP position, moreover, is better understood by the public. There is in truth, no party in the land whose aims are more clearly defined in the popular mind than ours. The trades unions have begun to rely upon us, and are depending upon our lead, and were we to abolish ourselves another ILP—perhaps owing to our desertion, a less resolute one— would inevitably take up our ground.[20]

What Glasier was doing was contrasting the ethical and nonconformist basis of much of the ILP support with the more economic-based Marxist tradition and was clearly exaggerating his case. But Glasier's views counted for a lot both in areas like the West Riding of Yorkshire, where the SDF had little support, and also amongst those ILPers who were also members of trade unions and were offended by Hyndman's well known opposition to industrial action. When faced with the decision to form socialist organisations in 1885, the socialists of Bradford and Leeds had opted to form branches of William Morris's Socialist League rather than Hyndman's SDF. The scandal of the SDF's acceptance of Tory money in contesting the 1885 election, the famous 'Tory Gold' issue, had also alienated many socialists from Hyndman and the SDF.

Not surprisingly, the National Administrative Council of the ILP supported Hardie's demand for federation and resolved that the decision between fusion and federation should be resolved by a new ballot of ILP members in which a three-quarter vote of the total membership in favour of fusion would have to be recorded if action were to be taken. The Conference accepted this advice and the vote was held in July 1898 when 2,397 voted for federation and 1,695 for fusion. The ILP leadership had, effectively blocked the prospect of a united socialist party being formed and H. W. Lee, stressed that the SDF was 'in favour of fusion'.[21] The discussions on socialist unity expired.

The belated efforts of Robert Blatchford to revive negotiations also failed. In spite of the *Clarion* decision to conduct a poll of its readers,

[20] *ILP Annual Conference Report*, 1898, 8.
[21] *Justice*, 27 August 1898.

which produced a vote of 4,429 for fusion and 3,994 for federation the ILP leaders were not inclined to be led from their refuge of 'federation'.[22]

The ILP leadership had thwarted the early attempts to form a socialist unity party in their desire to win trade union support. But how much support was there amongst the ILP rank and file for the socialist unity alternative? The available evidence suggests that there were deep divisions, very largely dependent upon geographical regions.

As both Martin Crick and Jeff Hill have suggested, there appears to have been strong support for the alliance idea in Lancashire, an area where both the SDF and the ILP were well entrenched. The idea of socialist unity appears to have emerged strongly in Salford in the early 1890s when the local SDF was active in the process which led to the formation of the local ILP and involved in the attempts to form a branch of the Gasworkers' Union at the Manchester and Salford Gasworks in the summer of 1889.[23] In other words, there was a sense of Labour solidarity evident in Salford, Manchester, Burnley, Blackburn and other centres. And Lancashire, as Watmough has pointed out, was, next to London, the most important centre of SDF activity—occasionally recording more members than the London branches were able to do.[24] Indeed, as Jeff Hill suggests, 'the most marked feature of SDF tactics in Lancashire was their flexibility.'[25] In the socialist unity debates of 1896 to 1898 support for fusion was firm from the Lancashire branches as indicated by the annual conference of 1896 when Fred Brocklehurst of Manchester introduced a motion to change the name the ILP's name to the 'National Socialist Party'. When it became known that the NAC had rejected the SDF's terms for fusion there was a strong and immediate reaction in Lancashire. Many branches felt that the NAC was cheating the party by insisting on an overwhelming vote in favour on the second ballot before the principle of fusion could proceed. The NAC attempted to justify its switch of policy with the SDF by asserting that 'In Blackburn, Nelson, Rochdale, Ashton and several other places the local branches of the ILP and SDF already work cordially side by side and for elections and many propaganda purposes are already virtually federated together'.[26] Many of the Lancashire ILP branches begged to differ and saw co-operation as the basis for fusion. Littleborough ILP called for 'one militant socialist party' whilst the branches at Droylsdon and Preston refused to enter the ILPs second ballot because they had already voted decisively for fusion.

[22] *Clarion*, 3 December 1898.

[23] Hill, 'Social-Democracy', 47, and *Justice*, 14 September 1889.

[24] P. A. Watmough, 'The Membership of the Social Democratic Foundation 1885–1902', *Society for the Study of Labour History Bulletin*, (Spring 1977), 35–40.

[25] Hill, 'Social Democracy', 51.

[26] *ILP Conference Report*, 1899.

Bolton West, Everton and Blackburn opposed the NAC, and Stockport announced its intention 'to withdraw from the party' as a protest against the undemocratic action of the NAC.'[27] Charles Higham, of the Blackburn ILP, emphasised the point at the 1899 national ILP conference when he claimed that the socialist co-operation in his own town illustrated the ridiculous position of the NAC and the ILP leadership.[28]

At the other extreme there was far less support for socialist unity in the textile region of the West Riding of Yorkshire, one of the major centres of ILP support. The West Riding was still one of the most active of the ILP areas even when ILP membership declined in the late 1890s. In 1897 the *ILP News* stated that 'Halifax has 730 paying members and these, being well organised, are probably the strongest socialist body in the country'.[29] At the same time the Bradford's branches recorded between 800 and 900 fee-paying members. The Keighley ILP had 120 members, the four main Huddersfield clubs had 235 members, and the Leeds, Hunslet and Holbeck branches had 237 members. Most other Yorkshire towns had small but viable branches. In fact, an examination of the 11,000 to 12,000 fee-paying members of the National ILP indicates that between 2,700 and 3,000 came from the West Riding.[30] The National ILP was strongly influenced by West-Riding opinion, which in turn was shaped by the attitudes of the powerful branches in Bradford and Halifax.

In Bradford the rejection of socialist unity was all too evident. In September and October 1897, there was almost total rejection of the idea. This is hardly surprising when one considers that the Bradford Labour Movement had built up a thriving club organisation of about twenty-seven or twenty-eight clubs and 2,000 members in the early 1890s, with considerable trade-union support. Even though their membership declined in the late 1890s they still provided social, educational and recreational activities for their members and their families and were a powerful political force within the working-class community.

There was no way in which the SDF could challenge the overwhelming dominance of the ILP. By the summer of 1895 it had only three modestly-sized branches in Leeds and smaller ones in Hull, Bingley and Low Bentham.[31] There was also a branch in Dewsbury

---

[27] Reports in the NAC Minute book, 16 June, 16 June–15 July and throughout August—September and November to December 1898. Also quoted in J. Hill, 'The ILP in Lancashire', in *The Centennial History of the ILP*, 50.

[28] Hill, 'The ILP in Lancashire', 50 and *ILP Conference Report*, 1899.

[29] *ILP News*, June 1897.

[30] *Ibid.*, September and October 1898 and March 1899.

[31] M. Crick, 'A Collection of Oddities': The Bradford Branch of the Social-Democratic Federation', *The Bradford Antiquary*, Third Series, number 5, 27.

which challenged and then took over the ILP and a small branch in Halifax. In August 1895, a Bradford branch was formed but it started with six members, never had more than 28, averaged about fifteen, and expired in 1897, and as Martin Crick states:

> Elsewhere in Yorkshire the outlook was similarly bleak. Of the three Leeds branches only Armley maintained an active existence. Low Bentham, Skipton and Sheffield branches clung tenuously to life until mid-1898 and they too collapsed. Those who were sympathetic to the SDF undoubtedly followed the example of W. P. Redfearn of Huddersfield who reported he had joined the ILP for want of a viable alternative and that he hoped eventually for the unity of the two parties. The only exception to this gloomy scenario was in Dewsbury, where an ILP branch had always supported socialist unity and had been sceptical as to the value of trade unions was 'organised out of existence' by a capable SDFer from Burnley.[32]

The fact is that the SDF presented no threat to the dominance of the ILP in the West Riding of Yorkshire and that the ILP branches, and particularly those in Halifax and Bradford, had established close links with the trade unions and were already pursuing the type of policies that Hardie was advocating. Thus, in 1896, the *Bradford Labour Echo* argued that 'The time has not come for the thorough fusion of forces which the creation of such a party would demand ... The formation of such a party before the time was ripe would bring nothing but mischief.'[33] Indeed, this was the dominant view, even though Keighley ILP voted in favour of fusion and the Morley branch seceded and the Dewsbury SDF and ILP branches fused.

Throughout 1898, when the Bradford ILP clubs were examining the possibility of reorganising the party into one centralised branch, rather than three constituency branches and numerous clubs, attempts to create a united socialist organisation failed. It is obvious that during the discussions various socialist societies had misinterpreted the intentions of the Bradford ILP when its general council had decided to meet a committee of 15 'outsiders'. This attempt to widen support was misunderstood. As the *Bradford Labour Echo* reflected:

> They the outsiders endeavoured to ignore the fact that the meeting was an ILP branch meeting, and proceeded to treat the gathering as one specially called to bring into being an entirely new Socialist party. Some of the outsiders who proposed to serve on the committee

[32] *Ibid.*, 28–9 and *Clarion*, 20 December 1901.
[33] *Bradford Labour Echo*, 11 April 1896.

withdrew their names, when the meeting passed the following resolution: 'That the fifteen members elected from the meeting should
declare themselves Socialists who were willing to become members
of the ILP under the reconstituted constitution.' Carried by an
overwhelming majority...

The *Bradford Observer* report, reprinted in the same issue of the *Echo*,
was even more direct: 'One fact made quite clear was that no fusion
of Socialist Sections is intended. The representatives of various smaller
Socialist bodies attended, and did their best to turn the discussion into
this groove, but entirely without avail.'

There was little support for the idea of fusion within the Bradford
ILP and equally little support for the idea in Halifax. The July 1898
issue of the *Record*, organ of the Halifax ILP, did refer to the 'One
Socialist Party' campaign going on in Bradford but played down its
importance, doubting its 'practical superiority' to the existing situation.
The report argued that the term fusion suggested a hardening of social
policies which did not fit the more general approach favoured by the
members of the Halifax ILP. Also most ILP members spent a working
week protected by trade-union surveillance, and weekends attending
Labour Church activities, glee club meetings and rambles. Satisfied
with their achievements they were not inclined to join forces with a
society which had little presence in Halifax and which appeared to
play down the value of trade unionism. On the whole one is left with
the impression that socialist unity barely merited serious consideration
in the ILP strongholds of Bradford and Halifax. Also, the Yorkshire
Divisional Council of the ILP had rejected the idea, by 32 voters to
sixteen, as early as October 1894.[34] In Bradford, Halifax and more
generally throughout the West Riding of Yorkshire there was little or
no inclination to join with an organisation that carried no political
weight or support. Martin Crick has suggested, the socialist unity
movement was probably a movement from the bottom up, but even
this is partial and barely evident in some areas, most notably the West
Riding of Yorkshire.

It would appear that there was little prospect that socialist unit would
be achieved in the late 1890s. There were four main reasons for this.
In the first place the ILP leaders and many of their supporters had
attached their flags to the trade union mast. Secondly, there were
intense rivalries within the broader socialist movement between Hardie
and Blatchford on the one hand, and between Hardie and Hyndman
on the other. Thirdly, if the ILP was driven by political expediency so
was the SDF, whose leadership showed no inclination towards socialist

---

[34] *Labour Leader*, 6 October 1894.

unity until it began to lose members in the late 1890s and once the Southampton parliamentary by-election faced it with financial embarrassment. Fourthly, whilst just under half the rank and file members of the ILP favoured fusion the other half, possibly the majority, favoured federation and it was this second body, firmly based in Yorkshire, which carried most political clout with the ILP leaders. Given these facts it is not surprising that the attempts at socialist unity in the 1890s ended in failure, and that future efforts would be blighted by similar problems.

It is true, as Martin Crick suggests, that there was nothing unusual in socialists having dual membership with the ILP and the SDF. Quite clearly it didn't matter to many socialists which organisation they joined for to them a socialist Britain was imminent. But after the 1895 general election defeats it was more difficult to sustain hope for the immediate success of socialism and electioneering and leadership considerations got in the way of sustaining any hopes of socialist success. Indeed, the experience of Lancashire should not be emphasised too much for, as Jeff Hill suggests, there were two factors that needed to be taken into consideration. One is that the Lancashire SDF branches acted more flexibly than their parent organisation did, and some branches still remained in the Labour Representation Committee even after their parent organisation had left. Secondly, they paid a price for their flexibility for, as Jeff Hill suggests, 'Though on the one hand local autonomy was a source of strength in that it allowed social-democrats to adapt to their immediate environment, on the other hand, it produced a movement notoriously prone to internal divisions over strategy and one which ultimately was unable to preserve its identity as a united socialist force.'[35]

Even if socialist unity had been achieved it seems unlikely that it would have survived. Most probably, the ILP would have split, with Hardie leading his West Yorkshire contingent and other supporters into an alternative ILP-like organisation. In effect the SDF would probably have been left with its own supporters and a few other socialists, much as occurred when the British Socialist Party was formed in 1911.

There was a second phase in the development of socialist unity at the beginning of the twentieth century. The Labour Representation Committee [LRC] was formed as a result of a conference held in February 1900 and, at first sight, appeared to have met the needs of both alternative strategies for the progress of the Labour movement. On the one hand, it was an alliance between the trade unions and the

---

[35] Hill, 'Social Democracy', 53.

socialist parties and, on the other, it brought the socialist parties, including the SDF and the ILP, into one organisation. Although the LRC was not a socialist organisation, as such, five of the twelve members of the Executive Committee were Socialists and there was a prospect that this alliance could be the basis of a closer co-operation between the SDF and the ILP. Yet within eighteen months of the founding conference the SDF voted to secede. This decision was taken because 'We were being committed to the support of men and measures with which we did not agree'.[36] Indeed, the ILP and SDF had clashed from the outset when the ILP failed to support the SDF resolution committing the LRC to socialist objectives.

The SDF's secession from the LRC was a mistake for it now cut itself off from the most influential independent political organisation of the working classes, although its action is explicable in terms of the internal difficulties within the party which led to the secession of two groups who formed the Socialist Party of Great Britain and the Socialist Labour Party, usually known as the 'Impossibilists'.

At this point the SDF appears to have revived its interest in socialist unity. Whether that was ever a realistic option seemed doubtful and David Howell has concluded that socialist unity had effectively been ruled out by the formation of the LRC: 'The logic of national events ... combined with local developments ... to erode the United Socialist alternatives, even in an environment where it had developed a significant presence.'[37]

Only Martin Crick seems to doubt this judgement. He bases his assessment upon a number of factors but, most importantly, the situation that existed in Lancashire, which has already been referred to. Quite clearly, there was a demand for socialist unity in Lancashire but this did not represent the dominant feeling of the ILP members many of who were drawn to the prospect of working through the LRC alliance at both the local and national levels. In any case, the Lancashire SDF branches, who had pushed the SDF towards affiliating with the LRC were dismayed by the withdrawal of their parent organisation and this appears to have caused something of a slump in the SDF activities in the county.

Crick's second line of argument is to stress that the Dewsbury parliamentary by-election of 1902 provided an insight of what could be achieved by socialist unity at a period when ILP and LRC parliamentary victories were still thin on the ground. His argument is that the SDF

---

[36] H. W. Lee and E. Archbold, *Social Democracy in Britain*, 159 quoted in Crick 'A Call to Arms', 187.

[37] D. Howell, 'Was the Labour Party Inevitable?', *The Bulletin of the North-West Labour History Society*, (1984), 17.

put forward Harry Quelch, the editor of *Justice*, as the SDF candidate because it feared that the local Trades Council and the ILP would impose a compromise Lib-Lab candidate, Sam Woods of the Wigan Miners, who might be accepted by the local Liberals. The Trades Council and ILP reaction of putting forward Edward Robertshaw Hartley, a butcher who was soon to become a member of both the SDF and the ILP, rebounded because he refused the candidature and gave his support to Quelch. He later added that 'The great work of the official section of the ILP at present seems not so much to push Socialism as to try and intrigue some half-a-dozen persons into Parliament.[38] And yet, despite the opposition of the Trades Council and the ILP, the electorate of Dewsbury gave 1,597 votes to Quelch, 517 votes more than Hartley had secured in the 1895 general election. Here was, as A. M. Thompson of the *Clarion*, wrote

> a crushing blow to the conflicting 'Leaders' and a triumphant vindication of Socialist Unity ... The rank and file of Dewsbury have shown the way. Socialists of all denominations have shut their eyes to the scowlings and nudgings of rival party officials and stood shoulder to shoulder for Socialism.[39]

The actions of the ILP were further criticised by a plethora of letters and articles in *Justice*, which, amongst other things, attacked the doctrines of the ILP as 'a heterogeneous conglomeration of absurdities and self contradictions. Their principles, as exemplified and illustrated by their tactics, are no principles but only political expediency.'[40]

Crick's viewpoint is highly biased in favour of the SDF and thus open to the criticism that it lacks balances. If, for instance, the Dewsbury parliamentary by-election of February 1902 caused a 'damaging split in the Labour movement' as Crick suggests, why should this necessarily revive the spirit of Socialist Unity?[41] There was, indeed, some criticism within ILP ranks about the effectiveness of the LRC but equally there was strong commitment to the view that trade unionists should be drawn into the independent political labour movement.

The ILP also retorted to the SDF's actions with a fusillade of abuse against the charge that the SDF had cheated by calling a joint meeting of all the Labour organisations to elect a candidate and then had pre-empted the meeting by announcing Harry Quelch to be their candidate.

[38] *Clarion*, 7 December 1901.
[39] *Ibid.*, 7 February 1902.
[40] *Justice*, 4 January 1902.
[41] M. Crick, 'Labour Alliance or Socialist Unity? The Independent Labour Party in the Heavy Woollen Areas of West Yorkshire, c. 1893–1902', in *'The Rising Sun of Socialism': The Independent Labour Part in the Textile District of the West Riding of Yorkshire between 1890 and 1914*, (eds.) K. Laybourn and D. James (1991), 38.

The *ILP News* reflected that

> The SDF has taken up the attitude of having its own isolated and impossibilist way, and setting up at defiance the ILP and the Trades Council. It is unity no doubt—the unity of itself. [...] We are disputing the pretence under which he has been placed in the field as 'the Socialist and Trade Union candidate', and we are disputing the suggestion that his candidature is anything but an unnecessary and humiliating reproach upon the reputation of Socialism. [...] An isolated SDF candidate would prove a very lamentable and futile political escapade, and would provide a very bad advertisement for Socialism in the West Riding of Yorkshire. Without the cardinal co-operation of the Trades Unions, no third, not to speak of a fourth candidate, would receive an effective vote in the division.[42]

And 1,597 votes was not that good when one considers that Hartley had contested the seat in 1895 when socialist fortunes were in decline. With more voters and a well-organised trade union movement the vote should have been much larger. Compared to the Conservative vote of 4,512 and the Liberal vote of 5,660, Quelch's vote was small, being about 14 per cent of the votes that were cast.[43]

The second phase of Socialist Unity, if it can be regarded as such, did not lead very far but Crick is quite correct to suggest that there were strong moves towards its further advocacy between 1904 and 1911, although that is not to suggest that it was a viable proposition. The SDF certainly changed its attitude towards Socialist Unity and fully embraced the Amsterdam Conference resolution of 1904 which instructed Socialist parties in all countries to amalgamate. It made approached to renew negotiations with the ILP in 1907, 1909 and 1910 but the ILP laid down the precondition that the SDF should re-affiliate with the SDF. It would also appear that the SDF became internally divided over the issues of industrial conflict and international relations as new figures in the party, such as Zelda Kahan, began to challenge Hyndman, Quelch and the other established leaders of the SDF/SDP. Undoubtedly the rising emphasis which the SDF placed upon Socialist Unity was a distraction from these internal conflicts but it was hardly going to offer a solution to the conflicts within the SDF/SDP nor a solution to the problem of policy as it emerged in the British Socialist

---

[42] *ILP News*, October 1901.

[43] K. Laybourn and J. Reynolds, *Liberalism and the Rise of Labour 1890–1918* (1984), 153. Ben Turner obtained 21.3 per cent of the vote in the 1906 general election and 20.2 per cent in the parliamentary by-election of April 1908.

Party. The SDF/SDP may have become less narrowly economically deterministic in its attitudes but the dominating influence of Hyndman's view was still present in the vital years when the BSP was being formed.

There were quite clearly other factors which encouraged the idea of reviving Socialist Unity apart from the convenience it offered to the SDF/SDP. The membership of all socialist organisations rose substantially between 1906 and 1909. In addition, the return of 29 LRC MPs to Parliament brought an optimism about social change that was not going to be realised, even by a Labour Party working upon a reforming Liberal government. The contrast between Labour Party inaction and rising socialist ambitions certainly increased tensions between some members of the ILP and the Labour Party.

Victor Grayson echoed this disillusionment on Parliament following his success in the Colne Valley parliamentary by-election in 1907. His views were outlined in a book entitled *The Problem of Parliament—A Criticism and a Remedy*, published in 1909 and dedicated to 'H. M. Hyndman, R. Blatchford and J. Keir Hardie, who can give this country a Socialist party tomorrow if they care to lead the way.'[44] At much the same time E. R. Hartley was arguing in a debate at Manchester that the ILP was 'swamped' within the Labour Party.[45] Indeed, between 1909 and 1911, 46 branches of the ILP collapsed. The moment seemed propitious for a renewal of the Socialist Unity debate.

Indeed, the criticism of the ILP intensified. Towards the end of 1910 four of the fourteen members of the NAC of the ILP signed the pamphlet *Let Us Reform the Labour Party*, better known as the 'Green Manifesto'. Written by J. McLachlan, a Manchester councillor, introduced by Leonard Hall, and contributed to by C. T. Douthwaite and the Rev. J. H. Belcher, it attacked the ILP and Labour Party tendency to sacrifice socialist principles in order not to embarrass the Liberal government. Subsequently, Fred Jowett criticised these men for their lack of loyalty and all lost their seats on the NAC at the annual conference in 1911.

Also, it should not be overlooked that in Birmingham, Manchester and many other towns, social representation committees were emerging to unite socialists of all persuasions. Many socialists were not attached to the two main socialist parties and a United Socialist Propaganda League was formed to combine them together and to spread the message to the rural areas.[46] Indeed, there was sufficient evidence to encourage Grayson, now free of his parliamentary duties and political

---

[44] Quoted in W. Kendall, *The Revolutionary Movement in Britain* (1971), 37.

[45] J. M. McLachlan and E. Hartley, *Should Socialists Join the Labour Party—A verbatim report of the debate* (1909).

[46] *Clarion*, 7 July 1911.

editor of the *Clarion*, that a call for socialist unity would be well received. As it was, within two months, it proclaimed that 'if the BSP has not up to the present absorbed at least thirty per cent of the Independent Labour Party our forms are liars and ought to be torn up.'[47] The *Labour Leader* countered with the suggestion that only about five per cent of ILPers had left for the BSP. However, there certainly seemed to be considerable support as Grayson toured the West Riding of Yorkshire and south Lancashire addressing 'a magnificent meeting at Colne Valley' and speaking to large audiences at St George's Hall, Bradford.[48]

But how many ILP members were won over to the BSP? There is no denying the divisive impact of Grayson's appeal upon the Yorkshire ILP branches. Apart from the Colne Valley Socialist League, the Wakefield ILP branch withdrew from the ILP and a new BSP branch of 70 members was formed.[49] A large number of individual members of the ILP also joined the BSP. Grayson's estimate of thirty per cent, however, may have been excessive. An estimate of twenty per cent would appear to be nearer the mark,[50] and Crick has suggest about twenty five per cent for Lancashire.[51] Within a couple of years the figures were to diminish significantly as individuals and branches drifted out of the BSP. J. Bruce Glasier's comment in October 1911 ultimately proved correct: 'The new party is merely the SDP under a new name.'[52]

In the meantime the SDF/SDP was conducting its own moves towards socialist unity and suggesting to its members that they should not complete the *Clarion* forms but await the Unity Conference at Manchester. Grayson's response to this was to suggest, in advance of Glasier's comment, that their plan will amount to 'little more than an enlargement of the SDF.'[53] Blatchford gave his support and suggested that beyond the basic principles of socialism the BSP would be a wide, all-embracing party, committed to both industrial and political action.[54] The potential was there for conflict but matters went smoothly on the weekend of 30 September to 1 October when the Socialist Unity Conference was held at Manchester, at which delegates claiming to represent 35,000 members, including 41 ILP branches, 32 Clarion clubs and fellowships, 85 SDF/SDP branches, 50 local Socialist Societies and

[47] *Ibid.*, 13 October 1911.

[48] *Ibid.*, 11 August and 22 September 1911.

[49] *Clarion*, 8 December 1911.

[50] Laybourn, 'A Story of Buried Talents and Wasted Opportunities', 22.

[51] M. Crick presented this percentage in a lecture at the Conference on the Centennial History of the ILP held at the University of Bradford, 30 January 1993 but some hint of this level is also indicated in D. Morris, 'The Origins of the British Socialist Party', *North West Labour History Society, Bulletin 8*, 1982–83, 34–5.

[52] L. Thompson, *The Enthusiasts: A Biography of John and Katherine Bruce Glasier* (1971), 169.

[53] *Clarion*, 11 August 1911.

[54] *Ibid.*

12 branches of the new BSP, plus other organisations, attended.

Yet the tensions soon surfaced for the Conference set up a Provisional Committee to prepare the constitution and Grayson, a member of that committee, soon realised that the SDP/SDF would not cease to exist as a separate organisation until the first annual conference in 1912. However, his main objection was that the Provisional Committee, of which he was a member, had not been given the authority to set up the BSP and he felt that the 'new Party must make a fresh start or it is doomed to failure.'[55] Nevertheless, the BSP was formed by the SDP and Grayson withdrew his support, many of his followers lost interest in the BSP and the Colne Valley Socialist League whilst still sending delegates to BSP conferences never paid its fees. The membership claimed by the BSP on the eve of the first annual conference were thus exaggerated. The 1,000 members claimed by the West Yorkshire District Council included several hundred members from Colne Valley who were not paying membership fees to the BSP and the 400 members claimed for Bradford seems something of an exaggeration.[56]

There is, perhaps, only a fine distinction to be drawn between the loss of support resulting from Grayson's departure and that which resulted from the internal difficulties within the movement, for both sprang from the dominance of the old inflexible SDF/SDP leadership which, as in the past, continued to undermine any possibility of achieving socialist unity. There may have been moments when the old SDF leadership proved less than dominant but not in the years 1911 and 1914. Hyndman's opening address to the first annual conference of the BSP in April 1912 also betrayed the contradictions within the Party. Whilst emphasising the success of the new body he admitted that there had been difficulties. Most revealing was his reference to the syndicalists, a group of industrial activists led by Tom Mann who hoped to capture the existing trade-union structure for the rank and file and to bring unity and militancy to trade unionism.[57] Although the BSP had declared itself for both industrial and political action, Hyndman returned to his old criticism of industrial action stating that 'of the futility of resuscitated syndicalism it is needless to speak. There is nothing real and nothing ideal in the floundering and hysterical propaganda of segregated grab.'[58]

Such a statement from the chair made the 'old guard' position clear. They would concede that 'The political and industrial organisations of the working class must be complementary to each other', but their

---

[55] Ibid., 5 January 1912, in an article written jointly by Tom Groom and Victor Grayson.
[56] Justice, 2 March 1912, and 9 December 1911.
[57] Conference BSP, 1912, 8.
[58] Ibid., 8.

view that the main function of the Socialist Party was the organisation of an independent political party of the working class' remained unchanged. Campaigning along this line appeared in the pages of *Justice* and the *British Socialist* before the first annual BSP conference in May 1912 and this thwarted the efforts by E. C. Fairchild, and other old SDF stalwarts, to synthesise political and industrial action.[59] Thus when, Leonard Hall, a syndicalist, moved an amendment at the first annual conference to reduce 'the organisation of an independent political party of the working class' to the one main function of the Party he met with vehement opposition. 'The Trades Union Congress was the expression of their industrial action', said Quelch, and it 'would be gross impertinence on their part to say the main functions of a Socialist Party was to organise and conduct industrial operations.' Hall's amendment was defeated but it had gained the support of about a third of the delegates with forty-six for and 100 against.

The syndicalist debate continued for several months with Hyndman and Harry Quelch attempting to counter the syndicalist articles and speeches of Gaylord Wilshire, Leonard Hall and Russell Smart. The eventual brake came in October 1912, when the BSP *Manifesto* was issued, emphasising the primacy of political over industrial action. Hall and Smart rejected the *Manifesto* and were supported by the Rev Conrad Noel, also a member of the Executive Council, who considered it to be 'disastrously one-sided' and felt that it did not express 'the feelings of the members of the British Socialist Party'.[60]

This division of opinion cut right across the BSP and halted its progress in its tracks. Fred Knee reflected this block to growth in his annual report in *The Socialist Annual* of 1913, commenting that

> I finished my last year's article on a note of exultant hope. This time I have to strike a lower key. Despite the unity achieved at Manchester in the autumn of 1911, and the subsequent formation of the British Socialist Party, the movement has not done well, the new body has spoken with too many tongues, and till now it has lacked anything like unity of purpose or of doctrine.[61]

Many BSP branches were clearly divided on the issue. The Huddersfield BSP, led by Arthur Gardiner, was a strong advocate of industrial action partly owing to the local popularity of H. Russell Smart, who had once contested Huddersfield in a parliamentary election, and also owing to the pioneer propaganda work on E.J.B. Allen, who lived locally.[62] It

---

[59] *Clarion*, 26 April 1912.
[60] *Justice*, 10 November 1912.
[61] *The Socialist Annual*, 1913, annual report of Fred Knee.
[62] Laybourn, 'A Story of Buried Talents and Wasted Opportunities', 25.

passed a resolution committing itself to socialist representation and 'to assist in the building up of a powerful union movement'.[63] In other areas there was serious division within the local BSP branch. This was most evident in the case of Birmingham where H. B. Williams, the Secretary of the local branch, found himself in conflict with Leonard Hall, Thomas R. Wintringham and others over industrial unionism, the 'Graysonian clot' on the party and other related issues.[64] Industrial unionism was to prove a stumbling block to the BSP as industrial action had proved to be to the SDF in earlier years.

This split was, however, just one of the tensions that divided the BSP. International affairs and defence matters continued as source of internal conflict for in December 1912 Zelda Kahan succeeded, by the narrowest of margins, in getting the BSP to oppose increased government naval expenditure in opposition to Hyndman.[65] As a consequence the old guard of the SDP/SDF rounded upon her and her supporters through articles in *Justice* to reverse the decision. As a result she resigned, citing the dangerously imperialistic attitudes of 'our Fuhrer' as being a cause of danger to the BSP but noting that the Executive has reversed the decision on armaments in the absence of four important opponents of the idea and with only five Executive Committee members present.[66]

Internal conflict, very much engendered by the intransigence of Hyndman and his supporters, led to the rapid decline of the BSP. Support had faded away, particularly in Yorkshire where only the slimmed down Bradford branches, and the Leeds branches directed by Bert Killip, appear to have carried any significant weight. Even then, the Leeds BSP decided in April 1913, by a large majority, to affiliate to the local Labour Party.[67] The BSP faced further problems as Twentieth Century Press, which produced *Justice* and other socialist journals, fell into the hands of the receivers as the new company failed to raise an eighth of the share finance it required.[68] The 'enrol a Million Socialists' campaign, begun in August 1912, also failed to get anywhere near the 100,000 it wished to win in less than a year, never mind the million it hoped for in five years.[69] In fact BSP membership fell from a claimed

---

[63] A. Gardiner Scrap Book. The source of the newspapers quotation is not indicated.

[64] BSP Papers 1910–1914 (Birmingham), in the British Library or Political and Economic Science, Coll. Misc. 155, M228, collected by H. B. Williams. Note particularly item 48/49/5-, and item 46, the letter from Wintringham to Williams.

[65] Look at Zelda Kahan's article 'Peace and its Perils' in *British Socialists*, I, 1912, 56–68 and *Justice* from December 1912 to March 1913.

[66] *Justice*, 15 March 1913.

[67] *Bradford Pioneer*, 11 April 1913.

[68] *Justice*, 8 February 1913.

[69] The *Clarion*, 21 June 1912 referred to the BSP decision to go for five million members during the next five years but in the same issue a report on the first annual conference of the BSP refers to H. Russell Smart stating the objective of raising 500,000 Socialists

40,000 in 1912 to a mere 15,313 by the time of the 1913 Blackpool Conference.[70] By 1913, the BSP was little more than the old SDP/SDF rump.

In such a climate of failure the BSP reversed overnight its policy of viciously attacking the Labour Party and the ILP and once again attempted to woo the ILP and the Labour Party. In the summer of 1913 the BSP leaders met with ILP and Fabian representatives to discuss the formation of a 'United Socialist Council', and membership of the Labour Party. Presiding over this love feast was the International Socialist Bureau. The suddenness of this transformation was remarkable for an organisation which had unstintingly criticised the Labour Party for its lack of class struggle and had complained that it was 'nothing more or less than the tail of the capitalist Liberal Party'.[71]

Nevertheless, many of the old guard came out in support of the new line, including H. M. Hyndman, Zelda Kahan, J. Hunter Watts, Fred Gorle, and Dan Irving and George Moore Bell, who summed up the new spirit when he wrote that

> The English people won't have a Socialist Party. They like compromise, and the Labour Party is a compromise. Up to date a very poor one; but it is *there* and we are *here*. It lacks spirit and courage, and knowledge. Are we going to help it get these things? Shall we take the field, or shall we leave it to the Liberals?[72]

These views were opposed by Harry Quelch, who was ill and died in September 1913, Thomas Kennedy and H. Russell Smart who felt that Socialism would be 'thrust into the background in favour of weak and ineffective reformist policy'[73]

Finally, the December 1913 Conference of the BSP decided to hold meetings with the ILP and the Fabians in order to organise four socialist demonstrations in 1914—at Cardiff on 1 March, Newcastle on 8 March, Glasgow on 15 March and at Leeds on 22 March, and others to be held later. The Third BSP Conference held in London 1914 went further and, having debated Socialist Unity decided upon holding a referendum of its members on Socialist Unity and affiliation to the Labour Party.[74] The result was a marginal victory in favour of affiliation to the Labour Party by 3,263 votes to 2,410.[75] As a result the BSP

---

and £10,000. Also look at the 'Enrol a Million Socialist Campaign' report in *Justice*, 31 August 1913.

[70] *Justice*, 31 August and 7 September 1912; Kendall, *Revolutionary Movement*, 312.

[71] *Justice*, 9 November 1912.

[72] *Ibid.*, 9 August 1913.

[73] *Ibid.*, 6 September 1913.

[74] *Ibid.*, 16 April 1914.

[75] *Ibid.*, 28 May 1914.

applied to join the Labour Party on 23 June 1914 and affiliated in 1916. In October 1916 a not very effective United Socialist Council was also formed.[76]

Stephen Yeo has written that the formative socialist period of the 1880s and 1890s was 'too exciting to last' and added that 'Socialism in that period had not yet become the prisoner of a particular elaborate party machine—a machine which would come to associate its own well-being with the prospects for Socialism.'[77] He was right for by the mid and late 1890s party electioneering was rapidly taking the place of the task of 'making socialists'. By that time, also, the ILP and the SDF had become almost sectarian in their approach which meant that there was little prospect of creating a Socialist Unity party. If it was the ILP leaders who were intransigent opponents of Socialist Unity in the 1890s, as they sought the support of the trade unions, it was equally the case that the SDF/SDP leaders of the 1911 to 1914 period were also intransigent for there was little evidence that Hyndman was going to change his mind on the issue of industrial action and defence. Martin Crick might be right that Hyndman's domination of the SDP/SDF was not total but it was still sufficient, until he was effectively ejected in 1916, to thwart attempts to united and keep socialists on one mass party.

In the final analysis, Socialist Unity was effectively a non-starter after the formation of the LRC in 1900, if not before, killed by the rigidity of both ILP and SDF leaders. Hardie, Hyndman and their close supporters had ensured that this would be the case. The fact that there were close relations between the ILP and the SDF branches, and dual membership, in some areas like Lancashire is of little significance because, as Jeff Hill noted, the sheer flexibility of the Lancashire SDF branches made them prone to internal strife and compromise. In any case areas like the West Riding of Yorkshire were dominated by the powerful Bradford and Halifax ILP organisations who would have no truck with Socialist Unity and were already operating a trade union alliance. By 1909 Victor Grayson's appeal to Hyndman, Blatchford and Keir Hardie 'who can give this country a Socialist party tomorrow if they care to lead the way' was already too late. As the Communist Party of Great Britain, the successor of the BSP, was to find, mass party socialism within a united socialist party in Britain has proved to be an appealing illusion.

[76] D. Marquand, *Ramsay MacDonald* (1977), 200, 208–9.
[77] Yeo, 'Religion of Socialism', 31.

LIBERAL TORYISM IN THE TWENTIETH CENTURY

By Michael Bentley

READ 25 SEPTEMBER AT THE UNIVERSITY OF SHEFFIELD

DUST has scarcely had time to settle on Lady Thatcher; yet already a thick sediment of historical significance attaches to the fifteen years of her ascendancy. The period between 1975 and 1990 looks likely to prove as significant for the political ideologies of the twenty-first century as that between, say, 1885 and 1906 currently looks for our own.[1] In the twilight world of John Major (who appears part-antidote, part-surrogate), Conservative ideology is becoming informed by reviews from both sides as they reflect on not only what went wrong but what it was that seemingly went so right, from a party point of view, for so long. We have just had placed before us, for example, John Campbell's admirable biography of Sir Edward Heath, on the one hand, and Alan Clark's transfixing diaries very much on the other.[2] Such documents supplement a mass of theorising and comment by political scientists and journalists, most of which dwells on the twin themes of discontinuity and dichotomy. The history of the Tory party is seen to enter a period of catastrophe by the end of the Heath government out of which there emerges a distinct party ideology which people call 'Thatcherism': a 'New Conservatism' radically distinct from the compromise and accommodation that marked politics after 1951. But that process was contested within the party—hence a dichotomy between two per-suasions: the hawks and the doves, the dries and the wets, the Tories and the Conservatives, the true blues and the Liberals. Language of this kind has a particular interest to historians. They want to raise issues about its chronological deep-structure: how 'new' was this 'New Conservatism'?. They recognise the need to situate the dichotomies of the moment in a wider context of Conservative experience: how singular is a doctrine of dichotomy within Conservative party doctrine? Above all they bring into question bald postulates about the nature of current Conservatism which do not compare experience across time.

One of the axes along which modern Conservative history might be

---

[1] It will be evident that this paper, first projected during the period of Mrs Thatcher's government, has been written for oral delivery. I have chosen to retain that patina for the printed version.

[2] John Campbell, *Edward Heath* (1993); Alan Clark, *Diaries* (1993).

aligned seems obvious to a nineteenth-century historian in the light of current comment. It concerns a tradition in Conservative thought and practice which, in its Victorian phase, is called Liberal Toryism and which, because of its historical and ideological implications, comments sharply on what may be happening during the last quarter of the twentieth century. From the very beginning of the Thatcherite contagion, its values and assumptions have helped form the language of discontinuity and dichotomy. Michael Wolff, senior speechwriter for Edward Heath, had exploded when the new order appeared in 1975: 'They want to destroy the past. It cannot be done and it should not be done.'[3] So much for continuity. Dichotomy, meanwhile, soon took upon itself the vocabulary of Liberalism as a term of abuse among those who voiced the new orthodoxies. Indeed, people like Douglas Hurd became resentful about being described as 'Liberal' simply because they had supported Heath against Thatcher.[4] It became a dry theme nonetheless that opposition to Mrs Thatcher and her works rested on a secret commitment to an unstated Liberal Toryism, a sin that dare not speak its name. Even before Mrs Thatcher had reached Downing Street, Maurice Cowling had warned about such loiterers in a polemical essay called 'The Present Position':

> [Mr St John Stevas and Sir Ian Gilmour] mistrust popular agitation and are using a 'moderate' position in order in part at least to expose the unreality of its expectations. This in a way could be salutary. The reason why it is not is that, in addition to rejecting the principles they associate with it, they are committed to another set of principles—the principles for which Lord Boyle died politically on the way to the University of Leeds and Mr David Lane on the way to the Race Relations Board—the principles of 'Liberal-Conservatism' in the form in which Lord Butler established them in the Conservative party between 1940 and 1964 ... Mr Lane, perhaps, is an unfortunate example; not everybody who praises liberal Conservatism actually believes in it.[5]

The Clark diaries suggest that this style of allegation held good to the end of the Thatcherite period. Thus Ian Gow's loathing for Peter Bottomley becomes interesting for its ground: that he regarded Bottomley as a 'closet Liberal'.[6] Even after Armageddon, at the first dinner

---

[3] Patrick Cosgrave, *Thatcher: the first term* (1985), 9.

[4] Witness Hurd's remark after he was attacked for the Peterhead prison riot in 1987. 'People pin the label "liberal" on me. In don't think I am.' *Sunday Telegraph*, 4 Oct. 1987.

[5] Maurice Cowling, 'The Present Position', in Cowling (ed.), *Conservative Essays* (1978), 13.

[6] Clark diary 26 Nov. 1985, in *Diaries*, p. 123. Bottomley had described herself to his local newspaper as 'basically a good Liberal'.

at Saltwood following the excitements in Paris, Clark was pleased to record, 'We are all (except for dear Tristan) true Tories', sounding quite as though Lord Bayford or Lord Eustace Percy were expected.[7] Contrast the tone and content of Douglas Hurd's attempt to defend Heath's manifesto of 1970 as an appropriate detergent for the Wilsonian stable. 'It is the note struck by Pym against the court of Charles I, by Pitt against the Fox-North coalition, by Gladstone against Disraeli, by the Conservatives in 1922 against Lloyd George. It is the outraged assertion of a strict view of what public life is about, after a period in which its rulers have been perverted and its atmosphere corrupted.'[8]

Because Liberal Toryism is an historical contention, it requires the perpetual use of the past by both its champions and detractors. Conservatives in any case spend their lives reversing into the future: one steers by keeping the wake straight as part of that 'enactment of historical vitality' that Professor Scruton placed near the centre of Conservative ideology in a well-known account.[9] But there is a strange asymmetry in party presentations of its own history. Rather in the way that Asquithian sympathies dominated the history of the Liberal party until the 1970s, so Conservative history has been filtered, not least because Liberal Tories have done much of the filtering, in order to represent one of the continuities in that history as though it were the central one, sometimes as though it were the only one. This impinges on a number of historical discussions of which the nature of Thatcherite Toryism is simply a prominent example. For if the Conservative party could acquire a more plural history as part of its canon of self-beliefs, some of the contentions currently made about continuity and internal fractures might come under question. This short paper can hardly supply the deficiency, but it may help concentrate the mind on one of the canon's most slippery elements. It will consider some formulations of Liberal Toryism as an organising principle and reject most of them before suggesting three propositions that may prove less vulnerable. What is to be gained from the astringency is the issuing of cautions against simply seeing a collection of discrete politicians as 'Tory men with Whig measures'[10] or, on the other side, giving Liberal Toryism some essentialist reading that enables supporters to state its core-beliefs with more assurance than plausibility. Besides, these people offer a

---

[7] *Ibid.*, 6 Jan. 1991, 387. The 'Tristan' was Tristan Garel-Jones.

[8] Quoted in Campbell, *Heath*, 271.

[9] Roger Scruton, *The Meaning of Conservatism* (1980), 21.

[10] J. H. Grainger, *Character and Style in English Politics* (Cambridge, 1969), 220. The problem derives from seeing men as different as Peel, Disraeli, Neville Chamberlain and Macmillan complicit in some linear tradition, or from hoping that a simultaneous presentation of the view of T. E. Utley, R. A. Butler and R. J. White will tell one 'what Tories think'. (216)

wonderful glimpse of what George Watson plaintively calls 'the haunting suspicions of the liberal mind.'[11]

One problem that pervades the entire discussion rests on a mistaken metaphor about the spatial nature of political positions; and since the notion of 'Liberal Toryism' drags two descriptions of very different things under a common cover, the potential for damaging the clarity of argument can be considerable. People speak not merely about 'right' and 'left' but about a political spectrum or a political space. Parties of the right merge into those of the Centre (whatever that is) and perhaps radicalise themselves—unless, confusingly, they be part of the Radical Right—into the red end of the rainbow pattern. Left to themselves these mental constructions do no more harm to the world than does Euclidean geometry to the chaos of shingle on a beach. But they are not left to themselves. By their frequent presence in conversation and books they establish an unspoken sense that the Conservative party really does have edges, that the left-hand one abuts or overlaps the right hand edge of the Liberal party and that if a dissident progressive Tory falls off the end of the Conservative world it is the Liberal one that prevents him from tumbling into nothingness. Definition becomes otiose: you know a Liberal Conservative because he lives, in Macaulay's phrase, 'not far from the common frontier' between the parties.[12] You know a non-Liberal Tory, according to Ian Gilmour, because 'though "right wingery" cannot be exactly defined, it is, like the elephant, easily recognised when it is seen.'[13]

A reaction against this peculiar ontology does not deny the possibility of Conservatives becoming Liberals—Gladstone, we recall, did so with some panache—nor to deny that they are more likely to do that than become socialists. It wonders only whether the temporal might not be more helpful than the spatial in characterising political sentiments within evolving groups. If parties are visualised as clusters of shared experience, scarred by a collective memory, ritualised through various formulae, prone to types of ethos, to use Drucker's *bon mot* of few years

---

[11] George Watson, *The English Ideology: studies in the language of Victorian politics* (1973), 104.
[12] T. B. Macaulay, *History of England from the Accession of James II* (1849–61, ed. Firth, 1913), I, 88. How prescient that he went on to observe: 'The extreme section of one class consists of bigoted dotards: the extreme section of the other consists of shallow and reckless empirics.' *ibid.* It is no less interesting that Macaulay made use of this language before it had become common to do so in connection with the idea of the state: for a perspective on this sense of 'frontier', see Michael Bentley, ' "Boundaries" in British Political Thought and Doctrine', in *The Boundaries of the State* (eds.) Simon Green and Richard Whiting (Cambridge, forthcoming).
[13] Ian Gilmour *Inside Right: a study in Conservatism* (1977), 12.

ago,[14] then a static boundary-language ill suits their nature. Seen from a distance we all acknowledge this: no tutor lets a student described Burke as 'right-wing' without a lesson in semantics. Closer to home, however, blindnesses occur which make it harder to see why more 'Liberal Tories' did not change their political allegiance or, when they did, why they did.

A second problem concerns terminology. The words 'Liberal' and 'Tory' carry resonances that vary with the assumptions of those who employ them. Among political philosophers, a distinction is frequently made between a 'liberal' tradition that grounds its recommendations in the ultimate reality of individuals with an accompanying image of society as a conglomerate of autonomous units and, conversely, what they see as 'Tory' ideology, stemming from a celebration of organicism and social cohesion, and resisting suggestions that the individual might not be coerced by the State since the State is itself the creator and guarantor of the individual's civic self. Transferred to party politics this version of reality has the comical result of making the so-called 'New Conservatism' a repository of Liberal Toryism because it most clearly, among the present tendencies of Conservative behaviour, approximates to the prescriptions of *laissez-faire*. Perhaps Wittgenstein had a point and we ought to look for meaning more in usage than stipulation. Certainly the term 'Liberal Toryism' will occur here as it does in most conversation about the subject—as a description of a form of Tory outlook that is taken to be tender rather than tough, moderate, flexible, caring, civilised, progressive, consensual and humane—all those characteristics that Mrs Thatcher never quite managed to embrace. By placing discussion in this frame it becomes possible to see linkages in Tory experience over the last century and a half that are missed by a less evolutionary approach that wants to see Thatcherism as a form of re-invented liberalism.

For a related reason, the apparatus of political economy seems a blunt instrument with which to tease out nuances within party politics, and easily degenerates into a conveyer-belt understanding of political change with politics forever being pulled along behind capitalist dynamics. Having discovered liberalism in Adam Smith and Cobden, one can go on to test for it in later generations by asking questions about the degree of state involvement that politicians or theorists are prepared to recommend. Since all Conservatives seem, from about 1948, ready to do so in some degree, then we need a new vocabulary to describe the events of the oil-inflated 1970s. Liberal Tories are re-described as Tories *tout court*; the Thatcherite tendency among them becomes 'social market

[14] H. Drucker, *Doctrine and Ethos in the Labour party* (1979)

Toryism'.[15] But this distinction, helpful in a review of changing economic attitudes, begs the questions that this study seeks to raise and applies to its evidence a litmus that becomes blotting paper, mopping into a diffuse stain the colours one had hoped to separate. It may be that they are all Liberal Tories now; but if the proposition is to become credible then it will need for its support something stronger than rhetorical claims by politicians anxious to define themselves as heirs to a tradition of far-seeing beneficence. To ask a politician, after all, if he has ceased to be a Liberal Tory, is rather like asking him whether he has ceased to be humble.

This worry over the rhetorical uses of Liberal Toryism certainly goes beyond prejudice. Sir Ian Gilmour exemplifies the strain with his persistent recourse to the past as a way of finding something optimistic to say; and here is a third strain of difficulty—the mangling of the past to create a Liberal Tory present. On inspection that past appears as a pre-formulated package, full of lessons about the importance of moderation as a Conservative device, 'stick[ing] as closely as possible to the centre,' as Gilmour wrote in a now famous passage, 'with a slight Right incline.'[16] History can be shaped around such a proposition but it looks very odd. 'British conservatives have not stuck dogmatically to free trade,' we are told, 'but have moved in between free trade and protection according to the circumstances of the time.'[17] Most historians who have worked on the subject would find this a bland resumé of a century of gut-tearing rancour that led to the attempted overthrow of leaders, the loss of general elections and the severing of personal relations. The same plasticity of temperament among Gilmour's historical figures makes them, *pace* his hero Disraeli, love coalitions. 'With the exception of Sir Alec Douglas-Home', we are told, 'every prime minister since Peel has at one time in his political career formed, considered forming, joined or attempted a coalition with other parties. Even allowing for the necessities of war, this surely shows a propensity towards coalitions.'[18] It shows in fact nothing of the kind other than that Conservatives prefer to be governing rather than not and camouflages the zeal with which luminous politicians, Peel included, have gone to special trouble to avoid having anything to do with Gilmour's vaunted 'centre'.

For R. A. Butler, often credited with having inaugurated this strain

[15] Eg. Andrew Gamble, *The Free Economy and the Strong State: the politics of Thatcherism* (1988).

[16] Gilmour, *Inside Right*, 130. Changing the metaphor to a more defensive mode, Gilmour also argued in 1975 that the party should not go 'digging [its] trenches further to the right.' Quoted in Campbell, *Heath*, 669.

[17] *Ibid.*, 116.

[18] *Ibid.*, 165.

of post-war Liberal Toryism, history played no less a role; only it was a different history. According to Gerald Sparrow, writing the valedictory biography once it had become clear that Butler had finally decided to go quietly by accepting the Mastership of Trinity College, Cambridge, the crucial period of the past for him had been that of Lord Randolph Churchill, with perhaps a dash of influence from Sir Geoffrey Butler, RAB's uncle. Originally Butler had fed from reading familiar among the youth of his generation: Bolingbroke, the Elder and Younger Pitt, Disraeli and so on; but his concept of a 'property-owning democracy' Sparrow credits to 'his uncle's historical precedents and rather cautious progressive planning'. Then one has one of those unfathomable remarks that often abound in this *genre* of influence-seeking. 'Once the idea had taken hold it was, of course, a modern development of the ideas with which Lord Randolph Churchill, had he lived, might well have introduced progressive Toryism into British public life forty-five years earlier.' Leaving aside the logical quibble that Butler's concept either was a development of earlier ideas or it wasn't, regardless of its taking hold, it remains difficult to place the post-1885 figure of Lord Randolph Churchill in a frame remotely like the one Sparrow believed appropriate in 1965. But then the lineage followed from the project that Sparrow had set himself in the first place: that of showing that Butler 'tore reactionary conservatism out of the Tory party and made it a liberal party for the people.'[19] Behind the specific point there stands a general one. Liberal Tories are anxious to claim a view of historical development which puts them in the mainstream of men of goodwill—a repellent phrase but a common one—and to claim licence for their position by relating it to the great works of Peel, Disraeli, Randolph Churchill, Balfour, Baldwin and Neville Chamberlain—anybody, in fact, among leading figures apart from the 3rd Marquis of Salisbury (who failed to introduce Old Age Pensions and was unsound on democracy and the gaiety of nations), Andrew Bonar Law (who put party before country over Ulster) and the 1st Earl of Birkenhead whose liberalism was confined entirely to his private life.[20] These claims promote cynicism but should not be dismissed on that ground alone. There are better reasons for suspecting that Sir Ian Gilmour is not Canning's spiritual heir.

The provenance of the concept of Liberal Toryism turns out to be more complicated than one might imagine and more relevant to a

[19] Gerald Sparrow, *'RAB': study of a statesman* (1965), 24.
[20] The present author is currently writing a study of Salisbury; for a good recent collection of essays, see *Salisbury: the man and his policies* (eds.) Robert Blake and Hugh Cecil (1987). Bonar Law is still best approached through Robert Blake's life, *The Unknown Prime Minister: the life and times of Andrew Bonar Law 1858–1923* (1955). For Birkenhead, see John Campbell, *F. E. Smith: first Earl of Birkenhead* (1983).

twentieth-century discussion than seems immediately apparent. For in large part the notion has a twentieth-century origin even though its dominating referent lies in the Liverpool ministry and its aftermath. Of course, Canning's contemporaries made hay with their hero's liberalism in foreign policy and the 'middle way' that Macmillan would want to revive a century later. 'I consider it to be the duty of British statesman,' Canning told the House of Commons in the year before his death, 'to hold a middle course between extremes: avoiding alike the extravagances of despotism and the licentiousness of unbridled freedom.' And Augustus Stapleton, for whom criticism of Canning could only imply failure of understanding, lost no opportunity in his biography to draw attention to the resolution with which Canning, 'a minister who looked not to temporary advantage, but to the attainment of lasting good,' brought philosophic calm to bear on every question and made each political act a feat of considered statesmanship.[21]

Out of all this attainment at the time, however, no clear principles seem to have emerged in the way that posterity would remark; indeed contemporaries often distanced themselves from liberalism by reminding their public about the ambiguities of Canning's language and action. Wellington had his own reasons for doing this with some pungency but the terms of his attack are worth recalling. 'We hear a great deal of Whig principles, and Tory principles, and Liberal principles and Mr Canning's principles; but I confess that I have never seen a definition of any of them, and cannot make to myself a clear idea of what any of them mean.'[22]

The clear idea was imposed retrospectively. Contemporary diarists certainly helped fix the image of Canning after his death. But it was the re-shaping of Tory politics in 1846 that accelerated the process. Like the controversy of 1922—that other seminal date for Liberal Tories—Peel's decision to liberalise policy over Maynooth and free trade became iconic both for a generation of well-wishers and for those harbouring bad blood. Many of Peel's followers defined themselves as 'Liberal Conservatives', 'ready', according to Professor Conacher, 'to accept the adjective "liberal" to indicate that a liberal view were compatible with a generally conservative position.'[23] One can find some warrant for that view among the Peelites themselves, expressly so in Aberdeen's generous if confused assurance that no government could be too liberal for him, providing that it did not abandon its Conservative

---

[21] Augustus Stapleton, *The Political Life of the Rt Hon George Canning* (3 vols., 1831), III, 4, 54–5.
[22] Quoted in G. Kitson Clark, *Peel and the Conservative Party* (1928), 34.
[23] J. B. Conacher, *The Peelites and the Party System* (Newton Abbot, 1972), 174.

character.[24] But with some simplicity of mind came also much ambiguity. The Peelites could hardly claim a direct descent from Canning when both Bentick and Disraeli had nettled their leader by claiming that he was responsible for Canning's premature death.[25] If one history had taken its origins in the adoring Stapleton, moreover, there were soon others finding Tory origins elsewhere. Pellew's life of Sidmouth, catching a tide in 1847, was every bit as dire as Stapleton's of Canning, and not one whit less adoring. What caught even Croker's eye when he reviewed it, though, was that once the narrative passed 1812 it failed to mention Canning at all.[26] So far as a coherent doctrine is concerned, one looks through the contemporary material in vain for articles or broadsides dwelling on Liberal Toryism as a virtue or curse, apart, perhaps, from one seventeen-year old observer who persuaded himself in 1854 that both Derby and Disraeli had a Liberal background and that this would save them from 'that horror of anything approaching to innovation' from which Tories had once suffered.[27] The silences and ambivalences are not surprising when one thinks about what 1846 had done. In so far as the Peelites used the term at all, they called themselves Liberal Conservatives to make a body of defectors alluring to the opposition rather than attractive to Tories. In so far as Tories disliked the Peelites they did so on the ground of a betrayal of public trust and private interest rather than out of a suspicion of Canningite proclivity. If anyone in Tory politics ought to have been free of Liberal imputation, after all, that person was surely Peel, the rat of 1827, the re-rat of 1829. As the Disraelian propagandist T. E. Kebbel recalled forty years later, 'the remark of Mr Greville, that Peel ought to have been a Whig, shows only that Greville did not understand what it was to be a Tory.'[28]

Disraeli's transmutation from cynical rebel to keeper of the covenant brought its own twists in his party's historical identity. Kebbel's history

[24] See Robert Stewart, *The Foundation of the Conservative Party 1830–67* (1978), 275. Cf. Lord Woolton's reflection on Sir Anthony Eden who had 'never wavered in his Conservatism, but had propounded Liberal principles.' *The Memoirs of the Rt Hon the Earl of Woolton* (1959), 418.

[25] Bentinck had first harried Peel for having 'chased and hunted' Canning to death: *Hansard* 3s, 8 Jun. 1846, LXXXVII, cols 177–84. Then Disraeli repeated the charge a few nights later: see Norman Gash, *Sir Robert Peel* (2 vols., 1972), II, 595–8.

[26] George Pellew, *The Life and Correspondence of the Rt Hon Henry Addington, First Viscount Sidmouth* (3 vols. 1847). For Croker's anonymous review, see the *Quarterly Review* (Mar. 1847), vol. 79, 554–5.

[27] Herbert Lowell, 'Conservative Reascendancy Considered', *Blackwood's* (Aug. 1854), 238–9. His age comes from the index entry in the *Wellesley Index of Victorian Periodicals* (ed. Walter E. Houghton), vol I (Toronto, 1966), 98. Derby had, of course, defected from the Whigs over the Irish Church issue in 1835. Disraeli's initial posture as a 'Radical' candidate in the 1830s must be what Lowell has in mind in his case.

[28] T. E. Kebbel, *Toryism*, 298n.

of Toryism, published in the year of the Home Rule crisis, may have been the last history to leave Canning's Toryness undisturbed. Kebbel did not dwell on Canning's difference from everyone else but on a longer perspective that saw an overriding unity where others had claimed fission. He offers Wellington's comments on an issue, for example, followed by the remark that Canning had said exactly the same. If the two men displayed differences in temperament, then so far as policy went those differences appear 'rather in degree than in kind'. If 'another Canning [were] to arise in our own generation his language would probably be different', we are told, but left in no doubt that it would be a Tory language. When Kebbel moves forward to Disraeli he can see a firm line running back to the horizon. 'Canning, in fact, was the first statesman who distinctly laid down the doctrine of English interests, afterwards acted on by Lord Palmerston and Lord Beaconsfield as the guiding star of English policy.'[29]

But this image of Liberal Toryism as simply a mild variant of Tory politics flickered with some violence in the later years of the nineteenth century as Liberals sought to acquire a stable past and an impeccable pedigree amid the welter of abuse and self-doubt accompanying Home Rule and the nervous language of resistance to socialism. Tories meanwhile could enjoy Salisbury's transparent absence of self-doubt and rid themselves of an unpleasant period. When the maestro of Edwardian Tory doctrine, Hugh Cecil, wrote his defence of the Conservative party as the House of Lords tumbled about his ears, it was no moment to dwell on the more simpering elements of Tory identity. He glided over Liberal Tory history in majestic silence, stopping only at Peel in order to silhouette him as 'an example of the mistake of supposing that even the highest practical abilities are sufficient, without philosophical insight, to save a politician from grave errors ... For consistency is a virtue that grows best in a mind trained to value the intellectual coherence of a sound political theory.'[30] The reasons for his silence and malignity go beyond the House of Lords and Hatfield. They reflect a suspicion, current by 1911, that Canning had been captured by the Liberal party for its own purposes.

Quite when this process had begun is difficult to date with precision, but F. H. Hill's contribution to Andrew Lang's memorable series of biographies called 'English Worthies' suggests that Canning in 1887 had begun to look different from the man appropriated by Kebbel the previous year. No longer a simple Tory, Canning becomes the spokesman for a hybrid political doctrine characteristic neither of radical Liberalism nor incipient Peelism. 'It would be difficult to extract from

[29] Kebbel, *ibid.*, 157.
[30] Hugh Cecil, *Conservatism* (1912), 68-9.

Canning's speeches or to see in his career', from where Hill was standing in 1887, 'any consistent scheme of partisan doctrine. The opponent of parliamentary reform and of the removal of Nonconformist disabilities cannot be called a Liberal; the advocate of Roman Catholic claims, the antagonist of the Holy Alliance, the promoter of Free Trade cannot be called a Tory.' But the impression gains ground that a reborn Canning would deal with the Concert of Europe quite as firmly as he was taken to have confronted the Holy Alliance—this a few years after Midlothian—and give the party a different tone from certain more recent persons.[31] This impression strengthens as one moves away from party history done by amateur enthusiasts to the professional scholarship that becomes available from the 1880s. Naturally this trail leads us in the direction of the period and place wherein reassessment was soon to begin of early-nineteenth century British politics from the perspective fostered by archival research and German method. It leads us towards Edwardian Cambridge.

There would be a pleasing symbolism in saying that it leads to Peterhouse and so, for a moment, it does. Harold Temperley's *Life of Canning* (1905) carried in a prefatory note a harbinger for later studies. He did not use the term Liberal Toryism but he did speak of 'Liberalism' by which he meant 'the progressive and enlightened domestic policy of Pitt, Canning and Huskisson', though he confused the issue by also intending 'the moderate Whigs led by Earl Grey'. He left no one in doubt that this special form of Liberalism illuminated the present and provided true hope as 'the polar star of our course':

> [Canning's] policy has two parts, a body and a soul, one fragile formed of the clay and dust of the wayside and the moment, the other compounded of more ethereal essences—serene, immortal and imperishable. In sorrow we turn from the accelerated decay of the one to behold the continued life of the other.[32]

Temperley's association with the conscience of Asquithian Liberalism—G. P. Gooch—says something of what impended. For the formation of Liberal Toryism as an overt organising device, however, we have to move down King's Parade towards Trinity College. J. R. M. Butler, Fellow of Trinity, had a distinguished background in the intellectual aristocracy and a surname heavy with Liberal Tory promise. His father, (Henry) Montagu Butler (1833–1918), had been headmaster of Harrow and Master of the College from 1886, had already lived through the spiral of memory that we are considering. 'The names of Chatham, Burke, Pitt ... Canning, Peel, Palmerston and Bright were at all times

---

[31] F. H. Hill, *George Canning* (1887), 218.
[32] H. W. V. Temperley, *Canning* (1905), 10, 268.

on his lips,' the son said in the biography he wrote of his father just after the First World War. 'A Peelite by tradition, a conservative Liberal by conviction, he passed gradually to liberal Conservatism, Gladstone's conversion to Home Rule and his failure to save Gordon proving important turning-points.'[33] Like father, very nearly like son. But J. R. M. Butler's well-known history of the great reform act, fastening on the period where it had all begun, did not contain Liberal Toryism as an analytical category when it appeared in 1914, probably because his immense regard for Sir Edward Grey read itself backwards into a devotion to the 2nd Earl whose decision to stay out in 1827 is made a commendable act of principle in rejecting association of one in whom Butler sees 'a degree of self-seeking and lack of straightforwardness'[34]; but then Butler was a party Liberal until after the war.

Where Liberal Toryism appeared with greater explicitness was rather in the early writing of Butler's friend and post-war colleague at Trinity, George Kitson Clark. Again a Liberal genealogy among the Kitsons left its mark in the highly-individual Toryism that Kitson Clark was to display all his adult life. His Anglican humanity, combined with an admiration for nineteenth-century Christian socialism, helped send him to the newly-opened Peel papers in a mood of evangelism in the 1920s. *Peel and the Conservative Party* (1928) thus became a tract for the times, putting Baldwin in the shadow of the greatest statesman of the nine-teenth century.[35] For the first time, probably, the concept of a distinct Liberal Toryism was also brought into play as a way of shaping the past. 'It was possible', Kitson Clark wrote, 'but it was not necessary for a Tory to hold with Eldon, that everything that existed, however corrupt, should be defended to the death lest all should fall together. In particular a group of liberal Tories were gathered round the splendid figure of George Canning, who was the disciple of Pitt if he was the enemy of Castlereagh.' Peel may not have moved intimately among them but the 'nascent Liberal' evident in Peel's youth reappears when Palmerston takes him to be, in Kitson Clark's words, 'so right-minded and liberal'; and the implication is strong that here we have invisible writing *avant la lettre* on Tamworth's wall.[36] Kitson Clark's writing stopped abruptly after *Peel and the Conservative Party* but he turned toward intensive teaching. It was in the atmosphere established in Trinity by J. R. M. Butler, Kitson Clark and G. M. Trevelyan, therefore, that the young W. R. Brock won the Thirlwall Prize Essay in 1939 with a short

---

[33] J. R. M. Butler, *The Passing of the Great Reform Bill* (1914), 94.
[34] Butler, *ibid.*, 46.
[35] The latter phrase was still echoing around his rooms in Trinity as late as the early 1970s, as members of his unforgettable graduate seminar in Cambridge will readily recall.
[36] G. Kitson Clark, *Peel and the Conservative Party* (1928), 3.

study whose picture of Liberal Toryism configured historical thinking until the 1970s. Perhaps Brock was surprised that Liberal Toryism did not appear in the primary sources he set himself to read. Certainly he felt it necessary to justify the term:

> The name is artificial—that is to say it is not found in the mouths of contemporaries—but because the High Tories accused the Government of 'liberalism', then a suspect and dangerous thing, because the 'liberals' who dominated the Cabinet felt acutely their estrangement from the 'ultras', and because the meaning of the phrase is readily intelligible to a later age, it is not inappropriate to speak of 'Liberal Toryism'[37]

Thus armed, Brock set about the defence of Canning against Castlereagh, or Churchill against Chamberlain, depending on how one reads a text whose proofs Brock corrected in a barrack-room in 1940 or 1941 and whose word-order he did not correct when he wrote of Canning: 'who would deny that ... he gave to England a policy and a tradition which she would do ill without.'[38] In the wake of Ranger and Trevor-Roper it has become irritating, boring even, to point to a tradition that turns out less traditional than its practitioners assume;[39] but the thought seems germane, granted the stridency with which present Liberal Tories lay claim to continuities in their own style of Tory language, that historical enquiry suggests a departure-point for that language in the frame of mind current between the wars of the twentieth century rather than in an identifiable body of doctrine in Disraelian reaches of the nineteenth.

For those people interested in maintaining a form of Liberal-Tory continuity, these considerations rather miss the point. The historical distinction that they wish to draw has little to do with academic speculation concerning the politics of the 1820s or 1840s or 1870s. It simply draws attention to a division between those who rest their Conservatism on a self-interested defence of property and the status quo, on the other hand, and to an every-growing element, on the other, who hope to use the state in order to improve the lives of its citizens. It is this tradition that is given a nineteenth-century origin. Even Hugh Cecil, for all his silence over Canning, spoke up for it in 1912. 'That authority should relieve suffering,' he wrote, 'that it should control and regulate trade; that it should restrain luxury; that it should suppress

---

[37] W. R. Brock, *Lord Liverpool and Liberal Toryism 1820 to 1827* (1941, 1967), preface.
[38] Brock, *op. cit*, 229.
[39] E. J. Hobsbawm and T. Ranger, *The Invention of Tradition* (Cambridge, 1992).

vice; that it should maintain religious truth: these were the principles which appealed to our forefathers as reasonable and especially to those among them who were Tories. And in the nineteenth century, when Liberalism enforced to the utmost the principle of personal liberty, it was among Conservatives that the authority and control of the State was defended and in some instances enlarged and strengthened.'[40] One way of deploying his vocabulary lay, therefore, in announcing that true Liberal Toryism consisted of the very opposite of Liberalism. And if this logic is followed through, then twentieth-century non-Liberal Tories become the champions, not of a Conservative heritage at all but of a Manchester Liberal one, and Margaret Thatcher comes into focus as a Cobdenite campaigner or at best as a sort of post-industrial whig, rolling back what she should be extending and tacking down.

A persuasion of this kind has appeared from time to time in the Liberal Tories' view of themselves and their past. Even so dry a commentator as Patrick Cosgrave gives it credence, from the other side of the fence, when he argues in his sympathetic study of the rise of Thatcherism that 'the old order in the Conservative Party—the order which opposed the Thatcher bid for the leadership—assumed a beneficent nature on the part of the state. Where inequality or poverty or unhappiness existed, the assumption was that the government of the day should do something about it.'[41] Gilmour himself makes considerable use of the contrast in order to suggest a new history of Conservatism that begins with Disraeli, who turns out to have invented two things: the view that the party must be a national party and the proposition that the condition of the people must become its abiding concern. Chris Patten, in his earlier incarnation, took up the same theme, ridiculing Joseph and his fellow travellers because they were too Liberal for their own good, and the coaxing out of the post-Disraelian chronology a theme of consistent social conscience reinforced by intelligent *étatisme*. His history comes out like this: 'Disraeli's government in the 1870s improved conditions at work and legalised trade union activity among much else. Neville Chamberlain [a big jump] in the 1920s and 1930s, and Lord Butler during the war, helped lay the foundations of the modern Welfare State ...' From there one is led on towards the need for well-adjusted housing and educational policies in the modern age.[42]

Now the history of Liberal Toryism as an embodiment of social reform appears flimsy on at least three levels. In the first place, the story itself seems garbled in the light of modern analyses of Conservative history. The days when Disraeli was hailed as the educator of his party

[40] Hugh Cecil, *Conservatism*, 170.
[41] Cosgrave, *Thatcher*, 20.
[42] Chris Patten, *The Tory Case* (1983), 16.

or Baldwin as embodiment of a dozy Liberalism have gone. The claims of Neville Chamberlain or Butler to party radicalism vis-a-vis the expansion of state responsibilities likewise need some qualification to bring the rhetoric into a relationship with the evidence.[43] The historiographical climate that has emerged over the past twenty years has engendered scepticism, with the result that the stature of such individuals is now frequently assessed in a different way and not taken verbatim from speeches in *Hansard* or party conference reports. A second problem, endemic in most forms of analysis of Liberal Toryism but glaring here, is that, to the extent that the dichotomy drawn can be demonstrated at all in Conservative history, Liberal Tories seem to fall on both sides of it. Tories from Canning through to Lord Robert Cecil have manifested a streak of Liberalism without committing themselves to any significant social reform and on occasion working assiduously against it. Tory social reformers, none more so than Disraeli, evolved a language of permissive state activity that never turned them into persons whom Liberals would be wont to admire.[44] Bonar Law, and Butler's *protégé* Enoch Powell, both wanted to do something with the state. Liberals (and many relaxed Tories) frowned on what they wanted to do. When historically a Tory has attracted the regard of Liberals, as Baldwin did in some of his postures, the reason for the acclaim had more to do with plangent rhetoric and moral tone than applause for remedial legislation or the doing of great deeds. But much the most forceful and important objection to the assumptions of Liberal Tory history takes the form of rejecting a convenient acceptance of social organicism or collectivism as the central thread in Tory development, while picturing Liberalism as an individualist tradition concerned to distance itself from the advance of the state.

The reduction of Toryism, as opposed to Conservatism, to a collectivist understanding of politics, was given support in an influential paper by Harvey Glickman some thirty years ago[45] and it has some force when one thinks that tariff reformers, for example, tended to be

[43] The Disraelian revision began most prominently with Paul Smith, *Disraelian Conservatism and Social Reform* (1967). Baldwin came under severe reconsideration in Keith Middlemas and John Barnes, *Baldwin* (1969); see, more recently, Philip Williamson, 'The Doctrinal Politics of Stanley Baldwin' in *Public and Private Doctrine: essays in British history presented to Maurice Cowling* (ed.) Michael Bentley, (Cambridge, 1993), 181–208. Neville Chamberlain's social-reform credentials are upheld largely in the first volume of David Dilks, *Neville Chamberlain* (Cambridge, 1984). Butler has yet to receive an astringent treatment; perhaps there is little evidence to be astringent about.

[44] Smith, *op. cit.*; but cf. Peter Ghosh, 'Disraelian Conservatism: a financial approach', *English Historical Review*, (1984), 268–96.

[45] Harvey Glickman, 'The Toryness of English Conservatism', *Journal of British Studies*, I (1961), esp. 124 and 129: 'Whereas Liberals begin with individuals, Tories begin with orders and classes. This is the key to the labyrinth of Tory beliefs.' (129).

non-Liberal in their politics. Naturally one can also find organic food for thought in that consensual 'middle opinion' so evident in the 1930s.[46] PEP, the Next Five Years Group and Macmillan's *Middle Way* could be taken to mark the origin of a sentiment that 'the rival principles and catch-words which marked the lines of political cleavage in the past are to a large extent irrelevant to the real issues now,'[47] and that modern Tories must embrace the state. Ignoring the thought that this strategy struck some contemporary Conservatives as an abdication of Toryism rather than a new wave of it, it should be emphasised that the confused ideological positions emphasised by the depression had their origin much earlier, and that social organicism had a different trajectory than these movements taken in isolation imply. Work on Liberal history in recent years has stressed the degree to which its theoretical equipment after Mill's death not only allowed the production of an organicist view of society but offered firmer grounds for it than anything Burke or Coleridge had said.[48] Liberal defences of individualism in Britain largely petered out from the second half of the 1870s. Conservative thinking, *per contra*, moved with Salisbury into resisting the allegation that property was theft and making allegations of its own that socialism and not a few forms of Liberalism amounted precisely to theft. Just as the Liberals retained their Cobdenites—their Morleys and their Hirsts—so the Conservative party continued to contain a band of collectivists who expressed themselves through organisations such as the party's Social Reform Committee in the years before the First World War. But to see the politics of both parties after 1900 determined by the demands of mid-Victorian Britain rehashes what contemporaries thought they were doing.

For one young Tory in the 1920s, admittedly, the situation of the country suggested a view of strategy that must have brought light to the shade of Canning:

> We shall 'dish the Whigs' & steal their clothes while they are bathing, in the true Disraelian style. We shall stand before the people as the only party capable of combining progress with sanity. That is our political duty & should always be our watchword...
>
> The Conservative party will of course go on, whatever Conservative

---

[46] See Arthur Marwick, 'Middle Opinion in the Thirties: planning, progress and political "agreement"', *English Historical Review*, LXXIX (1964), 285–98.

[47] *The Next Five Years* (1935), 5. On PEP and its related legacies, see John Pinder (ed.), *Fifty Years of Political and Economic Planning: looking forward 1931–81* (1981).

[48] A wide-ranging review of the relationship between Liberalism and organicism in political thought has been underway in a complex historiography over recent years. For some instances, see Michael Freeden, *The New Liberalism: an ideology of social reform* (Oxford, 1977) and Stephan Collini, *Liberalism and Sociology: L. T. Hobhouse and political argument in England* (Cambridge, 1979). Some lines of argument are suggested in Michael Bentley, *The Climax of Liberal Politics 1868–1918* (1987).

statesmen may do to wreck it ... But it will not, alas!, be the party of our dreams. It will become more and more the party of vested interests; of the rentier, not of the producer; of the middleman, not of the manufacturer, be he master or man ... It will sink to the position of a party dominated by middle-class aspirations, composed of middle-aged personalities, and attractive only to mediocre minds.[49]

Views of this kind catch the eye in Liberal-Tory retrospect and expand to fill the space available. But as one reviews the thirty-odd names that make up the central sponsorship of the Next Five Years Group in the 1930s, Macmillan seems marginal among a collection of non-Conservative affiliations. Beyond it, and inside Conservatism, there were those such as Lord Eustace Percy who ridiculed the false history of Liberal-Tory creation that saw 1922 as a missed opportunity for fusion.[50] As if to come full circle, we find Alan Clark (of all people) seizing on Macmillan as a personal icon just as Macmillan had seized on Disraeli; but what he wanted to remember was the First World War and 'the young classical scholar, less than a year out of Eton, pale and shaken but heroic', with all that he represented, the 'habitual bearing, stoicism, self-sacrifice, sense of "fair-play"; the whole *tenu* of the English upper class ...'[51] The inter-war years give rise not to one tradition, we should conclude, but to several and they intertwine disturbingly. If they recall Canning on the one hand they recall too Lord Clarendon's jibes about 'Tory illiberality and hindrance-spirit.'[52]

This jumble of positions emphasises two considerations. First, for every adumbration of *dirigisme* or *laissez faire* there appears a counterpoint of resistance and criticism—sometimes in the same text. Recall the famous review by Michael Oakeshott of Quintin Hogg's *The Case for Conservatism* (1947), easily the most distinguished Liberal-Tory polemic of this century. Apparently Hogg had set his heart on writing another Tamworth manifesto; he implied something of the kind in a letter to Butler.[53] But his message came out looking like a defence of old-fashioned individualism, or so Oakeshott believed, and thus gave rise

---

[49] Macmillan to Churchill, 1 January 1928, in Martin Gilbert, *Winston S. Churchill*, V (1976), 261–2.

[50] 'Such a fusion, under the heat generated by Lloyd George's energy and resourcefulness, would, they say and will say, have produced a healthier alternative party to Labour than the personal ascendancy which Baldwin was to win over a great body of non-partisan Liberal opinion in the constituencies. It would not have left a rump Liberal party struggling to retain a foothold in the House of Commons, but would have prepared a fold wide enough to receive the whole party on Asquith's death.' Lord Eustace Percy, *Some Memories* (1958), 86–7.

[51] Clark diary, 10 Feb. 1987, *Diaries*, 158.

[52] Clarendon to Reeve, 21 Dec. 1858, quoted in Angus Hawkins, *Parliament, Party and the Art of Politics in Britain, 1855–9*, (1987), 166.

[53] See Sparrow, 'RAB', 234.

to a critique that might stand as the ultimate *bouleversement* of Conservative logic: a liberal-minded Tory writes an individualist tract and then finds himself on a rack cranked by one of the century's most illiberal Tory minds for having made his account so individualist that it invites corruption into the worst forms of collectivism. Oakeshott frames the charge in a memorable passage that accuses Hogg of Enlightenment:

> ... we do not begin by being free; the structure of our freedom is the rights and duties which, by long and painful human effort, have been established in our society. Individuality is not natural; it is a great human achievement. The conditions of individuality are not limitations; there is nothing to limit. And the adjustment of those conditions are [*sic*] not interference ... they are continuations of the achievement. But the intellectual error involved in Mr Hogg's way of thinking would not be so damaging were it not for the fact that the step from these ideas of limitation and interference to the idea of adjustment by means of overhead planning, with physical controls, is as short as it is disastrous ... The bug of rationalistic politics has bitten the Conservative.[54]

Granting Oakeshott his theoretical point, which the party would have done had it been able to understand it, much room remained for voicing an hostility to these 'overhead adjustments' by the state more loudly than a love for society as man's better self. The ambivalence between this individualism and organicism as the appropriate Conservative aspiration also marked Keith Feiling's attempt to follow where Oakeshott had led, in his essay on the principles of Conservatism in 1953. Feiling knew from his studies of the early-nineteenth century that the Conservative party was not supposed to be individualist in a liberal sense and he bent every effort to make it something else. Authority could not reside in the community, he said, because Conservatives 'distrust general notions such as "the community".' But his analysis of what a community would be like if one were allowed to talk about it sounds closer to a bundle of sticks than a celebration of transcendence. 'It is individual personality', he writes as though mimicking W. H. Mallock, 'which creates the wealth of governments, and brings sap to the connected growths of interests, neighbourhoods and voluntary groupings.'[55] With friends such as Feiling, organicists hardly wanted enemies.

Yet the heart of these ambiguities and uncertainties seems less obscure if one places against them a second thought. Conservatives and Liberals

---

[54] Oakeshott, 'Contemporary British Politics', *Cambridge Journal*, I (1947–9), 488–9.
[55] Keith Feiling, 'Principles of Conservatism', *Political Quarterly*, (1935), 131.

want to be organic about society in different ways; and during the annealment of Toryism since the beginning of the twentieth century, Conservatives have come to feel organic about a particular value-structure rather than about the apparatus of government without whose help such values must remain elusive. Cry with the victorious Tessa Sanderson, as the Union Jack floats into the sky at the Olympic Games, and the Conservative party cries with you. Feel your heart go out to the blind and lame coming home from the Falklands and you feel something of what Conservative patriots feel. Yet neither the tears nor the sentiment validate, in Conservative eyes, the demand that your children's education be paid for by the state or that your mother's biopsy be hastened through the same instrumentality. They do not reverse the construction between north and south of a wall so impenetrable as to turn all organicist language to bathos. Rather than provide a touchstone by which to distinguish Liberal Tories from other kinds, the ideas of organicism and individualism offer nothing stronger than a collage of moods and intimations.

If Liberal Tories elude classification by their statism, perhaps they may be isolated by, say, their family background. This approximates to the commercial-traveller-versus-gent school of criticism. Liberality resides in great houses, rolling acres, panelled libraries, an education at an ancient university and a muscular view of man's purpose symbolised in rod, crop and gun. Illiberal Toryism has its home in Birmingham, Glasgow and Grantham. It is urban, provincial, hard-faced, hard-nosed; it has oil or flour on its hands and dirt on its money. In so far as it has an ideology, it centres on economic protection for the industry out of which it has grown and economic jealousy against immigrants and welfare scroungers. Lord Robert Cecil validated some of the latter accusation in his memoirs:

> ... the substitution of the moneyed for the landed interest as the dominant force on the Right brought a new conception of what was legitimate in party politics. The immediate result was the defeat, for good or evil, of those causes for which the old Tory party had fought for so long ... I cannot myself think that the eventual achievement of the Ottawa Agreements is worth the price the Conservatives had to pay for it.[56]

The image works well with this Cecil but hardly with his brother and still less with his father. It rings true for Sir Alec Douglas-Home, but leaves one furtive about generations of Westminsters and Mitfords. It

---

[56] Viscount Cecil of Chelwood, *All the Way* (1949), 107.

cuts close to the bone, after all, in implying that land liberalises when everyone knows that farming Toryism—'stick to the farmer who is on our side and never mind the labourer whose vote you won't get anyhow'[57]—has rarely had a liberal patina. It deflates Baldwin's liberal pretension, and to that extent deserves our thanks, but invites us to place most of the Tory intelligentsia—from Butler and Maudling to Powell and Cosgrave in very odd company. As a general conception of who Liberal Tories are, it leaves one sieving water.

The mention of intellectuals suggests an alternative tack. Perhaps Liberal Tories are clever Conservatives and illiberal ones examples of those whom Peel used to call 'blockheads', the bastions of the stupidest party. It is true that Bonar Law, whom few accuse of Liberalism, preferred the company of fools to that of cranks and that Sir John Marriott, cheated of office, shared a Liberal friend's bitterness that the Tory party had no use for brains.[58] But, again, the mistrust of men referred to by Reginald Northam as 'clever chaps' has always had a Liberal Conservative constituency quite as much as a reactionary one. R. J. White's reflections on *The Conservative Tradition* had endless goodwill (a Liberal Tory claim) and an encouraging smile for most people; but ideas received rough treatment when compared with the Coleridgean reality that lay beneath. 'The shape and pattern of Conservative politics,' he wrote, 'have rarely been imposed on the phenomena of nature, and of human nature, by clever men taking thought ... it is the by-product of real living, not the fabrication of unimpeded intellect. It has arisen out of nature, out of human nature, like the great, spare, necessary lines of a landscape seen in the perspective of history ...'[59] The reservation about pre-formulated doctrine is an important clue to hold in the mind. Suffice it meanwhile to suggest a scepticism over the implication that the intellectuality of Butler or Boyle's Conservatism constituted the defining characteristic of their liberalism. Powell became a professor long before his liberal critics.

In locating appropriate lineaments within all these positions, religion looks a possibility: perhaps beneficence and goodwill among Liberal Tories can be traced to One more mighty than Mr Major? But the sincerity with which some Liberal Tories have referred their liberality to some sense of Christian mission does not gainsay the sincerity of those who have based their aversion to liberality on precisely the same doctrines. Lord Robert Cecil, senior, taught Lord Robert Cecil, junior, much of what he knew about religion, after all, without bequeathing much of his politics. The Rev Dr Edward Norman's contributions to

[57] Sanders diary, 13 Nov. 1913, in John Ramsden (ed.), *Real Old Tory Politics*, (1984), 67.
[58] J. A. R. Marriott, *Memories of Four Score Years* (1946), 188.
[59] R. J. White, *The Conservative Tradition* (1950), 2.

the national book of goodwill have so far proved slimmer than his
Christian position might on this hypothesis predict. If Powell and
Macleod vied for precedence among Lord Butler's *Kindergarten*, then
Powell was the one who 'kept Sunday' while Macleod played bridge.
In a party that lacks a plausible equivalent to the Dissent that has
bulked so large in formulating Liberal party doctrine, Anglicanism in
the twentieth century has informed all Conservative positions and not
simply the progressive one. Reference to the Liberal Tory's inner man
will always be relevant but hardly discriminating.

So difficult is it, indeed, to create a spiritual, ideological or sociological
category that precisely defines what Liberal Tories are and believe, that
the temptation grows to see the phenomenon as little more than a
temperamental quirk on the part of individuals who otherwise remain
quite distinct from one another in their convictions. This thought
sometimes strikes home. Comparing the Tory diarists Crawford, Sanders
and Bridgeman provides glimpses, for example, of how parliamentary
politics may be differently conceived and expressed and often does
leave an impression that Liberal tories see that world in a distinctive
way. In Crawford's case, and occasionally in Bridgeman's, it comprises
a dislike for forms of party behaviour in which large issues are allowed
to fade in order to give priority to urgent considerations of electoral
advantage or the tactical needs of the leadership. So one notices
Bridgeman in the uncertain early months of Baldwin's leadership
'hat[ing] all this intriguing' and the counter-intriguing that he deemed
necessary to neutralise it.[60] This echoes Crawford's denunciation of
Derbys 'intriguing outlook' in 1931 or recalls his loathing of the party
atmosphere surrounding the rejection of Lloyd George in 1922.[61] From
Sanders, with his 'real old Tory politics' the image becomes confirmed
in negative—in his report, for example, that Alfred Lyttelton had been
criticised for being 'too kind to the other side', or in his jubilation
that Bonar Law's second eleven contained three men who had been
contemporaries in the upper sixth at Harrow, or in his pleasure many
years before when an MP of dubious reputation had been made the
victim of a 'rag' by 'a crowd of our boys'.[62]

Remarks about rags and boys are obviously unimportant in themselves. But a Liberal Tory, one suspects, would not report them or, if
he did, would use a language different from this elegiac mode depicting

[60] William Bridgeman to M. C. Bridgeman, 9 Dec. 1923, in Philip Williamson (ed.),
The Modernisation of Conservative Politics (19), 174.

[61] Crawford diary, 19 Nov. 1931, in John Vincent (ed.) *The Crawford Papers: the journals of
David Lindsey, twenty-seventh Earl of Crawford and tenth Earl of Balcarres, 1871–1940* (Manchester,
1984), 543. Cf. *ibid.*, 10 Octob. 1922; 'I hate these discussions about leadership and
electioneering' (449).

[62] Sanders Diary, 6 Apr. 1911 and 8 Jul. 1913, *ibid.*, 27, 65.

the party as an instinctive association with an unspoken *mentalité collective*. No sooner painted, however, than this picture crazes and flakes: it cannot take the weight that an explanation would impose. It is doubtless the case that Hugh Cecil 'love[d] the idea of a Constitutional row' because '[h]e always did, even at Oxford'; but then his brother Robert, whose politics took quite the opposite tinge, carried those equally back to his mother's knee where he would be 'chaff[ed] ... about my having always two grievances and a right!'[63] To see the same thing from the other direction, we note that even Sanders found F. E. Smith 'unnecessarily provocative' and the ironic Balfour 'rather flippant'. The categories established by responding to temperamental affirmations are not thereby compromised, but one would like their seams to feel a little more hermetic before resting a model of Liberal Tory behaviour on nothing more coherent than a personal idiosyncrasy or range of social tastes. As with the previous poles of argument, these considerations provide a clue but hardly a solution.

It is time to wonder whether these unsatisfactory elements can be made too say something more persuasive; and the three thoughts that seem most appropriate concern the question of chronology, the problem of category and the characteristics of a political language.

Continuity within any style of Conservatism over the century and a half since the Canningites mounted their attack on Wellingtonian Toryism is chimerical, and realism requires that at lest four sub-periods come into the picture. The first runs from the 1820s to the 1880s when the notion has little precise formulation and hinges for its meaning on the personalities at its centre, especially memories of Canning and Peel. A second period runs from the Liberal party's discovery of serious radicalism, which beckoned to a Tory past as a form of reassurance and the Conservative discovery of socialism and protectionism which made collectivism urgent to some and an anti-popular front to others. This epoch lasts until at least the First World War. The third period is the inter-war period, dominated electorally by the Liberal party's loss of its constituency and the need to radiate a sympathetic message to a discerned political centre to ensure that old Liberals became new Tories. A fourth grew out of the post-1948 consensus in which current Liberal Tories and their academic commentators grew up, and which they imagine to be an avatar of the Conservative past rather than a datable construction. That these moments comprise a series of sliding emphases is obvious enough, but then so is the danger of imagining that Liberal Toryism consists of a pattern of engraved prescription

[63] *Ibid.*, 18 Jul. 1911, 30; Cecil, *All the Way*, 13.

about civil rights, education or free trade.

The categories into which Liberal Tories are placed reflect this misunderstanding but then extend it by seeing the content of their recommendations as the key to what Liberal Toryism 'is' in some essentialist sense. Suppose, however, that this self-affirmed mode of otherness often works as a mask for another kind of distinction—one more subtle in its character and less attractive in its implications. The defining characteristic of Liberal Toryism seems to lie less in the content of its various doctrines than in the *function* that is permitted to any form of doctrine inside the Conservative party. Beneath the public, self-conscious clash over policy issues and strategic thinking, one can discern a more fundamental divergence about the legitimate use that a Conservative may make of ideology at all: progressive or reactionary, enlightened or unreconstructed.

A signpost towards this formulation appeared in an article by the late T. E. Utley, commenting in his *Times* column on Mrs Thatcher's keynote speech to the party conference in October 1987. His thoughts ran off at a tangent following the much-reported phrase about her election victory marking 'a staging post on a much longer journey':

> ... a mildly disrespectful idea occurred to me as I listened. If Mrs Thatcher's utopia were ever to be achieved, how much would she enjoy it? Her aim is a perfectly self-regulatory economy in which there is no further need for political intervention save of the most automatic kind. She wants a society governed by regular and general laws within the framework of which individuals are free to pursue their own ends. It is, in principle, an excellent objective, but where would it leave the likes of the Prime Minister—politicians with a passionate sense of political mission and an obsessive desire to move forwards? They would be obliged to think up some other sort of Utopia.[64]

Utley's alleged symbiosis of ideology and Thatcherite politics needed little acumen to identify since she went out of her way to allege it herself. She was never stronger than when sticking a knife into James Callaghan and drawing water, as at Cardiff Town Hall during the 1979 campaign. 'The Old Testament prophets', she told the party faithful, 'did not say "Brothers, I want a consensus." They said: "This is my faith. This is what I passionately believe. If you believe it too, then come with me." '[65] As with Sanders' boys and their rags, the point is that no Liberal tory would deploy such language: he or she would tend to *suppress* ideology as a dangerous lens that concentrates heat. 'Those

---

[64] *The Times*, 12 Oct. 1987.
[65] Quoted in Cosgrave, *Thatcher*, 64.

of the Right', Northam said (meaning *his* sort of Right) in 1939, 'develop no such obvious enthusiasm': 'Their guide is not some "high moral urge" or "penetrating spiritual insight" the result of which shall be some dramatic solution. These are expressions they do not use. In one sense they have no "principles", certainly not if principles mean an ideology.'[66] Gilmour has the same refrain. 'Nothing is more divisive than ideology'; divisions are to be avoided; ideology is to be avoided.[67] Quintin Hogg's formulation in 1947 remains, however, the most elegant. Conservatives (meaning Liberal Conservatives) are not even mainly interested in politics at all: 'religion, art, study, family, country, friends, music, fun, duty'—these all come first.[68] So far as the party is concerned, that too is a fraction of existence within politics:

> Unlike their opponents, the last thing Conservatives believe is that they have the monopoly of the truth. They do not even claim a monopoly of Conservatism. Modern Conservatives believe in the Liberal democratic state as it has gradually developed according to the British tradition. This means that ... the good of Britain would not be attained if the Conservatives held a monopoly of power ... They see nothing immoral or even eccentric in 'catching the Whigs bathing' and walking away with their clothes.[69]

Practice comes across as a transparency and ideology as a form of artificial colour. It did not seem so to Disraeli, in most of his moods, or Salisbury in any of them. It fails to catch the politics of many politicians since.

The final point reminds us that Liberal Toryism may most helpfully be regarded as a form of Conservative language rather than a precipitate of propositions or a core-collection of concepts. It has little resemblance to party Liberalism which is why even so proximate a figure as Lord Robert Cecil held back from joining the Liberal party when asked to do so in 1921.[70] Indeed most party Liberals hate the term 'Liberal Toryism' as a form of contradiction. Conservatives have needed to transcend the contradiction at a number of points in their history, ever since, in fact, Wellington's *parti conservateur* became Peel's Conservative party with all its ambivalences about amelioration, inclusiveness and

[66] Reginald Northam, *Conservatism* (1939), 40.
[67] Gilmour, *Inside Right*, 132.
[68] Hogg, *The Case for Conservatism*, 10. Patten's list of proper things to do (wry in face of recent prosecutions of Tory notables) therefore has a certain *deja vu*: 'books, music, pictures, work, friendship, admiring fine buildings and the countryside, enjoyment, having and bringing up a family.' *The Tory Case*, 22.
[69] *Case for Conservatism*, 13.
[70] See Michael Bentley, 'Liberal Politics and the Grey Conspiracy of 1921', *Historical Journal* (1977), 461–78.

progress. Avoiding the neo-platonism that attaches to seeing Liberal Toryism as a reified entity or the sillinesses that surround thinking of it as a piece of mapable territory saves us from some of its ineffability. But doing so leaves a larger task. For this collection of dialects about the past, the State, the economy, the international community, the people, the class system, the character of politics itself, requires an historical invigilation of a kind it has yet to receive. In this respect modern historians ride thirty years behind the early-modern, for whom the idea and implications of political languages are widely acknowledged.[71] What twentieth century Liberal Toryism requires, as I hope I have shown, is a recognition that it cannot be understand without its nineteenth-century relatives; but, even more than that, it requires an application of those historical procedures that have deconstructed seventeenth-century political ideas into their linguistic components and implied that historians still have a distinctive place in the history of political thought.

[71] Anthony Pagden (ed.), *The Languages of Political Theory in Early-Modern Europe* (Cambridge, 1987, 1990), comments on some case-studies. In general I have in mind the work of John Pocock, Quentin Skinner and those influenced by them since the 1960s.

'HARVESTING THE CUPBOARDS': WHY BRITAIN HAS PRODUCED NO ADMINISTRATIVE THEORY OR IDEOLOGY IN THE TWENTIETH CENTURY

By Peter Hennessy

READ 25 SEPTEMBER AT THE UNIVERSITY OF SHEFFIELD

MY purpose today is to do a kind of David Bellamy on the least promising patch of that unmapped, unloved bog-of-a-phenomenon we call 'The British Constitution'. You know the sort of thing—'this might just look like a boring old bundle of procedures and conventions to you, but there's life and insight in here!'

If ennui is already setting in, don't be upset. You are part of the grand tradition of our political nation. For my text today is from Mr Gladstone—his celebrated remark to the effect that:

> If there are two things on earth that John Bull hates, they are an abstract proposition and the Pope.[1]

Gently disposing of His Holiness, let me concentrate on what has been for the British that most abstract, and, sometimes, most resented of entities—the State. And I've introduced the Grand Old Man at the beginning quite deliberately. Because the administrative genes of the late-twentieth century British State—not its political or its electoral ones, but its administrative ones—are still mutations of that special cluster of DNA Mr G. spun into a kind of double helix in the mid- to late-nineteenth century. By this I mean the split between ministers and civil servants, the divide between the political and the administrative, the temporary government and the permanent government (to borrow Anthony Verrier's distinction), thus largely fulfilling the wish of his great mentor, Sir Robert Peel that Britain be administered and governed by impartial administration.[2] This, plus Gladstone's probity reforms, designed to keep the hands of public servants out of the public purse, was his and his century's greatest gift to our century. Yet for reasons I don't entirely understand, he put money matters on a statutory basis

[1] John H. Morgan, *John, Viscount Morley, An Appreciation and Some Reminiscences* (1924), 144.

[2] See Anthony Verrier, *Through the Looking Glass: British Foreign Policy in the Age of Illusions* (1983). Gladstone described Peel as 'my great master and teacher in public affairs' Lord Rosebery, *Sir Robert Peel*, (1899), 48.

with the Exchequer and Audit Act of 1866, but left the equally crucial people part of the reform to that convenient sleight-of-hand we know as the royal prerogative, making his changes (as Prime Ministers continue to do to this day) through civil service Orders in Council.

Some 120 years on, parliament is at last waking up to this curious asymmetry between statute and prerogative in Whitehall. As part of the current concern about civil service ethics and whether Whitehall is in danger of turning into 'Bluehall' after fourteen years of Conservative government, the all-party Treasury and Civil Service Select Committee is considering whether a Civil Service Act is now needed to entrench the Gladstonian principles, drawn from the Northcote-Trevelyan Report of 1854,[3] of a public service recruited solely on the basis of merit with a political neutrality that enables it to transfer its capacities and loyalties from one set of ministers to another at the flick of the electorate's wrist.[4]

There are good reasons for the Select Committee's concern whether or not one believes, as I do, that Sir Bernard Ingham or Sir Charles Powell apart,[5] senior civil servants did not 'go native' on Mrs Thatcher or her 'ism' between 1979 and 1990. For there were two assumptions implicit in Gladstone's and Robert Lowe's creation (through, mainly, the 1870 Order in Council) of a permanent career civil service.[6] First, that governments would change with reasonable regularity. Second, that the ideological differences between the competing parties would remain relatively limited in terms of policy, the mechanics of the state and the fundamentals of constitutional practice.

Mr Gladstone could not have foreseen the development of what Giovanni Sartori calls a modern 'predominant party system'[7] with four successive Conservative election victories, a phenomenon unknown in 1870 since pre-Reform Act days. Nor could he have anticipated the attitudinal gulf between the parties in the early to mid-1980s, especially on foreign and defence policy, which led the then Permanent Secretary to the Foreign Office, Sir Antony Acland, to declare in a radio interview,

> that if a government were to decide to take Britain out of Europe,
> that would be very unsettling and worrying for a large number of

---

[3] The easiest way of consulting the Northcote-Trevelyan Report in full is to consult Appendix 3 of the Fulton Report of 1968: *The Civil Service, Vol. 1: Report of the Committee 1966–68* (1968), 108–31.

[4] Treasury and Civil Service Committee, *The Role of the Civil Service: Interim Report*, I and II, Session 1992–93, Sixth Report, HC 390–I and 390 II.

[5] See my forthcoming 'The Civil Service since 1979' in *Turning Japanese?* eds. Helen Margetts and Gareth Smyth.

[6] For the post-1870 changes, see Peter Hennessy, *Whitehall* (1989), 47–51.

[7] Giovanni Sartori, *Parties and Party Systems: A Framework for Analysis* (Cambridge, 1976), 196.

members of the Foreign and Commonwealth Office, and I think for home civil servants as well. But there are other issues too which would cause them great anxiety: I think the withdrawal from NATO, or going wholly unilateralist, would also cause great anxieties in the minds of quite a number of us.[8]

Sir Antony was speaking in 1984, perhaps the moment of greatest polarisation in postwar British politics. It was a remarkable event—a career official saying, in effect, that a tranche of senior public servants might find themselves unable to serve wholeheartedly their Foreign Secretary in a democratically elected Labour government.

Those implicit assumptions in the Gladstonian settlement—central notions of his administrative reforms—were just that. They were not explicit theories to be encoded or embodied in statute. It was a pre-Weberian approach to the profession of government and it has endured. It is as if Mr G. and Robert Lowe felt it quite unnecessary for the 'true votaries',[9] as Lowe called them, in this new Whitehall to require such specifics. They, young men moving straight from university into public service, knew in their bones what was proper and improper. They carried checks and balances in their metabolism.

Clive Priestley, chief-of-staff in Mrs Thatcher's Efficiency Unit under Lord Rayner—and a great Northcote-Trevelyan man—once described this Whitehall equivalent of the 'Code of the Woosters' as the 'good chaps theory of government',[10] the argument being that a good chap knows what a good chap has to do and doesn't need to be told. (Interestingly enough, Mr Priestley was explaining this particular ingredient of the British public service ethos to a group of fairly bemused political-appointees in the Reagan Administration, in the entirely suitable surroundings of St George's, Windsor, at an Adam Smith Institute Conference in 1985).

Lowe himself captured the atheoretical, *ad hominem* essence of the Gladstonian reforms when he said in 1873 of the new 'competition wallahs' that they should have 'the best education that England affords: the education of public schools and colleges and such things, which give a sort of freemasonry among men which is not very easy to describe, but which everyone feels.'[11]

Such vagueness continued until Mrs Thatcher's time, when the Financial Management Initiative of 1982 and its successor initiatives took care of such woolliness in the era of 'performance indicators',

---

[8] Simon Jenkins and Anne Sloman, *With Respect, Ambassador* (1985), 103.

[9] James Winter, *Robert Lowe*, (Toronto, 1976), 264.

[10] Clive Priestley, 'Promoting the efficiency of central government', in *Managing the Bureaucracy*, eds. Arthur Shenfield *et al.* (1986), 117.

[11] Winter, *Lowe*, 264.

'mission statements', 'corporate plans' and 'Next Steps' agencies. In the mid-twentieth century, for example, the head of the civil service, Edward Bridges (son of the Poet Laureate, Etonian, classical scholar and Great War hero) treated a Cambridge audience to his 'Portrait of a Profession' in the 1950 Rede Lecture. Even at this stage in modern British administrative history—with Lasalle's 'night watchman state' long gone, a fully-fashioned welfare state up and running with over a million in the National Health Service and a nationalised industry workforce more than twice that—Bridges' portrait was a beautifully painted, almost dreamily impressionist affair which Gladstone and Lowe would have recognised instantly and approvingly. 'A Civil Servant's Life', Sir Edward began,

> makes him above all, a realist. He is less easily elated, less readily discouraged than most men by every-day happenings. Outwardly he may appear cynical or disillusioned, and perhaps to be disinclined to put up a fight for things which excite others. But that is because he has learnt by experience that the walls of Jericho do not nowadays fall flat even after seven circumambulations to the sound of the trumpet, and that many of the results which he wants to see come about in the most unexpected of ways. Once the crust of apparent disillusion is pierced, you will find a man who feels with the fiercest intensity for those things which he has learnt to cherish—those things, that is to say, which a lifetime of experience has impressed upon him as matters which are of vital concern for the continued well-being of the community.[12]

Thus, being a British civil servant has nothing to do with theory and everything to do with 'a lifetime of experience' and a notion of what is 'of vital concern for the continued well-being of the community'. In other words, it is a state of mind. Theory, if theory there be in Bridges' evocation of his craft, is one of guardianship of the essentials of continuity and those matters necessary for national well-being.

It was such notions as these which lay behind that rather marvellous scene in the War Cabinet Office in late 1941, when Bridges recruited Keith Hancock to supervise the preparation of a series of official histories of the war. 'Was there any point', Hancock asked, 'in starting to write the history of the war before we had won it?' Bridges replied that 'I would find ways of making myself useful in short term but I must also think in long term of the continuity of the State and the advantage of funding our experience for future use...'[13]

'Funds of experience' meant much in the Whitehall generation of

---

[12] Sir Edward Bridges, *Portrait of a Profession* (Cambridge, 1951), 31.
[13] W. K. Hancock, *Country and Calling* (1954), 196–7.

Edward Bridges and Norman Brook, a stark contrast to today when the official history side of the Cabinet Office's Historical Section is a much shrivelled thing and when so many official histories have been semi-privatised with, thankfully, foundations like Leverhulme stepping in to finance the *British Documents on the end of Empire* Series.[14]

The aura of Edward Bridges survived overtly amongst the cardinals of the British bureaucracy until fairly recent times. For example, on the day Sir Ian Bancroft took over the Curia, and became head of the home civil service in 1978, he said he wanted to set a tone as Sir Edward had done and he regarded his Service as a fixed national asset borrowed by successive sets of ministers.[15]

Administration-as-a-state of mind survived as the British way of central government from Mr Gladstone to Mrs Thatcher, through two world wars, the rise of the Labour party and its election into office, the waxing and waning of Empire and an increase in the reach of the State inconceivable and unconceived when the human specifications of the modern civil service were pieced together from 1854 to 1870. If I had to date its demise, it was shortly after the 1983 general election, when a note went forth from Sir Derek Rayner of Marks and Spencer, installed in the Cabinet Office as Mrs Thatcher's Efficiency Adviser, obliging all Permanent Secretaries to fulfil a certain management requirement. 'Is "must" a word to use to Princes?', minuted the head of the home civil service and Cabinet Secretary, Sir Robert Armstrong.[16] Sir Robert was echoing, I think, his hero, Lord Burghley, who had been to Elizabeth I what Armstrong was to Mrs Thatcher.

By the mid-1980s, Bridges' profession had ceased to be a largely self-regulating one. I shall come in a moment to the latest management reforms—theory-driven or otherwise—which replaced state of mind-cum-self-regulation as the operational ethic of the senior civil service.

I would like to turn first to the heart of central government administration—Cabinet and premiership—the core of the 'core executive' to use the rather ugly phrase recent political scientists have coined.[17] It was a pair of the best of the 'good chaps' that twentieth century Whitehall has groomed, who, in their different ways, turned my mind towards possible lines of research to see if, even her, it was Bagehot's

[14] See Peter Hennessy, 'The Spell of Palm and Pine', *Times Educational Supplement*, 8 October 1993.

[15] Hennessy, *Whitehall*, 150. For who owns Whitehall, see Lord Bancroft, 'Whitehall Management: A Retrospect' Lecture delivered by the Royal Society of Arts, 30 January 1984.

[16] Private information.

[17] See the special edition of *Public Administration*, LXVIII, 1, Spring 1990, Patrick Dunleavy, R. A. W. Rhodes and Brendan O'Leary (eds), on 'Prime Minister, Cabinet and Core Executive.'

'cake of custom'[18] rather than anything declaratory, systematic or explicit which might be found as the key to why and how our singular processes of government are carried out as they are.

First, Lord Trend, who, as Sir Burke Trend had served as Cabinet Secretary to Harold Macmillan, Alec Home, Harold Wilson and Ted Heath. He wrote a kind review of my study, *Cabinet*,[19] in which he had made much of Lord Haldane's 1918 report on the Machinery of Government.[20] Writing in 1986 Burke Trend said:

> A comprehensive job on the Haldane model badly needs to be done, not least because it could offer an opportunity, which is becoming overdue, to reassess the machinery of government in terms not simply of tinkering with departmental structures and organisation but of tackling the conceptual problem of the correct relationship between a government's social and economic policies and its administrative machinery which will take us into the twenty-first century.[21]

I called on him and asked him to elaborate. Trend regarded Haldane as a one-off in terms of the British administrative tradition, his thought the fruit of a marriage between a university department of philosophy and the War Office. 'He'd been Secretary of State for War. He thought in terms of military planning ... [and] ... he was a philosopher a Hegelian,' Trend explained.[22] It was exactly these traits which led that most pragmatic connoisseur of British governmental practice, Roy Jenkins, to dismiss Haldane as a politician with 'a strong and persistent taste for rather cloudy metaphysics'.[23] But Trend was 'a great admirer, though'; he went on , 'I didn't read him attentively until I was thinking about the Central Policy Review Staff [the famous Cabinet Office "think tank"] in 1970.'[24]

This recollection of Trend's was what raised the possibility in my mind that here, at least, there might be an intellectual, even perhaps, a theoretical pedigree between the Haldane Report of 1918 and *The Reorganisation of Central Government* White Paper of 1970, which embodied, not just the 'think tank' idea but that bundle of efficiency reforms (fewer and larger government departments, a smaller Cabinet, a zero-based budgeting system called programme and analysis review)[25] which

[18] Walter Bagehot, *Physics and Politics* (1872), Kegan Paul edition (undated), 27.

[19] Peter Hennessy, *Cabinet* (1986).

[20] *Report of the Machinery of Government Committee*, Cd 9230 (1918). For Lord Trend's review see Burke Trend, 'Machinery under pressure', *Times Literary Supplement*, 26 September 1986, 1076.

[21] *Ibid.*

[22] Conversation with Lord Trend, 1 October 1986.

[23] Roy Jenkins, *Asquith* (Fontana ed. 1967), 34.

[24] Conversation with Lord Trend, 1 October, 1986.

[25] *The Reorganisation of Central Government*, Cmnd 4506, (1970).

was to comprise the Whitehall component of what Edward Heath called his 'quiet revolution'.[26] The White Paper containing them was drafted, incidentally, chiefly by Trend, Sir William Armstrong, then head of the home civil service and Ian Bancroft who was to be his successor-but-one.[27]

The Haldane Report is generally remembered for a single passage, a gem of understatement recalled each time a government rushes into a policy initiative as ill-thought out as it is significant—'We have come to the conclusion ... that in the sphere of civil government the duty of investigation and thought as preliminary to action, might with great advantage be more definitely recognized.'

On this side of its findings, the Haldane Report has become rather like the People's Charter of 1838—a laundry list whose demands/recommendations can be checked off as many, though not all, became a reality with the passage of time.

> Research councils (with the foundation of the Social Science Research Council in 1965 the arc was almost complete, though even after the 1993 White Paper, we still await one for the Humanities).[28]
>
> A ministry of research (in a way the Central Policy Review Staff fulfilled that function between 1971 and 1983, though Haldane did not get a bespoke department with its own Cabinet minister until William Waldegrave was appointed Minister for Public Service and Science in 1992).
>
> Standing committees of parliament to cover the main divisions of government (A 61-year time lag here ending with the creation of the new departmentally-related select committees of the House of Commons in 1979).

But what Trend had in mind was Haldane's delineation of the chief functions of the Cabinet and the fistful of conditions whose fulfilment was 'essential, or, at least desirable' if those functions were to be carried out efficiently. First, the trio of functions:

(a) the final determination of the policy to be submitted to Parliament;
(b) the supreme control of the national executive in accordance with the policy prescribed by Parliament; and
(c) the continuous co-ordination and delimitation of the activities of the several Departments of State.

Next, the quintet of conditions:

[26] John Campbell, *Edward Heath: A Biography* (1993), 311.
[27] Private information.
[28] See the latest Government White Paper on science policy, *Realising Our Potential: A Strategy for Science, Engineering and Technology*, Cm 2250, (1993).

(a) the Cabinet should be small in number—preferably ten, or, at most, twelve;
(b) it should meet frequently;
(c) it should be supplied in the most convenient form with all the information and material necessary to enable it to arrive at expeditious decisions;
(d) it should make a point of consulting personally all the Ministers whose work is likely to be affected by its decisions; and
(e) it should have a systematic method of securing that its decisions are effectually carried out by the several Departments concerned.[29]

An Audit here reminds me of Mount Everest pre-1953, a host of heroic attempts ending in failure: how often did we hear (and still do as the battle of the memoirs rages) of full Cabinet being reduced to the imprint of a handbag during the Thatcher years or of the persistent difficulties of integrating complicated policies which cross departmental boundaries.

A smaller Cabinet has proved immensely difficult to achieve in peacetime, though Attlee, Churchill and Heath tried. Briefing for ministers on Cabinet matters that do not closely affect their departmental interests remains a problem and the few individual ministers who have attempted a remedy (Callaghan at the Home Office after 1967;[30] William Rodgers at Transport after 1976[31]) have failed within a few months. The problems of policy implementation have vexed every Cabinet and premier since Armistice Day.

The 1970 White Paper struck a succession of Haldanian themes and notes—the need to blend functions and unify policy, 'a radical improvement in the information system available to Ministers', the need to avoid overload and duplication, 'a strategic definition of objectives' and 'a capability at the centre for assessment of policies and projects in relation to strategic objectives', with common information 'free from purely departmental considerations'.[32]

Yet even that latter day Haldanian, Burke Trend, brought the full power of the grand pragmatic tradition to the running of this new 'capability unit'.

'I wanted to call it "the Think Tank",' Heath told an RIPA lecture audience a decade later.[33] 'The Secretary of the Cabinet won and we called it the Central Policy Review Staff.' Trend objected. Why? 'It

[29] Cd. 9230.
[30] James Callaghan, *Time and Chance* (1987), 232.
[31] Conversation with William Rodgers, 8 September 1993.
[32] Cmnd 4506, 6–13.
[33] Edward Heath, *The First Keeling Memorial Lecture*, Royal Institute of Public Administration, 7 May 1980.

became known as the Think Tank' he said later, 'but they weren't quite the words you could see on the front of a White Paper. I remember scratching my head and sucking my pencil and thinking, "What on earth are we going to call this thing?" And then it seemed to me that if you took the words which we finally did adopt, they came as near as I could come to being accurate about it. It *was* central, it *was* concerned with policy; and it *was* concerned with reviewing policy centrally and it consisted of a staff, not a political unit.'[34]

I mentioned an intellectual, perhaps even a theoretical thread from Haldane to Heath. Where is the evidence for this? Could the research angle, that very notion of a 'think tank' whose Herman Kahnish Americanness[35] so offended Trend's Englishness, be the strand which links? (Though, Trend should not have been alarmed. According to legend 'think tank' was originally a very English invention—Cockney, no less. Like the term 'brain box', it was a synonym for grey matter.[36])

There have, after all, been a series of attempts to boost the analytical capability at the very centre of government from Baldwin's Committee of Civil Research, with its brief to produced 'connected forethought from a central standpoint to the development of economic, scientific and statistical research in relation to civil policy and administration',[37] (under the chairmanship of that supreme political intellectual, Arthur Balfour), through Ramsay MacDonald's Economic Advisory Council, Attlee's, Morrison's and Cripps' Central Economic Planning Staff, and Churchill's Statistical Section (in both its war and peace incarnations) with Lloyd George's Prime Minister's Secretariat, the famous 'Garden Suburb', as the prototype of all of them.

This, I think, is more than stretching a point, it's snapping a non-existent piece of elastic. The problems these bureaucratic accretions bolted, at various times and in various ways, to the Whitehall super-structure, were intended to address had their similarities—the need for agreed data especially on the economic and industrial intractabilities of a country with an ever more 'thinly lined Exchequer' (to use Paul Gore-Booth's apt phrase[38]). But to see a theoretical link between them is far fetched—though occasionally, thought was given to earlier models, Trend-and-Haldane style, before a new marque was designed. And in one case the human link was real enough—Lord Plowden the former

[34] Conversation with Lord Trend, 7 November 1983, for BBC Radio 3's *Routine Punctuated by Orgies*.

[35] For its US development see James A. Smith, *The Idea Brokers: Think Tanks and the Rise of the New Policy Elite*, (Washington, 1991), xiii–xiv.

[36] Peter Hennessy and Simon Coates, *Little Grey Cells: Think Tanks, Governments and Policy Making*, Strathclyde Analysis Paper No 6, (1991), 1.

[37] Henry Roseveare, *The Treasury, The Evolution of a British Institution* (1969), 172.

[38] Paul Gore-Booth, *With Great Truth and Respect* (1974), 232.

head of the Central Economic Planning Staff being counted among the more important of Edward Heath's advisers in the late 1960s on the 'think tank' idea.[39]

Beyond these tenuous connections, it was all expediency and *ad hoccery* rather than anything worthy of the name of a British synthesis on how best to provide extra, enhanced advice and analysis to ministers or prime ministers, at the apex of power. The search for a special British theory of administration here was plainly doomed.

Why not, therefore, embrace reality by recognising that pragmatism is the only common theme? Here I come to the second of my *animateurs*, another supreme insider and a Cabinet Secretary like Lord Trend, the present incumbent Sir Robin Butler. The occasion was a conversation in the Cabinet Office in July 1990 for the purposes of one of my 'Whitehall' Watch' columns in *The Independent*. We talked about the possibility of a hung parliament after the next election and I asked him how he, the Queen's Private Secretary and the Prime Minister's Principal Private Secretary would proceed in such an eventuality? 'You try to make sure you get the documents in hand', Sir Robin replied. 'A lot of things have been done in the past in the three weeks before an election. The documents are always in the cupboards.'[40]

Here again, precedent, not theory is king, or, rather queen. Even though, in the event, the result was clear cut (though the three men concerned just happened to be dining together on election night[41]), my curiosity remained aroused by this very British way of proceeding at a moment, potentially, of intense political uncertainty. If *they* 'go to the cupboards', I thought, *I* will too—or at least to those cupboards whose contents have been emptied at the Public Record Office. Having found but one file on the royal prerogative at election time, that dealing with the 1959 general election,[42] I made pleas to the palace and the Cabinet Office to have the hundred year rule for palace-related material reduced to thirty. To my great pleasure the *Open Government* White Paper of July 1993 acceded to my request.[43]

'Weeding' is now under way, and No 10 is considering giving it priority.[44] As yet, we cannot carry out a quality audit on the result. So this is very much a report on 'work in progress'.

[39] Conversation with Lord Plowden, 13 October 1983.

[40] Conversation with Sir Robin Butler, 24 July 1990. I have Sir Robin's permission to quote him.

[41] Private information.

[42] Public Record Office, PREM 11/2654.

[43] *Open Government*, Cm 2290, (1993), 68.

[44] Letter from John Holroyd, Departmental Record Officer, No 10 Downing Street, to Peter Hennessy, 5 August 1993.

But the real gold seam is the Cabinet Office's own 'cupboard' category—the CAB 21 series—which contains the working files of what must be dubbed the lead constitutional department in Whitehall. And, rummaging through them this summer, I came across a couple of cross-references to a file from 1954 which had not reached Kew. It's title? 'British Constitutional System'.

It was almost one of those moments which occasionally cause embarrassment and mirth in the PRO reading room—when a researcher feels like 'The Guy Who Found the Lost Chord' and succumbs to a Jimmy Durante impression. Encouraged by the new climate of openness, I wrote swiftly to the Cabinet Secretary asking for the file to be found, reviewed and released. It was, and such is the new climate, I was invited into the Cabinet Office to consult it. What did I find? The Holy Grail? The genetic code of the system? A theoretical treatise? No.

I found a letter to Sir Ivor Jennings following up a chat he'd had with Sir Norman Brook in the course of updating his *Cabinet Government* in the late 1940s. A rather useful organogram of 'The Central Executive Government of Great Britain' in November 1944. A list of 'certain matters which, by convention, are not made the subject of collective decision by the Cabinet'. A description of the functions of the Cabinet Office in January 1953 and what looks like a lecture on 'Cabinet Government' delivered by the Cabinet Secretary, probably in the late 1940s, which ends with the following paragraph, rather germane to today's theme:

> The existing system of Cabinet Committees is in fact a typically British mixture of empiricism and conscious form. It is constantly being adapted to changing circumstances—by the severely prag-matical test of 'What works best'—and it makes no pretence to schematic perfection.[45]

There is a brief from August 1948, created for reasons unknown, on the Cabinet system (starting off with Haldane's three chief functions) and including the relationship of ministers to their departments and officials. And the *pièce de résistance*, a list drawn up by Stuart Milner-Barry, of the Treasury's organisation and methods division, of the growth of government institutions and personal offices, sixty-one pages of it, beginning with the office of Lord Chancellor in the eleventh century and finishing on 1 April 1956 with the transfer of the admin-istration of agricultural research grants from the Ministry of Agriculture to the Agricultural Research Council.[46]

[45] 'Cabinet Government', undated, PRO, CAB 21/4548, British Constitutional System.
[46] *Ibid.*

And that's it. So much for Jimmy Durante. The search for the code, if not the chord, goes on.

Other files in CAB 21 are more promising, however. Take first, the early versions of *Questions of Procedure for Ministers*, the ministerial rulebook first distributed by Attlee within a few days of becoming P.M.[47] In May 1949, Sir Norman Brook's private secretary, Ronald Fraser, undertook a grand consolidation embracing the scattering of directives Attlee issued in his first $3\frac{1}{4}$ years in office. The CAB 21 files show graphically how Fraser worked in blending the ingredients into this particular 'cake of custom'.[48]

The constitutional status of '*QPM*', as it's known in Whitehall, is ambiguous. I have long regarded it as the nearest we have in Britain to a written constitution for Cabinet government, a kind of 'surrogate' for it.[49] Burke Trend said *QPM* was 'not a constitution, merely some tips for beginners—a book of etiquette'.[50] Sir Robin Butler, regarded by the present premier, as the Michael Mates affair showed,[51] as not just custodian, but interpreter of *QPM*, does not regard the document as enjoying the status of a constitutional convention, maintaining that it is 'discretionary' and could be dispensed with tomorrow if a new Prime Minister so chose. Though I have to say that if one accepts Dicey's classic definition of a convention as expressing 'the constitutional morality' of our system of government or, my own favourite, the Le May definition of 'the general agreements among public men about the "rules of the game" to be borne in mind in the conduct of political affairs', it is hard to see what *QPM* amounts to, taken together, if not a constitutional convention.[52]

Sir Robin's own metaphor for the organic nature of the British constitution is taken from the forests—'... it grows like a Christmas tree with new things added to it ... We have an unwritten constitution and to that extent it develops by custom and practice,'[53] he told the Treasury and Civil Service Select Committee earlier this year, while

---

[47] Initially, the instructions to ministers took the form of two Cabinet papers—'Cabinet Procedure' and 'Miscellaneous Questions of Procedure'. PRO, CAB 66/67; CP (45)99, 8th August 1945.

[48] PRO, CAB 21/1624, 'Cabinet Procedure: Consolidated Version of the Prime Minister's Directives'.

[49] Hennessy, *Cabinet*, 8.

[50] Conversation with Lord Trend, 1 October 1986.

[51] According to Mr Major's leaked off-the-record comments to the Political Editor of ITN, Michael Brunson, the PM explained: 'As the Cabinet Secretary told me, "It was an act of gross injustice to have got rid of him [Mates]"'. Anthony Bevin's, 'Why does a complete wimp keep winning?' *The Independent*, 27 July 1993.

[52] Private information; A. V. Dicey, *Introduction to the Study of the Law of the Constitution* (1885), 424. G. H. L. Le May, *The Victorian Constitution* (1979), 1.

[53] *The Role of the Civil Service: Interim Report*, 24–5.

discussing the significance of *QPM* and the 'Armstrong Memorandum' on *The Duties and Responsibilities of Civil Servants in Relation to Ministers*.[54]

QPM is the most glittering twentieth century example of this 'Christmas tree' phenomenon, growing from thirty-seven paragraphs in its August 1945 prototype to sixty-four paragraphs by the time it left Ronald Fraser's hands in 1949. Intriguingly, it had shrunk to fifty-seven paragraphs when Macmillan re-issued it in February 1958[55] though it was up once more to eighty-five paragraphs by the time Wilson had won the election in 1966.[56]

When Callaghan replaced Wilson in April 1976, *QPM* was a mighty 132 paragraphs[57]. By 1983 under Mrs Thatcher, it had added another two,[58] and there it remained when John Major, breaking with the tight secrecy of the past, declassified it in May 1992.[59] By the time the next version appears it will, I reckon, have risen to 135 to take account of the 'Lamont contingency' arising from his financial difficulties with his tenant, 'Miss Whiplash'.[60]

I carried the file containing the first substantial postwar revision of *QPM* with me to Edinburgh this summer and placed it in the hands of R. P. Fraser who had not seen it for over 43 years. As he leafed through it, we chatted about its significance.

Hennessy: It just grows, like coral, doesn't it?

Fraser: I think that is an apt simile, indeed.

Hennessy: I have thought for some time that whenever this side of the British constitution is developed, it's a young man or woman in their late twenties in the Cabinet Secretary's Private Office who does it.

Fraser: Probably, probably. But one didn't see it in those terms. One was conscious that it provided something to be going on with in a purely practical way. I don't think we saw our role as having anything more than a limited, day-to-day significance. One rarely had time to reflect.[61]

[54] *The Duties and Responsibilities of Civil Servants in Relation to Ministers: Note by the Head of the Home Civil Service*, Cabinet Office, (1985).

[55] PRO, CAB 129/91, 'Questions of Procedure for Ministers', C (58)45, 24th February 1958.

[56] C (P) 665, 'Questions of Procedure for Ministers', 5 April 1966. Still unpublished. Acquired privately.

[57] C (PR) (76) 1, 'Questions of Procedure for Ministers', 23rd April 1976. Still unpublished. Acquired privately.

[58] C (P) (83)5, 'Questions of Procedure for Ministers', 27 June 1983. Still unpublished. Acquired privately.

[59] *Questions of Procedure for Ministers*, Cabinet Office, (1992).

[60] *Payment of Legal Expenses Incurred by the Chancellor of the Exchequer*, House of Commons Committee of Public Accounts, 25th Report, 1992–93 Session, 22 April 1993.

[61] Conversation with R. P. Fraser, 26 August 1993.

Yet Mr Fraser did recall an artefact alluded to in several CAB 21 documents but never released *in toto*—'The Precedent Book'. Some fragments have been declassified including a very useful file on 'The Function of the Prime Minister and His Staff' drafted by a certain William Armstrong in the Treasury's machinery of government division in 1947 after a request for a briefing from the Institute of Public Administration when one of its members had to deliver a paper on the subject at an international conference in Berne in July that year.[62]

By the time Fraser became involved with the file it had plainly become part of 'The Precedent Book' and it had been expanded to include a fascinating section on the most special of special relationships, that between Monarch and Premier, which has baffled every observer since Bagehot.[63]

'The Precedent Book', Fraser explained, had been started by his predecessor, the same William Armstrong, because a sputtering argument about the use of official papers by former ministers wishing to write their memoirs had caused him to go back and look up the precedents since Lloyd George. Fraser himself handed on these fruits of experience to his successor, A. W. Bavin, in the form of 'quite voluminous notebooks'.[64] 'It was very much the way these things are discharged', he continued, clearly recognising the entirely reactive nature of the process, before delivering the best answer (from insider or outsider) I have encountered to the question that is my theme today.

> I suppose, in a sense we saw our role as a gathering of the harvest over long years of experience. Our function was to explain the relevance of that for the modern age or the situation that confronted us on the general premise that there would be a number of principles that governed the way the system operated.[65]

'Christmas trees', 'coral', 'precedent books', 'funds of experience', 'a gathering of the harvest'. There you have it. Not a theory in sight and no ideology, save an unswerving devotion to the pragmatic or what Whitehall, generation on generation, has liked to call 'the practical'.[66]

May I offer some afterthoughts on the so-called 'new public management' of the late 1980s and early 1990s? It is plain that at the very core of the 'core executive', the Cabinet and premiership terrain, that

[62] PRO, CAB 21/1638, 'Function of the Prime Minister and his staff'.

[63] Walter Bagehot, '*The Monarchy*' in Norman St John Stevas, *The Collected Works of Walter Bagehot*, V, (1974), 243.

[64] Conversation with R. P. Fraser, 26th August 1993.

[65] *Ibid.*

[66] Quoted in Peter Hennessy and Simon Coates, *The Back of the Envelope: Hung Parliaments, the Queen and the Constitution*, Strathclyde *Analysis* Paper No 5. (1991), 17.

the old ways of ordering and adjudicating affairs are intact, that the ancient constitution, if you like, is still operational if messily and opaquely. Though the Cabinet Secretary, Sir Robin Butler, did admit, during questioning by the Treasury and Civil Service Select Committee this spring that on *Questions of Procedure for Ministers*, civil service ethics and related matters, that he was 'the supreme judge of whether or not constitutional conventions are being broken.' (the phrase is Giles Radice's; the MP who was putting the questions).[67]

But what of 'Next Steps' agencies, Citizens' Charters and market testing. Does this, at last, amount to an administrative ideology of state?

I have argued in the past that the Next Steps was 'At last the 1909 show', a belated recognition that since, to pick an obvious benchmark, a national network of Labour Exchanges was established, and, post office apart, the state created a visible outlet for itself in every high street in the land, an increasing proportion of civil service manpower and money has been invested in public businesses. Until the late 1980s, such new standing armies of bureaucracy were treated almost as territorials, as something to be grafted on to an early nineteenth century bone structure of small, hierarchically taut policy departments in which something approaching genuine political control was possible. Hence, in spinning out the big public businesses from the narrow confines of core ministries, the 'Next Steps' was at last recognising a 'New Liberal' reality rather than any Thatcherite philosophy of state, that Mrs T. was treading where LG and Churchill should have trod eighty years before.[68]

The Citizens' Charter is misnamed. It should be called the 'Consumers' Charter'[69] for two reasons: all 57 million of us remain the Queen's subjects, we are not citizens; secondly it is a list of aspirations not a Bill of Rights. It was drawn up quite deliberately to be resistant to judicial review.[70] It has yet to be tested in the courts. But the Charter's design team in the Cabinet Office confidently expect the judges' hands to slip off it. The notion was political, not philosophical in origin. A 'big idea' was needed for Mr Major to carry round the nation as the election approached which would distinguish him from his predecessor. A 'big idea' was found largely in the fertile mind of Sarah Hogg, the

[67] *The Role of the Civil Service: Interim Report*, 25.

[68] Peter Hennessy, 'Whitehall by the year 2000: The FDA Christmas Lecture', 7 December 1992, extracts from which were published in *FDA News*, January 1993.

[69] The alternative name was originally applied by Sue Richards of the Office of Public Management and a special adviser to the Treasury and Civil Service Committee.

[70] Conversation with Brian Hilton, Head of the Citizen's Charter Unit in the Cabinet Office, 25 September 1991.

head of his Downing Street policy unit.[71] It was an attempt to marry the 'accountancy' of government, at which the Prime Minister excels, with the 'poetry' of politics, at which he does not.[72]

What, finally, of market testing for which great claims have been made, especially by the Financial Secretary to the Treasury, Stephen Dorrell, who has talked of a 'long march' which will not be ended until the state has been diminished to its 'inescapable core'?[73] This is more a loss of nerve about the public sector's capacity to conduct any activity more efficiently than the private sector (and in that sense it's purely ideological in political terms) rather than a philosophy of a 'well managed state' to use Clive Priestley's phrase.[74] It is an in-house version of a wider attempt to push further privatisation, the aspect of Mrs Thatcher's stewardship still regarded as 'one of the clear successes of the last 14 years', as Mr Dorrell put it.[75] It could be seen, uncharitably, as a classic case of political displacement activity—when all else proves politically intractable, governmentally impossible and personally souring, return to the totem pole, touch it and flaunt it for the purposes of reassurance.

If the efforts of Mr Major, Mr Dorrell, William Waldegrave and Sir Peter Levene, the current Efficiency Adviser to the PM, were directed to returning the British State to its 'nightwatchman' mode—to 'At last the 1870 show'—it might amount to an administrative ideology of state in at least this area of public or formerly public, services. But, so far, the enterprise is unworthy of such a description. It is not so much a philosophy, more a case of economy-driven expediency, with a dash of hand-washing Pontius Pilatery, with a presentational overlay intended to portray Mr Major as more radical and more determined, in this area, at least, than was his predecessor.

So whether it be in its policy-making functions, its management activities or in bonding its series of special internal interrelationships, the British state still awaits that singular combination of Charles Trevelyan, Max Weber and R. B. Haldane to give it what it has always lacked—a genuine administrative theory. Why? Because no premier or Cabinet or Select Committee has commissioned such a *tour de force*. (Haldane and the 1970 White Paper dealt with but a fragment, though

---

[71] Private information. Though to be fair to Mr Major he had pressed the case for improved public services when chief secretary to the Treasury.

[72] This apt distinction belongs to John Biffen. See his 'How Major can heal the Tory Wounds', *Evening Standard*, 20 September 1993.

[73] Stephen Dorrell, 'Redefining the Mixed Economy', speech to the Centre for Policy Studies, 23 November 1992. For William Waldegrave's version of the new philosophy see his speech to the Public Finance Foundation of 5 July 1993.

[74] Priestley, 'Promoting the Efficiency of Central Government', 115.

[75] David Owen, 'Treasury signals further sell-offs' *Financial Times*, 24 September 1993.

a central one) and because nobody in what Edward Shils might have called Britain's 'intellectual penumbra'[76] has felt moved to provide one unasked. In fact, the whole question has left successive generations of the British political and administrative classes unmoved because, as Jim Callaghan said when I asked him about its royal prerogative/hung parliament aspect:

> Well, it works, doesn't it? So I think that's the answer, even if it is on the back of an envelope and doesn't have a written constitution with every coma and every semi-colon in place. Because sometimes they can make for difficulties that common sense can overcome.[77]

There in the voice of Britain's last Labour Prime Minister, we hear the authentic notes of our ancient constitution, all improvisation and 'tacit understanding', to use Sydney Low's delicious phrase.[78] In Jim Callaghan, as in all previous Labour premiers, it could not have found a better bugler.

---

[76] Edward Shils, *The Intellectuals and the Powers and Other Essays* (Chicago, 1972), 21.
[77] Quoted in Hennessy and Coates, *The Back of the Envelope*, 18.
[78] Sydney Low, *The Governance of England* (1904), 12.

WOMEN AND THE NORMAN CONQUEST

By Pauline Stafford

READ 15 OCTOBER 1993

IN 1779 William Alexander published what is probably the first history of women in English.[1] The work is in the eighteenth-century Enlightenment tradition of Montesquieu or the Scot Millar in its wide comparative reference; it ranges over ancient and modern societies, civilised and savage. Alexander was interested, like Millar,[2] in the historical changes which had produced change for women; and convinced, like so many eighteenth-century thinkers, that change was a western phenomenon. In his story, the first great change after Rome came with the arrival of the Germans, who gave 'law and custom to all Europe' and who brought with them a new view of women. 'Their women were in many respects of equal and sometimes even greater consideration and consequence than their men'.[3] His sentiments echo those of the French writer Thomas, whom he had certainly read. In 1772 Thomas had begun his essay on the character, manners and spirit of women in different centuries by dividing the world into savages, who oppress as tyrants, orientals, who are driven to oppress due to an excess of love, and the denizens of temperate climates, where less passion allows greater freedom. It was thus from the cold 'shores of the Baltic and forests of the North' that the primitive Germans brought to Europe their spirit of gallantry and great respect for women.[4] Both Thomas and Alexander echoed and adapted Tacitus' classic picture of Germanic women. Tacitus had long since written of the high regard in which the German women were held: of the mothers and wives who urged their sons and husbands to valour, of their inspirational chastity, of the austere frugality of Germanic marriage, of wives whose controlled

[1] I am grateful to Professor Jane Gardner, Dr Ann Hughes and Dr William Stafford for guidance on aspects of the historiography of this topic.

[2] J. Millar, *The Origin of the Distinction of Ranks* (Edinburgh, 1779).

[3] W. Alexander, *The History of Women from the Earliest Antiquity to the Present Time: giving some account of almost every interesting particular concerning that sex, among all nations, ancient and modern* (1779), 10. For discussion of this rather confused work and of the Enlightenment traditions which influenced it see e.g. J. Rendall, *The Origins of Modern Feminism, Women in Britain, France and the United States, 1780–1860* (1984) and S. Tomaselli, 'The Enlightenment debate on women', *History Workshop Journal*, XX (1985), 101–24.

[4] A-L. Thomas, *Essai sur le Caractère, les Moeurs et l'Esprit des Femmes dans les différens Siècles* (Paris, 1772), reprinted with introduction and notes by Colette Michael (Paris and Geneva, 1987).

passions loved the married state itself rather than their husbands.[5]

First-century Rome and late eighteenth-century Paris and Britain may seem strange places to begin a consideration of women and the Norman Conquest, but they are significant ones. My major concern is with the question of the status of women in early English society and with the specific question of whether the Norman Conquest of 1066 ended a sort of Golden Age for women. Those questions have a long history; indeed they would not be framed in this way without that history. To approach them through their history is to appreciate their tenacity and deep roots, to understand something of where they fit in the overall development of the writing of the history of English women and to recognise the problems and pitfalls in an approach to that history which seeks Golden Ages, or indeed any simple unilinear development.

Tacitus, Alexander and Thomas were each concerned with Germanic women in general. Kemble, in his *Saxons in England* published in 1849, focussed attention specifically on the English branch of the Germanic peoples, on the foremothers of the English. For the Anglo-Saxons, as for the Germans in general, the home was a sacred place where woman was 'near akin to divinity'.[6] John Thrupp, in his study of the Anglo-Saxon home in 1862 agreed that 'the home is the wife's kingdom'. Thrupp argued for improvement during the Saxon period, culminating in the ninth and tenth centuries when 'the high education bestowed on women during the last era of Anglo-Saxon civilisation and the independent position they attained, tended to place them on an equality with the male sex; and, combined with the chastity and sobriety which generally distinguished them, offered a sound foundation for the chivalrous respect and devotion of after times'.[7] Although Thrupp does not comment specifically on the effects of the Norman Conquest on women, he feels that a sort of Golden Age certainly existed by these late Saxon times: 'no family solicitor of the present day could have wished for anything more formal' than the property rights of Anglo-Saxon widows, and the legal situation of Anglo-Saxon women included privileges 'they do not possess at the present day, except under peculiar circumstances in the city of London'.[8]

In the 1890s in America, Florence Buckstaff made the critical link between such rights and privileges and their ending at the Norman

[5] Cornelii Taciti, *De Origine et Situ Germanorum*, ed J. G. C. Anderson (Oxford, 1938), chaps 7, 18 and 19.

[6] J. M. Kemble, *The Saxons in England, a History of the English Commonwealth till the Period of the Norman Conquest* (1849), 233.

[7] J. Thrupp, *The Anglo-Saxon Home: a History of the Domestic Institutions and Customs of England from the Fifth to the Eleventh century* (1862), 74.

[8] Thrupp *op cit*, 69 and 71.

Conquest. Her treatment of the question is sophisticated ﹒
change came gradually, was not much apparent in Dome﹒
were important into the early twelfth century; her meticulous ﹒
is still an important introduction to the subject. But the change wh﹒
had come by the time of Glanvill was a Norman import, a feudal
family law; it was 'Norman dower ... which superseded the community
of property of our Anglo-Saxon forefathers'[9] and which still formed the
basis of law on the subject eight centuries later. From the high status
of Germanic women via that of their specifically English daughters we
have come at last to the deterioration of that status which the Norman
Conquest is alleged to have brought. The view was stated succinctly
by Doris Stenton in 1956. 'The evidence which has survived from
Anglo-Saxon England indicates that women were then more nearly the
equal companions of their husbands and brothers than at any other
period before the modern age. In the higher ranks of society this rough
and ready partnership was ended by the Norman Conquest, which
introduced into England a military society relegating women to a
position honourable but essentially unimportant ... [a] subjection which
feudal law imposed on all wives.'[10] Whilst far from unquestioned,[11] it is
a view which has become something of an orthodoxy. A recent article
on Anglo-Norman slavery ended with the ironic observation that the
Normans after 1066 may have freed the remaining slaves but 'this must
be set against their debasement of women in general'.[12]

All these accounts offer to a greater or lesser extent a view of a
Golden Age for women pre 1066. They call for more consideration of
Golden Ages in general, and of these Golden Ages in particular.[13]

[9] F. G. Buckstaff, 'Married women's property in Anglo-Saxon and Anglo-Norman law
and the origin of common-law dower', *Annals of the American Academy of Political and Social
Science*, IV (1893), 233–64 at 264.

[10] D. M. Stenton, *The English Woman in History* (1956), 348.

[11] M. Chibnall, 'Women in Orderic Vitalis', *Haskins Society Journal*, II (1990), 120 and
fn. Change within the period before 1066 is argued by A. Klinck, 'Anglo-Saxon women
and the law', *Journal of Medieval History*, VIII (1982), 107–21; M. A. Meyer, 'Land charters
and the legal position of Anglo-Saxon women', in *The Women of England, from Anglo-Saxon
times to the present*, ed B. Kanner (1980), 57–82 is a nuanced and thoughtful review. Literary
views of Anglo-Saxon women are reviewed by S. Hollis, *Anglo-Saxon Women and the Church*
(Woodbridge, 1992), Introduction.

[12] J. S. Moore, 'Domesday Slavery', *Anglo-Norman Studies*, XI (Woodbridge, 1989), 220
and fn.

[13] See D. Lowenthal, *The Past is a Foreign Country* (Cambridge, 1985), esp 21–28, 372.
For specific discussion of Golden Ages in women's history rebutting the idea of an early
modern Golden Age see Olwen Hufton, 'Women in History: Early Modern Europe',
Past and Present, CI (1983), 125–41 and Amanda Vickery, 'Golden Age to separate spheres?
A review of the categories and chronology of English women's history', *Historical Journal*,
XXXVI (1993), 383–414. For a rejection of such a Golden Age in the late medieval
English countryside see J. Bennett, *Women in the Medieval English Countryside* (Oxford, 1987),
4–6 and passim.

Golden ages—or their silver cousins 'the good old days'—are interpretations of the past which always do violence to it. They are simplifications. It is in their nature to be defined in relation to our concerns not those of the past, to subordinate the past to the present in a kind of historical imperialism or colonisation. The Golden Age appeals to both conservative and radical alike. For one it can be a nostalgia for a time of clear and unquestioned hierarchies and relationships, for the other an inspiring and reassuring reminder that changes sought now are merely a return to the past, are possible now because they existed then. It can be antithesis of present ills or perfection of present aspirations, but the present is usually its referent. It allows continual reformulation as the concerns of the present change. As in so many critiques of the here and now, women and gender are often used as a tool of argument. The apparent unanimity over the Golden Age for women in early England masks a debate over the position of women in civil society which has produced differing definitions of those halcyon times.

Tacitus' Germanic women, for example, were a foil to the decadence of contemporary Rome, which he, like many of his contemporaries, blamed on women. Society for him is healthy when women are chaste, mothers and controlled by their husbands, not when they visit the theatre and the baths, exchange love letters with their lovers and fail to breastfeed. Tacitus constructs a Germanic woman with which to beat the Romans of his own day.[14]

Kemble, using Anglo-Saxon women against the feminists of his own day, was happy to echo the ancient Roman. He placed Anglo-Saxon women and their high status firmly within the home, that sacred place where women were 'near akin to divinity'. But there they should stay. To complete the quotation 'not one of them ever raved that the *femme libre* could be woman'. Early English women happily accepted men's representation of them in public life, content to be beings of a higher nature. They did not clamour and rave for the rights of women. Kemble's Teutonic women are a mid-nineteenth-century conservative male pipe dream.

Florence Buckstaff, by contrast, redefined the Anglo-Saxon Golden age as one of legal rights and landholding. She castigated late nineteenth-century America with precisely that tradition of Anglo-Saxon liberties so important to American constitutional debate. '*Norman* dower ... which superseded the community of property of our *Anglo-Saxon* forefathers is still the rule eight centuries later in a large number of the laws of a race [i.e. America] which has no prouder name for itself

---

[14] In doing so he, like Alexander, also utilised another concept, that of the 'noble savage' or 'barbarian-as-superior'.

than Anglo-Saxon.'[15] Buckstaff shifted the debate on to the legal and landholding issues which have dominated it since. Buckstaff was the first woman regent of the University of Wisconsin and later organiser of social welfare services in that state.[16] She shifted the debate at least in part as a response to the feminist agenda of her day, one which sought legal and property rights for women.

In 1919 George Forrest Browne, bishop of Stepney and later of Bristol, gave yet another formulation to the Golden Age of Anglo-Saxon women. He emphasised the 'acumen, wit and wisdom, the intellectual promptness and vigour' of Abbess Hilda and her like.[17] Bishop Browne was a staunch supporter of women's education, involved in the admission of women to Cambridge and the foundation of Newnham.[18] For him Anglo-Saxon England was a Golden Age of religious women as educators.

Given the ability of Golden Ages to metamorphose constantly to suit current needs, it is not surprising that the most recent incarnation of Anglo-Saxon woman is as the liberated controller of her own body, a view informed by the radical feminist analysis, agenda and practice of the 1970s. Reading E. W. Williams' article 'What's so new about the sexual revolution? some comments on Anglo-Saxon attitudes towards sexuality in women based on Exeter Book riddles'[19] would surely have left Kemble's chaste Angel of the Hearth in a swoon.

Anglo-Saxon England has thus been a Golden Age variously of women's domestication, women's legal emancipation, women's education and women's sexual liberation. The length of a tradition which has changed so fundamentally over time is no guarantee of its veracity. A cursory view of a range of evidence from either side of the 1066 divide casts immediate doubt on the idea of a brutal Norman ending of the Golden Age. The raw statistics of Domesday, for example,

[15] Buckstaff, *op cit*, 264.

[16] S. M. Stuard, 'A new dimension? North American Scholars contribute their perspective', in *Women in Medieval History and Historiography*, ed. S. M. Stuard (Philadelphia, 1987), 85.

[17] G. F. Browne, *The Importance of Women in Anglo-Saxon Times: the Cultus of St Peter and St Paul and other Addresses*, Studies in Church History (1919), 24.

[18] See Alice Gardner, *A Short History of Newnham College Cambridge* (Cambridge, 1921), 11–12. He was secretary to the syndicate for local lectures in Cambridge which was so important in fostering the foundation of Newnham. He supported the proposals in the 1880s to provide some more stable form for the instruction and examination already being provided for women and was involved in the drawing up of the 'Graces' which formed the basis of Newnham.

[19] *Texas Quarterly*, XVIII (1975), 46–55. For parallel arguments that the early nunneries in Europe secured women the personal freedom of supportive all-female institutions, provided an environment which allowed them to free their bodies, souls and brains from male domination see S. Wemple, *Women in Frankish Society, Marriage and the Cloister 500–900* (Philadelphia, 1981), 163, 190.

suggest a different picture of England on the eve of the Norman arrival. No more than five per cent of the total hidage of land recorded was in the hands of women in 1066. Of that five per cent, 80–85% was in the hands of only eight women, almost all of them members of the families of the great earls, particularly of earl Godwine, or of the royal family.[20] By the tenth and eleventh centuries women other than the queen are virtually absent from the witness lists of the royal charters,[21] and thus apparently from the political significance such witness lists record.

By contrast Norman and Anglo-Norman women strike an early English historian by the range and prominence of their activity. In Musset's edition of the acts of William the Conqueror and Mathilda for the abbeys of Caen, for example, thirty documents are printed. Twenty-three of them mention women either as signatories, grantors, consenting to grants or as involved in some way in the making of the grant.[22] No collection of pre-1066 English documents shows the same proportions.[23] Twelfth-century Anglo-Norman charters regularly record the consent of wives, of mothers and sometimes even of daughters to land grants. It was only after 1066 that an English king attempted to arrange the succession for his daughter. Henry I should not be remembered in women's history as the English king who produced more known bastards than any other, but as the man who tried to pass the throne to his daughter Mathilda.[24] He may well have been the first

[20] Figures calculated by M. A. Meyer, 'Women's Estates in later Anglo-Saxon England: the politics of possession', *Haskins Society Journal*, Studies in Medieval History, ed. R. B. Patterson, III (1991), 111–29, at 113–17.

[21] Queens as witnesses: A. Campbell ed., *Encomium Emmae Reginae*, Camden Soc, Third Series, LXXII (1949), appendix 2; F. Barlow, *Edward the Confessor* (1970), 77, 93, 163 and S. Keynes, *The Diplomas of King Æthelred 'the Unready', 978–1016* (Cambridge, 1980), 187. Note in addition the witness list of S 582 [S = P. H. Sawyer, *Anglo-Saxon Charters, an annotated list and bibliography*, (1968)] where Ælfgyth *magistra* of Wilton witnessed a charter of 955 A.D. in favour of the nuns of Wilton.

[22] L. Musset, ed., *Les Actes de Guillaume le Conquérant et de la Reine Mathilde pour les Abbayes Caennaises*, Memoires de la Société des Antiquaires de Normandie, XXXVII (Caen, 1967), nos 2–16, 18–22, 25, 27. No 17 is a list of parishioners of Bourg l'Abbé, including six women out of some 67/68 people. The above list includes many *signa* and activities of Queen Mathilda, but also covers many transactions involving other women. I am grateful to Dr David Bates for pointing out the utility of the Caen charters for the study of women.

[23] The *Libellus Æthelwold* is the only English collection which approaches this for evidence of female activity. Like the Norman charters it covers private grants and disputes rather than royal. Forthcoming edition by S. Keynes, see for the present *Liber Eliensis*, ed. E. O. Blake, Camden Soc, Third Series, XCII (1962).

[24] The most recent discussion of Mathilda's claim and Henry's plans is M. Chibnall, *The Empress Mathilda* (Oxford, 1991), 50–53. Gilbert Foliot, abbot of Gloucester, felt able in 1142–3 to make a case for a daughter's inheritance based on divine, natural and human law which is unparalleled pre-1066. Chibnall *op cit*, 84–7 discusses this letter and

English king to put down in written form the right of a daughter to inherit land.[25]

This evidence sits ill with a periodisation which would see 1066 and the coming of the Normans as heralding a decline in women's status. As does the career of such a Norman woman as Mabel, daughter of Talvas, heiress of Bellême in the eleventh century. The mothering of nine children did not prevent her from actively defending her inheritance, travelling, we are told, with a retinue of one hundred armed men when necessary. She seized at least one castle and disposed of rivals, accidentally poisoning her own brother-in-law in the process. She was finally murdered, resting after her bath, by a man whom she had deprived of land. Her death, Orderic tells us, occasioned rejoicing at her ruin. Her epitaph described her as, 'A shield of her inheritance, a tower guarding the frontier; to some neighbours dear, to others terrible. She died by the sword, by night, by stealth, for we are mortals all … Pray for her.' It was not her low status activities which called for such intercession.[26] All this evidence needs careful interpretation and discussion. None of it speaks transparently about the status of women as a group or as individuals. Yet it begs for reconsideration of the tradition of seeing pre-1066 England as a sort of Golden Age of women and of deterioration with the arrival of the Normans.

That tradition unites two important Golden Ages, that of high status Germanic women and of the Norman Yoke on Anglo-Saxon liberties. High status Germanic women dated back to first-century Rome. The idea of Anglo-Saxon liberties goes back to the seventeenth century.

---

its arguments. It is printed in *The Letters and Charters of Gilbert Foliot*, eds A. Morey and C. N. L. Brooke (Cambridge, 1967), 60–6. For Henry of Huntingdon on women's claims to rule see below n. 105.

[25] This is how the implications of the *Statutum Decretum* may be interpreted. This lost royal decision, referred to as a *Statutum Decretum* in *Regesta Regum Anglo-Normannorum*, iii, eds. H. A. Cronne and R. H. C. Davis (Oxford, 1967), 39 no 106, was concerned with the division of land among daughters. Cf. S. F. C. Milsom, 'Inheritance by women in the twelfth and thirteenth centuries', in *On the Laws and Customs of England, Essays in Honor of S. E. Thorne*, eds M. S. Arnold, T. A. Green, S. A. Scully and S. D. White (Chapel Hill, 1981), 77–8. Milsom remarked that 'it took some step beyond Henry I's coronation charter in establishing female inheritance itself'. J. C. Holt, 'The heiress and the alien', *Supra*, ser 5, XXXV (1985), 11–14 argues convincingly for a date for this decision between 1130 and 1135. M. Chibnall, *Anglo-Norman England* (Oxford, 1986), 174 sees it as the preservation of traditional custom rather than deliberate change. What it did provide was the first recorded written acceptance of daughters' inheritance. It is worth speculating whether such a change was politically important to Henry I in securing the throne for his daughter.

[26] V. Chandler, 'Intimations of authority: notes on three Anglo-Norman countesses', *Indiana Social Studies Quarterly* (1978), 5–17; Orderic Vitalis, *The Ecclesiastical History*, ed M. Chibnall, especially Vol 3, Book 5 (Oxford, 1972), 134–8 for her death and epitaph.

The two traditions made ideal partners in the context of nineteenth-century Teutonism. The status of women had already emerged in the late eighteenth and early nineteenth centuries as a litmus test of civilisation and a marker for change and periodisation.[27] It pleased Kemble that his admired Teutonic ancestors, the Anglo-Saxons, treated their women better than the French Normans.[28] The Saxons never purchased their wives in the 'truly gross and vulgar sense of such purchases among those whom writers of Romances represent as the chivalrous Normans'. In claiming a loss of status for women at this alleged critical turning point of English history, Buckstaff made overt what Kemble left implicit. Women's status was linked to the idea of 1066 as a turning point of great significance, to a view of Anglo-Saxon England as the land of lost content, and to a debate long framed in legal and constitutional terms. Were it not for that critical tradition late eleventh- and twelfth-century women might have been seen differently and the period before 1066 would not have been treated as a unity in women's nor in any other area of English history.[29]

Writing whether about Germanic, Anglo-Saxon, or Anglo-Saxon and Norman women has always been in the context of debate—the history of women has been written when 'women' and their status were issues.[30] Although the tradition has developed with the advancing state of the evidence,[31] the most fundamental differences lie not in the

[27] Thus, for example, Fourier, 'As a general proposition: social advances and changes of period are brought about by virtue of the progress of women towards liberty and social retrogression occurs as a result of a diminution in the liberty of women ... The extension of privileges to women is the fundamental cause of all social progress'. *Théorie des Quatre Mouvements et des Destinées Générales*, (Paris, 1846) in *The Utopian Vision of Charles Fourier*, eds J. Beecher and R. Bienvenu (1972), 195–6.

[28] Kemble *op cit*, ii, 97. For Kemble's commitment to German scholarship and his correspondence with Jakob Grimm see R. A. Wiley, 'Anglo-Saxon Kemble: the life and works of John Mitchell Kemble, 1805–1857, philologist, historian, archaeologist', *Anglo-Saxon Studies in Archaeology and History*, B. A. R. British Series, LXXII, (Oxford, 1979), 165–273.

[29] I shall be concerned particularly with the questions of 'status' and 'women'. It should also be pointed out that 'Anglo-Saxon' is an equally debatable term in this tradition. Abbess Hilda from the seventh century is too readily cited alongside the landholding women of the tenth and eleventh centuries in a common category 'Anglo-Saxon women' which does little justice to the differing circumstances necessary to an understanding of either.

[30] B. A. Hanawalt, 'Golden Ages for the history of medieval English women', in *Women in Medieval History and Historiography*, ed. S. M. Stuard (Philadelphia, 1987), 1–24. For a similar history of writing about Greek women see M. Katz' forthcoming article on Greek women in *History and Theory*.

[31] If Doris Stenton's views differ from those of Kemble it is in large part because of the growth of knowledge of legal and social history in the intervening years. The evidence on which so many of these statements, particularly since Kemble, have been based requires careful consideration not blanket rejection.

evidence but in the criteria used for the definition of status. All have been in agreement that Anglo-Saxon women were of high status; they differ in what they understand by 'high status'. All the writers quoted were responding in some way to a 'woman-question', in which the subject of the question has already been generalised as 'woman'.[32] Change after 1066 has been the explicit formulation of the question; questions about status and women have often been left insidiously implicit or unasked. Some historians were aware of the problems of these terms. Doris Stenton carefully restricted her comments about deterioration to upper-class women, and Eileen Power asked whether there was such a thing as 'the position of medieval women'.[33] Their caution is essential.

If Anglo-Saxon England was an age of high status for women, which women are we discussing? Noble women only? Noble daughters, wives or widows? An individual noble woman in a particular family context? Was there any common legal status of daughters, wives or widows which would encourage such generalisation? And if there was should we not allow for the enormous variation which a particular legal framework allows as it intersects with political, economic and individual family situations?

If Anglo-Saxon England was a period of high status for women, how do we judge that status? Of its nature the tradition has no agreed set of criteria, nor have modern historians. Should we judge by landholding rights, or by power through the family.[34] Since different statuses need not coincide, these approaches are not necessarily mutually exclusive.[35] Perhaps no agreed set of criteria is possible as long as the 'status of women' is a live political issue. But can we proceed by bundling all existing ones together when the criteria themselves are debatable, when few are transparent guides to status? When Marjorie Chibnall states that Norman and Anglo-Norman women were 'effective and powerful

---

[32] For the question of whether there can or should be a history of women see D. Riley, *Am I that name, Feminism and the category of 'women' in history* (1988), H. Bloch, *Medieval Misogyny and the invention of western Romantic Love* (Chicago, 1991), Introduction.

[33] Stenton *op. cit* and Eileen Power's opening remarks in 'The position of women', in *The Legacy of the Middle Ages*, eds G. C. Crump and E. F. Jacob (Oxford, 1926), 401, reprinted in her *Medieval Women*, ed M. M. Postan (Cambridge, 1975).

[34] Stenton e.g. judges by landholding and legal rights. Marjorie Chibnall 'Women in Orderic', 120 and fn, has recently criticised this approach for a failure to take account of status within or through the family.

[35] For the problems of measuring female status H. Moore, *Feminism and Anthropology* (Cambridge, 1988), chap 2; S. C. Rogers, 'Woman's place: a critical review of anthropological theory', *Comparative Studies in Society and History*, XX (1978), 122–62; discussion in C. Meyers, *Discovering Eve, Ancient Israelite Women in Context* (Oxford, 1988), 33–37 and P. Reeves Sanday, *Female Power and Male Dominance, on the Origins of Sexual Inequality* (Cambridge, 1981), 114, 120–1, 163 etc.

by virtue of their position in the family' she does not have in mind that sacred and separate family sphere which underlies Kemble's ideology. For her and others, it is precisely the lack of that clear distinction of public and private spheres which allows if not requires women like Mabel of Bellême to be both the mother of nine children and the active shield of her inheritance.[36] We must ask not merely was 1066 a turning point, but were women a group and how is status to be measured.

Since Buckstaff much debate has centred on landholding and legal questions, the long-standing terms of the 1066 debate. Although some have continued to speak of 'women', the central issue has been the status of *noble*women as landholders. The social, economic, legal and political similarities of this group have justified some generalisation of them. But it can be questioned whether the legal and political framework of this group and its landholding changed dramatically in and after 1066, whether they can be generalised as a group and whether their landholding can be translated simply into their status.

Over the past twenty years and more Professor Holt's work has brilliantly demonstrated the dialogue of royal power, noble inheritance, family organisation and politics in the Anglo-Norman period.[37] From 1066, or more correctly from 1087, he sees a situation where challenge to noble inheritance was possible, where there was significant royal interference in that inheritance opened up by distant and debatable claims but chiefly by the political incentive for the king to intervene, and at the same time where the means to resist that intervention existed. All this left noble inheritance in a state of flux and flexibility not ended until 1154 and after. Henry I's coronation charter and Magna Carta were major statements in this dialogue, the mid-century Civil war its violent expression. The results of this for noble women were diverse. Both families and king sought to control their inheritance and marriage. But, between the two, some individual women were able to act more independently. Both Holt and Doris Stenton have hailed Magna Carta clauses 7 and 8, and the earlier proffers a widow made

[36] Chibnall, *op cit.* For Kemble the family was the private world in which women belonged. The more recent views of e.g. J. McNamara and S. Wemple, 'The power of women through the family in medieval Europe', in *Clio's Consciousness Raised*, eds, M. Hartmann and L. W. Banner (New York, 1974) and much reprinted, or P. Stafford, 'Sons and mothers, family politics in the early middle ages' in *Medieval Women*, ed D. Baker (Oxford, 1978), 79–100 take issue openly or implicitly with the idea of a clear public/private distinction in the early middle ages. For specific discussion of this issue see J. Nelson, 'Review Article, The problematic in the private', *Social History*, XV (1990), 355–64.

[37] J. C. Holt, 'Feudal society and the family, I to IV', *Supra*, ser 5, 32–35 (1982–85); his 'Politics and property in early medieval England', *Past and Present*, no LVII (1972), 3–52, and *Magna Carta* (Cambridge, 1965).

to the king to choose her fate, as steps forward in the legal emancipation of English women.[38] This dialogue was older than 1066; royal intervention begins as early as the late ninth century; already succession dispute and foreign invasion allowed noble resistance, already attempts were being made to find agreements on this issue between the king and other groups.[39] What were the ramifications of this for women?

There is evidence to suggest that the king was already interfering in noble marriage by 1016 and before. Cnut's laws forbade the marrying off of widows and demanded that women consent to marriages; this implies that some widows and daughters at least were married off without their consent.[40] Cnut's statement comes in a section dealing with the abuses of the king's power and by extension that of other lords.[41] Individual cases reinforce the view that Cnut was dealing here with an established practice of royal intervention in noble marriage.

In the mid tenth century Ælfgar ealdorman of Essex left two daughters as his heirs. I deliberately do not state that he had no sons; we do not know. The wills of Ælfgar himself and of the two women concerned have survived.[42] The elder daughter, Æthelflæd, married first the king, Edmund, and then a south Midlands ealdorman; the younger, Ælfflæd, married Ælfgar's replacement as ealdorman of Essex, Byrhtnoth, an incomer sent to Essex by the king. Ælfgar's will made his daughters great heiresses, but also tied their inheritances to grandchildren, and in the event of failure of heirs provided for reversion to the church. The case strongly suggests the manipulation of female inheritance in political ways. Did Byrhtnoth have the good fortune to fall in love with one of the richest women in Essex, or was pressure involved in the marriage of the daughter of one ealdorman to his

---

[38] J. C. Holt, *Magna Carta* (Cambridge, 1965), 46 saw the proffers by which widows gained some freedom of choice in marriage as 'one of the first great stages in the emancipation of women', though as J. S. Loengard remarked, much depends on the size of the proffer, ' "Of the gift of her husband": English dower and its consequences in the year 1200', *Women of the Medieval World*, eds J. Kirshner and S. Wemple (Oxford, 1985), 235 fn; Doris Stenton *op cit*, 51 hailed Magna Carta clause 8 as a 'tentative beginning of the emancipation of English women from the legal subservience which had followed the Norman Conquest'.

[39] P. Stafford, 'The Laws of Cnut and the history of Anglo-Saxon royal promises', *Anglo-Saxon England*, ed P. Clemoes et al, X (1981), 173–90 and *Unification and Conquest, a Political and Social History of England in the Tenth and Eleventh Centuries* (1989), especially chaps 2, 8, 9 and 10.

[40] II Cnut 73 and 74 printed in F. Liebermann, *Die Gesertze der Angelsachsen* (Halle, 1903–16), vol I, and with translation in A. J. Robertson, ed., *The Laws of the Kings of England from Edmund to Henry I* (Cambridge, 1925).

[41] I have argued a case for seeing Cnut's laws as, if not a coronation charter, at least the expression of a political agreement between king and nobles in 'The Laws of Cnut...'.

[42] D. Whitelock, *Anglo-Saxon Wills* (Cambridge, 1930), nos 2, 14, 15.

successor?[43] Was that pressure the king's? Did royal pressure extend to pressure on the father to endow his two daughters so liberally? Can we even rule out a choice of women as heirs with a view to such important marriages? The difficulty of reconstructing the full circumstances of tenth-century documents make all these hypotheses. But it would be unwise to assume that the Normans brought to England the practice of the king or others manipulating the inheritance and marriages of noble women.[44] One of the grand narratives of medieval social history, that of the interaction of lord, family and inheritance was already in place.

Some noble families were already reacting by attempting to tie up future inheritance, to see women as conduits of land rather than as heirs. Ælfgar tied the succession of his land via his daughters to his grandchildren, and in their absence, to the church. Ælfgar was passing his inheritance in the direct female line at the expense of collateral male heirs and attempting to ensure the next stage of that direct succession.[45] He was doing so under possible pressure of external interference, perhaps in fear of future interference to the detriment of

[43] The witness lists indicate a gap between Ælfgar and Byrhtnoth, but the idea of a politically arranged marriage is not thereby invalidated. The king may have had plans for Ælfgar's daughters, including his own marriage to one of them, whilst their father was ealdorman, and his plans may have included the future succession of the ealdormanry. Ælfgar's disappearance from the witness lists does not necessarily argue for his death and if there was an ealdorman whose office separates that of Ælfgar and Byrhtnoth, the appointment of a new man and his marriage to a woman whose landholding has been confirmed for his benefit may mark renewed royal intervention in Essex. We may be misled in seeing a tenth- or eleventh-century will as a simple arrangement of post obit bequests rather than the confirmation of a series of gifts and arrangements, some already made *inter vivos*, dowry possibly among them.

[44] Two cases in the *Chronicon Abbatiae Ramesiensis*, ed W. D. Macray, Rolls Series, (1886) 49, where Archbishop Oda received lands for petitioning Eadred that Edwyn might marry the daughter of Ulf, and 135, where a follower of Cnut receives royal permission to marry an English widow. For another probable case see A. Williams, 'The king's nephew: the family and career of Ralph, earl of Hereford', *Studies in Medieval History Presented to R. Allen Brown*, eds. C. Harper Bill, C. Holdsworth and J. Nelson (Woodbridge, 1989), 327–43. Williams sees Ralph's English fortunes founded on an advantageous arranged marraige. Her identification of his wife Gytha links her with a family which certainly had male members and thus potential male heirs in 1066. A choice of the woman as heir followed by her marriage to a royal relative seems possible here. J. Nelson, 'Commentary on the papers of J. Verdon, S. F. Wemple and M. Parisse', in *Frauen in Spätantike und Frühmittelalter, Lebensbedingungen—Lebensnormen—Lebensformen*, ed. W. Affeldt (Sigmaringen, 1990), 332 suggests Alfred may already have been interfering in the fate of noble women, directing them, for example, to nunneries.

[45] Cf one of the earliest wills, that of ealdorman Alfred in the late ninth century, ed. F. Harmer, *Select English Historical Documents of the Ninth and Tenth Centuries* (Cambridge, 1914), no 10 for a similar attempt to pass land to a female heir in the direct line, but allowing for the repurchase of the land by paternal relatives in the event of her failure to produce an heir. This case is muddied by the existence of a son whom some have argued as illegitimate.

his direct heirs. He was simultaneously using the protection of that external power, the king, to secure such a narrowing of the inheritance. Post-1066 historians might call this a shift towards patrilineal primogeniture and the narrowing of the inheriting family to the direct heirs in each generation.

Ælfgar negotiated all this in his will, with the agreement of the king. Already the dialogue of noble inheritance and royal power was producing individual agreements, and by 1016 collective ones. The prehistory of Magna Carta should include not only the coronation charter of Henry I after 1066, but before that date the laws of Cnut, the specific agreements recorded in the shire and borough customs in Domesday which derive in part or in whole from the pre-Conquest situation,[46] and arguably the wills of the tenth century. This series of agreements between individual nobles and the king, between noble, shire and town communities and English kings, chart the painful evolution of inheritance towards closer definition in the face of royal interference.

When those agreements were collective 'women' or at least groups of women were generalised: widows and unmarried women in the laws of Cnut: widows in the coronation charter of Henry I;[47] daughters in families without direct male heirs in the mid-twelfth-century *statutum decretum*.

But turning from collective agreements to individual royal interventions, before or after 1066, a more complex picture emerges in which individual women benefit and lose. Royal interference worked both for and against noble women. The king intervened to ensure the successful outcome of the widow Æthelgifu's dispute over dower in the tenth century, at a price.[48] And for an even higher price Henry I allowed countess Lucy to administer her own lands in the late 1120s.[49] The king guaranteed many of the women's wills from the tenth and eleventh centuries, after suitable payment.[50] But the king's involvement

---

[46] Stafford, 'The Laws of Cnut ...', S. Reynolds, 'Towns in Domesday', *Domesday Studies*, ed. J. C. Holt (Woodbridge, 1987) 295–309; and Stafford, *Unification and Conquest* (1989), chapter on 'Ruling the Kingdom', and 213, 159–61.

[47] Coronation Charter of Henry I, caps 3 and 4, *Stubbs Select Charters*, 9th edition (Oxford, 1913), 118.

[48] *Will of Æthelgifu*, ed D. Whitelock, Roxburgh Club (Oxford, 1968).

[49] *Magnum Rotulum Scaccarii vel magnum rotulum pipae de anno tricesimo primo regni Henrici Primi*, ed J. Hunter (1833), 110.

[50] The similarity between such payments and proffers for dower after 1066 would bear exploration. Few women testators proffered the heriot which was the normal payment made by men, but most proffered some combination of land and cash to the king, and occasionally to the queen. The relevance of the queen to noble women's landholding in the tenth century and the significance of heriot in gender definition are issues to which I hope to return elsewhere.

in inheritance and land dispute worked differently for different women. Whilst some benefited from protection of their wills or intervention in land dispute on their behalf, others lost. In the 990s, Æthelred II refused to accept the heriot or death payment proferred by one noble widow for the control of some or all of her husband's lands.[51] Her husband was accused of treason. The truth of the accusation cannot be known, though the delay in prosecution of the case until the widow came forward is suspicious. The woman was forced to seek an advocate, the archbishop of Canterbury, and paid for his support in loss of land. This noble widow was vulnerable to the king's intervention and had to relinquish land to gain a powerful protector.

None of these examples supports a simple statement about high or low status for women, before or after 1066. The series of collective agreements shows some definition of groups of women, as heiresses, or as widows, which legitimises a qualified discussion of at least 'noblewomen' in a general way. That series begins before 1066 and the stimulus to definition was a debate over inheritance and women as carriers of it forced in large part by royal intervention, which spanned the tenth to twelfth centuries. The individual cases, however, illustrate the difficulty of generalising the impact even of a specific factor, here royal intervention in inheritance, for a specific social group, noble widows. The collective agreements may allow us to speak of the 'rights' of widows or heiresses, though with the heavy qualifications such a statement must have before the existence of a legal profession. Either side of 1066 we are dealing with the implications for noble women of a flexible legal situation[52] and of royal interference within it. If a turning point is to be sought, and all such are debatable, it might be found in the restriction of flexibility in inheritance of the late twelfth century; in the working of the possessory assizes and the attempts at legal standardisation.[53]

Tracing the relationships of individual noble women with kings also reveals the importance of family circumstances in understanding their lives. The paucity of evidence for the period before 1066 makes family reconstruction and history almost impossible. Where reconstruction can be achieved, its critical importance in interpreting what is happening becomes clear. My discussion of the family of Ælfgar of Essex was

[51] *Wills* no 16.2. It is not clear whether Ætheric's widow was seeking all his land, or merely her dower. The outcome involved her gift of her morning-gift to Christ Church Canterbury, and it may be that it was chiefly this and her dower with which she was concerned.

[52] Below n 75 for more discussion of the legal framework.

[53] S. F. C. Milsom, 'Inheritance by women in the twelfth and thirteenth centuries', *On the Laws and Customs of England*, ed M. S. Arnold et al (Chapel Hill, 1981), 60–89 and *The Legal Framework of English Feudalism* (Cambridge, 1976).

speculative; ironically 1066 itself, a foreign conquest, allows the fullest examination of individual family circumstances. The Norman Conquest had a dramatic effect on the production and survival of documents. The early English noblewomen whom we can see most clearly are those who lived on either side of and in the thick of these great events.

Domesday Book shows how far women's enrichment paralleled that of their families in general; the widows of earls Harold and Godwine stand out from the rest. Domesday and the fuller chronicle sources reveal how far women shared the fate of their families. Gytha, Godwine's widow and Harold's mother, was rapidly dispossessed—perhaps as Harold's mother, perhaps for her support of her grandsons in rebellion. Earl Leofric's widow and daughter-in-law by contrast seem to have retained some of their lands for longer, mirroring the political fortunes of their sons and grandsons.[54] Women, even of the same social group, are divided by the differing fortunes of the families of which they form part.

Women are also individuals, more than the expression of roles within families. No eleventh-century evidence permits a full assessment of individual action, but the sources after 1066 provide tantalising glimpses. Gytha, Godwine's widow and Harold's mother, carved a political role for herself. She sought her dead son's body, supported her grandsons, was involved in rebellion and then went into exile in Flanders, the traditional retreat of eleventh-century English malcontents; from there she appears to have contacted other of William's enemies in Scandinavia.[55] Her actions were those of a mother, of a widow, of an eleventh-century English noble; of Harold's mother, and Godwine's widow and a Scandinavian noble woman; of an individual woman at a particular critical point in eleventh-century history. Her career demonstrates those family roles which shaped and allowed women's actions, roles which remain constant over a long historical period which spans 1066.[56] It demonstrates those roles within a specific family and political context. But it strongly suggests that an active individual woman seized, utilised and developed the opportunities of her roles and her context. Gytha is no proof of the specially high status of Old

---

[54] P. Stafford, 'Women in Domesday', *Medieval Women in Southern England*, Reading Medieval Studies, XV (Reading, 1989), 75–94.

[55] The fullest account of Gytha remains the various references in vols I to IV of E. A. Freeman, *The History of the Norman Conquest of England, its Causes and Results* (Oxford, 1870–79).

[56] P. Stafford, 'Sons and Mothers ...' and *Queens, Concubines and Dowagers, the King's Wife in the Early Middle Ages* (1983). There are important similarities in the opportunities which the roles of wife, widow, mother allow women throughout the medieval period as the growing literature on noble and royal women demonstrates, e.g. J. Ward, *English Noblewomen in the Later Middle Ages* (1992); M. K. Jones and M. G. Underwood, *The King's Mother, Lady Margaret Beaufort, Countess of Richmond and Derby* (Cambridge, 1992).

English noble women. To generalise her even as 'Anglo-Saxon noble woman', let alone as 'Anglo-Saxon woman' is to do some violence to historical understanding.

Either side of 1066 noble women had claim to land as heiresses, and often held it as widows. It is not easy to move from such a statement to an assessment of their status. The situation of the heiress exemplifies this. Shifts towards patrilineal primogeniture and the narrowing of the inheriting family to direct heirs produces heiresses. There is a constant proportion of failures in the direct male line; as the claims of collateral males were restricted, so the likelihood of female heirs increases.[57] The Empress Mathilda's claim on the English throne is the most obvious example. It resulted from a desire to cut out collateral heirs, in this case Henry I's nephews, coupled with the accidental death of her only legitimate brother in the disaster of the White Ship.

Does the heiress's land make her a high status woman? The more land a woman holds the more likely she is to be controlled and manipulated by male relatives or lords.[58] This point is readily conceded for the pathetic heiresses of the high middle ages, passed from hand to hand and bed to bed as the pawns of male politics. What reason is there to suppose that heiresses before 1066 were any different? Indeed Ælfgar's daughters suggest the similarities. Before and after 1066 women had claims on land which could make them vulnerable and manipulable. Their claims could also be challenged or overridden. If the empress Mathilda was the greatest English heiress of the twelfth century, she did not secure her inheritance. Her cousin Stephen was crowned king. Direct primogeniture was far from triumphing over collateral claims when the direct heir was a woman, on either side of 1066. About 1000 A.D. the great midland noble, Wulfric Spott, passed over his daughter and left the bulk of his land to his brother, nephews and Burton abbey; so much for the special position of Anglo-Saxon women. It is easy to see the heiress as victim, not a high status woman.

But that is too simple. Æthelflæd and Ælfflæd may have been manipulated heiresses in their youth, but they made wills which show at least a limited freedom of action over their inheritance as widows. Mathilda's failure to secure coronation does scant justice to the impact of her claim to the throne on her life. That claim legitimised and allowed extensive political even military activity. It affected her relationship with

[57] J. Martindale, 'Succession and politics in the Romance-speaking world, c. 1000–1140', in *England and her Neighbours, 1066–1453*, essays in honour of Pierre Chaplais, eds. M. Jones and M. Vale (1989), 19–41.

[58] J. Nelson, 'Commentary on the papers of J. Verdon, S. F. Wemple and M. Parisse', in *Frauen in Spätantike und Frühmittelalter, Lebensbedingungen—Lebensnormen—Lebensformen*, ed W. Affeldt (Sigmaringen, 1990), 331, arguing that the property claims of women already made them manipulable in ninth-century Frankia.

her sons if not with her husband Geoffrey.[59] It is impossible to generalise to all heiresses from Mathilda or from Æthelflæd; it is against such generalisation that I have argued. But a balance sheet on the status of heiress would have to include opportunities as well as manipulations.[60]

These women realised some of the opportunities of the heiress as a wife and mother or widow. Land, its provenance and claims on it affects the dynamics of power within families. So too does emphasis on legitimacy which is a corollary of emphasis on direct lineal descent. The woman who is the vehicle of that descent, the wife, the legitimate bearer of heirs, takes on a new prominence. An ecclesiastical reform movement which was stressing legitimate Christian marriage reinforced that status. In the private charters of post-1066 England the consent of wives to gifts is commonplace, their involvement in joint gifts regular. Consent and involvement cover their claims to dower, dowry or their own inheritance. The wife's prominence also defines that narrow inheriting family in which the wife and mother is a key figure. The inheritance structures which produced some heiresses and excluded other daughters brought wives to the fore.[61] Can a particular inheritance practice or even women's landholding be taken as a simple guide to the status of women when the implications of landholding and inheritance practice can be ambiguous and varied, not only for different women, but at different stages of the same woman's life?

These approaches could be applied to specific areas of debate, for example the transition from morning gift to *maritagium* and its alleged significance for women. Morning gift was a marriage gift made to a woman herself at marriage, a marital prestation which passed from the husband and his family to the wife. Morning gift is seen as a gift to the woman herself, as land over which she had special freedom of control. It has become one index of pre-1066 liberties.[62] *Maritagium*, a dowry payment, was made by the bride's family to the husband. It was land which he then held. It is seen as a Norman introduction and is associated with the low status of women after 1066.[63]

[59] The claim and its negotiation may have contributed both to the breach and reconciliation with Geoffrey, see M. Chibnall, *The Empress Mathilda*, 55–62. Some Angevin chroniclers stress that she brought the promise of power to Geoffrey. Their joint action on the continent is discussed in *ibid* 62–72. Henry II and her other sons were brought up in her household, often in her own land of Normandy. Relations between mother and sons are discussed in *ibid* esp 143–63.

[60] Including the advantages of a higher degree of male commitment to marriage to an heiress and a greater intensity in the husband and wife relationship, J. Gillingham, 'Love, marriage and politics in the twelfth century', *Forum for Modern Language Studies*, XXV (1989), 292–303.

[61] They had different implications for another group of women, concubines.

[62] C. Fell, *Women in Anglo-Saxon England* (1984), 56–7. Buckstaff *op cit*, 242–5.

[63] Classic general discussion of the shift in a European framework in D. Owen Hughes,

The freedoms of morning gift in the tenth and eleventh centuries are easily exaggerated by a readiness to seek signs of women's high status then. The clearest statement is in the early tenth-century Fonthill case, where a woman asserts her freedom to sell her morning gift.[64] The context is, as so often, dispute, in which it was in the interests of the purchaser to emphasise a freedom of disposal which may have been far more debatable; he certainly took care to have the sale guaranteed by king Alfred and other prestigious witnesses. The Fonthill account does not make it clear whether the woman was a wife or a widow; other evidence suggests that morning gift was collapsing close to dower arranged at marriage by the tenth century. Ælfflæd in her will leaves her morning gift to her husband's foundation at Ely, emphasising its association with land on which his family retained a claim, a situation closer to dower than to the alleged freedoms of a wife's control of morning gift.[65] The laws of Cnut specifically associate morning gift with all a woman received from her husband.[66] It is not clear that tenth-century morning gift and twelfth-century dower are as different as a desire for a 1066 transition would make them.[67]

Far from guaranteeing its sacrosanct nature, Cnut states that morning gift will be forfeit if a woman remarries within a year. Though this particular provision may refer to the ecclesiastical reforming impetus to stress freedom of consent in marriage, and to the perennial desire of husbands' families to prevent dower land passing to a second husband, other evidence shows a morning gift, and the dower from which it is becoming difficult to distinguish it, already under threat from the growth of royal powers of forfeiture. Ætheric's widow had to promise hers to Christ Church Canterbury in order to gain her dead husband's lands from the king.[68] Cnut's threat of loss if a woman is forced into remarriage is a reminder of the ambiguity of landholding for women; a widow with substantial dower and/or morning gift was likely to find herself forced into marriage. Already dower was subject

---

'From brideprice to dowry in mediterranean Europe', *Journal of Family History*, III (1978), 262–96. Whitelock, *Wills*, 179, claims dowry as foreign to Anglo-Saxon marriage customs.

[64] Harmer, 18.

[65] Wills, 15.

[66] II Cnut, 73a.

[67] Against this it must be pointed out that the *Leges Henrici Primi*, ed and trans L.J. Downer (Oxford, 1972), cap 70.22 distinguish dos, maritagium and morning gift. There may be some antiquarian compliation here. *Be wifmannes beweddung*, printed and translated D. Whitelock, *English Historical Documents*, I, (second ed. 1979), no 50, stresses gifts to the bride for her acceptance and does not mention dowry. But the document is clearly in the context of the growing stress on Christian marriage, witness the reference to the presence of a priest, and the mention of the gift which symbolised the wife's consent would be critical. It may not be wise to place too much emphasis on its omissions.

[68] Wills, 16.2.

to the sort of agreements between kings and communities which royal intervention called forth;[69] whilst in practice it varied in amount depending on individual circumstances.

Dowry, far from being a Norman import, was given in pre-1066 England. The will of Thurketel of Palgrave speaks of land received when he took his wife, and there are instances where Domesday refers to land given as dowry.[70] And just as morning-gift and dower are no simple guide to women's high status, nor is dowry to deterioration. By 1086 Norman widows were holding dowry and dower;[71] although it initially passes to the husband, dowry contributes to the extensive landholding of widows; life cycle is essential in interpreting the significance of any inheritance practice for women. Dowry must always be interpreted in its social context. Domesday sometimes states that a husband was holding his wife's dowry of his father-in-law.[72] This confirms the use of marriage as a link between men, but the creation and sustaining of a link between a woman's family and her husband is also critical. Such a link serves as protection; the severance of a woman from her natal family at marriage can leave her exposed and vulnerable.[73] The idea of a sharp turning point in 1066 has produced partial readings of morning gift, dower and dowry both before and after that date. As an index of status none of them should be divorced

[69] See e.g. the Nottinghamshire and Derbyshire customs in Domesday which appear to exempt dower from forfeiture, DB I 280v.

[70] Wills, 24 and DB II, 195r the case of Bishop Ælmær; DB II, 431v, land Edmund the priest received with his wife; DB II, 264r refers to land which Reinold the priest held 'with the daughter of Payne' which may be dowry. DB I, 252v is a Shropshire case of dowry given pre-1066, in land which the father held 'as a canon'. The bishop of Durham in the late tenth century gave his daughter together with lands of St Cuthbert to Uhtred, see the tract *De Obsessione Dunelmi* in *Symeonis Monachi Opera Omnia*, ed T. Arnold, Rolls Series, LXXV vol I (1882), 215–20, translated C. R. Hart, *The Early Charters of Northern England and the North Midlands* (Leicester, 1975), 146–50. The geographical spread will not allow Fell's and Whitelock's interpretation of a Scandinavian custom. A common theme is church land. Since it seems odd to argue that ecclesiastical husbands and fathers were unique in giving and receiving dowry, this should probably be interpreted as a desire to record dowry when church land or claims were involved in some way.

[71] See e.g. Azelina widow of Ralf Taillebois, sheriff of Bedfordshire who was holding lands *de maritagio* and *de dote* in 1086, DB I, 218r.

[72] See e.g. DB I, 48rv and 356v Guy holding Warnborough, Claxby and Sloothby from Hugh son of Baldric with his daughter; DB I, 48v Fatherling held Woodcutt from William Bellett with his daughter. If Reinhold the priest above is to be interpreted as holding dowry the practice was not new in 1066; he was holding from his wife's brother.

[73] The *Leges Henrici Primi*, caps 70.12 and 70.23 show how incomplete the transfer of a woman from her natal family was. The undatable tract *Be wifmannes beweddung*, clause 7, stresses that it is when a woman moves from her natal family [and lord?] and their protection that she is most vulnerable. Like the *Leges* it underlines the lack of total separation at this date by insisting that a woman's family shall continue to help her pay compensation after marriage.

from social and political context or from life-cycle.

The tradition has shaped the debate over women in ways which have given undue prominence to 1066. The practices of family inheritance and royal power which are seen as critical to the framework of noble women's lives, span that divide. So too do movements of ecclesiastical reform and economic growth. If I have touched only briefly on these latter, that reflects not their relative importance, but their peripheral place in the 1066 debate.[74] We need a new periodisation covering the late-ninth to mid-twelfth century to explore a common range of factors.[75] Women's landholding admits of no simple translation into high or low status. A woman's own life-cycle and family situation interpreted those factors even as those factors opened or closed opportunities for her. The traditional legal and constitutional nature of the Norman Conquest debate may have helped obscure this interaction. We cannot assess status by family *or* landholding; the two are intertwined. The tradition has generalised women, partly as a result of that same legal and constitutional emphasis, more because it reflects a modern debate which itself generalises women. Clearly we cannot stop using that collective noun;[76] but its use must be accompanied by realisation of the great variety of experience it conceals. I would certainly not suggest that no change may have occurred across this period, but the idea of a sharp break is unsustainable and the questions Holt has raised about family and royal power could fruitfully be applied to the tenth and eleventh centuries.

One reason why they have not been is the paucity of pre-1066 evidence. Indeed the view of an Anglo-Saxon Golden Age is sustained by an over-interpretation of a handful of tenth- and eleventh-century

---

[74] Again the nature of the 1066 debate may here have artificially separated factors which in fact interacted. The religious/reform context of the growth of English royal power in the ninth and tenth century was a factor drawing both king and churchmen further into interference in family life and inheritance e.g. their joint punishment of marital offences involving loss of land, further comment in Stafford, *Unification and Conquest* (1989), p 168.

[75] Such a periodisation would also make more sense for the legal framework. This is not the place to discuss the framework, or the disagreements about it, in detail. Note for example the difference between S. D. White, *Custom, Kinship and Gifts to the Saints, The Laudatio Parentum in Western France 1050–1150* (Chapel Hill, 1988), esp 70–3, arguing that the mid twelfth century saw a shift from one legal framework of norms, legitimating strategies, flexibility and custom continually remade to another of strong government, routine, regularity, the application of rules by trained professionals, and that of W. Davies, P. Fouracre et al., *The Settlement of Disputes in Early Medieval Europe* (Cambridge, 1986), 237–40 emphasising that state intervention was not the key development of the twelfth century, but was already well-established. Where both are in agreement, however, is in the substantial continuity of the situation at least from the tenth to the mid twelfth century.

[76] Though there are problems, see above n 32.

documents. A small number of documents often bereft of context have had a pernicious effect on our view of tenth- and early eleventh-century women. Such women rise up before us like lone archetypes, make their wills or speak their piece in court and then melt back into darkness. For all the world like some historical equivalent of witches on the blasted heath, they loom up at us, figures of power in their very isolation. A false contrast is produced with the twelfth century when the wealth of family charters and other evidence show us women enmeshed in family and legal coils.[77] Any move towards a greater understanding of women's situation between the tenth and twelfth centuries must begin with a rigorous scrutiny of the late Anglo-Saxon documents and as full a restoration of their context as possible. It must also include a reading of the twelfth-century documents which is more open to the powers of women they suggest. The latter must be left for further study;[78] some of the tenth and eleventh century evidence can be tackled immediately.

The Herefordshire woman who allegedly disinherited her son in favour of her kinswoman in the reign of Cnut is a *cause celèbre*.[79] Shorn of all context the scene has great power. Thegns arrive from the Herefordshire shire court to ask a woman about land which her son is disputing. Their questions move her to wrath. She summons her kinswoman Leofflæd and states that she grants her 'her land, her gold, her clothing and raiment and all that she possesses'. She turns to the men and tells them to 'act well like thegns' and take her message to the meeting. It is hard to read it without supplying the tones of an eleventh-century Lady Bracknell, or a latter-day Iron Lady scornfully bidding them to 'Be men'.

Details and full context tell a different tale. The woman was not in court herself, her statement had to be delivered by proxy. She is not even named, though the man whose claims were being extinguished is.

---

[77] On such false contrasts and their relationship to 'feudalism' see M. Clanchy, *England and its Rulers, 1066–1272* (1983), 84.

[78] That there is much to be said is suggested by the fact e.g. of Robert of Gloucester's wife, Mabel, fulfilling his treaty with the Earl of Hereford in 1142, *Earldom of Gloucester Charters*, ed. R. B. Patterson (Oxford, 1973), 95–7; the charge which she took over his affairs when he was captured, *Willelmi Malmesbiriensis Monachi Historia Novella*, ed K. R. Potter (1955), 68; and from the land which accumulated in the hands of women in a family which produced a succession of female heirs and widows like that of the Arches in twelfth-century Yorkshire and from their apparent power over it at certain stages of life. The fortunes of this family may be followed in W. Farrer, *Early Yorkshire Charters*, I–III (1914–16), nos 534–6, 538, 541, 545–6, 548, 553, 555, 1331–8.

[79] A. J. Robertson, *Anglo-Saxon Charters* (Cambridge, 1956), no 78. Whitelock, *English Historical Documents* I, 602 remarks that 'it shows how freely a woman could dispose of land in Anglo-Saxon times', and D. Stenton, *op cit* 26–7 comments on the freedoms of Anglo-Saxon women it suggests.

The kinswoman to whom she promises her land is the wife of Thurkil the White. It was Thurkil who had spoken on the claim in the shire court; it was he who rode to Hereford to have the case recorded in the Herefordshire Gospel Book where it still survives. In 1066 it was he and the clergy of Hereford who are said to hold the land in question.[80] The court proceedings were under the joint presidency of the English bishop of Hereford and the new Danish earl Ranig. Thurkil himself has a Danish name and looks suspiciously like one of Cnut's followers newly established in the west midlands who has married an English wife.[81] Beyond that we cannot go in reconstructing the context of this case.

But it is far enough to suggest the need for careful reading. The judgement delivered land arguably to the English wife of an incoming Dane, and ultimately to her husband, and to the church of the ecclesiastical president of the shire court. The surviving documents will never tell us what distortions of judgement in the woman's favour occurred. But we can suspect an editing of claims on the land to emphasise her freedom to give, a wider range of arguable family claims than the document admits.[82] The case shows a society in which women's landholding could be defended, and in which choice of heir among family members was possible, including among women. Inheritance was flexible, and political pressure could act on it. But we would be unwise to argue from this case for the general freedom of eleventh-century women to disinherit their sons, to bequeath land to others freely or to defend their cases in court. It has to be read as the power a particular woman could have in a particular situation, with all the qualifications and limitations that situation suggests. It is no proof of the rights of Anglo-Saxon women.

[80] DB vol I, 182R and 187R.

[81] For a comparable case in the East Midlands see above n. 44.

[82] Such editing was far from unknown; see a series of ninth-century Worcester cases. *English Historical Documents*, I, no. 81 lays great stress on the right of a mother to dispose of her lands to the church, and specifically envisages trouble with the Berkeley people; the land in question ended up in the possession of the church of Worcester and in the Worcester Cartulary. This record follows a record of a dispute between those same Berkeley people over the land. Did the woman have such clear rights to dispose of her land? Or is that Worcester's claim, made precisely in the context of the dispute with Berkeley? Cf *English Historical Documents*, I, nos. 68 and 75 in which a grandmother appears to bequeath a monastery at Withington to her granddaughter who in turn grants it to the bishop of Worcester. The girl's mother is presented as disputing the original bequest, but her action is presented as an illegitimate intervention. Both documents are recorded in the Worcester cartulary. It was in the bishop's interests to present a simple line of inheritance and transmission in which the rights of grandmother and granddaughter to pass on the land were uncomplicated and other claims indefensible. We might at least suspect that legitimate family claims were much wider and rights of disposal more problematic than either document would suggest.

Leofflæd was still holding land, though not this land, in 1066. She is one of the small proportion of women listed in Domesday Book. Such women are too few in number in 1066 to sustain the Golden Age view of pre-Conquest England; nor are they easy to interpret.[83] Domesday is no more transparent than the Herefordshire legal record. Domesday consistently underestimates women landholders, on either side of 1066; the figures for the number of hides held by women quoted earlier are no simple index of women's landholding. The women who are included, either side of 1066, are there largely because their landholding touches the royal interest, or that of some Norman claimant.[84] Only in certain cases is Domesday concerned with the internal arrangements of family land for dower or dowry which were the most important ways women held land. Those internal family provisions were common to English and Norman society. The underestimation is consistent across 1066 because the sources of women's landholding and the way they held it had not changed; nor had fundamental ideas on inheritance and women's claims on it.

The Normans used marriage to English women to negotiate the new situation in England.[85] If Thurkil was a Dane, perhaps his marriage to Leofflæd was designed to achieve the same results after the conquest of 1016. The Normans sought legitimacy and land. To marry a woman for this reason was also to choose her as heir, to vest in her the wider family claims in land which the incomer sought to extinguish, to attempt to do through marriage what the Herefordshire legal record did in writing. The flexibility of inheritance which could recognise a woman as heir in this way survived 1066. Had it not been understood and practised by the Normans it is hard to imagine them marrying to gain legitimacy.

Leofflæd like the other women in Domesday has to be read with caution. She may be further testimony to the ambiguity of women's landholding and its interpretation for women's status; an heiress because a politically powerful husband chose her as one. She and some other women named as landholders in Domesday may be landholders for the same reasons they are named, because their landholding suited or

[83] P. Stafford, 'Women in Domesday', *Medieval Women in Southern England*, Reading Medieval studies, XV, ed K. Bate et al (Reading, 1989), 75–94.

[84] P. Hyam, '"No register of title", the Domesday inquest and land adjudication', *Anglo-Norman Studies*, IX (1987), 127–41 draws attention to the fact that predecessors were probably named by Norman tenants in 1086. J. C. Holt, '1086', in *Domesday Studies*, ed. J. C. Holt (Woodbridge, 1987), 41–64 sees Domesday as a super charter in which Normans sought to secure their holding: the extinction of earlier claims by naming the predecessor entitled to transfer them is central to such a view.

[85] E. Searle, 'Women and the legitimisation of succession at the Norman Conquest', *Proceedings of the Battle Conference on Anglo-Norman Studies*, III, ed R. Allen Brown (1981) 159–70 and 226–9.

affected the strategies of a man. The Normans used women and ideas about inheritance to negotiate 1066; the very flexibility of women's landholding made them usable and vulnerable.[86] It meant they could be chosen but also bypassed.[87] If inheritance was tightened for whatever reasons in the course of the twelfth century it is far from clear that that tightening was automatically bad for women.[88] By the same token a flexibility which allows women to be named as heirs brings its own opportunities. There is no room here for simple tales of progress or retreat; and much need to scrutinise the documents with great care.

Domesday freezes two moments in eleventh-century English history, 1066 and 1086, spanning the critical decades of the Norman Conquest. It has been surprisingly little used to illuminate the experience of the Conquest by the women who lived through it.[89] Again the terms of the older debate have diverted attention towards the long term and away from questions about the immediate impact, or about the part played in the unfolding of the Conquest itself by women like Gytha. Had William the Conqueror thought about women and the Norman Conquest he would certainly have thought about her, at large with her daughters in Flanders, perhaps plotting the sort of political comeback queen Emma had staged a generation before. He would have thought of Edith, Gytha's daughter and the Confessor's widow, who had remained in England: Edith, hoping to retain some of her power after 1066, a symbol perhaps for the remnant of English nobles who hoped to survive 1066;[90] a symbol too for William, the legitimate English king, respecter of his predecessor's widow. People would surely have pointed to Mathilda, William's wife;[91] rule of England and Normandy made

[86] The frequency of dispute about women's land suggests a gender-specificity about such flexibility, exploited by the Normans. At the same time we should note the reorganisation of claims around male heirs after 1066 suggested by A. Williams, 'A vice-comital family in pre-Conquest Warwickshire', *Anglo-Norman Studies*, XI (Woodbridge, 1989), 279–95.

[87] For an earlier example of by-passing see Will of Wulfric Spott, *Wills* no 17 in which he disinherited his daughter in favour of his brother and nephew. The political context is again crucial, but so is recognition that flexibility is by no means simply good for women's claims on land.

[88] Loengard *op cit* on dower, and cf R. M. Smith, 'Women's property rights under customary law; some developments in the thirteenth and fourteenth centuries', *Supra*, ser 5, XXXVI (1986), 165–94 for the complex and by no means simply unfavourable influence of the precision of Common law on women's landholding among peasants.

[89] As in the case of Gytha E. A. Freeman must stand as an honourable exception to this generalisation.

[90] See the men who surrounded her at Wilton in 1072 when she witnessed the record of the sale of Combe, F. H. Dickinson, 'The sale of Combe', *Somerset Archaeological and Natural history Society Proceedings*, XXII (1876), 106–13.

[91] Mathilda's career, like that of Gytha, would repay detailed examination for the interaction of the sort of forces I have been discussing. In the charters of great nobles of the late eleventh and early twelfth centuries we find frequent reference to prayers and

her a regent and helped set a pattern for queenly regency which would benefit her daughter-in-law, Edith/Mathilda, wife of Henry I—a *Norman* woman contributing to a tradition of *English* queenly power. They would have spoken of Emma, Norman wife of Ralph of Gael, who defended Norwich castle after her husband's rebellion in 1075. By the 1080s William and others would be thinking uneasily of the wives, widows and daughters of Norman sheriffs whose dower lands had swelled in the aftermath of the great land grab after 1066.[92] People would surely have remarked on the English women dispossessed, fleeing to nunneries, on those whom Normans had married to legitimise their landtaking, perhaps too on the number of English widows who survived the immediate upheaval.[93]

Women experienced 1066 variously as daughters, wives, mothers, widows; as nobles; as Norman or English; as members of particular families; as individuals—not as some collective group 'women'. Some English and Norman women benefited from a Conquest which posed as a legitimate takeover. Many widows survived 1066 with some of their lands intact; Norman sheriffs enriched their wives' dowers with the legitimate pickings of the predatory Old English state.[94] William acted the ideal Old English king in his protection of widows; he showed that king's other face in his readiness to marry them off to his

---

gifts for the soul of the whole royal family—defined as the king, his sons and their mother the queen see e.g. W. Farrer, *Early Yorkshire Charters*, I–III (1914–16), nos 559, 1002; IV (1935), no 1; VI (1939), no 1 etc. Such constant nods in the direction of the throne bespeak the same sort of anxiety in the face of royal power expressed by tenth-century nobles in their wills. The definition of the royal family is an index of the insecurity of an upstart dynasty anxious to emphasise its hereditary claim on a conquered throne. The inclusion of the queen as high-born and legitimate mother highlights that specific insecurity even as it expresses the more general emphasis on direct line. Queen Mathilda was not just wife and mother; but the wife of William I and the mother of his heirs. She was also the daughter of the count of Flanders, a fact which Norman charters recognise and stress see e.g. Caen charters, no 12. Like her granddaughter and namesake Mathilda, her particular status is that of heiress, wife and mother in a specific political family situation. As an English queen she was heiress of yet another tradition. In the Caen charters she appears as a woman who bought and sold land, exercised patronage, favour and was actively sought out. She later backed her son in his rebellions against his father. Again it is hard to read her simply as an emanation of her roles, as 'woman' in any of her eleventh-century guises.

[92] Stafford, 'Women in Domesday', 78–9, for more details.

[93] See Godgifu and Ælfgifu widows of earls Leofric and Ælfgar and a range of lesser women like Wulfeva widow of Finn, DB I 98rv; Sæwulf's widow, 51v; Godgifu, 168v; the widow of Wulfweard the White, 87r; Leofgeat, Ælfhild, Ealdhild, Wenesi's widow 74f; Edric's widow, 70r and many others. Many of the above are not simply widows, but widows of royal officials another group with a high survival rate across 1066.

[94] Above n 92 for the Domesday interest in sheriff's wives, see e.g. the 48 lands of the wife of Hugh son of Grip in Dorset where she is listed as a separate tenant-in-chief.

followers when it suited him.[95] The traditions of pre-1066 England were formative—Mathilda inherited a tradition of English queenly power; but those traditions could be built on, as they were in her activities as regent which extended to the hearing of legal cases.[96] As vulnerable daughters and as widows English women carrying claims to land were married by incoming Normans; but the status of widow brought opportunity to an Edith. Women shared the fate of their families, but had the special protections of widows, a kind of freedom from family and its ties; but an ambiguous freedom in which royal servants often ended up holding these women's lands.[97] All the problems of generalising status or women appear in the diversity of female experience of 1066.

When the author of Queen Edith's *Life of Edward* argued his patroness's case for survival in these difficult days, he drew on the eleventh-century past. He also drew on gender notions, presenting her as an ideal daughter, wife and widow, creatively handling her failure to produce an heir with a picture of the daughter-wife who was almost identified with the kingdom and its fate. Orderic Vitalis, like some latter-day Homer, tells the story of the Norman Conquest through marriages promised and aborted.[98] The way eleventh- and twelfth-century chroniclers themselves talked about women and the Norman Conquest has, ironically, evoked little modern comment. This is doubly ironic since gender constantly informed the discussions of Germanic and English women from Tacitus to the nineteenth century.[99] In ending by looking at how two chroniclers close to the event talked about women and the Norman Conquest I have no qualms about generalisation. The generalisations are theirs, and it is their gender notions and anxieties which those generalisations reveal.

By the early twelfth century the causes of the Norman Conquest were being discussed in gendered terms. Bishop Wulfstan of Worcester is said to have foretold the defeat of longhaired Englishmen.[100] Men,

---

[95] DB I, fo 167r for example, where he married the widow of an Old English sheriff Ælfwine, to Richard.

[96] DB I, 238v and 48v.

[97] See e.g. Wulfeva whose lands in Suffolk came to be held by Robert Malet the sheriff and his mother and Wulfwen of Creslow whose lands in Dorset, Somerset, Middlesex, Buckinghamshire and Wiltshire came into the hands of Edward of Salisbury. DB I, fos 80v, 150v, 69v etc.

[98] Eleanor Searle, *op cit*, 163.

[99] J. Wallach Scott, 'Gender: a useful category of historical analysis', *American Historical Review*, XCI (1986), 1053–1075 has pointed out how often gender relations and identities are defined with reference to contemporary social and political debate. This applies as much to the twelfth as to the nineteenth century.

[100] *The Vita Wulfstani of William of Malmesbury*, ed. R. R. Darlington, Camden Soc, Third Series, XL (1928), 23.

he claimed, who were ashamed to be as they were born but imitated women would be as useless as women at the defence of their homeland. He used often to cut a lock of hair from a man's head using the knife with which he cleaned his fingernails, and then bade them shear the rest to match. These are not prophetic visions of 1066 but a later interpretation of defeat as a result of effeminacy. It is impossible to know whether the anxieties they speak were those of Wulfstan himself, of Coleman his biographer, or those of William of Malmesbury who translated and preserved that biography. His words and actions are full of the inconsistency of gender anxiety. Short hair is not intrinsic to some unchanging male nature; but it was the fashion of the military men of about 1100 A.D. It is evoked in an attempt to assert clear gender boundaries and to threaten the dire results of disturbing them. His remarks do not accord with the contributions of women like Gytha or Emma to the Conquest. The actions of such women disturbed gender expectations. They went beyond the management to the defence of the household; beyond acceptable maternal grieving to verge on unacceptable female vengeance. It may be in part the actions of women which prompted the anxieties Wulfstan expresses.

Orderic betrayed some of these anxieties in his story of Mabel of Bellême. Her tale ends with murder, not on the battlefield or in castle siege, but in her own stronghold, after a bath, relaxed, vulnerable, female. No doubt Orderic reports the embellished truth; the story as it stands has certainly provoked scepticism.[101] The death of the oppressor of St Evroul who was also a belligerent woman drew from Orderic a story which is as revealing about him as about the manner of Mabel's end. Mabel had been a woman out of place; in her death she is firmly in it. Orderic may not be entirely at ease with fighting women.[102] Mabel's bath, like Wulfstan's knife speak of gender boundaries disturbed

[101] Chibnall, *Orderic Vitalis, Ecclesiastical History*, III, Book 5, 137, fn notes an epic, legendary quality in the story.

[102] The belligerence of Norman women has been discussed by Eleanor Searle, 'Emma the Conqueror', in *Studies in Medieval History Presented to R Allen Brown*, eds C. Harper Bill et al (Woodbridge, 1989), 281–8. In view of the arguments about declining status and the role of a military society in this decline, the belligerence of Norman women is ironic. One of the first Norman women mentioned after 1066 is Emma, daughter of William Fitz Osbern and wife of Ralph of Gael; we hear of her because she is in control of a castle during the rebellion of her husband in 1075. The castle as a confusion of stronghold and home is an ideal foyer for women's military activities. Orderic often speaks approvingly of the Norman fighting women. Isabel of Montfort is likened to Camilla and the Amazon queen when she rides out amongst the men, *Orderic Vitalis, Ecclesiastical History*, ed Chibnall, IV, Book 8, 212–4. But did he realise how ambiguous Amazons are as a symbol of female military activity? They lose and are restored to correct female status. There is an extensive literature on them as inversion figures in antiquity see e.g. L. Hardwick, 'Ancient Amazons—heroes, outsiders or women', *Greece and Rome*, XXXVII (1990), 14–36. At best Orderic is divided on this issue.

and unstable. Both have much to tell of the expectations and fears of men and perhaps of the powers of women of about 1100 A.D.

It is Orderic who recounts the strange story of the lascivious Norman wives after 1066.[103] Some Normans, he states, returned early after the initial conquest at the promptings of their wives. Certain Norman women 'consumed by fierce lust' had threatened to pollute their beds with adultery and stain their offspring with infamy unless their husbands returned immediately to their conjugal duties. And so, as a result of these wanton women, inheritances were lost which these men's successors had still not recovered. The story provides an honourable excuse for the nobles who quit England.[104] It provides an explanation consistent with male honour for actions which deprived male heirs of the land which supported honour. The wicked wives faced them with an impossible choice. Orderic's is a world where male honour and *honores* are meshed in the politics of marriage. His story reveals that world's obsession with legitimacy and the anxieties about paternity and suspicion of women it produces. His wanton Norman wives throw a shaft of light into its heart. Those anxieties recall the ambiguous importance of heiresses, wives and mothers. If some early twelfth-century writers were concerned about gender boundaries, it may have less to do with the militarisation of men than with the powers of women, not to mention the ambiguous position of celibate monks.[105] In the twelfth century as in the nineteenth, the use of women to talk about 1066 tells us less about women's role in the Conquest and its effects upon them than it does about the concerns of the male authors of the day. Yet the creative use of gender stereotypes to defend Edith's position reveals that even such apparently confining notions had possibilities which women themselves could exploit. Limitations and opportunity are so often inextricably mixed.

*   *   *

---

[103] Orderic Vitalis, *Ecclesiastical History*, II, Book 3, 218–20.

[104] The story may be told in this place to contrast their motives and behaviour with the looting mercenaries whose pay off is recorded immediately afterwards.

[105] The two authors whom I have cited are both monastic. A rather different view might be derived from the works of more secular clerical writers, such as Henry of Huntingdon, Geoffrey of Monmouth or Geoffrey Gaimar. Henry, for example, does not comment on women and 1066, but his discussion of Æthelflæd, Lady of the Mercians in the early tenth century and widow of the last Mercian king Æthelred, is of great interest. He is fulsome in praise of a regnant woman, who is almost a king, and mistakenly makes her her husband's daughter, a significant error in view of the contemporary debate about Empress Mathilda's rights to rule. The readiness to argue for female rule after 1066 is clear. Such readiness is not, of course, a guide to Henry's views on gender in general. These questions would repay further study. I am grateful to John Gillingham for drawing my attention to this.

There is no serious argument for adding gender-bending to the causes of the Norman Conquest, but there are many for abandoning the idea of 1066 as a turning point of great significance in the history of English women, and for jettisoning the Anglo-Saxon Golden Age. Both ideas are more a product of the political concerns of past historians than of the experience of the eleventh century. They threaten to obscure the continuities of the English early middle ages. They generalise women and ignore problems of status measurement. Even in their most sophisticated forms they have long diverted attention from the experience of 1066 by the women who lived through it, and from the gendered discussion of it by near contemporaries. A wider framework would allow for the continuities, though it must include latitude for varied interpretation in individual women's lives. Within that framework and without preconceptions of deterioration or Golden Ages changes between the tenth and the twelfth centuries may well be discovered. The evidence on either side of 1066 will need careful scrutiny to explore the power as well as the limitations on women, both in the twelfth as in the tenth century. The powers of tenth- as of twelfth-century women will look more complex when seen in full context, but that complexity will reveal more about what gives power to women, about how and when they are able to exercise it. Women's history is now too sophisticated for 'Golden Ages' or for simple stories of advance or retreat. It is time to restore the lives of tenth-, eleventh- and twelfth-century women to them.

METAPHORS OF THE MIDDLE: THE DISCOVERY OF THE PETITE BOURGEOISIE 1880–1914

By Geoffrey Crossick

READ 10 DECEMBER 1993 AT THE UNIVERSITY OF NOTTINGHAM

AFTER a long period of neglect, during which historians had looked towards the petite bourgeoisie primarily to heap upon it the responsibility for fascism, the last fifteen years has seen a growing research interest in the social and political history of the world of small retail, artisanal and manufacturing enterprise.[1] The result of this attention has been paradoxical, on the one hand establishing the petite bourgeoisie as a focus for sustained research, while on the other confirming how difficult it is to see the owners of small retail and manufacturing enterprise as a coherent social group or social class. The combination of the owner's labour and capital within family-centred enterprises might indicate a distinct position for the petite bourgeoisie within the social structure, but various forces militated against a social or demographic identity for the proprietors of small enterprise: the high rate of business turnover, the limited proportion of petits bourgeois who remain in that position through their careers, and the low rate of continuity between generations. Although political struggle was important in the formation of any class, one could go further with respect to the petite bourgeoisie and suggest that it was only at times of political crisis and action, only through the discourse and actions of its organisations, that a petit-bourgeois identity might emerge. It is not surprising, therefore, that research has focused above all on those years between the 1880s and the First World War, when the emergence of interest

---

[1] This growth of interest can first be seen in two special issues of *Le Mouvement social*: 'L'atelier et la boutique', 108 (1979), and 'Petite entreprise et politique', 114 (1979). Subsequent publications include *Shopkeepers and Master Artisans in Nineteenth-Century Europe* (eds.) Geoffrey Crossick and Heinz-Gerhard Haupt (1984); Philip G. Nord, *Paris Shopkeepers and the Politics of Resentment* (Princeton, 1986); *Splintered Classes: Politics and the Lower Middle Classes in Interwar Europe (ed.)* Rudy Koshar (New York, 1990); *L'univers politique des classes moyennes* (eds.) Georges Lavau et. al. (Paris, 1983); Steven M. Zdatny, *The Politics of Survival. Artisans in Twentieth-Century France* (New York, 1990); *Aux frontières des classes moyennes. La petite bourgeoisie belge avant 1914* (eds.) G. Kurgan and Serge Jaumain (Brussels, 1992); Jonathan Morris, *The political economy of shopkeeping in Milan 1886–1922* (Cambridge, 1993). I am grateful to Peter Heyrman, Serge Jaumain and Leen Van Molle for helpful discussions in the early stages of this research, and also to Heinz-Gerhard Haupt and Sylvie Taschereau for valuable comments on an earlier version of this paper.

groups and increasing political mobilisation seemed to offer evidence of a real petit-bourgeois identity.

There are other ways, however, in which social groups can come into existence. The petite bourgeoisie may have been discovered by historians over the last decade, but they had been discovered before. While those studying the petite bourgeoisie in Britain have wrestled with patchy sources that were often only incidentally concerned with the world of small enterprise, those working on Germany, Belgium and France have been drawn to a substantial body of writings published in the quarter century before the First World War. The material on Germany is well known, for its connections to the process known as *Mittelstandspolitik* made it central to political analysis and formation. The discovery of the petite bourgeoisie in France and Belgium has been less well explored, yet in these countries too the petite bourgeoisie became an issue in social thought as well as political action in those years, and it is that process of discovery which is the concern of this paper.

More precisely, it is the discovery within particular strands of catholic and conservative thought upon which this paper focuses, for there were indeed other discourses. Liberals in Belgium, the Radical Party in France, and the more ambivalent and ultimately negative socialist groups in Belgium and then France, all struggled to shape a vision of the world of small enterprise. In these two countries, however, it was amongst social catholics and Le Playists that the most sustained and public analysis took place, constructing a discourse which was to influence not only the movements of petits bourgeois themselves, but also debates on these intermediary social groups in subsequent decades.[2] This paper is an exploration of that discovery. A necessary element in any act of discovery is the process of naming. The discourse upon which this paper focuses sometimes used the term *petite bourgeoisie* to describe the owners of small enterprise, primarily in Belgium, but the term *classes moyennes* was more common in both Belgium and France. Rather than translating it inaccurately as *middle classes*, it will be kept in its French form in quotations, thus retaining the resonances of both middle and average bound up in the French expression.

Georges Blondel, Parisian economist and a leading member of the *Société d'économie sociale*, the society devoted to following the ideas and methods of Frédéric Le Play, observed in 1908 that 'the problem of the *classes moyennes*, which nobody used to speak about some fifteen or

---

[2] These other strands of analysis have received little attention. For French radicalism and the *classe moyenne*, see Serge Berstein, 'Le Parti Radical-Socialiste, de la défense du peuple à celle des classes moyennes', in Lavau, *L'univers politique*, 71–93. For French socialists Madeleine Rebérioux, 'Les socialistes français et le petit commerce au tournant du siècle', *le mouvement social*, 114 (1981), 57–70.

twenty years ago, is beginning to concern a good number of people.'[3] A literature had developed during those years which argued insistently that the petite bourgeoisie was in crisis, that its very survival was at stale, and that it could be crushed beneath the wheels of the juggernaut of progress and economic concentration. It was a literature which saw the moral organisation of society as intricately bound up with the problems of the petite bourgeoisie, and which saw the individualisation of rights and relationships which flowed from 1789 as undermining the cohesive institutions of an ordered society, but pride of place in the analysis of petit-bourgeois problems was given to the economic trends of the previous fifty years. Large-scale capital was invading more and more branches of manufacturing, and it was now attacking retailing through the rise of department stores and multiple chains. Furthermore, the technological revolution in transport, together with the emergence of large-scale merchant activity, had also destroyed the protections that distance had once given to local producers and traders, and the subsequent decline in local markets and loyalties undermined the moral as well as the economic bases of viable small enterprise. Statistics that revealed numbers of small workshops rising at the start of this century provided little comfort, for the issue was not existence but prosperity, and an increasing proportion of small firms seemed no more than precarious outworkers for department stores.[4]

The problems faced by the petite bourgeoisie, it was argued in this literature, were exacerbated by the way that those seeking to reestablish social stability were concerned exclusively with the working class. Inquiries and research—such as the 1886 Labour Commission in Belgium that followed the riots of that year or the work of the Labour Department established by the French government in 1891—focused only on the situation of wage workers. Governments and social investigators had lost sight of the reality of *la question sociale*, the social question, and now confused it with *la question ouvrière*, the working-class question. Oscar Pyfferoen, the young Belgian social catholic whose work on the Ghent municipal enquiry into the petite bourgeoisie marked his conversion to the cause, wrote that 'for many years the attention of the intellectual and political worlds has been preoccupied

[3] Georges Blondel, 'Le problème des classes moyennes. Aperçus français', *Bulletin de l'Institut international pour l'étude du problème des classes moyennes*, May 1908, cited henceforward as *IICM Bulletin*. I have not succeeded in tracking down a complete set of this *Bulletin* for the period 1905–1914, though the combined holdings of the Catholic Documentation Centre (KADOC), at the Catholic University of Louvain, and Louvain Municipal Library between them cover most of these years.

[4] Victor Brants, *La petite industrie contemporaine* (2nd edition, Paris, 1902), 68 ff; Maurice Dufourmantelle, 'La défense des classes moyennes', *La réforme sociale*, LVII (1909), 765–6; Paul du Maroussem, *La question ouvrière* (4 vols., Paris, 1891–94).

with measures to help the working class. That is what is known as the social question. In truth it is only one aspect of that question, for workers do not constitute the whole of society ... Alongside the interests of workers are those of the petite bourgeoisie, the *classes moyennes*, who are no less worthy of being taken into consideration.[5] For Paul du Maroussem, whose studies of Parisian small trades for the Labour Department have provided a rich source for historians, the legislation and social benefits devised to help the working class served only to make life more difficult for small enterprise, so that 'each attempt to solve the *working-class question* serves only to deepen and to aggravate the *social question*.'[6] Within this analysis, only the strengthening of the *classes moyennes* could offer a solution to the social question, yet they seemed to be threatened with disappearance in the face of what both liberal and Marxist writers insisted upon seeing as progress.[7] Blondel concluded from the 1901 Congress of the Petite Bourgeoisie held in Namur that 'it is not only a matter of finding the means by which the *classes moyennes* might participate in progress; it is a matter of finding out whether progress itself is going to be the cause of their death.'[8]

Hector Lambrechts, the Belgian lawyer and civil servant who was an indefatigable presence formulating and publicising policy on behalf of the petite bourgeoisie and whose inelegant writings provide the most informative as well as the dullest point of entry to this literature, stressed that 'the *classes moyennes* ... are dying, and their disappearance will prove fatal to the social order, for their existence is a condition of both progress and peace'.[9] Here was the discourse of discovery, in which the world of small enterprise that was felt to be threatened with extinction was presented as the key to maintaining social order and building social peace. The vice-chairman of a catholic petit-bourgeois association in Brussels told the very first congress of the Petite Bourgeoisie held in Antwerp in 1899, that 'our only concern, our only programme is to

---

[5] Oscar Pyfferoen, 'La petite bourgeoisie d'après une enquête officielle à Gand (1)', *La réforme sociale*, XXXVII (1899), 285.

[6] Paul du Maroussem, *La question ouvrière*. vol 3: *Le jouet parisien. Grands magasins. 'Sweating-system'*, (Paris, 1894), 202–3.

[7] For example, Théophile Funck-Brentano, *La Politique. Principes. Critiques. Réformes* (Paris, 1893), 186.

[8] Georges Blondel, 'La petite bourgeoisie', *La réforme sociale*, XLII (1901), 836.

[9] Hector Lambrechts, 'La concentration, commun dénominateur de la question sociale', *Revue sociale catholique*, XVII (1912–13), 186. Lambrechts published extensively in a variety of journals, including *La réforme sociale, Revue d'Economie Politique, Revue des Questions Scientifiques*, and *IICM Bulletin*. As *Hego* he wrote a series of interesting popular articles in the Antwerp newspaper *La métropole* between 1895 and 1906, many of which tackled questions relating to the petite bourgeoisie. His most important books include *Le problème social de la petite bourgeoisie envisagé au point de vue belge* (Brussels, 1902) and his institutional memoirs, *Trente années au service des Classes Moyennes* (Dison, 1931).

improve the lot of the *classes moyennes* of the petite bourgeoisie, such an interesting social stratum *which does exist* and which *we have not invented*.[10] By the end of this paper we might disagree with him, and suggest that the *classe moyenne* which was invested with such importance in these years was indeed an invention, an idealised *classe moyenne* that was constructed to be used in argument and debate by intellectuals and reformers anguished at social developments which they sought to control.

It is a mistake to compartmentalise late nineteenth-century intellectual movements too closely, for those concerned with developing social science, as a means to manage a social world threatened by disorder, were eclectic in their contacts.[11] Nevertheless, this concern for the petite bourgeoisie was to be found primarily within the world of social catholicism and amongst the followers of the mid-century French metallurgist turned sociologist, Frédéric Le Play. Social catholicism, growing since mid-century but only becoming a major current of ideas from the 1870s, sought to resolve through catholic teaching the social problems born out of the industrial revolution and economic liberalism, problems that came to be designated the social question. Social catholicism contained a diverse range of reform ideas, from the corporatist theories of Albert de Mun and La Tour du Pin; through free associations and *cercles* in which workers might organise under the leadership of church and elite; to a commitment to traditional employer paternalism (*patronage*) in which employers' care for the material, moral and religious needs of their workforce would counter the demoralising individualism of modern employment relations and bridge the new gulf between rich and poor. The papal encyclical *Rerum Novarum* in 1891 drew together these threads in a critique of a world in which employers and workers, rich and poor faced each other across an abyss of incomprehension. Social catholics could read what they wanted to in the encyclical which, although serving to increase catholic commitment to social action, offered little coherent guidance to policy. The common thread of social catholicism remained a belief that collaboration between different social milieux in a moral and religious framework would provide the basis

[10] *Compte rendu sténographique du Congrès International de la Petite Bourgeoisie, tenu à Anvers le 17 et 18 septembre 1899* (Brussels, 1900), 713. Original emphasis. His words suggest an implicit response to discordant voices denying the reality of the *classes moyennes*.
[11] See for example the variety of intellectual tendencies gathered from the 1870s in Emile Boutmy's *Ecole libre des sciences politiques*: Christophe Prochason, *Les années électriques 1880–1910* (Paris, 1991), 212 ff. The coexistence of eclectic and even contradictory ideological groups in late nineteenth- and early twentieth-century French reform movements is a recurrent theme in Sanford Elwitt, *The Third Republic Defended. Bourgeois Reform in France, 1880–1914* (Baton Rouge, 1986), though his study reduces them to a single underlying project.

for social peace. This would constitute a third way between socialism and liberalism, one in which family, intermediary associations and catholic works would provide the alternative to individualised solutions on the one hand and collectivist ones on the other.[12]

Although Le Playism was not necessarily social catholic, it was there that it increasingly found its followers.[13] They drew from their master's ideas—both before and after his death in 1886—elements close to those of social catholicism: a belief that moral reform alone could resolve the social question; a rejection of both individualist and statist prescriptions; a strong attachment to the policy of *patronage*; and a special emphasis on the family, both its structure and its role in property transmission, in achieving social stability. Le Playists went beyond this however, taking Le Play's innovation in social science methodology, the monographic case study of workers' families, and constructing it as a scientific basis for the conditions of social peace.[14] These published monographs constituted in reality little more than anecdotes upon which an excessive ideological weight was loaded, to sustain the Le Playist belief that type of family and type of employment regime were the bases for analysing the conditions for social stability. The goal of Le Playist social science was social peace. As the first editor of *La Réforme sociale*, the principal Le Playist journal, explained in its inaugural issue in 1881, 'the main issue today, far less than that of increasing wealth, is to assure stability, social peace, in a word that sum of well-being to which man can legitimately aspire.'[15]

The *Société d'économie social*, founded by Le Play himself in 1856, and its monthly papers and discussions which were subsequently published in its journal, *La Réforme sociale*, constituted in France the institutional base for those interested in analysing the petite bourgeoisie. There was close interaction in these years between Belgian and French catholic

---

[12] Jean-Marie Mayeur, 'Catholicisme intransigent, catholicisme social, démocratie chrétienne', *Annales E. S. C.*, XXVII (1972), 483–99; Gérard Cholvy and Yves-Marie Hilaire, *Histoire religieuse de la France contemporaine, Vol 2 1880–1930* (Toulouse, 1986), 73 ff and 150 ff; *Een Kantelend Tijdperk. De wending van de Kerk naar het volk in Noord-West-Europe* (ed.) Emiel Lamberts (Louvain, 1992), especially essays by Mayeur on France and Paul Gérin on Belgium.

[13] On the ideas of Le Play and the Le Playist movement, see Michael Z. Brooke, *Le Play: engineer and social scientist. The life and work of Frédéric Le Play* (1970); Catherine Bodard Silver (ed.), *Frédéric Le Play on Family, Work and Social Change* (Chicago, 1982); Antoine Savoye, 'Les continuateurs de Le Play au tournant du siècle', *Revue française de sociologie*, XXII (1981), 315–44; Matthew H. Elbow, *French Corporative Theory, 1789–1948. A Chapter in the History of Ideas* (New York, 1953), 48 ff.

[14] Jean-René Tréanton, 'Faut-il exhumer Le Play? ou les héritiers abusifs', *Revue française de sociologie*, XXV (1984), 458–83.

[15] Edmond Demolins, 'L'école de la Réforme sociale. Son programme', *La Réforme sociale*, I (1881), 4.

intellectuals, and its Belgian sister organisation, the *Société belge d'économie sociale,* established in 1881 by the Louvain economist and historian Victor Brants, was the main channel of Le Playist ideas into Belgium, its *Revue social catholique* carrying regular articles on the petite bourgeoisie and the social crisis. One can appreciate the intellectual plausibility of embracing the cause of the middle as a solution to a polarised society, but it must be stressed that only a minority of social catholics, even of Le Playists did so.[16] A glance at the contents of these journals and the congresses of the two societies makes that clear, but so too does the almost total neglect of the petite bourgeoisie by the influential *Musée social* from its foundation in 1894. Its wide-ranging inquiries and discussions of the social question from both social catholic and solidarist perspectives were concerned almost exclusively with the world of labour, the working-class and social reform.[17]

Le Playist intellectuals straddled the worlds of social science and conservative politics, and their role in government social inquiries increased their connection to the state, above all in Belgium where a distinct political situation forced the petit-bourgeois question onto the agenda.[18] Not only was the Catholic Party in power in Belgium from 1884 to the end of our period, but its franchise reform of 1893 created universal manhood suffrage tempered by plural voting related to property and education. The petite bourgeoisie's consequent electoral importance could not be matched in France, where the question of the *classe moyenne*, surfacing only on the fringes of political debate, was never as closely linked to party politics or strategy, though the Nationalists' victory in the 1900 Paris elections warned French radicalism that its traditional social base was by no means secure, and alerted others to the potential for electoral organising amongst an increasingly disenchanted shopkeeper class. However much political circumstances pushed the issue of petits bourgeois—normally shopkeepers—intermittently into prominence, and however much political threads were wound around petit-bourgeois organisations, the petit-bourgeois dimension remained peri-

---

[16] The division amongst the followers of Le Play, which produced an alternative tendency around the journal *La Science sociale* (founded 1886), was as much to do with personalities as theories, but it is noteworthy that *La Science sociale*, which was explicitly concerned with the development of Le Playist theory rather than social action, gave relatively little attention to the *classes moyennes*.

[17] See the publications of the Musée social, its *Annales* as well as its *Mémoires et Documents*. Étienne Martin Saint-Léon's report on '*Le IIIe Congrès international des classes moyennes*' in *Le Musée social*, December 1911, 357–79 is a rare and low-key exception. On the institution itself, see Sanford Elwitt, 'Social reform and social order in late nineteenth-century France: the Musée Social and its friends', *French Historical Studies*, XI (1979–80), 431–51.

[18] Le Playists played a major role in the Belgian *Commission du Travail* (1886) and *Commission Nationale de la Petite Bourgeoisie* (1902–6) as well as in the enquiries undertaken by the *Office du Travail* in France from 1891.

pheral to the strategies of political parties, even to most catholic politicians.

The main sphere of action for the intellectuals, lawyers, writers and reformers who engaged with the question of the petite bourgeoisie in these years was the Le Playist societies and journals already referred to, and the national and international congresses, beginning at Antwerp in 1899, at which the needs of small enterprise could be debated, and at which the leaders of petit-bourgeois organisations could be taught the means by which their class could be saved. The International Institute for the Study of the Problem of the *Classes Moyennes*, founded in 1903 and based in Brussels, had the tireless Hector Lambrechts as its Secretary. It was the organisational base for a succession of congresses, but above all for the spread of information on matters such as comparative legislation and self-help associations that were so dear to the heart of those who were defining a social role and a route to social survival for the *classes moyennes*.[19]

Yet as one reads the early writings in *la Réforme sociale* and elsewhere, and as one considers the imperatives of catholic social reform, the less inevitable it appears that the petite bourgeoisie would be discovered as a major force for stability. Indeed, the world of small enterprise could appear as an obstacle rather than an aid to strategies for social peace. Consumer cooperative societies formed one stumbling block. Although Belgian social catholics were still hesitant about cooperatives in the 1880s, fearful of workers' autonomy and socialist ideas, the 1890s saw them become a major part of catholic strategy for working-class (as well as agrarian) improvement.[20] Oscar Pyfferoen praised them in 1892 as the only way for workers to obtain the material benefits of lower prices, and the moral benefits of the absence of credit and an encouragement to thrift. For Pyfferoen, the excessive number of small shops all too often meant high prices and low quality, and other social catholics agreed.[21] Socialist cooperatives might be regretted on political

[19] For the development of the International Institute, see its own publications, above all the *IICM Bulletin*; Lambrechts, *Trentes années*; M. Dufourmantelle, 'Le Decennium de l'Institut International des Classes Moyennes', *La Réforme sociale*, LXVII (1914), 56–61; Serge Jaumain, 'Les petits commerçants belges face à la modernité 1880–1914', Doctoral thesis, Université Libre de Bruxelles, 1991, 395–400.

[20] Paul Gérin, 'Les mouvements populaires en Belgique', in Lamberts *Kantelend Tijdperk*, 159. At its 1893 Congress, the Catholic *Ligue démocratique belge* formally supported the spread of consumer cooperation: *Congrés International de la Petite Bourgeoisie 1899*, 124. For agrarian cooperatives, see the excellent study by Leen Van Molle, *Chacun pour tous. Le Boerenbond Belge 1890–1990* (Louvain, 1990).

[21] Oscar Pyfferoen, 'Les boulangeries coopératives', *La Réforme sociale*, XXIII (1892), 340–53; though compare Pyfferoen's changed tone just seven years later in 'La petite bourgeoisie'. Hubert-Valleroux similarly defended consumer cooperatives, and questioned the proliferation of individual retailers, in 'Les origines de la co-opération en France et en Angleterre et les tendances actueles des coopérateurs', *La Réforme sociale*, XXV (1893), 445–65. The early Le Playist attraction to consumer cooperation is most clearly shown

grounds, especially the *Vooruit* in Ghent, but even their benefits were acknowledged. Small shopkeepers may have been an obvious target, but criticism of bad working conditions in small enterprise extended to artisanal workshops. *Patronage*, paternalism under enlightened catholic large employers, seemed a far better prospect for creating decent conditions and moralising communities, and the power of *patronage* amongst those influenced by Le Play made the attractions of small enterprise seem limited. The annual meeting of the *Société d'économie sociale* took a trip to the Louvre department store in 1891, one of the targets of the shopkeeper movement, and the members were impressed by what they saw on their tour and by a clever speech by the Director who laid great emphasis on the possibilities for *patronage* offered by businesses such as his: good pay, retirement benefits, medical services, savings banks, canteens, supervision by employers.[22] The department store's potential for *patronage* seemed at this stage far more attractive than the myriad of small shopkeepers it threatened to displace. From the perspective of the early 1890s, the commitment of even these sections of social catholicism was clearly not fixed, and few would have argued with the view expressed by Brants in his 1885 lectures on political economy that, given doubts about how effectively small enterprise could be saved, the real need was to attend to the situation of factory labour.[23]

Nevertheless, to sections of catholic conservatism, the *classe moyenne* gradually emerged as a force that was essential to the health of society and to the social peace that was the goal of Le Playist social science. As a meeting in Lyon was told, 'history teaches us ... that when, in a nation, the *classe moyenne* ceases to exist, that nation loses it vitality, and loses little time before it too disappears.'[24] It was essential to social peace because it was the middle, the average, the *moyenne*. Here was an insistently used metaphor which came to pervade the discourse—the metaphor of the middle. There was not one but many such

---

in the *Société d'économie sociale*'s discussion on the subject at the 1890 annual meeting. Whereas Dr Goddyn's savage onslaught on consumer cooperatives as the work of socialists and anarchists was excluded from the full report, M. Gruner's moderate assessment of their advantages, given the exploitation of workers by overnumerous intermediaries, was reproduced in full. Compare the report of the working session in 'Les sociétés coopératives en Belgique. La coopération, son domaine, ses limites,' *La Réforme sociale*, XX (1890), 33–37, with the full report 'La coopération. Son domaine et ses limites', *ibid.*, 577–98.

[22] J. Angots des Retours, 'Les Grands Magasins du Louvre', *La Réforme sociale*, XXII (1891), 95–9. See also Demolins' defence of the department store in his 'La question des grands magasins', *La Science sociale*, IX (1890), 289–319.

[23] Victor Brants, *La Lutte pour le Pain Quotidien. Précis des leçons d'économie politique* (Paris, 1885), 195.

[24] Max Turmann, 'Un aspect du problème des classes moyennes', *La Chronique sociale du France*, XVIII (1909), 461.

metaphors, and all rested on the presence of a middle which would prevent the polarisation of classes and the consequent destruction of the social order. 'The day will come,' wrote Théophile Funck-Brentano, 'when the working classes, whose demands are already overwhelming us, and the *classes moyennes* will form but a single class, the poor, and that day will see reborn the horrors of ancient Greece and Rome.' Decline in the ancient world was evoked with striking frequency, often citing Fustel de Coulanges on the horrors that followed, their polarised societies producing a decadence that seemed matched in the present. Paul du Maroussem's analysis of the cabinet-makers of the faubourg Saint-Antoine in Paris led him to observe that the Greek republics declined when they lost 'the intermediary stages on the social scale, those classes which united wealth to poverty'.[25]

There were many metaphors of the middle. The first placed it within a spatially conceived social structure, a scale that saw the socially mobile move in and out of the middle. For Pyfferoen, the worker could hope to become a small shopkeeper or small manufacturer, and 'thus raise himself towards wealth by passing through the *classes moyennes*'.[26] Here was one of the most recurrent images, but so too was the second sense, of the middle as a buffer between the classes. Du Maroussem told the 1910 Congress of the *Société d'économie sociale* which devoted itself to the *classes moyennes* that they consulted *un état de milieu*, 'a middling estate, a group of classes which form a buffer between the rich and the poor'.[27] For Pyfferoen they 'absorb the shocks between the social extremes'.[28] The Aristotelian middle constituted the third sense of the metaphor, the ideal which was such precisely because it avoided the extremes—Martin Saint-Léon referred explicitly to the *classes moyennes* as a *juste milieu* within contemporary society.[29] Formal references to Aristotle were not surprising, given the subject and given the neo-Thomist revival in social catholic thought.[30] Georges Duplat cited Aristotle's praise of the *moyenne*, arguing that there is a force, in society as much as in biology, whose natural tendency is to maintain or reestablish equilibrium. That force was 'the *moyenne* which separates

---

[25] Th. Funck-Brentano, *Politique*, 141; Paul du Maroussem, *La Question ouvrière. vol 2 Ebénistes du Faubourg St-Antoine* (Paris, 1892), 277. See also *Congrès International de la Petite Bourgeoisie 1899*, 92 (Frantz Funck-Brentano) and 231 (G. Verbiest).

[26] Oscar Pyfferoen, 'La formation technique des classes moyennes', *La Réforme sociale*, L (1905), 838.

[27] Paul du Maroussem at Closing Banquet, *Les Classes Moyennes dans le Commerce et l'Industrie. XXIXe Congrès de la Société internationale d'économie sociale* (Paris, 1910), 128.

[28] Pyfferoen, 'Formation technique', 838.

[29] Étienne Martin Saint-Léon, 'L'organisation corporative des classes moyennes', *La Réforme sociale*, LX (1910), 204.

[30] The classic statement in Aristotle's own writings is in *The Politics* Book 4, Chapter 11.

antagonistic extremes'.[31] The fourth sense is the normative definition, in which the social location produced moderate social and political values, in which the average nature of the class's virtues constituted its value. Blondel wrote of 'the ideas of moderation and good sense to which they are naturally inclined'.[32] These moderate values flowed from the fifth sense of the middle, the fact that it mixed together elements such as labour and capital, property and work, production and consumption, which were dangerous when concentrated yet wholesome when mixed. Duplat asked why they were called *moyennes*. He answered that it was because 'the support of possessions is not enough for carrying out of their economic function. They must add labour. Furthermore, it is because this union of labour and property ... produces an average (*moyenne*) between possessions and labour which is the basis of social equilibrium.'[33] Finally, there was the middle as 'the necessary links in the chain'.[34] As, Brants wrote, the *classe moyenne* 'represents the personal and moral link between employers and workers, it is a personal link between producer and customer, it is, as one says, a system of social peace.'[35]

This praise of the middle as a force for moderation and stability, and the attachment of a group defined by moral criteria to a specific location in the social structure, had a long heritage. The struggle by constitutional radicals in the Britain of the 1790s against Pitt's assessed taxes proposal spoke in defence of a social middle that was ground down by government policies, a group whose virtues and independence made them the core of the social order. Yet these middle groups were rarely defined in other than moral and educational terms.[36] Similarly with the appeals of Guizot and Orléanist discourse in France or of the reform Whigs in the 1820s and 1830s, seeking the rule of the middle groups, the *juste milieu*, for this was a political and ideological centre which was only implicitly social.[37] Indeed, in the Orléanist case, the

---

[31] Georges Duplat, *La classe moyenne. Son rôle social. Son action politique. Sa situation économique. Les réformes urgentes* (Brussels, 1914), 97–8. See also Frantz Funck-Brentano, *Grandeur et décadences des classes moyennes* (Paris, 1903), 48–9; Lambrechts, *Trente Années*, 79.

[32] Blondel, 'Le problème', *IICM Bulletin*, May 1908.

[33] Duplat, *Classe moyenne*, 12.

[34] Edouard Aynard, 'Le petit commerce et l'industrie', in *Les Classes Moyennes dans le Commerce et l'Industrie*, 12.

[35] Brants, *Petite industrie*, 30. For an interesting critical discussion of the implications of the word *moyenne*, see Henri Mougin, 'Un projet d'enquête sur les classes moyennes', in R. Aron *et. al.*, *Inventaires III: Classes Moyennes* (Paris, 1939), 296 ff.

[36] Dror Wahrman, 'Virtual representation: parliamentary reporting and languages of class in the 1790s', *Past and Present*, 136 (1992), 83–113.

[37] Vincent E. Starzinger, *Middlingness. Juste Milieu Political Theory in France and England, 1815–1848* (Charlottesville, 1965); Klaus-Peter Sick, 'Le concept de classes moyennes. Notion sociologique ou slogan politique?', *Vingtième siècle*, XXXVII (1993), 16–18.

concept of the *classe moyenne* designated the conclusion of historical evolution, as that part of society which was the embodiment of French liberty and order finally came to power. Appeals to the virtues and qualities of the middle thus had many precedents. The difference with social catholic and Le Playist discourse, apart from the fact that the idea of the middle was now firmly attached to the cause of conservatism, was that the late-nineteenth century invention of this middle did not rest with its normative definitions but pinned it to precise occupational categories. The problem then became, as we shall see, the need to escape from the fact that these precisely identified groups did not always meet the requirements of the ideology that had designated them.

What were the supposed characteristics of the world of small enterprise? The Comte de Boissieu painted an attractive picture. 'In the course of our inquiries', he wrote, 'more than one of us has come across the normal, prosperous, family workshop, providing the moralising qualities that the factory could never offer, however Christian it might be. This workshop teaches its members the value of the family home, maintains an intimacy between husband and wife and within the family which is always endangered by factory life, and ensures the recruitment of an elite of workers, endowed with the happy qualities of initiative and independence.'[38] At the heart of the idealised world of the *classes moyennes* lay the intimate interaction of workplace, family and enterprise from which so many of the moral benefits flowed. Étienne Martin Saint-Léon's portrait of the independent shop told of 'the owner who, with the help of his son or daughter, attends to the practical side of the job; the owner's wife is on the till; family life and professional life coincide. As for the young employee, the shopgirl, the female assistant, they work under the eye of their master.'[39] The family provided the natural setting for work, for the master could move between home and work without disruption, and because the employees ate at the family table. Workers were not abandoned to individual pleasures, but embraced the stabilities of family life. The women of the family were bound into the enterprise, which prevented the deformation and corruption of their character that followed work outside the home, while at the same time allowing their natural character to suffuse the world of workshop

[38] Le Comte de Boissieu, 'Le moteur éléctrique et l'industrie à domicile dans la région lyonnaise', *La Réforme sociale*, LV (1908), 656. For an enthusiastic description of harmonious family life in a shoemaker's workshop, see René Beckers, 'La cordonnerie à Louvain', in Commission Nationale de la Petite Bourgeoisie (Belgium), *Enquêtes écrites, Monographies*, I (1904), 284–6.

[39] Etienne Martin Saint-Léon, *Le Petit Commerce français. Sa lutte pour la vie* (Paris, 1911), 97–8.

or shop. As the 1910 Congress was told, 'women have a substantial presence in small enterprise; they play a major role, with their ingenuity, their love of order, and the charm of their relations with customers.'[40] The nature of an occupation and its setting was a key determinant of moral well-being, and small enterprise provided the ideal setting. Pyfferoen wrote of the *classes moyennes*' 'spirit of work and of order, their honest and simple habits, their calm and modest tastes'.[41] These were no chance qualities, for they were the natural consequence of a life of independence where savings, hard work and frugality were the only basis for success, and they were deeply engrained in the moral character of the *classes moyennes*. In Martin Saint-Léon's words, 'all the faculties of the mind are brought into play, all the force of the will is directed towards a single goal, and when the human spirit is subjected to such a test, to this moral gymnastics, it develops, grows, learns under the stimulus of necessity.'[42] And here was a life to which others could aspire, for only small enterprise could offer resourceful and intelligent workers the opportunity to escape their lot. As Frantz Funck-Brentano explained, 'the *classe moyenne* is the broad and open road by which the frugal, skillful and diligent worker can become an employer. Even those who do not get there can keep alive the hope, for them and for their children. And everyone knows that man lives by hope more than he does by reality.' If denied the opportunity of upward mobility, it was repeatedly argued, intelligent and ambitious workers would become the leaders of revolutionary politics.[43]

These were the characteristics of a social group whose survival and renewal would provide the solution to the social question, a question which was redefined to focus it upon their presence. Joseph Bernard, writing of French shopkeepers, spoke of 'their social role whose importance, I must admit, is much greater than their economic value'.[44] It was for these social and moral reasons that they had to survive. The problem was that this was an idealisation of the world of small enterprise which continually threatened to unravel, as it faced the tensions within its own ideas as well as the reality of small enterprise. At the heart of the discourse lay its most serious problem: the world that it described was one cast in an artisanal mould, yet the petite bourgeoisie which was organising in France and Belgium to overcome is problems was primarily made up of shopkeepers. The greatest pressure on *artisans* in

[40] Aynard, 'Le petit commerce et l'industrie', 23.

[41] Pyfferoen, 'La petite bourgeoisie', 292.

[42] Martin Saint-Léon, *Le Petite Commerce français*, 93-4.

[43] Frantz Funck-Brentano in *Congrès International de la Petite Bourgeoisie 1899*, 91. See also Pyfferoen, 'La petite bourgeoisie', 293.

[44] Joseph Bernard and Louis Hoffmann, 'Le petit commerce et les grands magasins', *La Réforme sociale* LXI (1911), 303.

industrialising western Europe was experienced during the middle third of the nineteenth century, at a time when the structure of politics generally kept them within the radical popular milieu to which they had been historically committed. For independent *retailers*, however, these were generally optimistic decades of growth, and economic and social difficulties for them grew only in the later nineteenth century, and in a very different political context. If the process of discovery took some impetus from petit-bourgeois movements, as it certainly did, then it was largely shopkeeper movements to which it was compelled to respond. The pattern was significantly different in Germany, where artisans played the major role in organisations as well as in the responses of parties and government. In this context, the influence of Germany on Belgian and French ideas was especially important. When Hector Lambrechts was charged by the Belgian government in 1896 with setting up a service for the *classe moyenne* within the Labour Department, his first step was to tour German and Austrian towns to learn what was being done there.[45] Key figures from German state bureaucracies, chambers and associations participated in both the International Institute and the major petit-bourgeois congresses. The footnotes of the main figures in the intellectual movement—Brants, Lambrechts, Martin Saint-Léon and the rest—reveal how much, as well as how circumspectly, they drew on the German experience.[46]

However, the German and Austrian situations were seen as deriving from different historical conditions, and rarely accepted uncritically, especially with respect to the corporatist ambitions of German reformers. Victor Brants spoke for many when he recognised the benefits of corporations, which had once delivered many of the resources that were now needed, such as technical education, apprenticeship, moral regulation, and solidarity of the trade. Like others, he saw the attractiveness of the advance in trade organisation in the German countries, advances of which he was perhaps the most effective publicist in Belgium. He was clear, however, that the past could not be reconstructed in the present.[47] Le Playists were not of one opinion on the question of corporations. A lecture on Limousin corporations in the three centuries before their abolition saw them as nothing but selfish monopolies—in the speaker's view the good relations in the Limousin trades on the eve

---

[45] Lambrechts, *Trente années*, xiv.

[46] The German example is a continuing thread in Brants, *Petite industrie*, but one over which he is cautious.

[47] Brants, *La petite industrie*, 67–8 and his 'La petite industrie et la restauration corporative (Loi du 15 mars 1883)', *La Réforme sociale*, XVII (1889), 224–37. Georges Blondel, more acquainted with German and Austrian developments than others in France, was vigorous in his rejection of corporate legislation in Austria: 'Le problème', *IICM Bulletin*, May 1908.

of the Revolution were the result not of corporations but of the natural benefits of the small workshop and sound religion. Most recognised that the individualism introduced by the French Revolution had been destructive of order and morality in economic and therefore social life.[48] 'The Revolution,' wrote Edmond Demolins, 'in substituting the spirit of individualism for the old spirit of association, has created a society destined for weakness and discord.'[49] Although some like Martin Saint-Léon were more tempted by the corporatist vision, most rejected the backward-looking solutions it seemed to offer, solutions unsuited to the economic and political world in which they lived. Lambrechts was not alone in finding the statist and centralising approach of the German reforms disturbing. Free associations and private initiative were the only way forward, and in this respect the Le Playists increasingly stood out from the corporatist emphases which came to dominate French (though not Belgian) social catholicism.[50] In France, corporatism carried an implicit challenge to the Republic and its removal of privileged bodies separating the citizen from the state. Le Playists, on the liberal wing of social catholicism, were unwilling to commit themselves to the political implications of such a position.

Nonetheless, the German influence reinforced the tendency to trace the image of the *classes moyennes* from an artisanal template, in much the same way that those who sought to ridicule the *classes moyennes* tended to ignore artisans and write of shopkeepers.[51] The character of the *classe moyenne* upon which its special role rested was constructed upon an image of the artisanal family enterprise that was fashioned out of the past more than the present. It was not always clear in the discourse whether the artisanal character being described represented a present condition or a potential drawn from a retrievable past. One only needs to set the admittedly extreme case of the degraded Parisian small producers examined by Paul du Maroussem against the artisanal past presented by Albert Babeau and a clutch of lesser mythologisers, whose widely-read histories of artisanship written in just these years helped fas-

---

[48] Louis Guibert, 'Les anciennes corporations de métiers en Limousin', *La Réforme sociale*, VI (1883), 445–54.

[49] Edmond Demolins, report on 'Une conférence sur le mouvement corporatif', *La Réforme sociale*, V (1883), 519–20.

[50] Hector Lambrechts, 'L'œuvre sociale du Reichstag allemand en 1886', *Revue des Questions Scientifiques*, XLI (1897), 104 ff. Le Play himself had admired the guilds of the *ancien régime*, but a concern for freedom of occupation made him unwilling to accept a continued role in the nineteenth century: Elbow, *French Corporative Theory*, 48–9. A more corporatist social catholic concern for small enterprise can be found in the *Union fraternelle du commerce et de l'industrie* set up by Léon Harmel in 1891. See Nord, *Paris Shopkeepers*, 395 ff.

[51] E.g. Georges Deherme, *Les classes moyenne. Etude sur le parasitisme social* (Paris, 1912), which stressed not only shopkeepers but civil servants as well for the purpose of ridicule.

hion the artisanal ideal. Babeau wove together such elements as the home, patriarchy, continuity of place, personal relations with clientèle, simple and honest traders, care for apprentices, workplace discipline, economy, the wife's lack of vanity and her involvement in the business, religion, and the sociability of the trade. It was not only Victor Brants who saw this idealised picture of what once existed as a description of what could still be found in small towns, and which could be built again everywhere, given the importance of historical identity for small-scale industry.[52]

The image of the shopkeeper, on the other hand, was too uncomfortable to make him an attractive model, especially if one dwelt on his relationship with working-class customers. When Louis Rivière gave one of the opening lectures at the *Société d'économie sociale*'s 1910 Congress, he spoke of artisans when discussing the qualities of the *classes moyennes*, but concentrated on small shopkeepers when examining their faults.[53] It was a tension which repeatedly surfaced, for the social value of small retailers was so much more difficult to construct. Stress could be laid on their local identity and commitment, and their service to working-class customers was identified, providing credit in times of hardship, but even that was a two-edged weapon, for credit was seen as an obstacle to working-class frugality.[54] The solution was also found, as we shall see, by setting the value of shopkeepers as the obverse of the dangers and immorality encouraged by the institutions of large capital which threatened them. Most of all, however, shopkeepers were presented as part of a wider *classe moyenne* with shared characteristics, largely assuming that what was written about the qualities of artisans applied to everyone in small enterprise.[55]

The idealisation of the role of the *classes moyennes*—artisans as well as shopkeepers—was thus in tension with the reality, in which neither was the character lived up to nor the role fulfilled. As Henry Clément observed in 1912, 'if these *classes moyennes* have a necessary role to play in society, it is clear that in general they are fulfilling it very badly.[56]

[52] Albert Babeau, *Les Artisans et les Domestiques d'autrefois* (Paris, 1886). For such atempts to root the image of artisans in their past, see François Husson, *Artisans français. Les serruriers. Etude historique* (Paris, 1902). Examples of the uses of Babeau's influential study include Brants, *La petite industrie*, 27 ff and Rivière, 'La notion des classes moyennes', in *Les Classes Moyennes dans le Commerce et l'Industrie*, 4.

[53] Louis Rivière, 'La notion', 8.

[54] Victor de Clerck, 'Les co-opératives d'achats en gros entre petit commerçants et petits industriels', *La Réforme sociale*, LX (1910), 648.

[55] This was an assumption which shopkeeper representatives might contest, as when they insisted that associations could not bring to retailers the benefits which artisans might enjoy. See the interventions by Moens and Attout-Van Cutsem too the session on associations at the 1899 Congress, *Congrès International de la Petite Bourgeoisie 1899*, 363–8.

[56] Henry Clement, 'Les classes moyennes', *La Réforme sociale*, LXIV (1912), 706. The essay is a review of the book by Georges Deherme referred to above.

Criticisms may have taken second place to the idealisations on which I have concentrated, but they were nonetheless evident. Victor Brants was more explicit than most, for he was not only a perceptive commentator but also a tardy and never complete convert to the cause of the *classes moyennes*. 'It would be puerile to represent the *classe moyenne* as a paragon of virtue', he argued. 'We have already spoken of abuses in the workplace. Irreligion, avarice, harshness, pride, and unfair commercial practices can be found amongst them as amongst all classes, as well as sensuality, vanity, jealousy. We certainly do not dispute the merits which the *classes moyennes* could possess, but it is false and ridiculous to attach these to them as some kind of fundamental privilege, and to attribute to them a sort of social immunity.'[57] The criticisms did not end with retailers who overcharged or defrauded customers, but pointed out that, notwithstanding expectations of harmony, work conditions were poor in many small workshops.[58] The very individualism which the *classes moyennes* were supposed to correct appeared at times to be more deeply rooted amongst them than amongst any other social class. 'Its egoism and narrowness of spirit are faults which are very apparent and far too common,' a meeting of Lyonnais social catholics was told.[59] The charge of egoism became more insistent after 1900 as petits bourgeois seemed resistant to the advice to associate that was so insistently directed at them. P.-J. de Clercq explained that the characteristics of those workers who sought to set up for themselves— resistance to authority, stubborn pride, vigorous independence—were precisely those which made it hard for them subsequently to cooperate.[60]

There was a further problem, expressed neatly by Henry Clément. 'Their goal,' he wrote of the petite bourgeoisie, 'is not to defeat those who are creating problems for them, but to suppress them with the help of the public authorities.'[61] In the eyes of social catholics, the demands of petit-bourgeois organisations amounted to little more than asking the state to legislate against their large-scale competitors or to tax them out of existence. This was particularly uncomfortable for Le Playists, concerned to accommodate many liberal economic ideas, reluctant to countenance the accretion of yet more power to the state, and convinced of the moralising power of associational solidarity. The demand of many organisations—not least the fragile but threatening autonomous petit-bourgeois movement in Belgium during the 1890s— for simple legislative solutions to complex economic problems was

---

[57] Brants, *La petite industrie*, 167.
[58] *ibid.*, 159; Fr. Funck-Brentano in *Congrès International de la Petite Bourgeoisie 1899*, 94.
[59] Turmann, 'Un aspect du problème', 461.
[60] P.-J. de Clercq, 'Les Artisans', *IICM Bulletin*, December 1908.
[61] Clement, 'Classes moyennes', 707

unacceptable: prohibitions on consumer co-operatives, the ban on civil servants joining or running co-operatives, taxing large-scale retailers out of existence. M. Geûens told the *Société d'économie sociale belge* that 'two tendencies divide the Belgian petite bourgeoisie ... Firstly there are the malcontents who never cease complaining and moaning ... The second group, on the other hand, tells them that they are the principal architects of their own salvation. In the first system, the state is expected to organise and save the petite bourgeoisie almost in spite of itself; according to the second school, the principle of renewing the *classe moyenne* lies above all with the *classe moyenne* itself.'[62] The origins of this distrust were various, not least the political conjuncture where, in Belgium, those lauding the petite bourgeoisie were involved with a ruling Catholic Party that needed to avoid the divisions that would have followed strong intervention on behalf of small enterprise. The roots in social catholic ideology, however, did not require the specificities of the Belgian situation: there was the belief in subsidiarity, that social and political health rested on allowing the maximum to be done by levels below that of the central state, especially by self-organised voluntary associations. As Brants observed, 'the State has a strong capacity to destroy, but it is weak when it has to build.'[63] The state's role was to support associations rather than replace them. Duplat argued that 'if the state's legislation rests on two forces, local associations and communal authorities, it will create a harmony that is both valuable and effective, because it will be maintaining and confirming industrial and commercial relations in their true centre which, for the *classe moyenne*, is the corporation and the town.'[64] The localism of the petite bourgeoisie seemed to make them a natural agent of subsidiarity, if they could only be dissuaded from their demands of the state.

Tensions such as these need not have inhibited the emergence of a discourse which idealised the *classe moyenne*, and they did not do so. Nevertheless, as discussion of the world of small enterprise and the ideal of the *classe moyenne* grew from the 1890s, so there emerged a variety of means by which those tensions were rendered less significant. One was to look to the future and recast the *classe moyenne* in broader terms, to incorporate the old petite bourgeoisie within a redefined middle that included managers and heads of department in large enterprises, white-collar workers, minor civil servants, even shareholders. Nowhere did the conceptual weakness of the metaphor of the middle become more apparent than in these debates, where the middle

---

[62] M. Geûens, 'Le crédit à la petite bourgeoisie. La loi et l'initiative privée', *La revue sociale catholique*, XVII (1912–13), 35.

[63] Brants, *La lutte*, 262.

[64] Duplat, *Classe moyenne*, 74.

was identified less by occupation than by such criteria as income and character. For Charles Morisseaux, director of the Belgian Labour Department in 1895, precise occupations were not the issue, asking 'what is it that constitutes this class, if not a certain degree of morality, of foresight, of education, of well-being?'[65] Although most writers concerned with the petite bourgeoisie did at times play with the idea of a wider *classe moyenne*, they resisted until the more serious attempts to construct a conceptual unity appeared during the inter-war period.[66] Autonomy built on labour and capital remained the requirement if this class were to play its appointed role. As Brants observed, including white-collar occupations assumed that middling incomes and middling social rank were the issue, but these professions lacked the independence which gave pride, strength, and social endurance.[67] Paul du Maroussem asked whether one could see in the employees of department stores 'a new *classe moyenne* which seems to have been reborn on the ruins of the old,' but concluded that without heredity or independence, even for the minority of employees who did climb the career ladder, there could be no real reconstruction of the *classe moyenne*.[68] It was in fact defenders of the new commercial and industrial order who held most firmly to the idea that new occupations were broadening the *classe moyenne*, writers such as Pierre Moride who was so impressed by the new retail chains. They could not be destroying the *classes moyennes*, he insisted, because 'the *classes moyennes*, in our sense, does not include only small shop-keepers. The term *classes moyennes* means "classes which enjoy—thanks to their labour or their capital—an average income." ' That meant white-collar workers, small shopkeepers, civil servants, and the managers of shops in retail chains.[69] Voices such as these, however, were very

[65] Charles Morisseaux, *La législation du travail*, I (Brussels, 1895), 292–3. See also Armand Julin, 'Les industries à domicile et les moteurs électriques', *La Réforme sociale*, XLIV (1902), 322.

[66] Luc Boltanski, *Les cadres. La formation d'un groupe social* (Paris, 1982); Maurice Halbwachs, 'Les caractéristiques des classes moyennes', in Aron, *Inventaires III*, 28–52. See also a discussion rooted in the debates of the interwar period, Leo Moulin and Luc Aerts, 'Les classes moyennes. Essai de bibliographie critique d'une définition', *Revue d'histoire économique et sociale*, (1954), 168–186, 293–309.

[67] Victor Brants, 'Les employés', *La Réforme sociale*, LVIII (1909), 619. As early as 1883 Feyeux was rejecting the possibility that managers and employees could play such a role: A. Feyeux, 'La question des grands et des petits magasins', *La Réforme sociale*, V (1883), 361.

[68] Du Maroussem, *La question ouvrière. vol 3: Le jouet parisien*, 37 and 241–62.

[69] Pierre Moride, *Les Maisons à succursales multiples en France et à l'étranger* (Paris, 1913), 192–3. Note the *or*, in 'their labour or their capital', removing the key linkage that described the classic petite bourgeoisie. For a similar argument, this time from the Director of the *Statistique générale de la France*, see Lucien March, 'La concentration dans les industries de fabrication, d'entretien, etc', in *La Concentration des entreprises industrielles et commerciales. Conférences faites à l'Ecole des Hautes Etudes sociales* (ed.) A. Fontaine (Paris, 1913), 71. Social catholic defenders of consumer co-operatives followed an equivalent path,

much the minority. For the defenders of the petite bourgeoisie, on the other hand, the idealisations of the middle required that it rest upon small, independent and family-centred enterprise. Indeed, their savage criticisms of the growth of *fonctionnarisme*, of minor civil servants, rendered impossible their acceptance within the *classe moyenne*. Civil servants were anathema to these critics of the modern state, an incubus that weighed down the independence of society and distorted the nature of ambition. The fact that the children of shopkeepers and small masters flocked to such posts (as they increasingly did) was a sign of pessimism and degradation. In Frantz Funck-Brentano's words, 'they are forced by necessity to seek not a trade but a career.'[70] The distinction was important.

If looking to the future to recast the *classes moyennes* had only limited success in these years, another solution to the tensions within the discourse was to look to the past and assert the historic role of the petite bourgeoisie in the struggle for communal freedoms and public liberty. 'In former times they have constituted the rampart of our communal liberties', claimed Pyfferoen with respect to Belgium.[71] Louis Rivière's opening address to the 1910 Congress presented the *classes moyennes* as central to France's national traditions of freedom and moderation, seeing them amongst those who established the communal liberties of fifth-century urban centres, and tracing them from the freemen at the foot of the feudal chateau or abbey, through the medieval artisanat, to the emerging Third Estate.[72] Théophile Funck-Brentano gave them an even greater lineage, tracing the *classes moyennes* through 'the equestrian order under the Romans, the free citizen of the Greek city-state, the corporations and masters of the middle ages, the Third Estate during the Renaissance, and the modern small proprietors, manufacturers and shopkeepers'.[73] Here then was a historic commitment to liberty and independence, to communal rights and local liberties, which gave the *classes moyennes* an identity in the past which might take precedence over tensions in the present, and which could reinforce the local attachments that were seen as fundamental to the moralising qualities of the *classes moyennes*.

Far more important than these forward-looking or backward-looking

---

presenting the managers of co-operative stores and the workers who accumulated savings through their dividend as forces constructing a new *classe moyenne*. See the contributions of Welche and Récamier to the discussion on consumer co-operation at the *Société d'Economie sociale*, in *La Réforme sociale*, XXV (1893), 461–4.

[70] *Congrès International de la Petite Bourgeoisie 1899*, 89.
[71] Pyfferoen, 'La petite bourgeoisie', 292.
[72] Rivière, 'La notion', 4–5.
[73] Th. Funck-Brentano, *Politique*, 53–4.

approaches, however, were three distinct perspectives which streng-thened the place of an idealised middle and helped it to prevail within the discourse: optimism about the direction of economic processes was the first, articulated above all through an electrical utopianism; the *classe moyenne* as moral inversion the second; and a strategy to encourage small enterprise towards modernisation though association the third. Optimism about the direction of economic processes was necessary to the ideology, explicitly pitted as it was against both Marxist and liberal economic assertions of the inexorable character of economic concentration.[74] It was not enough to find a continuing but subordinate role for small enterprise, for example through the corner ship or artistic production, for such economic marginalisation could not sustain the social role of the middle. Signs were therefore sought that concentration was not inevitable. As early as 1883 the *Société d'économie sociale* had been told that overcoming the problems of distributing power to small workshops would soon produce a flourishing industrial peasantry, and the electric motor was subsequently seized upon as the solution.[75] In a flourish of electrical utopianism, the first form of artificial energy capable of being transmitted over long distances to drive small motors was presented as the force which would reverse the process of industrial concentration. One writer claimed that with electricity 'the end of factory concentration and the rebirth of the family workshop were no longer mere hopes but tangible possibilities.'[76] Opening the pavilion on artisanal technology at the 1905 International Exhibition in Liège, the director of the Institut Montefiore declared that with better equipment and cheap power small masters would be able 'to regain their place in the sun'.[77] Here was a faith in the potential of electricity which fitted poorly to the reality, but it was an incantation regularly repeated. When Henry Morel-Journel lectured to the *Société d'économie politique et économie sociale* of Lyon on the awakening of the *classes moyennes* he spoke almost entirely about shopkeepers, but the subsequent discussion was

---

[74] For an explicit challenge from Victor Brants to the supposedly inexorable nature of economic laws, see Brants, *La petite industrie*, 5–9.

[75] M. Denayrouze, 'La décentralisation des forces motrices et la reconstitution des ateliers domestiques', *La Réforme sociale*, V (1883), 613–18.

[76] E. Dusaugey, Director of the *Société d'énergie électrique de Grenoble*, quoted in Ernest Dubois and Armand Julin, *Les Moteurs électriques dans les industries à domicile* (Brussels, 1902), 274. Optimistic faith in the power of electricity was widespread in these years—one historian has written of an 'electromania' seizing French society in the last twenty years of the nineteenth century. See Alain Beltran, 'Du luxe au coeur du système. Électricité et société dans la région parisienne (1880–1939)', *Annales E. S. C.* (1989), 1114. It is interesting to note how this enthusiasm was used by different groups to sustain such very varying views of progress.

[77] *IICM Bulletin*, August 1905

dominated by the way the electric motor could save the artisan.[78]

The reality was far more limited than the utopian dreams, as the investigators sent out by the Belgian government to explore the potential of the electric motor in small workshops regularly reported. Julin and Dubois insisted that it should not be seen as 'a sort of panacea, as a magic wand capable of changing into an idyllic form the conditions of labour in large and small-scale industry'.[79] Their comparative studies of Swiss watchmaking, and the silk trades of Lyon and Saint-Étienne, concluded that the electric motor could neither save nor revitalise workshop production where the situation was not favourable, but that where there were other economic reasons favouring dispersed production (as in the Stéphanois ribbon-weaving trades) then it could play a positive role. Even here they concluded that the benefit was less in increasing competitiveness than in reducing the physical strain of work. 'One must not see the electric motor as the instrument to liberate decentralised production.'[80] Or as Victor Brants warned, 'do not cry Eureka too soon.'[81] Such warnings did not prevent the widespread faith that electricity would save small-scale production, and with it the *classe moyenne*.

These hopes vested in the electric motor not only serve to remind us of the extent to which the artisan rather than the shopkeeper was the model for those who espoused the cause of the *classe moyenne*— after all, with respect to retailing, electricity was mostly referred to disparagingly in describing the seductive bright lights of the department stores—but they also lead us back to the nature of Le Playist interest in small enterprise. For Frédéric Le Play, there were two models of employment relationships which would harmonise industrial society. The first was to be found in the French tradition of *patronage*, in which the devout and enlightened large employer provided the institutions and influences to moralise and stabilise his workforce. The other was

[78] Henry Morel-Journel, 'Le Réveil des classes moyennes en France', in Société d'Economie politique et d'Economie sociale de Lyon, *Compte Rendu Analytique des Séances de l'Année 1910–1911* (Lyon, 1911), 54–103.

[79] Julin and Dubois, *Moteurs électriques*, 274.

[80] Julin, 'Les industries à domicile', 232. See also Julin and Dubois, *Moteurs électriques;* de Boissieu, 'Le moteur électrique'; Armand Julin and Ernest Dubois, 'Les moteurs électriques dans les industries à domicile', *La Revue sociale catholique*, VI (1901–2), 158–66; Armand Julin, 'L'outillage mécanique de l'atelier familial', *La Revue sociale catholique*, IX (1904–5), 289–317; Le Comte de Boissieu, 'L'emploi du moteur mécanique dans la petite industrie parisienne', *La science sociale*, XXXVI (1903), 314–33.

[81] Brants, *La petite industrie*, 151. Indeed, Brants took Lambrechts to task for making concentration the common denominator of the social question. Brants insisted that it was not concentration but the moral order that was the essential issue, for all techniques and all forms of enterprise had both advantages and disadvantages. See the discussion of Lambrechts, 'Commun dénominateur', 187.

the *fabrique collective*, in which dispersed domestic artisans, preferably with a small plot of land, produced for the merchant-capitalist (*fabricant*) who organised the industry. Interest in the latter revived from the 1890s, as the electric motor seemed to make family-based dispersed production once again possible.[82] It was not so much the independent workshop master as the domestic producer who was the hero of electrical utopianism, though talk of the *classes moyennes* rarely acknowledged the distinction. A specific Le Playist attachment to domestic industry and to an associated package of values thus came to be transmuted into a distinct interest in a larger *classe moyenne*.

The second perspective which helped the idealised middle to prevail within the discourse was the *classe moyenne* as moral inversion. It was not simply that the petite bourgeoisie itself was a source of good within the social order, but that the forces which were undermining the petite bourgeoisie were at the same time introducing into society values and practices that damaged morality and social peace. Some of these— such as the granting of long-term credit to bourgeois customers— directly hurt small enterprise. Pyfferoen devoted almost all of his opening address to the 1901 petit-bourgeois Congress to the way the rich abused credit, and he called for the creation of a *Ligue des honnêtes gens* to eradicate such practices.[83] Here was a sign of moral decline, as the well-to-do's decision to spend on pleasure, rather than paying their tradesmen, consigned small business to repeated crises.[84] Most moral critiques of this kind, however, were directed at the competitors rather than the customers of small enterprise. The demoralising nature of the factory came under attack. The transition from workshop to factory brought with it the uprooting of people from '*le clocher, la terre, le foyer*' (parish, land and home). Whereas workshops and small towns were conducive to 'good morality', factories saw the workers unsupervised

---

[82] Julin, 'L'outillage mécanique', 310; Julin and Dubois, *Moteurs électriques*, 13; Armand Julin, 'Le travail des femmes belges dans la grande et la petite industrie', *La Réforme sociale*, XLII (1901), 381–408; Robert Picot in *Les Classes Moyennes dans le Commerce et l'Industrie*, 85. Brants was, as ever, more careful about these distinctions: Brants, *La Lutte*, 192.

[83] Oscar Pyfferoen in *Comte rendu sténographique du 2ème Congrès international de la Petite Bourgeoisie, tenu à Namur le 15 et 16 septembre 1901* (Namur, 1902), 64–5. The brief emergence of consumer associations directed to encouraging ethical shopping practices, such as the responsible settlement of debts to shopkeepers and the purchase only of produce manufactured without sweated labour, responded to the same anxieties. See Maurice Deslandres, *L'Acheteur, son rôle économique et social: les ligues sociales d'achteurs* (Paris, 1911); the report of *La Ligue nationale du paiement comptant* (Belgium) in *Compte Rendu Sténographique du IVème Congrès national de la petite bourgeoisie tenu à Saint-Trond les 4, 5 et 6 août 1907* (Saint-Trond, 1907), 87–94; and the brief discussion in Rosalind H. Williams, *Dream Worlds: Mass Consumption in Late Nineteenth-Century France* (Berkeley, 1982), 303–10.

[84] Hego (Hector Lambrechts), 'Vous dépensez trop', *La Métropole*, 6 September 1900.

and family ties weakened. As Maurice Vanlaer concluded in his lectures to students at the Catholic Institute in Paris, economic progress had been favoured at the expense of moral.[85] The rise of mass production and the decline of quality were similarly denounced. 'Industry kills arts', concluded Hector Lambrechts. With mass production, 'the public aesthetic sense has been lost'.[86] One consequence was the morally corrosive impact of modern consumerism, a force created by mass production and large-scale distribution. Lambrechts argued that if one examined modern consumer psychology one would find 'in the lowering of the level of morality, in the substitution of appearance for reality, and in the intense desire for pleasure, the ideal cultural terrain for the first stage of mass production—imitations and junk—to take over'.[87] Albert Feyeux bemoaned the changes in the bakery trade, with fancy breads and elaborate displays everywhere, compared with his childhood when the baker had no more than a simple wooden counter, with a parrot in a wire cage as the only touch of ornamentation. 'Simple morals developed easily in such modest but adequate establishments.'[88] People now bought for excitement and display rather than need as the consumer frenzy took control, and the greatest culprit was that bête noire of both shopkeeper movements and those lauding small enterprise, the department store. Its moral faults were overwhelming. Paul du Maroussem graphically showed the way direct purchasing by Parisian department stores constructed the sweating system where an independent artisanat had once stood.[89]

Most criticism, however, centred on the moral consequences of department stores for customers and employees alike. With their bright lights, exotic displays, seasonal novelty and endless sales, they replaced the wholesome acquisition of necessities with a passion for excitement and newness, for shopping for its own sake. They created 'illusory needs' and 'a hysteria for buying'.[90] Their employees, regimented in an unhealthy environment, forced to leave home for long hours of work, and to bow to every caprice of their customers as they competed for their sales bonuses, were denied the moral certainties of family life

---

[85] Maurie Vanlaer, 'L'atelier moderne et l'évolution économique', *La Réforme sociale*, XLVII (1904), 440–3.

[86] Hector Lambrechts, 'De l'Avenir des Classes Moyennes', *IICM Bulletin*, February 1911. See also Théophile Funck-Brentano, 'Préface', in Paul du Maroussem, *La Question ouvrière. vol. 1. Charpentiers de Paris. Companons et Indépendents* (Paris, 1891), 16.

[87] *IICM Bulletin*, June/July 1911, 456. See also Martin Saint-Léon, *Petit commerce*, 16.

[88] Albert Feyeux, 'Un nouveau livre des métiers—1. La boulangerie parisienne', *La science sociale*, IV (1887), 341.

[89] Du Maroussem, *Question ouvrière*, passim.

[90] Blondel, 'Le problème', *IICM Bulletin*, April 1908. For contemporary critiques of the department store, see Michael B. Miller, *The Bon Marché. Bourgeois Culture and the Department Store, 1869–1920* (Princeton, 1981), 190 ff.

and the family work unit.[91] The image of women in this catholic discourse was an essentially passive one, with the assistants portrayed as victims and the shoppers as weak and impressionable. The moral role of women in society was undermined in many ways—female employees were unprotected, and the delights of shopping not only diverted female customers from their home responsibilities, the entice-ment to wasteful purchases and even shoplifting also destroyed their intrinsic feminine moral qualities. Funck-Brentano told the graphic tale of Mlle Marguerite Boulanger, a virtuous young woman destroyed by the power of the department store. She was accused of stealing a small piece of lace which had been caught up in her belongings, forced to endure a distressing interrogation in which she was stripped naked, and the search of her home while her elderly mother looked on in a state of shock. 'The next day,' he told his audience, 'she died in atrocious pain, proclaiming her innocence ... and covered with the tears of her helpless mother, sister and brother.' This was more than a sad tale. It was evidence of the consequences of the disorganisation of society that followed when the old traditions of work, production and sale were lost.[92] In the critique of the morally corrosive influence of department stores, one sees the reverse of the moral qualities of the *classe moyenne*, which was erected as an ideal with which to beat the undesirable aspects of modern life, while presenting that ideal as if it were the description of a real social group. Disorder in work and exchange could only be defeated by a new order for human tastes and desires, and the nature of consumption therefore needed to be reconstituted if the *classes moyennes* were to be saved. The first petit-bourgeois Congress was told that in the face of the individualism of modern taste, only the family and 'local solidarity' could provide the orderly setting for consumption.[93] Saving the *classes moyennes* required saving the moral order of society.

The final strategy was the most active, for it meant the construction of a concrete programme by which the movements of the petite bourgeoisie could be directed away from appeals to the state and attacks on large-scale economic activity, and towards a constructive programme for improvement. Books and articles, lectures and debates were repeatedly structured around a single polarity—'the appeal to the state' on the one hand, 'free initiative' on the other. Oscar Pyfferoen identified the strategy clearly. A certain number of men of science, he explained, have collaborated with the petit-bourgeois movement to

---

[91] Du Maroussem, *La question ouvrière. vol 3: Le jouet parisien*, 254; Martin Saint-Léon, *Petit commerce*, 98; Joseph Bernard, *Du mouvement d'organisation et de défense du petit commerce français*, Thèse de droit, University of Paris (1906), 51–3.

[92] Fr. Funck-Brentano, *Congrés International de la Petite Bourgeoisie 1899*, 81–3.

[93] G. Verbiest, *ibid.*, 219–33.

open its eyes to what he termed 'the true remedy' for their problems: associations, credit, technical education.[94] This process of persuasion from outside was directed above all at the associational solution—a powerful social catholic ideal that was given substance and encouragement, especially in Belgium, by the success of agrarian self-help associations such as the *Boerenbond belge*.[95] Intermediate bodies between the individual and the state were needed but, as Victor Brants argued, the role once played by commune and corporation would now have to be fulfilled by voluntary associations.[96] After a lack of focus in the 1890s, the turn of the century saw a clear programme directed at the petite bourgeoisie. It was a programme embodied in books and articles about small business, and repeated almost *ad nauseam* in the themes and structure of the many national and international congresses of the petite bourgeoisie, animated and directed by that milieu of social catholics and Le Playists which has been the subject of this paper.[97] Concessions were certainly granted to petit-bourgeois demands for state support, calling for greater fairness in taxation, and over the law on such matters as bankruptcy and credit, together with closer regulation of itinerant traders. The real strategy, however, sought to divert the organisations of small enterprise away from more extravagant demands of the state, and towards using associations to achieve an improvement in the competitive position of small enterprise.[98] 'One can say without exaggeration,' proclaimed Hector Lambrechts, 'that upon a rapid and compact process of organisation of the petite bourgeoisie rests its principal chance of survival and, without doubt, its entire prospects for technical and commercial progress'.[99] Trade associations would provide professional education, co-operatives for credit as well as purchasing, and technical improvement. When one shopkeepers' association had the temerity to tell the 1899 Congress that too much was being expected

[94] Pyfferoen, 'Formation technique', 840–1.

[95] Van Molle, *Chacun pour tous*. For France, *Les Classes Moyennes dans le Commerce et l'Industrie*, 71–2.

[96] Brants, *La Lutte*, 263–5.

[97] In addition to the international congresses of 1899 and 1901 cited above, the *Institut international pour l'étude des problèmes des classes moyennes* organised further congresses including one in Munich in 1911, whose proceedings were published as *III. Congrès international des classes moyennes* (Munich, 1912). The Belgian *Association nationale pour l'étude et la défense des intérêts de la petite bourgeoisie*, founded in 1900 as a result of the 1899 Antwerp congress, organised a series of national congresses, all of whose proceedings were published. The proceedings of the 4th Congress at Saint-Trond are cited above.

[98] For the operation of that strategy in Belgium, see Serge Jaumain and Lucia Gaiardo, ' "Aide-toi et le gouvernement t'aidera' ". Les responses de l'état à la crise de la petite bourgeoisie (1880–1914)', *Revue belge d'histoire contemporaine*, XIX (1988), 417–71. Bernard, *Du mouvement d'organisation* is a detailed study directed at just such a strategy of turning shopkeepers away from demands of the state.

[99] Lambrechts, *Le problème social*, 254.

of associations as a way to combat consumer co-operatives, it was firmly put in its place by the chairman.[100] The association was more than simply instrumental, however, for it was a moral device for social catholics—the way to create social cohesion and solidarity in a domain where individualism and isolation reigned.

As this paper has shown, a complex discourse took shape which for the first time made the fate of small enterprise and the fate of the middling groups a major social question. It was a discourse which presented a social group and described its identity. The many debates about what to call them indicate a real terminological uncertainty,[101] and if *classe moyenne* (whether singular or plural) came to prevail, it was partly because of its historic resonances, drawing on an older vision which saw the *classe moyenne* as the force for liberty and independence in French and Belgian life. In this sense the term narrowed in a similar way to that of the *Mittelstand* in Germany, focusing on only a part of what had once been a larger group. The term was above all attractive, however, because the concept of the *moyenne*—the average and the middle—provided the metaphorical purchase needed for a group that was to moderate and stabilise society.

The identity of small enterprise did not come from a single discourse, however insistently that was diffused in the fifteen years before the First World War. A social group was indeed constructed in the discourse of these years, one whose character and role were both ambiguous and mythologised, and it is in this sense that one can talk of the invention, and not simply the discovery, of the petite bourgeoisie. As Edouard Aynard told the 1910 Congress, 'the *classes moyennes*, educated by your school, will learn what they are and what they are worth.'[102] There was another process of construction going on, however, for these were the years during which the owners of small enterprise were themselves being increasingly sought as voters, and in which they were increasingly organised in economic associations and pressure groups, in trade congresses, and in fragile national federations.[103] Sections of small

[100] A note from the *Association des commerçants de la Louvière* was read out by the Chairman of the session on co-operatives: *Congrès International de la Petite Bourgeoisie 1899*, 217–19.

[101] Hector Labrechts was later to recall 'the fluctuating terminology at the time'. Lambrechts, *Trente Années*, 316.

[102] Edouard Aynard, at Closing Banquet, *Les Classes Moyennes dans le Commerce et l'Industrie*, 124.

[103] Brants acknowledged this, writing that 'it is the movement, the agitation which has provoked the research, and we are sure that this time it has not been without value to science.' Brants, *La petite industrie*, 5–6.

enterprise in these countries were now asserting themselves.[104] It was in the interaction between these various spheres that a petit-bourgeois identity took shape—the political conjuncture that made middling independents more relevant electorally, the process of organising that gave small enterprise a more public presence, and the discourse of those who invested the *classe moyenne* with a new role and a new significance. The discoverers spread their ideas to petit-bourgeois organisations whenever they could—visiting and addressing them, and seeking to direct their efforts into appropriate activities. Occasionally, summoned to congresses to be preached at, leaders of local associations of shopkeepers and master artisans expressed their resentment. One Brussels baker, angry at the way opening and working hours were on the agenda at a congress, complained that 'it is thoroughly regrettable to see that the spokesmen and flag-bearers ... are gentlemen who are not petits bourgeois at all and who understand not the slightest aspect of commercial affairs.'[105] Vander Cruyssen, of the Ghent carpet-makers association, resented an opening speaker at the 1901 Congress who had told them that 'we are the doctors and we wish to cure the sick, even in spite of themselves.' Vander Cruyssen called such outsiders 'you others, who designate yourselves the defenders of the petite bourgeoisie'.[106] Such outbursts were not common, for the congresses were too carefully managed for that,[107] but the distance between those who described and those whom they described was a continuing tension within the discourse as it has been within this paper. If the organised petite bourgeoisie increasingly drew on a larger discourse to assert its importance to the health of society, it is a cautionary note to see that a more prosaic terminology existed at the level of local organisations, one that rarely talked of petits bourgeois or *classes moyennes*, but spoke of bakers and ironmongers, at best of small shopkeepers.[108] Petits

---

[104] There is an increasing literature on these movements, of which the most important works are Nord, *Paris Shopkeepers*, Jaumain, 'Petits commerçants', 473–527. See also various essays, especially the national surveys, in Crossick & Haupt, *Shopkeepers and Master Artisans*.

[105] M. Lebon, to *Congrès international de la boulangerie, 28 & 29 août 1910* (Louvain, 1910), 90.

[106] *Congrès international de la Petite Bourgeoisie 1901*, 114–15.

[107] For this careful management, see Jaumain, 'Petits commerçants', 456 ff.

[108] The terminology of description merits further attention, distinguishing not only between countries and languages, but also between different actors, such as outside observers, national leaders, local organisations and so on. For some preliminary findings on Belgium, see G. Kurgan-Van Hentenryk, 'A la recherche de la petite bourgeoisie: l'enquête orale de 1902–1904', *Revue belge d'histoire contemporaine*, XIV (1983), 295–7. The generalisation on self-description rests upon my reading of various shopkeeper newspapers for Lyon in the decade or so before the First World War, especially *L'Alliance* and *Le Courier du Commerce*. Geoffrey Crossick, 'From gentleman to the residuum: languages of social description in Victorian Britain', in *Language, History and Class* (ed.) Penelope J. Corfield (Oxford), 1991), 150–78, a general discussion of the vocabulary of social

bourgeois were perhaps thus fated to constitute a *classe objet* in the sense which Pierre Bourdieu applied to the peasantry—a social group constructed and defined far more firmly from the outside than it ever was from within.[109] The process by which the question of the *classe moyenne*—its social role and the threat to its survival—was placed on the agenda in these countries is a complex one. The academics, churchmen, politicians and civil servants whose discovery of the petite bourgeoisie as a major social question has been explored in this paper, invented neither small enterprise nor its owners. In their idealised notion of the *classe moyenne*, however, they constructed a vision which was to resonate in both politics and ideology in the decades that were to follow.

---

description in Britain, contains brief comments on the English terminology of lower middle class, 173–4.

[109] Pierre Bourdieu, 'La paysannerie, une classe objet', *Actes de la recherche en sciences sociales*, 17–18 (1977), 2–5.

THE ROYAL HISTORICAL SOCIETY
REPORT OF COUNCIL, SESSION 1993–1994

THE Council of the Royal Historical Society has the honour to present the following report to the Anniversary Meeting.

1. Review of the Society

The Council has proceeded during the course of the year to act upon some of the recommendations of the Final Report on its Review (1992–93) of the activities and future direction of the Society. Among changes it has already set in train are the following: a contract with Cambridge University Press to become the publisher of the Society's major publications from January 1995; the institution of the new category of Member of the Society to be formally introduced in November 1994; a proposed new framework of subscriptions for Fellows and Members; an evolving pattern of lectures and conferences; a review of the Society's By-laws.

Council intends to pursue further other issues which were raised by the Review. It has already established Working Parties on the Corresponding Fellowship and on promotion and publicity. It is also looking closely at the range of its Prizes and Awards. During the year the Librarian completed his review of the Society's Library holdings and arranged for the sale of books which were deemed to be peripheral to the policy of consolidating and augmenting the Library's series of record publications. The income from this sale will be used both to improve the bindings of some of the Society's older and more valuable books and to augment the Society's Research Support Fund.

2. Issues of concern to historians

Council believes that the Society, as the senior society of professional historians in the United Kingdom, should play an active part in promoting and defending the interests of historical scholarship and study in this country. Among issues on which the President and Council have made representation during the year are the following:
- the revised proposals for the National Curriculum for History in England and Wales;
- the impact of proposed changes in local government on local record offices;

- a proposal by a major private corporation to offer some of its early holdings of books and records for sale abroad;
- the Research Assessment Exercise to be conducted by the Higher Education Funding Councils, 1996.

The President gave an address on the problems confronting learned societies at a meeting held at the British Academy on 26 May 1994. A one-day conference has been arranged by the Society in January 1995 to discuss the state of postgraduate studies, and the funding thereof, in History.

3. Bibliographies

The Society continues to support two major bibliographies which are being prepared under its aegis.

a) *The Annual Bibliography of British and Irish History* prepared under the editorships of Dr. Barbara English and Dr. John Palmer at the University of Hull. The Society provides financial support for the employment of a part-time assistant for the project.
b) The *British History Bibliographies* project which is being prepared under the general editorship of Dr. John Morrill with its headquarters at the University of Cambridge. The Council was greatly gratified to learn that substantial grants have been made by the Leverhulme Trust, the British Academy and other bodies which enable this project to be extended to a new termination date of September 1996.

Council is actively considering the future of these two major projects and the future relationship between them. It wishes to place on record its great sense of indebtedness to the general editors, the volume and section editors, and the team of contributors (numbering well over 100 people) who are contributing to the success of these two invaluable projects.

4. Other activities

a) The Society continues its close link with the British National Committee of the International Congress of Historical Sciences as described in last year's Report. The first conference to be arranged under the aegis of the new BNC is to be held in St. Andrews in April 1995. Preparations are afoot to provide support for the scholars from Britain invited to deliver papers at the Quinquennial Congress in Montreal August 1995.
b) The Society has renewed its funding for a Research Fellowship at the Institute of Historical Research. It also contributes to the Young Historian Scheme of the Historical Association and provides prizes for outstanding A-level students.

c) The Society is holding a reception for Japanese historians at the first Anglo-Japanese Conference at the Institute of Historical Research September 1994.

5. Meetings of the Society

The Society held two Council meetings and paper readings outside London, at the University of Nottingham and the University of Glasgow; both events were well attended and were followed by receptions which enabled Council to meet local members. As in 1992–93, the success of these meetings owed much to the hospitality provided by resident members of the Society and by the host Universities. The Society has arranged to meet at Leicester and Bristol during the 1994–95 session.

The annual one-day conference in September was held at the University of Sheffield. A two-day conference was held in Oxford in January 1994 to commemorate the bicentenary of the death of Edward Gibbon. Arrangements are in hand to hold a one-day conference in London in September 1994 and a two-day conference at Selwyn College, Cambridge in March 1995.

An evening party was held for members and guests in the Upper Hall at University College London on Wednesday, 7 July 1993. 169 replies were received, and it was well attended.

6. Prizes

(i) The Whitfield Prize for 1993 was awarded to Dr. J.M. Neeson for her book *Commoners: common right, enclosure and social change in England, 1700–1820,* (Cambridge University Press). The assessors also declared Dr. Jane H. Ohlmeyer *proxime accessit* for her book *Civil War and Restoration in the Three Stuart Kingdoms – the career of Randal MacDonnell, marquis of Antrim, 1609–1683,* (Cambridge University Press). The assessors commented on the high quality of the entries received.

(ii) The Alexander Prize for 1994 was awarded to Assistant Professor Joseph C. Heim, from California University of Pennsylvania, for his essay *Liberalism and the Establishment of Collective Security in British Foreign Policy,* which was read to the Society on 27 May 1994.

7. Publications

Transactions, Sixth Series, Volume 4; 'Miscellany XXXII', (Camden, Fifth Series, Volume 3); *The Derby Diaries,* ed. J. Vincent, (Camden, Fifth Series, Volume 4), and *Historians' Guide to Early British Maps,* ed. H. Wallis, (Guides and Handbooks, No. 18), went to press during the session and are due to be published in 1994.

The Society's *Annual Bibliography of British and Irish History, Publications of 1992,* was published by Oxford University Press.

The following four volumes in the STUDIES IN HISTORY series went to press during the session: Alexandra Walsham *Church Papists: Catholicism, Conformity and Confessional Polemic in Early Modern England,* (Volume 68); Glyn Stone, *The Oldest Ally: Britain and the Portuguese Connection, 1936–1941,* (Volume 69); Michael Braddick, *Parliamentary Taxation in seventeenth-century England: local administration and response,* (Volume 70); and Robin Harris, *Valois Guyenne: Politics, Government and Society in Late-Medieval France,* (Volume 71).

8. Papers read

At the ordinary meetings of the Society the following papers were read:

'Prince and States-General: Charles V and the Netherlands' by Professor H. Koenigsberger (7 July 1993: Prothero lecture).

'Women and the Norman Conquest' by Dr. Pauline Stafford (15 October 1993).

'Metaphors of the Middle: the Discovery of the "Petite Bourgeoisie", 1880–1914' by Professor Geoffrey Crossick (10 December 1993).

' "My special friend?" The Settlement of Disputes and Political Power in the Kingdom of the French, Tenth to Early Twelfth Centuries' by Dr. Jane Martindale (4 March 1994).

'The structures of politics in early Tudor England' by Dr. Steven Gunn (29 April 1994).

At the Anniversary meeting on 19 November 1993, the President, Professor R.R. Davies, delivered an address on 'The Peoples of Britain and Ireland, 1100–1400: I. Identities'.

A one-day conference entitled 'Political Ideologies in Twentieth Century Britain' was held at the University of Sheffield on 25 September 1993, at which the following papers were read:

'The failure of Socialist Unity in Britain, c. 1893–1914', by Professor Keith Laybourn;

'Liberal Toryism in the Twentieth Century', by Dr. Michael Bentley; and

'Why has Britain produced no administrative ideology in the Twentieth Century', by Professor Peter Hennessy.

A two-day conference entitled 'Gibbon and Empire' was held at Magdalen College, Oxford on 7 and 8 January 1994, at which the following papers were read:

'Gibbon and the Roman Empire in the fourth and fifth centuries', by Dr. John Matthews;

'Gibbon and the Roman Empire in the sixth century', by Professor Averil Cameron;

'Gibbon and Byzantine diplomacy and warfare' by Dr. Jonathan Shepard;

'Gibbon and the later Byzantine Empires' by Professor Anthony Bryer;

'Gibbon, Hodgkin and the invaders of Italy' by Dr. Thomas Brown;

'Gibbon and Clovis' by Dr. Ian Wood;

'Gibbon and the early middle ages in eighteenth century Europe' by Dr. Rosamond McKitterick;

'Religion and Revision in The Decline and Fall' by Dr. David Womersley;

'Gibbon and the imperial idea in early modern Europe' by Dr. John Robertson;

'Gibbon: an Enlightened historian of empire?' by Professor Jeremy Black;

'Gibbon and the concept of Decline and Fall' by Mr. Peter Ghosh;

'Churchill and Gibbon' by Dr. Roland Quinault.

The proceedings were summed up by Lord Dacre of Glanton and Professor John Burrow.

Dr. J. Howard-Johnston was unable through illness to read his paper on 'Gibbon and the Middle period of the Byzantine empire'.

9. Annual Report

The Society's investment income again fell slightly despite the efforts of our investment managers (Messrs Cazenove). There was a small deficit on the year. This was expected due to Council's decision to delay raising subscription rates until the Review of the Society's activities was completed. Since the Review is now complete proposals for revised subscription rates will be put to the 1994 Anniversary meeting. Other measures designed to increase the income of the Society are also proposed as a result of the Review and are described earlier in this Report.

Council records with gratitude the following benefactors to the Society:

Mr. L.C. Alexander
The Reverend David Berry
Professor Andrew Browning
Professor C.D. Chandaman
Professor G. Donaldson
Mrs. W.M. Frampton
Mr. E.L.C. Mullins
Sir George Prothero
Professor T.F. Reddaway
Miss E.M. Robinson
Professor A.S. Whitfield

10. Membership

Council records with regret the deaths of 25 Fellows, 4 Associates and 1 Corresponding Fellow. They included Honorary Vice-President— Professor D. Hay, Fellows—Mr. A.T. Milne, a former Honorary Librarian; Professor G. Holmes, a former Member of Council; Mr. M.F.B. Fitch a benefactor of historians, and Corresponding Fellow— The Rev. Dom J. Leclercq.

The resignations of 4 Fellows, 1 Associate and 10 Subscribing Libraries were received. 33 Fellows and 4 Associates were elected and 2 Libraries were admitted. 17 Fellows transferred to the category of Retired Fellow. The membership of the Society on 30 June 1994 comprised 2120 (including 37 Life Members, 305 Retired Fellows, 38 Corresponding Fellows and 141 Associates). There were 648 Subscribing Libraries and the Society exchanged publications with 15 Societies, British and foreign.

11. Officers and Council

At the Anniversary Meeting on 19 November 1993, the Officers of the Society were re-elected.

The Vice-Presidents retiring under By-law XVII were Mr. M. Roper and Professor C.S.R. Russell. Miss V. Cromwell and Professor H.C.G. Matthew were elected to replace them. The members of Council retiring under By-law XX were Dr. C.M. Barron, Professor N. Hampson, Professor A.J. Pollard and Professor M.C. Prestwich. Following a ballot of Fellows, Professor P.R. Coss, Professor L.J. Jordanova, Professor F. O'Gorman and Dr. J.R. Studd were elected in their place.

Messrs. Davies Watson were appointed auditors for the year 1993– 94 under By-law XXXIX.

12. Representatives of the Society

The representation of the Society upon various bodies was as follows: Mr. M. Roper, Professor P.H. Sawyer and Mr. C.P. Wormald on the Joint Committee of the Society and the British Academy established to prepare an edition of Anglo-Saxon charters;
Emeritus Professor H.R. Loyn on a committee to promote the publication of photographic records of the more significant collections of British Coins;
Professor G.H. Martin on the Council of the British Records Association;
Emeritus Professor M.R.D. Foot on the Committee to advise the publishers of *The Annual Register*;
Dr. R.C. Mettam on the History at the Universities Defence Group;

Professor C.J. Holdsworth on the Court at the University of Exeter;
Professor A.G. Watson on the Anthony Panizzi Foundation;
Professor M.C. Cross on the Council of the British Association for Local History;
Professor J. Sayers on the National Council on Archives;
Miss V. Cromwell on the Advisory Board of the Computers in Teaching Initiative Centre for History;
Dr. A.M.S. Prochaska on the Advisory Council of the reviewing committee on the Export of Works of Art;
Professor R.A. Griffiths on the Court of Governors of the University College of Swansea;
Professor A.L. Brown on the University of Stirling Conference; and
Professor W. Davies on the Court at the University of Birmingham.

Council received reports from its representatives.

During the year, Dr. R.D. McKitterick agreed to succeed Professor E.B. Fryde on a committee to regulate British co-operation in the preparation of a new repertory of medieval sources to replace Potthast's *Bibliotheca Historica Medii Aevi*; Professor M.C. Cross agreed to succeed Professor C.N.L. Brooke on the British Sub-Commission of the Commission International d'Histoire Ecclesiastique Comparee; Dr. G.W. Bernard agreed to succeed Dr. R.C. Mettam on the History at the Universities Defence Group.

Miss V. Cromwell agreed to represent the Society on the Advisory Committee of The TLTP History Courseware Consortium, and Professor P.K. O'Brien agreed to represent the Society on the ESRC Working Group on *Quality and Data Collection*.

THE ROYAL HISTORICAL SOCIETY

BALANCE SHEET AS AT 30TH JUNE 1994

	Note	1994 £	1994 £	1993 £	1993 £
FIXED ASSETS					
Tangible assets	2		1,503		2,051
Investments	3		1,649,119		1,653,640
			1,650,622		1,655,691
CURRENT ASSETS					
Stocks	1(c)	1,483		7,803	
Debtors	4	14,731		16,336	
Cash at bank and in hand	5	16,530		17,449	
		32,744		41,588	
LESS: CREDITORS					
Amount falling due within one year	6	88,190		92,421	
NET CURRENT (LIABILITIES)			(55,446)		(50,833)
NET TOTAL ASSETS			1,595,176		1,604,858
REPRESENTED BY:					
General Fund			1,501,906		1,510,817
Miss E.M. Robinson Bequest			60,558		60,252
A.S. Whitfield Prize Fund			31,935		30,904
Studies in History			777		2,885
			1,595,176		1,604,858

THE ROYAL HISTORICAL SOCIETY

Income and Expenditure Account for the Year Ended 30th June 1994

GENERAL FUND

	Note	1994 £	1994 £	1993 £	1993 £
INCOME					
Subscriptions	7		59,385		60,899
Investment Income			64,640		67,291
Royalties and reproduction fees			5,466		5,360
Donations and sundry income			1,084		3,021
			130,575		136,571
EXPENDITURE					
SECRETARIAL AND ADMINISTRATIVE					
Salaries, pensions and social security		24,012		23,115	
Computer consumables, printing and stationery		5,550		3,144	
Postage and telephone		1,968		2,063	
Bank charges		1,968		2,073	
Audit and accountancy		3,290		3,231	
Insurance		601		536	
Meetings and travel		17,431		10,905	
Conference fees recoverable		(1,268)		—	
Repairs and renewals		577		741	
Depreciation	1(b)	1,121		1,130	
			55,250		46,938
PUBLICATIONS					
Publishing costs	8(a)	(3,863)		16,782	
Provision for publications in progress	8(b)	72,450		67,900	
Other publication costs	8(c)	5,826		4,277	
			74,413		88,959
LIBRARY AND ARCHIVES	1(d)				
Purchase of books and publications		1,128		918	
Binding		2,553		2,457	
			3,681		3,375
			133,344		139,272
OTHER CHARGES					
Centenary fellowship		5,650		5,658	
Alexander prize		499		297	
Prothero lecture		254		(100)	
Grants		175		4,125	
Research support grants		12,015		11,680	
Donations and sundry expenses		653		1,241	
A-level prizes		900		900	
Young Historian Scheme		1,994		1,993	
British History Bibliographies		2,000		2,000	
			24,140		27,794
			157,484		167,066
(Deficit) for the year			(26,909)		(30,495)
Surplus on sale of Investments			108,281		11,348
(Deficit)/surplus on revaluation of quoted investments			(90,283)		703,668
			(8,911)		684,521
Balance brought forward at 1.7.93			1,510,817		826,296
Balance carried forward at 30.6.94			1,501,906		1,510,817

THE ROYAL HISTORICAL SOCIETY

Income and Expenditure Account for the Year Ended 30th June 1994

SPECIAL FUNDS

	£ 1994	£	£ 1993	£
MISS E.M. ROBINSON BEQUEST				
INCOME				
Investment income		2,279		3,782
EXPENDITURE				
Grant to Dulwich Picture Gallery	2,000		3,000	
Other expenses	149		24	
		(2,149)		(3,024)
Surplus for the year		130		758
Surplus on disposal of investments		24,762		4,000
(Deficit)/surplus on revaluation of quoted investments		(24,586)		32,173
		306		36,931
Balance brought forward at 1.7.93		60,252		23,321
Balance carried forward at 30.6.94		60,558		60,252
A.S. WHITFIELD PRIZE FUND				
INCOME				
Investment income		1,173		1,322
EXPENDITURE				
Prize awarded	1,000		1,000	
Other expenses	77		—	
		1,077		1,000
Surplus for the year		96		322
Surplus on disposal of investments		—		3,519
Surplus on revaluation of quoted investments		935		10,910
		1,031		14,751
Balance brought forward at 1.7.93		30,904		16,153
Balance carried forward at 30.6.94		31,935		30,904
STUDIES IN HISTORY				
INCOME				
Royalties		2,080		1,583
Investment income		429		690
		2,509		2,273
EXPENDITURE				
Honorarium	3,500		3,500	
Editor's expenses	981		967	
Ex gratia royalties and sundry expenses	136		98	
		(4,617)		(4,565)
(Deficit) for the year		(2,108)		(2,292)
Balance brought forward		2,885		5,177
Balance carried forward		777		2,885

1. ACCOUNTING POLICIES
   (a) *Basis of accounting*
       The accounts have been prepared under the historical cost convention as modified by the revaluation of quoted investments to market value.
   (b) *Depreciation*
       Depreciation is calculated by reference to the cost of fixed assets using a straight line basis at rates considered appropriate having regard to the expected lives of the fixed assets.
       The annual rates of depreciation in use are:
       Furniture and equipment   10%
       Computer equipment   25%
       Prior to 1st July 1987 the full cost of fixed assets was written off to General Fund in the year of purchase.
   (c) *Stocks*
       Stock is valued at the lower of cost and net realisable value.
   (d) *Library and archives*
       The cost of additions to the library and archives is written off in the year of purchase.

2. TANGIBLE FIXED ASSETS

	Computer Equipment	Furniture and Equipment	Total
	£	£	£
Cost			
At 1st July 1993	8,681	620	9,301
Additions during year	573	—	573
At 30th June 1994	9,254	620	9,874
Depreciation			
At 1st July 1993	6,878	372	7,250
Charge for the year	1,059	62	1,121
At 30th June 1994	7,937	434	8,371
Net book value			
At 30th June 1994	1,317	186	1,503
At 30th June 1993	1,803	248	2,051

The cost of additions to the library and archives is written off in the year of purchase.
Prior to 1st July 1987 the cost of furniture and equipment was written off in the year of purchase. Items acquired before that date are not reflected in the above figures.

3. INVESTMENTS

	1994	1993
	£	£
Quoted Securities, at cost	950,614	824,670
Surplus on revaluation	632,817	746,751
Quoted Securities at market value	1,583,431	1,571,421
Money invested at call	65,688	82,219
	1,649,119	1,653,640

Quoted Investments are stated at market value in the Balance Sheet as at 30th June 1994.
The surplus arising on re-valuation plus profits (less losses) realised on disposals of investments is credited to Income and Expenditure Account in the case of investments held on General Fund and to the relevant fund accounts where investments are held for specific funds.
Movements in quoted investments during year were:

	£
Cost at beginning of year	824,670
Additions during year	280,190
Disposals during year	(154,246)
Cost at end of year	950,614

4. DEBTORS

	1994 £	1993 £
Sundry debtors	10,272	12,917
Prepayments	4,459	3,419
	14,731	16,336

5. CASH AT BANK AND IN HAND

	1994 £	1993 £
Deposit accounts	15,106	13,656
Current accounts	1,424	3,793
	16,530	17,449

6. CREDITORS

	1994 £	1993 £
Sundry creditors	1,000	1,000
Subscriptions received in advance	9,282	12,532
Accruals	5,458	10,989
Provision for publications in progress	72,450	67,900
	88,190	92,421

7. SUBSCRIPTIONS

	1994 £	1993 £
Current subscriptions	55,000	56,134
Subscription arrears received	1,997	2,149
Income tax on covenants	2,388	2,616
	59,385	60,899

8. PUBLICATIONS

	1994 £	1993 £
(a) Publishing costs for the year		
List of Fellows	3,858	—
Transactions, sixth series Vol. 2	(1,008)	17,172
Transactions, sixth series Vol. 3	19,065	—
Camden, fourth series Vol. 43	—	22,262
Camden, fourth series Vol. 44	—	16,708
Camden, fifth series Vol. 1	11,790	151
Camden, fifth series Vol. 2	19,300	—
Camden, fifth series Vol. 3	315	—
Guides and Handbooks No. 18	6	—
Indirect costs, paper storage and usage and insurance	7,235	8,608
Printing costs for circulation to members	3,476	2,481
	64,037	67,382
Less: Provision b/fwd	(67,900)	(50,600)
	(3,863)	16,782
(b) Provisions for publications in progress		
Transactions, sixth series Vol. 3	—	18,300
Transactions, sixth series Vol. 4	16,100	—
Camden, fifth series Vol. 1	—	18,550
Camden, fifth series Vol. 2	—	18,550
Camden, fifth series Vol. 3	16,000	—
Camden, fifth series Vol. 4	18,850	—
List of Fellows	3,000	2,500
Guides and Handbooks No. 18	18,500	10,000
	72,450	67,900

(c) Other publication costs															
Annual Bibliography	8,115	6,586
Less: royalties received	(2,289)	(2,309)
	5,826	4,277

R. R. DAVIES, *President*
P. M. THANE, *Treasurer*

REPORT OF THE AUDITORS TO THE MEMBERS OF THE ROYAL HISTORICAL SOCIETY

We have audited the accounts on pages 288 to 293 which have been prepared under the historical cost convention and the accounting policies set out on page 291.

Respective responsibilities of the Council and Auditors
The Council is required to prepare accounts for each financial year which give a true and fair view of the state of affairs of the Society and of the profit or loss for that period.
In preparing those accounts, the Council is required to:
—select suitable accounting policies and then apply them consistently;
—make judgements and estimates that are reasonable and prudent;
—prepare the accounts on the going concern basis unless it is inappropriate to presume that the Society will continue in business.
The Council is responsible for keeping proper accounting records which disclose with reasonable accuracy at any time the financial position of the Society. They are also responsible for safeguarding the assets of the Society and hence for taking reasonable steps for the prevention and detection of fraud and other irregularities.
As described above the Council is responsible for the preparation of accounts. It is our responsibility to form an independent opinion, based on our audit, on those accounts and to report our opinion to you.

Basis of opinion
We conducted our audit in accordance with Auditing Standards issued by the Auditing Practices Board. An audit includes examination, on a test basis, of evidence relevant to the amounts and disclosures in the accounts. It also includes an assessment of the significant estimates and judgements made by the Council in the preparation of the accounts, and of whether the accounting policies are appropriate to the Society's circumstances, consistently applied and adequately disclosed.
We planned and performed our audit so as to obtain all the information and explanations which we considered necessary in order to provide us with sufficient evidence to give reasonable assurance that the accounts are free from material misstatement, whether caused by fraud or other irregularity or error. In forming our opinion we also evaluated the overall adequacy of the presentation of information in the accounts.

Opinion
In our opinion the accounts give a true and fair view of the state of the Society's affairs as at 30th June 1994 and of its deficit for the year then ended.

18 SOUTH STREET, DORKING
23 September 1994.

DAVIES WATSON & CO
Chartered Accountants
Registered Auditors

293

ROYAL HISTORICAL SOCIETY
THE DAVID BERRY ESSAY TRUST

Balance Sheet as at 30th June 1994

	1994 £	1994 £	1993 £	1993 £
FIXED ASSETS				
1117.63 units in the Charities Official Investment Fund				
(Market Value £7,298:1993 £6,709)		1,530		1,530
CURRENT ASSETS				
Bank Deposit Account	9,957		9,404	
LESS: CREDITORS				
Amounts falling due within one year	4,076		4,076	
NET CURRENT ASSETS		5,881		5,328
NET TOTAL ASSETS		7,411		6,858
Represented by:				
Capital Fund		1,000		1,000
Accumulated Income Account		6,411		5,858
		7,411		6,858

Income and Expenditure Account for the Year Ended 30th June 1994

	1994 £	1994 £	1993 £	1993 £
INCOME				
Dividends		338		334
Bank Interest Receivable		215		372
		553		706
EXPENDITURE				
Adjudicator's Fee		—	84	
		—		84
Excess of income over expenditure for the year . .		553		622
Balance brought forward		5,858		5,236
Balance carried forward		6,411		5,858

1. ACCOUNTING POLICIES
    Basis of accounting. The accounts have been prepared under the historical cost convention.
    The late David Berry, by his Will dated 23rd April 1926, left £1,000 to provide in every three years a gold medal and prize money for the best essay on the Earl of Bothwell or, at the discretion of the Trustees, on Scottish History of the James Stuarts I to VI, in memory of his father the late Rev. David Berry.
    The Trust is regulated by a scheme sanctioned by the Chancery Division of the High Court of Justice dated 23rd January 1930, and made in action 1927 A 1233 David Anderson Berry deceased, Hunter and Another v. Robertson and Another and since modified by an order of the Charity Commissioners made on 11 January 1978 removing the necessity to provide a medal.
    The Royal Historical Society is now the Trustee. The investment consists of 1117.63 Charities Official Investment Fund Income units. The Trustee will in every second year of the three year period advertise inviting essays.

REPORT OF THE AUDITORS TO THE TRUSTEES OF THE DAVID BERRY ESSAY TRUST

We have audited the accounts on pages 281 to 290 which have been prepared under the historical cost convention and the accounting policies set out on page 282.

Respective responsibilities of the Council and Auditors
    The Trustees are required to prepare accounts for each financial year which give a true and fair view of the state of affairs of the Trust and of the profit or loss for that period.
    In preparing those accounts, the Trustees are required to:
—select suitable accounting policies and then apply them consistently;
—make judgements and estimates that are reasonable and prudent;
—prepare the accounts on the going concern basis unless it is inappropriate to presume that the Trust will continue in business.
    The Trustees are responsible for keeping proper accounting records which disclose with reasonable accuracy at any time the financial position of the Trust. They are also responsible for safeguarding the assets of the Trust and hence for taking reasonable steps for the prevention and detection of fraud and other irregularities.
    As described above the Trustees are responsible for the preparation of accounts. It is our responsibility to form an independent opinion, based on our audit, on those accounts and to report our opinion to you.

Basis of opinion
    We conducted our audit in accordance with Auditing Standards issued by the Auditing Practices Board. An audit includes examination, on a test basis, of evidence relevant to the amounts and disclosures in the accounts. It also includes an assessment of the significant estimates and judgements made by the Trustees in the preparation of the accounts, and of whether the accounting policies are appropriate to the Trust's circumstances, consistently applied and adequately disclosed.
    We planned and performed our audit so as to obtain all the information and explanations which we considered necessary in order to provide us with sufficient evidence to give reasonable assurance that the accounts are free from material misstatement, whether caused by fraud or other irregularity or error. In forming our opinion we also evaluated the overall adequacy of the presentation of information in the accounts.

Opinion
    In our opinion the accounts give a true and fair view of the state of the Trust's affairs as at 30th June 1994 and of its surplus for the year then ended.

118 SOUTH STREET, DORKING   DAVIES WATSON & CO
                                                            Chartered Accountants
                                                            Registered Auditors

ALEXANDER PRIZE

The Alexander Prize was established in 1897 by L.C. Alexander, F.R.Hist.S. The prize is awarded annually for an essay on a historical subject, which has been previously approved by the Literary Director. The essay must be a genuine work of original research, not hitherto published, and not previously awarded any other prize. It must not exceed 8,000 words, including footnotes, and must be sent in by 1 November. Further details may be obtained from the Executive Secretary. Candidates must *either* be under the age of 35 *or* be registered for a higher degree *or* have been registered for a higher degree within the last three years. The winner of the prize is awarded £250.

1994 PRIZE WINNER

Joseph C. Heim, BA, MA, PhD,
'Liberalism and the Establishment of Collective Strategy
in British Foreign Policy'

DAVID BERRY PRIZE

The David Berry Prize was established in 1929 by David Anderson-Berry in memory of his father, the Reverend David Berry. The prize is awarded every three years for an essay on Scottish history, within the reigns of James I to James VI inclusive. The subject of each essay must be submitted in advance and approved by the Council of The Royal Historical Society. The essay must be a genuine work of research based on original material. The essay should be between 6,000 and 10,000 words excluding footnotes and appendices. Further details may be obtained from the Executive Secretary.

1991 PRIZE WINNER

M. H. Brown
' "That Old Serpent and Ancient of Evil Days"
Walter, earl of Atholl and the Murder of James I'

WHITFIELD PRIZE

The Whitfield Prize was established by Council in 1976 out of the bequest of the late Professor Archibald Stenton Whitfield. The prize is currently awarded to the best work on a subject of British history published in the United Kingdom during the calendar year. It must be the first solely authored history book published by the candidate and an original and scholarly work of research. Authors or publishers should send three copies (non-returnable) of a book eligible for the competition to the Executive Secretary before the end of the year in which the book is published. The award will be made by Council and announced at the Society's annual reception in the following July. The current value of the prize is £1,000.

1993 PRIZE WINNER

Janet M. Leeson, BA, PhD
'Commoners: Common Right, Enclosure and Social Change
in England, 1700–1820'

Commoners is a social history of the smallest landholders and users of commons in eighteenth and early nineteenth century England. It argues that common right ensured the survival until parliamentary enclosure of a peasantry whose social relations were in part shaped by access to land, common agriculture and shared use rights. It looks at entitlement to commons, the co-operative regulation of common fields and pastures, the harvests taken from uncultivated common waste. It suggests why and where common right survived until enclosure, and it reviews the contemporary debate on the social implications of common right and the public policy issues at the heart of parliamentary enclosure. Finally, it describes a vigorous opposition to enclosure and a significant decline of small landholders when common lands were enclosed. In short, *Commoners* makes shared land use a prism through which to see both the economies and the social relations of common-field villages. In doing so it challenges the views that England had no peasantry or that it had disappeared before industrialization. It shows how parliamentary enclosure shaped social relations, sharpened antagonisms, and imprinted on popular culture a pervasive sense of loss.

THE ROYAL HISTORICAL SOCIETY

STANDING COMMITTEES 1994

Finance Committee

PROFESSOR O. ANDERSON
PROFESSOR M.D. BIDDISS, MA, PhD
MISS V. CROMWELL
P.J.C. FIRTH, MA
PROFESSOR R.A. GRIFFITHS
PROFESSOR E.P. HENNOCK
DR. P. MATHIAS, CBE, MA, DLITT, FBA
DR. J.R. STUDD
And the Officers

Publications Committee

PROFESSOR J.M. BLACK
PROFESSOR P.R. COSS
PROFESSOR C.R. ELRINGTON, MA, FSA
PROFESSOR H.C.G. MATTHEW
DR. R.D. McKITTERICK
DR. J.S. MORRILL
PROFESSOR D.M. PALLISER
PROFESSOR A.G.R. SMITH
And the Officers

Research Support Committee

PROFESSOR J. GOOCH (Chairman)
DR. K. BURK
PROFESSOR P.A. CLARK
MISS V. CROMWELL
DR. A.M.S. PROCHASKA
And the Officers

Membership Committee

PROFESSOR O. ANDERSON
DR. G.W. BERNARD
PROFESSOR H.T. DICKINSON
PROFESSOR L. JORDANOVA
DR. R.C. METTAM
And the Officers

General Purposes Committee

PROFESSOR A.J. FLETCHER
DR. F. HEAL
PROFESSOR C.J. HOLDSWORTH
PROFESSOR F. O'GORMAN
And the Officers